Visions
AND Values

Readings in the Human Experience

Third Edition

ROBERTA VANDERMAST · JEFFERY DONLEY
DAN DUTKOFSKI · DIANN ROTHWELL LAPIN

HOUGHTON MIFFLIN COMPANY
Boston · New York

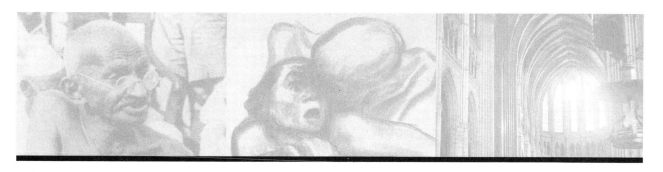

Custom Publishing Editor: Kyle Henderson
Custom Publishing Production Manager: Kathleen McCourt
Custom Publishing Project Coordinator: Kim Gavrilles

Cover Design: Ryan Duda
Cover Photograph: PhotoDisc, Inc.
Text Design and Production: Jeff Potter/Potter Publishing Studio

Printed in the United States of America.

ISBN-13: 978-0-618-22645-0
ISBN-10: 0-618-22645-1
N-00666

4 5 6 7 8 9 – VG – 06

Houghton Mifflin
Custom Publishing

222 Berkeley Street · Boston, MA 02116

Address all correspondence and order information to the above address.

Contents

About the Book...v

CHAPTER **1** **Identity**

Identity · ROBERTA VANDERMAST.............................1

Mirrorings · LUCY GREALY.....................................4

Beethoven's Silent Testament · DAN DUTKOFSKI.................11

I Was a Slave · FREDERICK DOUGLASS.........................15

Beyond Appearance: Rembrandt's Search for Self

　　　DIANN ROTHWELL LAPIN.................................21

How Don Quixote Became a Knight · MIGUEL DE CERVANTES....25

Martha Graham: Dancer · ERNESTINE STODELLE.................29

The Bicentennial Man · ISAAC ASIMOV.........................34

CHAPTER **2** **Work**

Work · JEFFERY REX WAYNE DONLEY...........................53

Michelangelo: The Reluctant Painter · DIANN ROTHWELL LAPIN..56

The Giant Pyramids: Their Rise and Fall · MARK LEHNER.........62

Dorothea Lange, Photographer · CHRISTOPHER COX.............67

The Samurai Warrior · D. T. SUZUKI............................76

The Myth of Sisyphus · ALBERT CAMUS........................80

Liberation Management · TOM PETERS.........................82

CHAPTER **3** **Love**

Love · DAN DUTKOFSKI...87

Stone Cold Love · DIANN ROTHWELL LAPIN.....................90

The Falconer and the Lady · GIOVANNI BOCCACCIO.............94

The Taj Mahal · JEFFERY REX WAYNE DONLEY...................98

A Summer Tragedy · ARNA BONTEMPS.........................103

Frida's Love Letter · RONALD TAMPLIN........................108

The Tragedy of Love · VIRGIL.................................112

Hills Like White Elephants · ERNEST HEMINGWAY..............120

Othello · WILLIAM SHAKESPEARE.............................123

CHAPTER **4** **Family**

Family · DIANN ROTHWELL LAPIN 127

The Making of a Scientist · RICHARD P. FEYNMAN 130

Waiting for the Mahatma · R. K. NARAYAN.................... 134

The Roman House · JEFFERY REX WAYNE DONLEY 144

Mary Cassatt · ROBERTA VANDERMAST 151

Hector and Andromache · HOMER........................... 158

The Blood of the Conquistadores · JULIA ALVAREZ 161

Everyday Use · ALICE WALKER 172

In the Gloaming · ALICE ELLIOTT DARK 177

CHAPTER **5** **Morality**

Morality · DAN DUTKOFSKI 187

Winter · KIT REED 190

The Ring of Gyges · PLATO.............................. 194

"Momma, the Dentist and Me" · MAYA ANGELOU 196

A Lesson Before Dying · ERNEST J. GAINES 200

The Horrors of War: Goya, Picasso, and Dali

    ROBERTA VANDERMAST 204

Night · ELIE WIESEL 212

The United Nations Declaration of Human Rights 219

Where Have All The Good Deeds Gone? · CHRISTINA SOMMERS .. 223

CHAPTER **6** **God**

God · JEFFERY REX WAYNE DONLEY 228

When Bad Things Happen to Good People · HAROLD KUSHNER .. 230

The Sermon on the Four Noble Truths · GAUTAMA BUDDHA..... 237

The Koran · AS REVEALED TO MUHAMMAD 280

The Sermon on the Mount 246

The Cathedral at Chartres: A Bible in Stone

    ROBERTA VANDERMAST 248

The Dedication of the Great Pyramid of the Aztecs

    GARY JENNINGS 257

Creation Legends of the Hopi

    MARGOT EDMONDS AND ELLA E. CLARK 267

Heaven and Earth in Jest · ANNIE DILLARD 274

Acknowledgments 279

About the Book

L EARNING ABOUT HUMANITIES TODAY is an imposing challenge for both the student and the teacher. The world has become a smaller place and the "global community" a nearer reality. Rapid-fire communications let us learn about events in the world as they occur. In our rush to access the present, we often feel the past is irrelevant or, at best, not very interesting. Yet it is the past, as well as the present, that determines who we are and also points us to the future. Thus, humanities is about who we are, who we were, and who we will be, for it is the study of human kind and its achievements, both glorious and humble. It is also the study of the human experience, an experience that is universal and timeless.

The human experience is composed of our shared thoughts, feelings, and beliefs down through the ages. Humans have always looked at the present and dreamed of what the future can be; these ideals form our visions, our inward expression of thought and feelings. In turn, we have defined modes of behavior; these models are our values, our outward expression of our beliefs. Together, humans' visions and values have shaped each culture in unique, yet universal, ways. These collective thoughts and achievements are unique in that they represent particular individuals at particular points in history. They are also universal because we can all share in the ways in which they relate to each of our lives. This anthology of readings has been specially developed to focus on these shared ideals and models — humankind's universal visions and values.

The readings are divided into six chapters, each of which focuses on one of the following constants or themes in the human experience: identity, work, love, family, morality, or God. Down through the ages, men and women in all cultures have been challenged by their sense of their own self, their daily activities, their close relationships, the ways in which they make decisions and act, and their beliefs in a greater power. These constants have been the source of literary and artistic expression for many centuries.

Each chapter is composed of an introduction to the theme of that chapter. The introduction probes both the inner and outer dimensions of this key constant in the human experience. Following the introduction are seven or eight articles that relate the theme in its many dimensions to the broader human experience. These articles have been specially written or selected because they support the chapter theme. Whether it is a Japanese author describing the work of the medieval Samurai Warrior or a contemporary American consider-

ing the morality of the discrimination she suffered as a child, each article brings out a special point that relates directly to the chapter's theme.

A wide range of cultural and ethnic viewpoints and a broad sampling of key historical eras are contained in the articles. African-American, Asian, European, Hispanic, and Native American writers and artists are included. Primary source materials from the Ancient World up through modern times have been selected to vary the historical perspective, as well as the cultural orientation.

A wide variety of genre types and subject areas has also been included. In addition to primary source materials, there is poetry, fiction, non-fiction essays, biography, and art and architecture analysis. The subject areas covered are the traditional humanities disciplines and, in an attempt to broaden these limits to include other vital areas of human experience, science, business, politics, and social science are also presented.

Although written or chosen to support the chapter theme, each ar-

ticle is self contained and can be used by itself. Each selection includes: a brief overview that highlights the author and sets out a context for the article; a graphic time line that precedes the article and lists key dates for the author and his/her historical era; six questions at the end of each article that can be used to stimulate class discussion, for writing assignments, or to prompt personal reactions; and, suggested recommendations for further reading following each article.

The goal of this anthology is to provide readers with a source that challenges their awareness of their own place in the world. To build this awareness, it is important to survey a wide range of human experiences. In order to define our own visions and values, we must understand the lessons of the past, the challenges of the present, and our hopes for the future. Understanding ourselves, our culture — past and present — and the cultures of others can lead us to a closer connection between our personal experiences and those of humankind.

Langston Hughes

Lucy Grealy

Ludwig van Beethoven

Frederick Douglass

Rembrandt van Rijn

Miguel de Cervantes

Martha Graham

Isaac Asimov

CHAPTER **1**

Identity

I T IS EASY TO IDENTIFY with the assignment given to Langston Hughes in "Theme for English B." At some point in our education, most of us have been asked to write a "page come out of you" — something that reflects the way we see ourselves. When Langston Hughes looks at himself, he first sees his age and race, and then moves from there to his birthplace and to his college classroom where he is "the only colored student in his class." He doesn't stop with his appearance, however; he also writes of what makes him unique, "a pipe for a Christmas present, or records, Bessie, bop or Bach," as well as what makes him universal, "I like to eat, sleep, drink, and be in love." In this poem, he moves the reader from outward appearances to inner realities and illustrates several ways in which we establish our identities. We may base our identities on appearance, like race, birthplace, and status in life, or on our uniqueness — our individuality. We may see

LANGSTON HUGHES
Theme for English B

The instructor said,

Go home and write
a page tonight.
And let that page come out of you —
Then, it will be true

I wonder if it's that simple?
I am twenty-two, colored, born in Winston-Salem.
I went to school there, then Durham, then here
to this college on the hill above Harlem.
I am the only colored student in my class.
The steps from the hill lead down into Harlem,
through a park, then I cross St. Nicholas,
Eighth Avenue, Seventh, and I come to the Y,
the Harlem Branch Y, where I take the elevator
up to my room, sit down, and write this page:

It's not easy to know what is true for you or me
at twenty-two, my age. But I guess I'm what
I feel and see and hear, Harlem, I hear you:
hear you, hear me — we two — you, me, talk on
     this page.
(I hear New York, too.) Me — who?

Well, I like to eat, sleep, drink, and be in love.
I like to work, read, learn, and understand life.
I like a pipe for a Christmas present,
or records, Bessie, bop, or Bach.
I guess being colored doesn't make me *not* like
the same things other folks like who are other races.
So will my page be colored that I write?

Being me, it will not be white.
But it will be
a part of you, instructor.
You are white —
yet a part of me, as I am part of you.
That's American.
Sometimes perhaps you don't want to be a part of me.
Nor do I often want to be a part of you.
But we are, that's true!
As I learn from you,
I guess you learn from me —
although you're older — and white —
and somewhat more free.

This is my page for English B.

ourselves divided from the rest of humanity or a part of it, but no matter how we see ourselves, identity defines the very core of our existence.

Advertisements saturate our materially-oriented society. Those ads encourage us to identify ourselves by our outward appearances. If we identify ourselves mainly by our appearances, then we will be more likely to buy the products we see advertised. If we believe the advertisements we see or hear, we believe that, in order to establish an identity, we should buy the sexiest perfume, wear the most fashionable clothes, drive the hottest car, and vacation at the most expensive ski resort. Ads imply that if our material possessions are the latest and most expensive, then we will be the best person we can be. In stressing appearance, advertisements hope to convince us that "to consume is to be." It seems that this approach works. Millions of dollars are spent each year as many of us attempt to build the type of identity portrayed by these ads. Yet how many of us step back and think about the effects of building our identity in this way? What does it mean to our sense of self if we equate ourselves with our appearance?

A sense of self built on the basis of appearances can be restrictive and dangerous. If we are slaves of fashion, it requires not only an expensive and constantly changing wardrobe, it means that our sense of self must change as often as the styles do. While keeping up with the latest may be appealing, it can lead to being pushed and pulled in a number of directions as different brands vie for our attention and our money. Our sense of self can become fragmented by this constant change in directions and by dependence on fashion "gurus" who define the latest trends. Even if we are not slaves to fashion, we can be enslaved by other aspects of appearance. Instead of what we wear, it might be how "fat" we are, how much hair we have, our age, or our race. Yet any sense of self built on outward appearances is dependent on others' definitions of being beautiful or ugly. Those who are slaves to fashion, physical appearance, or race, restrict their identities by substituting stereotypes for reality. These stereotypes exalt the perfect man or woman, not in terms of how people really are in their infinite variations, but in terms of how they should be: all alike. These images reduce identity to one dimension — appearance — and give others power over us by letting them dictate to us what we think of ourselves. Thus, a sense of self built on outward appearances can offer no sense of individuality. This is the danger of equating identity with appearance.

A firm foundation for personal identity can be built upon uniqueness, autonomy, and integrity. Uniqueness is founded in the sense that you are one of a kind. It stems from the recognition that each person can see herself from within, rather than from without. Each of us can realize that there is more to ourselves than what is visible. Beyond what others see, there is what "I" think and feel, my own special way of experiencing the world which belongs to me alone. Along with uniqueness comes the recognition that each of us can act independently from the desires or influences of others. This is autonomy. We can override the effects of advertising, parents, and peers to act independently and freely. Acting autonomously makes each one of us the force behind who we are. It requires that we understand our actions and our motivations. Autonomy gives us the power to act independently. Immanuel Kant, a nineteenth-century German philosopher, noted that the literal meaning of the word autonomous is "one who gives laws to himself." This is the foundation of human dignity and worth. However, uniqueness and autonomy must be accompanied by integrity, a sense of being consistent and unified. In order for our actions to be consistent and unified, we need a set of self-chosen principles to guide us. These principles lay out broad bases for actions. These principles can range from being honest with yourself to treating others as you would like to be treated. Choosing and acting consistently on these principles gives us integrity, a sense of being consistent and whole, and results in the sense that we have unique identities.

In this chapter, each author explores the nature of identity. Some fall prey to, and break free from, the power of appearances. Others challenge the power of stereotypes and demonstrate lives built on uniqueness, autonomy, and integrity. Some are dancers and writers; others, former slaves and composers. A few are victims of disease and of human cruelty. Like Langston Hughes, each of these authors demonstrates that a sense of identity built on a firm foundation allows us to see ourselves reflected in others. As Hughes writes in "Theme for English B," identity can exist beyond appearances and beyond differences.

"You are white —
yet a part of me, as I am part of you.
That's American.
Sometimes perhaps you don't want to be a part of me.
Nor do I often want to be a part of you.
But we are, that's true!
As I learn from you,
I guess you learn from me —

We can choose to let appearances separate us and see ourselves divided from the rest of humanity, or we can look beyond appearances to understandings we might share. Hughes hopes his instructor can see past age, race, and background to see him as he really is. Hughes' poem leaves us hoping that his professor will be able to see not what he appears to be, but who he actually is.

THINK ABOUT IT

1. What are the dangers in basing identity on appearance?
2. Why are the concepts of uniqueness, autonomy, and integrity related to each other?

TALK ABOUT IT

3. Programs for children, especially animated series which are designed to sell a line of toys, stress the importance of consumerism. What do these shows teach children about their identities?
4. Consider some of the famous figures of our time. Which have identities defined by appearance? Which have identities defined by uniqueness, autonomy, and integrity? Are these distinctions applicable only to Americans? What about other cultures?

WRITE ABOUT IT

5. Describe a fictional character from a book, movie, or television show whom you feel demonstrates a clear sense of identity. On what basis does this character establish his/her identity?
6. What is the basis for your identity? Describe an incident which demonstrates who you are and explain how it reveals the basis for your identity.

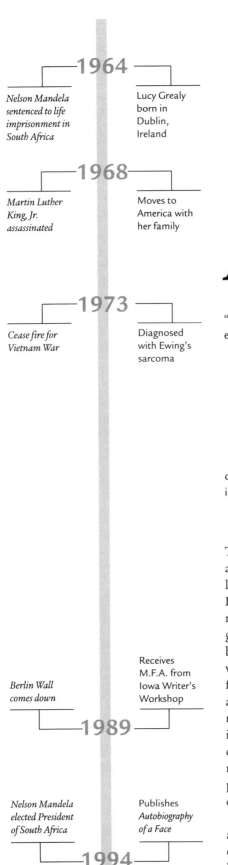

1964

Nelson Mandela sentenced to life imprisonment in South Africa

Lucy Grealy born in Dublin, Ireland

1968

Martin Luther King, Jr. assassinated

Moves to America with her family

1973

Cease fire for Vietnam War

Diagnosed with Ewing's sarcoma

Berlin Wall comes down

Receives M.F.A. from Iowa Writer's Workshop

1989

Nelson Mandela elected President of South Africa

Publishes *Autobiography of a Face*

1994

L U C Y   G R E A L Y

Mirrorings

"Mirrorings" by Lucy Grealy was selected for inclusion in *The Best American Essays 1994,* edited by Tracy Kidder. In the Biographical Notes included for each author, it says:

> Lucy Grealy is an award-winning poet. Her work has appeared, among other places, in The Paris Review and the London Times Literary Supplement. She has received a fellowship from the Bunting Institute, been a guest of the Yaddo Corporation, and been a fellow at the Fine Arts Work Center in Provincetown. Her memoir, *Autobiography of a Face,* is based on the essay in this book, which won a National Magazine Award. She lives in Manhattan.

> In "Mirrorings," Ms. Grealy pursues the effect disfigurement has on one's sense of self and comes to an interesting conclusion about the power of perception in forming identity.

THERE WAS A long period of time, almost a year, during which I never looked in a mirror. It wasn't easy, for I'd never suspected just how omnipresent are our own images. I began by merely avoiding mirrors, but, by the end of the year, I found myself with an acute knowledge of the reflected image, its numerous tricks and wiles, how it can spring up at any moment: a glass tabletop, a well-polished door handle, a darkened window, a pair of sunglasses, a restaurant's otherwise magnificent brass-plated coffee machine sitting innocently by the cash register.

At the time, I had just moved, alone, to Scotland and was surviving on the dole, as Britain's social security benefits are called. I didn't know anyone and had no idea how I was going to live, yet I went anyway because by

happenstance I'd met a plastic surgeon there who said he could help me. I had been living in London, working temp jobs. While in London, I'd received more nasty comments about my face than I had in the previous three years, living in Iowa, New York, and Germany. These comments, all from men and all odiously sexual, hurt and disoriented me. I also had journeyed to Scotland because, after more than a dozen operations in the States, my insurance had run out, along with my hope that further operations could make any real difference. Here, however, was a surgeon who had some new techniques, and here, amazingly enough, was a government willing to foot the bill: I didn't feel I could pass up yet another chance to "fix" my face, which I confusedly thought concurrent with "fixing" my self, my soul, my life.

Twenty years ago, when I was nine and living in America, I came home from school one day with a toothache. Several weeks and misdiagnoses later, surgeons removed most of the right side of my jaw in an attempt to prevent the cancer they found there from spreading. No one properly explained the operation to me, and I awoke in a cocoon of pain that prevented me from moving or speaking. Tubes ran in and out of my body, and because I was temporarily unable to speak after the surgery and could not ask questions, I made up my own explanations for the tubes' existence. I remember the mysterious manner the adults displayed toward me. They asked me to do things: lie still for x-rays, not cry for needles, and so on, tasks that, although not easy, never seemed equal to the praise I received in return. Reinforced to me again and again was how I was "a brave girl" for not crying, "a good girl" for not complaining, and soon I began defining myself this way, equating strength with silence.

Then the chemotherapy began. In the seventies, chemo was even cruder than it is now, the basic premise being to poison patients right up to the very brink of their own death. Until this point I almost never cried and almost always received praise in return. Thus I got what I considered the better part of the deal. But now it was like a practical joke that had gotten out of hand. Chemotherapy was a nightmare and I wanted it to stop; I didn't want to be brave anymore. Yet I had grown so used to defining myself as "brave" — i.e., silent — that the thought of losing this sense of myself was even more terrifying. I was certain that if I broke down I would be despicable in the eyes of both my parents and the doctors.

The task of taking me into the city for the chemo injections fell mostly on my mother, though sometimes my father made the trip. Overwhelmed by the sight of the vomiting and weeping, my father developed the routine of "going to get the car," meaning that he left the doctor's office before the injection was administered, on the premise that then he could have the car ready and waiting when it was all over. Ashamed of my suffering, I felt relief when he was finally out of the room. When my mother took me, she stayed in the room, yet this only made the distance between us even more tangible. She explained that it was wrong to cry before the needle went in; afterward was one thing, but before, that was mere fear, and hadn't I demonstrated my bravery earlier? Every Friday for two and a half years I climbed up onto that big doctor's table and told myself not to cry, and every week I failed. The two large syringes were filled with chemicals so caustic to the vein that each had to be administered very slowly. The whole process took about four minutes; I had to remain utterly still. Dry retching began in the first fifteen seconds, then the throb behind my eyes gave everything a yellow-green aura, and the bone-deep pain of alternating extreme hot and cold flashes made me tremble, yet still I had to sit motionless and not move my arm. No one spoke to me — not the doctor, who was a paradigm of the cold-fish physician; not the nurse, who told my mother I reacted much more violently than many of "the other children"; and not my mother, who, surely overwhelmed by the sight of her child's suffering, thought the best thing to do was remind me to be brave, to try not to cry. All the while I hated myself for having wept before the needle went in, convinced that the nurse and my mother were right, that I was "over-

doing it," that the throwing up was psychosomatic, that my mother was angry with me for not being good or brave enough.

Yet each week, two or three days after the injection, there came the first flicker of feeling better, the always forgotten and gratefully rediscovered understanding that to simply be well in my body was the greatest thing I could ask for. I thought other people felt this appreciation and physical joy all the time, and I felt cheated because I was able to feel it only once a week.

Because I'd lost my hair, I wore a hat constantly, but this fooled no one, least of all myself. During this time, my mother worked in a nursing home in a Hasidic community. Hasidic law dictates that married women cover their hair, and most commonly this is done with a wig. My mother's friends were now all too willing to donate their discarded wigs, and soon the house seemed filled with them. I never wore one, for they frightened me even when my mother insisted I looked better in one of the few that actually fit. Yet we didn't know how to say no to the women who kept graciously offering their wigs. The cats enjoyed sleeping on them and the dogs playing with them, and we grew used to having to pick a wig up off a chair we wanted to sit in. It never struck us as odd until one day a visitor commented wryly as he cleared a chair for himself, and suddenly a great wave of shame overcame me. I had nightmares about wigs and flushed if I even heard the word, and one night I put myself out of my misery by getting up after everyone was asleep and gathering all the wigs except for one the dogs were fond of and that they had chewed up anyway. I hid all the rest in an old chest.

When you are only ten, which is when the chemotherapy began, two and a half years seem like your whole life, yet it did finally end, for the cancer was gone. I remember the last day of treatment clearly because it was the only day on which I succeeded in not crying, and because later, in private, I cried harder than I had in years; I thought now I would no longer be "special," that without the arena of chemotherapy in which to prove myself no one would ever love me, that I would fade unnoticed into the background. But this idea about not being different didn't last very long. Before, I foolishly believed that people stared at me because I was bald. After my hair eventually grew in, it didn't take long before I understood that I looked different for another reason. My face. People stared at me in stores, and other children made fun of me to the point that I came to expect such reactions constantly, wherever I went. School became a battleground.

Halloween, that night of frights, became my favorite holiday because I could put on a mask and walk among the blessed for a few brief, sweet hours. Such freedom I felt, walking down the street, my face hidden! Through the imperfect oval holes, I could peer out at other faces, masked or painted or not, and see on those faces nothing but the normal faces of childhood looking back at me, faces I mistakenly thought were the faces everyone else but me saw all the time, faces that were simply curious and ready for fun, not the faces I usually braced myself for, the cruel, lonely, vicious ones I spent every day other than Halloween waiting to see around each corner. As I breathed in the condensed, plastic-scented air under the mask, I somehow thought that I was breathing in normality, that this joy and weightlessness were what the world was composed of, and that it was only my face that kept me from it, my face that was my own

mask that kept me from knowing the joy I was sure everyone but me lived with intimately. How could the other children not know it? Not know that to be free of the fear of taunts and the burden of knowing no one would ever love you was all that anyone could ever ask for? I was a pauper walking for a short while in the clothes of the prince, and when the day ended I gave up my disguise with dismay.

I was living in an extreme situation, and because I did not particularly care for the world I was in, I lived in others, and because the world I did live in was dangerous now, I incorporated this danger into my secret life. I imagined myself to be an Indian. Walking down the streets, I stepped through the forest, my body ready for any opportunity to fight or flee one of the big cats that I knew stalked me. Vietnam and Cambodia, in the news then as scenes of catastrophic horror, were other places I walked through daily. I made my way down the school hall, knowing a land mine or a sniper might give themselves away at any moment with the subtle metal click I'd read about. Compared with a land mine, a mere insult about my face seemed a frivolous thing.

In those years, not yet a teenager, I secretly read — knowing it was somehow inappropriate — works by Primo Levi and Elie Wiesel, and every book by a survivor I could find by myself without asking the librarian. Auschwitz, Birkenau: I felt the blows of the capos and somehow knew that because at any moment we might be called upon to live for a week on one loaf of bread and some water called soup, the peanut-butter sandwich I found on my plate was nothing less than a miracle, an utter and sheer miracle capable of making me literally weep with joy.

I decided to become a "deep" person. I wasn't exactly sure what this

would entail, but I believed that if I could just find the right philosophy, think the right thoughts, my suffering would end. To try to understand the world I was in, I undertook to find out what was "real," and I quickly began seeing reality as existing in the lowest common denominator, that suffering was the one and only dependable thing. But rather than spend all of my time despairing, though certainly I did plenty of that, I developed a form of defensive egomania: I felt I was the only one walking about in the world who understood what was really important. I looked upon people complaining about the most mundane things — nothing on TV, traffic jams, the price of new clothes — and felt joy because I knew how unimportant those things really were and felt unenlightened superiority because other people didn't. Because in my fantasy life, I had learned to be thankful for each cold, blanketless night that I survived on the cramped wooden bunks, my pain and despair were a stroll through the country in comparison. I was often miserable, but I knew that to feel warm instead of cold was its own kind of joy, that to eat was a reenactment of the grace of some god whom I could only dimly define, and that to simply be alive was a rare, ephemeral gift.

As I became a teenager, my isolation began. My nonidentical twin sister started going out with boys, and I started — my most tragic mistake of all — to listen to and believe the taunts thrown at me daily by the very boys she and the other girls were interested in. I was a dog, a monster, the ugliest girl they had ever seen. Of all the remarks, the most damaging wasn't even directed at me, but was really an insult to "Jerry," a boy I never saw because every day between fourth and fifth periods, when I was cornered by a particular group of kids, I was too ashamed to lift my eyes off the floor. "Hey, look, it's Jerry's girlfriend!" they shrieked when they saw me, and I felt such shame, knowing that this was the deepest insult to Jerry that they could imagine.

When pressed to it, one makes compensations. I came to love winter, when I could wrap up the disfigured lower half of my face in a scarf: I could speak to people and they would have no idea to whom and to what they were really speaking. I developed the bad habits of letting my long hair hang in my face and of always covering my chin and mouth with my hand, hoping it might be mistaken as a thoughtful, accidental gesture. I also became interested in horses and got a job at a rundown local stable. Having those horses to go to each day after school saved my life; I spent all of my time either with them or thinking about them. Completely and utterly repressed by the time I was sixteen, I was convinced that I would never want a boyfriend, not ever, and wasn't it convenient for me, even a blessing, that none would ever want me. I told myself I was free to concentrate on the "true reality" of life, whatever that was. My sister and her friends put on blue eye shadow, blow-dried their hair, and spent interminable hours in the local mall, and I looked down on them for this, knew they were misleading themselves and being overly occupied with the "mere surface" of living. I'd had thoughts like this when I was younger, ten or twelve, but now my philosophy was haunted by desires so frightening, I was unable even to admit they existed.

Throughout all of this, I was undergoing reconstructive surgery in an attempt to rebuild my jaw. It started when I was fifteen, two years after chemo ended. I had known for years I would have operations to fix my face, and at night I fantasized about how good my life would finally be then. One day I got a clue that maybe it wouldn't be so easy. An older plastic surgeon explained the process of "pedestals" to me, and told me it would take ten years to fix my face. Ten years? Why even bother, I thought; I'll be ancient by then. I went to a medical library and looked up the "pedestals" he talked about. There were gruesome pictures of people with grotesque tubes of their own skin growing out of their bodies, tubes of skin that were harvested like some kind of crop and then rearranged, with results that did not look at all normal or acceptable to my eye. But then I met a younger surgeon, who was working on a new way of grafting that did not involve pedestals, and I became more hopeful and once again began to await the fixing of my face, the day when I would be whole, content, loved.

Long-term plastic surgery is not like in the movies. There is no one single operation that will change everything, and there is certainly no slow unwrapping of the gauze in order to view the final, remarkable result. There is always swelling, sometimes to a grotesque degree, there are often bruises, and always there are scars. After each operation, too frightened to simply go look in the mirror, I developed an oblique method, with several stages. First, I tried to catch my reflection in an overhead lamp: the roundness of the metal distorted my image just enough to obscure details and give no true sense of size or proportion. Then I slowly worked my way up to looking at the reflection in someone's eyeglasses, and from there I went to walking as briskly as possible by a mirror, glancing only quickly. I repeated this as many times as it would take me, passing the mirror slightly more slowly each time until finally I was able to stand still and confront myself.

The theory behind most reconstructive surgery is to take large chunks of muscle, skin, and bone and slap them into the roughly appropriate place, then slowly begin to carve this mess into some sort of shape. It involves long, major operations, countless lesser ones, a lot of pain, and many, many years. And also, it does not always work. With my young surgeon in New York, who with each passing year was becoming not so young, I had two or three soft-tissue grafts, two skin grafts, a bone graft, and some dozen other operations to "revise" my face; yet when I left graduate school at the age of twenty-five I was still more or less in the same position I had started in: a deep hole in the right side of my face and a rapidly shrinking left side and chin, a result of the radiation I'd had as a child and the stress placed upon the bone by the other operations. I was caught in a cycle of having a big operation, one that would force me to look monstrous from the swelling for many months, then having the subsequent revision operations that improved my looks tremendously, and then slowly, over the period of a few months or a year, watching the graft reabsorb back into my body, slowly shrinking down and leaving me with nothing but the scarred donor site the graft had originally come from.

It wasn't until I was in college that I finally allowed that maybe, just maybe, it might be nice to have a boyfriend. I went to a small, liberal, predominantly female school and suddenly, after years of alienation in high school, discovered that there were other people I could enjoy talking to who thought me intelligent and talented. I was, however, still operating on the assumption that no one, not ever, would be physically attracted to me, and in a curious way this shaped my personality. I became forthright and honest in the way that only the truly self-confident are, who do not expect to be rejected, and in the way of those like me, who do not even dare to ask acceptance from others and therefore expect no rejection. I had come to know myself as a person, but I would be in graduate school before I was literally, physically able to use my name and the word "woman" in the same sentence.

Now my friends repeated for me endlessly that most of it was in my mind, that, granted, I did not look like everyone else, but that didn't mean I looked bad. I am sure now that they were right some of the time. But with the constant surgery, I was in a perpetual state of transfiguration. I rarely looked the same for more than six months at a time. So ashamed of my face, I was unable even to admit that this constant change affected me; I let everyone who wanted to know that it was only what was inside that mattered, that I had "grown used to" the surgery, that none of it bothered me at all. Just as I had done in childhood, I pretended nothing was wrong, and this was constantly mistaken by others for bravery. I spent a great deal of time looking in the mirror in private, positioning my head to show off my eyes and nose, which were not only normal but quite pretty, as my friends told me often. But I could not bring myself to see them for more than a moment: I looked in the mirror and saw not the normal upper half of my face but only the disfigured lower half.

People still teased me. Not daily, as when I was younger, but in ways that caused me more pain than ever before. Children stared at me, and I learned to cross the street to avoid them; this bothered me, but not as much as the insults I got from men.

Their taunts came at me not because I was disfigured, but because I was a disfigured woman. They came from boys, sometimes men, and almost always from a group of them. I had long, blond hair, and I also had a thin figure. Sometimes, from a distance, men would see a thin blonde and whistle, something I dreaded more than anything else because I knew that as they got closer, their tune, so to speak, would inevitably change; they would stare openly or, worse, turn away quickly in shame or repulsion. I decided to cut my hair to avoid any misconception that anyone, however briefly, might have about my being attractive. Only two or three times have I ever been teased by a single person, and I can think of only one time when I was ever teased by a woman. Had I been a man, would I have had to walk down the street while a group of young women followed and denigrated my sexual worth?

Not surprisingly, then, I viewed sex as my salvation. I was sure that if only I could get someone to sleep with me, it would mean I wasn't ugly, that I was attractive, even lovable. This line of reasoning led me into the beds of several manipulative men who liked themselves even less than they liked me, and I in turn left each short-term affair hating myself, obscenely sure that if only I had been prettier it would have worked — he would have loved me and it would have been like those other love affairs that I was certain "normal" women had all the time. Gradually, I became unable to say "I'm depressed" but could say only "I'm ugly," because the two had become inextricably linked in my mind. Into that universal lie, that sad equation of "if only . . ." that we are all prey to, I was sure that if only I had a normal face, then I would be happy.

The new surgeon in Scotland, Oliver Fenton, recommended that I undergo a procedure involving something called a tissue expander, followed by a bone graft. A tissue expander is a small balloon placed under the skin and then slowly blown up over the course of several months, the object being to stretch out the skin and create room and cover for the new bone. It's a bizarre, nightmarish thing to do to your face, yet I was hopeful about the end results and I was also able to spend the three months that the expansion took in the hospital. I've always felt safe in hospitals: they're the one place I feel free from the need to explain the way I look. For this reason the first tissue expander was bearable — just — and the bone graft that followed it was a success; it did not melt away like the previous ones.

The surgical stress this put upon what remained of my original jaw instigated the deterioration of that bone, however, and it became unhappily apparent that I was going to need the same operation I'd just had on the right side done to the left. I remember my surgeon telling me this at an outpatient clinic. I planned to be traveling down to London that same night on an overnight train, and I barely made it to the station on time, such a fumbling state of despair was I in.

I could not imagine going through it again, and just as I had done all my life, I searched and searched through my intellect for a way to make it okay, make it bearable, for a way to do it. I lay awake all night on that train, feeling the tracks slip beneath me with an odd eroticism, when I remembered an afternoon from my three months in the hospital. Boredom was a big problem those long afternoons, the days marked by meals and television programs. Waiting for the afternoon tea to come, wondering desperately how I could make time pass, it had suddenly occurred to me that I didn't have to make time pass, that it would do it of its own accord, that I simply had to relax and take no action. Lying on the train, remembering that, I realized I had no obligation to improve my situation, that I didn't have to explain or understand it, that I could just simply let it happen. By the time the train pulled into King's Cross station, I felt able to bear it yet again, not entirely sure what other choice I had.

But there was an element I didn't yet know about. When I returned to Scotland to set up a date to have the tissue expander inserted, I was told quite casually that I'd be in the hospital only three or four days. Wasn't I going to spend the whole expansion time in the hospital? I asked in a whisper. What's the point of that? came the answer. You can just come in every day to the outpatient ward to have it expanded. Horrified by this, I was speechless. I would have to live and move about in the outside world with a giant balloon inside the tissue of my face? I can't remember what I did for the next few days before I went into the hospital, but I vaguely recall that these days involved a great deal of drinking alone in bars and at home.

I had the operation and went home at the end of the week. The only things that gave me any comfort during the months I lived with my tissue expander were my writing and Franz Kafka. I started a novel and completely absorbed myself in it, writing for hours each day. The only way I could walk down the street, could stand the stares I received, was to think to myself, "I'll bet none of them are writing a novel." It was that strange, old, familiar form of egomania, directly related to my dismissive, conceited thoughts of adolescence. As for Kafka, who had always been one of my favorite writ-

ers, he helped me in that I felt permission to feel alienated, and to have that alienation be okay, bearable, noble even. In the same way that imagining I lived in Cambodia helped me as a child, I walked the streets of my dark little Scottish city by the sea and knew without doubt that I was living in a story Kafka would have been proud to write.

The one good thing about a tissue expander is that you look so bad with it in that no matter what you look like once it's finally removed, your face has to look better. I had my bone graft and my fifth soft-tissue graft and, yes, even I had to admit I looked better. But I didn't look like me. Something was wrong: was this the face I had waited through eighteen years and almost thirty operations for? I somehow just couldn't make what I saw in the mirror correspond to the person I thought I was. It wasn't only that I continued to feel ugly; I simply could not conceive of the image as belonging to me. My own image was the image of a stranger, and rather than try to understand this, I simply stopped looking in the mirror. I perfected the technique of brushing my teeth without a mirror, grew my hair in such a way that it would require only a quick, simple brush, and wore clothes that were simply and easily put on, no complex layers or lines that might require even the most minor of visual adjustments.

On one level I understood that the image of my face was merely that, an image, a surface that was not directly related to any true, deep definition of the self. But I also knew that it is only through appearances that we experience and make decisions about the everyday world, and I was not always able to gather the strength to prefer the deeper world to the shallower one. I looked for ways to find a bridge that would allow me access to

both, rather than riding out the constant swings between peace and anguish. The only direction I had to go to achieve this was to strive for a state of awareness and self-honesty that sometimes, to this day, occasionally rewards me. I have found, I believe, that our whole lives are dominated, though it is not always so clearly translatable, by the question "How do I look?" Take all the many nouns in our lives — car, house, job, family, love, friends — and substitute the personal pronoun "I." It is not that we are all so self-obsessed; it is that all things eventually relate back to ourselves, and it is our own sense of how we appear to the world by which we chart our lives, how we navigate our personalities, which would otherwise be adrift in the ocean of other people's obsessions.

One evening toward the end of my year-long separation from the mirror, I was sitting in a café talking to someone — an attractive man, as it happened — and we were having a lovely, engaging conversation. For some reason I suddenly wondered what I looked like to him. What was he actually seeing when he saw me? So many times I've asked this of myself, and always the answer is this: a warm, smart woman, yes, but an unattractive one. I sat there in the café and asked myself this old question, and startlingly, for the first time in my life, I had no answer readily prepared. I had not looked in a mirror for so long that I quite simply had no clue as to what I looked like. I studied the man as he spoke; my entire life I had seen my ugliness reflected back to me. But now, as reluctant as I was to admit it, the only indication in my companion's behavior was positive.

And then, that evening in that café, I experienced a moment of the freedom I'd been practicing for behind my Halloween mask all those years ago. But whereas as a child I expected my liberation to come as a result of gaining something, a new face, it came to me now as the result of shedding something, of shedding my image. I once thought that truth was eternal, that when you understood something it was with you forever. I know now that this isn't so, that most truths are inherently unretainable, that we have to work hard all our lives to remember the most basic things. Society is no help; it tells us again and again that we can most be ourselves by looking like someone else, leaving our own faces behind to turn into ghosts that will inevitably resent and haunt us. It is no mistake that in movies and literature the dead sometimes know they are dead only after they can no longer see themselves in the mirror; and as I sat there feeling the warmth of the cup against my palm, this small observation seemed like a great revelation to me. I wanted to tell the man I was with about it, but he was involved in his own topic and I did not want to interrupt him, so instead I looked with curiosity toward the window behind him, its night-darkened glass reflecting the whole café, to see if I could, now, recognize myself.

THINK ABOUT IT

1. How did Ms. Grealy's childhood shape her adult image of herself?
2. Why was Ms. Grealy finally able to see herself as an attractive person?

TALK ABOUT IT

3. Is it possible to discount how a person looks?
4. Why does our society place so much emphasis on how we look? Is this true of other cultures?

WRITE ABOUT IT

5. Is looking different (or being different) a curse or a blessing?
6. What do you find "ugly" about yourself? What would it take to make you shed this ugliness?

READ MORE ABOUT IT

Grealy, Lucy. *Autobiography of a Face.* Boston: Houghton Mifflin, 1994.

Grealy, Lucy. "The Face in the Mirror." 13 *Vogue* October 1994: 92.

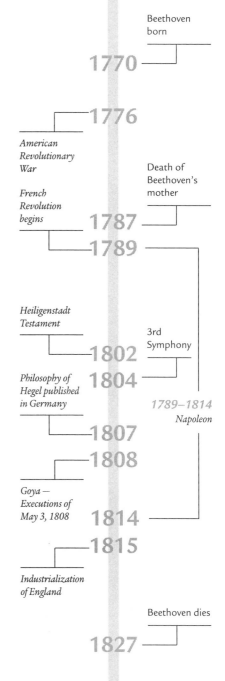

DAN DUTKOFSKI

Beethoven's Silent Testament

Dan Dutkofski is a member of the Interdisciplinary Studies faculty at Valencia Community College in Orlando, Florida. Although his advanced degrees are in philosophy and theology, he has always had an interest in music, whether as a member of a choir, an instrumentalist, or simply as one who loves to hear music for what it is: a profound means of communication which transcends time and culture to speak to all who listen.

Ludwig van Beethoven (1770–1827) is perhaps one of the best known classical composers, famous for music which has uplifted spirits, roused national pride, and captured the emotions of millions over the years. His musical works range from symphonies and concertos to string quartets and solo piano pieces. Among his more famous works are the Fifth and the Ninth Symphonies because of their familiar melodies, and the Third Symphony, originally written as a tribute to Napoleon, but later named Eroica (Hero).

WHO DOES NOT KNOW or recognize the name of Ludwig van Beethoven? Who cannot whistle (or at least hum) that immortal phrase from the *Fifth Symphony?* Yet for all this familiarity, few of us are able to say that we know that much about the person and the troubled life he led. Beethoven's life and circumstances were not the stuff of fairy tales; he had to overcome great pressures and adversity to achieve the degree of success he enjoyed.

As a young boy, Beethoven's father was anxious to have his son recognized as a child prodigy. His first public concert was on March 2 and was advertised to introduce the six-year-old Beethoven to the Court of Bonn. If you noticed that he was born in 1770, you know he was 8, not 6.

For many years, Beethoven believed that he had been born in 1772, but later records indicate that his father had claimed his son was younger to heighten his image as a child prodigy. Beethoven's father placed him under enormous pressure to achieve greatness very early in his life; all his free time away from school was to be spent practicing. This pressure caused Beethoven to spend a great deal of time alone. It is no wonder then that later in life his social skills lacked refinement.

In late 1792, Beethoven went to Vienna to study under another great composer, Haydn, who was at the height of his career. Because of Haydn's busy schedule, there were few lessons from the master and Beethoven studied under another teacher, Johann Schenk. As a student, Beethoven was hardheaded and obstinate and by late 1797, when he was just 17, he discovered that he was losing his hearing. The great tragedy for the young Beethoven is that by 1800, just as he was being recognized as a composer in his own right and being placed on the same level as Mozart and Haydn, he knew that he would soon be completely deaf.

Given Beethoven's lack of social skills and the pressure placed on him from his youth to become a great musician, how would he respond to the news of his deteriorating hearing? At first, he was able to overcome much of the strain because of his success: Prince Lichnowsky acted as his patron and provided him with the financial security he required to compose quietly. While composing can be done in private, performing as a virtuoso musician required public appearances. How would Beethoven respond to the great demands that would be placed on him as a performing musician?

Perhaps most telling is a document known as the Heiligenstadt Testament, written by Beethoven in 1802, in which he presents something of an explanation to his brothers (and to us as well) concerning his increasing irritability and depressed state of mind. It reveals clearly Beethoven's perception of himself, as well as his understanding that others perceived him as a moody and reclusive man.

Heiligenstadt, October 6, 1802
For My Brothers Carl And [Johann] Beethoven

Oh my fellow men, who consider me, or describe me as, unfriendly, peevish or even misanthropic, how greatly do you wrong me. For you do not know the secret reason why I appear to you to be so. Ever since my childhood my heart and soul have been imbued with the tender feeling of goodwill, and I have always been ready to perform even great actions. But just think, for the last six years I have been afflicted with an incurable complaint which has been made worse by incompetent doctors. From year to year my hopes of being cured have gradually been shattered and finally I have been forced to accept the prospect of a *permanent infirmity* (the curing of which may take years or may even prove to be impossible). Though endowed with a passionate and lively temperament and even fond of the distractions offered by society I was soon obliged to seclude myself and live in solitude. If at times I decided just to ignore my infirmity, alas! how cruelly was I then driven back by the intensified sad experience of my poor hearing. Yet I could not bring myself to say to people? 'Speak up, shout, for I am deaf'. Alas! how could I possibly refer to the impairing of *a sense* which in me should be more perfectly developed than in other people, a sense which at one time I possessed in the greatest perfection, even to a degree of perfection such as assuredly few in my profession possess or have ever possessed — Oh, I cannot do it; so please forgive me, if you ever see me withdrawing from your company which I used to enjoy. Moreover my misfortune pains me doubly inasmuch as it leads to my being misjudged. For me there can be no relaxation in human society, no refined conversations, no mutual confidences. I must live quite alone and creep into society only as often as sheer necessity demands; I must live like an outcast. If I appear in com-

pany I am overcome by a burning anxiety, a fear that I am running the risk of letting people notice my condition-And that has been my experience during the last six months which I have spent in the country. My sensible doctor by suggesting that I should spare my hearing as much as possible has more or less encouraged my present natural inclination, though indeed when carried away now and then by my instinctive desire for human society, I have let myself be tempted to seek it. But how humiliated I have felt if someone standing beside me heard the sound of a flute in the distance and I *heard nothing,* or if someone heard a *shepherd sing* and again I heard nothing—Such experiences almost made me despair, and I was on the point of putting an end to my life. The only thing that held me back was my art. For indeed it seemed to me impossible to leave this world before I had produced all the works that I felt the urge to compose; and thus I have dragged on this miserable existence—a truly miserable existence, seeing that I have such a sensitive body and that any fairly sudden change can plunge me from the best of spirits into the worst of [humors—*Patience*—that] is the virtue, I am told, which I must now choose for my guide; and I now possess it—I hope that I shall persist in my resolve to endure to the end, until it pleases the inexorable Parcae[1] to cut the thread; perhaps my condition will improve, perhaps not; at any rate I am now resigned—at the early age of 28 I was obliged to become a philosopher, though this was not easy; for indeed this is more difficult for an artist than for anyone else—Almighty God, who look down into my innermost soul, you see into my heart and you know that it is filled

---

1 *Parcae* is the Latin name for the Fates who in Roman mythology governed human destiny.

with love for humanity and a desire to do good. Oh my fellow men, when someday you read this statement, remember that you have done me wrong; and let some unfortunate man derive comfort from the thought that he has found another equally unfortunate who, notwithstanding all the obstacles imposed by nature, yet did everything in his power to be raised to the rank of noble artists and human beings.—And you, my brothers Carl and [Johann], when I am dead, request on my behalf Professor Schmidt,[2] if he is still living, to describe my disease, and attach this written document to his record, so that after my death at any rate the world and I may be reconciled as far as possible—At the same time I herewith nominate you both heirs to my small property (if I may so describe it) — Divide it honestly, live in harmony and help one another. You know that you have long ago been forgiven for the harm you did me. I thank you again, my brother Carl, in particular, for the affection you have shown me of late years. My wish is that you have a better and more carefree existence than I have had. Urge your children to be *virtuous,* for virtue alone can make a man happy. Money cannot do this. I speak from experience. It was virtue that sustained me in my misery. It was thanks to virtue and also to my art that I did not put an end to my life by suicide—Farewell and love one another—I thank all my friends, and especially *Prince Lichnowsky and Professor Schmidt. I* would like Prince Lichnowsky's instruments to be preserved by one of you, provided this does not lead to a quarrel between you. But as soon as they can serve a more useful purpose, just sell them; how glad I shall be if in my grave I can

LUDWIG VAN BEETHOVEN, C. 1818.
Carl Friedrich Von Kloeber
Pencil drawing.
Beethovenhaus, Bonn, Germany

---

2   Schmidt was the physician Beethoven was seeing at this time. Schmidt had a reputation for miraculous work with deaf patients.

still be of some use to you both—Well, that is all—joyfully I go to meet death-should it come before I have had an opportunity of developing all my artistic gifts, then in spite of my hard fate it would still come too soon, and no doubt I would like to postpone its coming—Yet even so I should be content, for would it not free me from a condition of continual suffering? Come then Death, *whenever* you like, and with courage I will go to meet you—Farewell; and when I am dead, do not wholly forget me. I deserve to be remembered by you, since during my lifetime I have often thought of you and tried to make you happy—Be Happy

Ludwig van Beethoven

For my brothers Carl and [Johann]

To be read and executed after my death

Heiligenstadt, October 10, 1802
Thus I take leave of you — and, what is more, rather sadly — yes, the hope I cherished — the hope I brought with me here of being cured to a certain extent at any rate that hope I must now abandon completely. As the autumn leaves fall and wither, likewise-that hope has faded for me. I am leav-

ing here — almost in the same condition as I arrived — even that high courage which has often inspired me on fine summer days —has vanished-Oh Providence — do but grant me one day of pure joy — for so long now the inner echo of real joy has been unknown to me — Oh when oh when, Almighty God — shall I be able to hear and feel this echo again in the temple of Nature and in contact with humanity Never? — No! — Oh, that would be too hard.[3]

This last will and testament was never read by his brothers during Beethoven's lifetime. It was discovered after Beethoven's death, carefully folded and preserved in a desk drawer. The Testament reveals a darker side of Beethoven which does not seem to match the mood of many of the optimistic and uplifting works composed after 1802. In his own way, Beethoven overcame the adversity of his deafness and presented to the world some of the most memorable works of classical music.

---

[3] This translation of the Heiligenstadt Testament is taken from Philip G. Downs, *Classical Music: The Era of Haydn, Mozart, and Beethoven* (New York, 1992), 5:63–65.

THINK ABOUT IT

1. How did Beethoven's early life influence the adult he became? Did the early pressure in his life help or hinder him as he tried to determine what he would become?

2. How important are the senses for artists? Do musicians need to hear? Do painters need keen eyesight?

TALK ABOUT IT

3. How often do the opinions of other cause some people to give up on their dreams because they are told to be more realistic?

4. Are there people today who are overcoming great odds to achieve success in a field for which no one would think them competent?

WRITE ABOUT IT

5. If you were a public relations expert, how would you go about improving Beethoven's Image? What recommendations would you make to him to improve his "marketability"?

6. Have you been reluctant to reveal some aspect of your life for fear of ridicule and misunderstanding? How had this affected your sense of identity?

READ MORE ABOUT IT

Cooper, Barry, ed. *The Beethoven Compendium: A Guide to Beethoven's Life and Music.* London: Thames and Hudson, 1991.

Downs, Phillip G. *Classical Music: The Era of Haydn, Mozart, and Beethoven.* New York: Norton, 1992.

Scherman, Thomas, and Louis Biancolli, eds. *The Beethoven Companion.* New York: Doubleday, 1972.

Wegeler, Franz Gerhard. *Beethoven Remembered: The Biographical Notes of Franz Wegeler and Ferdinand Ries.* Arlington, VA: Great Ocean Publishers, 1987.

FREDERICK DOUGLASS

I Was a Slave

More than anyone else in the nineteenth century, Frederick Douglass was, in his life and work, a voice yearning for a higher plane of awareness against the prejudice, separation, injustice, indignity, and mute agony of millions of slaves in the United States. Douglass was born about February 7, 1817, in Tuckahoe, Maryland. After escaping slavery in 1838, he stated he was "like one who had escaped a den of hungry lions." He became an eminent American human rights leader, abolitionist, and reformer, as well as a brilliant orator and writer.

A self-made man, he wrote his own autobiography, *The Narrative of the Life of Frederick Douglass,* in 1845 (from which this excerpt is drawn). In addition, he published his own abolitionist newspaper, the *North Star* (later called *Frederick Douglass's Paper*), in Rochester, New York, from 1847 until 1863. He supported women's rights, was a temperance advocate, headed the Rochester station of the Underground Railroad, and was a consultant to Abraham Lincoln during the Civil War. Douglass became the first black citizen to hold high rank in the U.S. government, first as the Assistant Secretary of the Santo Domingo Commission *(1871),* then as Marshall in the District of Columbia *(1877–81),* and finally as minister and consul general to Haiti *(1889–91).* Frederick Douglass, man of integrity, died in Washington on February 20, 1895. *The Narrative of the Life of Frederick Douglass* is Douglass at his best, displaying the penetrating details of nineteenth-century slavery.

I WAS BORN in Tuckahoe, near Hillsborough, and about twelve miles from Easton, in Talbot county, Maryland. I have no accurate knowledge of my age, never having seen any authentic record containing it. By far the larger part of the slaves know as little of their ages as horses know of theirs, and it is the wish of most masters within my knowledge to keep their slaves thus ignorant. I do not remember to have ever met a slave who could tell of his birthday. They seldom come nearer to it than planting-time, harvest-time, cherry-time, spring-time, or fall-time. A want of information concerning my own was a source of unhappiness to me even during childhood. The white children could tell their ages. I could not tell why I ought to be deprived of the same privilege. I was not allowed to make any inquiries of my master concerning it. He deemed all such inquiries on the part of a slave improper and impertinent, and evidence of a restless spirit. The nearest estimate I can give makes me now between twenty-seven and twenty-eight years of age. I come to this, from hearing

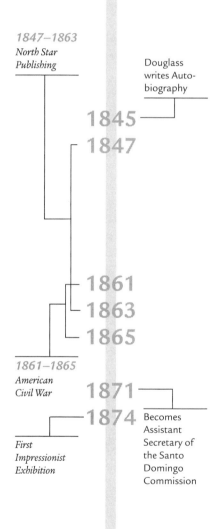

Death of Napoleon — 1817 — Douglass born

1821

July Revolution in Paris — 1830

1847–1863 North Star Publishing — Douglass writes Auto-biography

1845

1847

1861

1863

1865

1861–1865 American Civil War — 1871 — Becomes Assistant Secretary of the Santo Domingo Commission

1874

First Impressionist Exhibition

Douglass dies

1895

my master say, some time during 1835, I was about seventeen years old.

I have had two masters. My first master's name was Anthony. I do not remember his first name. He was generally called Captain Anthony — a title which, I presume, he acquired by sailing a craft on the Chesapeake Bay. He was not considered a rich slaveholder. He owned two or three farms, and about thirty slaves. His farms and slaves were under the care of an overseer. The overseer's name was Plummer. Mr. Plummer was a miserable drunkard, a profane swearer, and a savage monster. He always went armed with a cowskin and a heavy cudgel. I have known him to cut and slash the women's heads so horribly, that even master would be enraged at his cruelty, and would threaten to whip him if he did not mind himself. Master, however, was not a humane slaveholder. It required extraordinary barbarity on the part of an overseer to affect him. He was a cruel man, hardened by a long life of slaveholding. He would at times seem to take great pleasure in whipping a slave. I have often been awakened at the dawn of day by the most heartrending shrieks of an aunt of mine, whom he used to tie up to a joist, and whip upon her naked back till she was literally covered with blood. No words, no tears, no prayers from his gory victim seemed to move his iron heart from its bloody purpose. The louder she screamed, the harder he whipped; and where the blood ran fastest, there he whipped longest. He would whip her to make her scream, and whip her to make her hush; and not until overcome with fatigue, would he cease to swing the blood-clotted cow-skin. I remember the first time I ever witnessed this horrible exhibition. I was quite a child, but I well remember it. I never shall forget it whilst I remember any thing. It was the first of a long series of such outrages, of which I was doomed to be a witness and a participant. It struck me with awful force. It was the blood-stained gate, the entrance to the hell of slavery, through which I was about to pass. It was a most terrible spectacle. I wish I could commit to paper the feelings with which I beheld it.

Chapter III

To describe the wealth of Colonel Lloyd would be almost equal to describing the riches of Job.[1] He kept from ten to fifteen house-servants. He was said to own a thousand slaves, and I think this estimate quite within the truth. Colonel Lloyd owned so many that he did not know them when he saw them; nor did all the slaves of the out-farms know him. It is reported of him, that, while riding along the road one day, he met a colored man, and addressed him in the usual manner of speaking to colored people on the public highways of the south: "Well, boy, whom do you belong to?" "To Colonel Lloyd," replied the slave. "Well, does the colonel treat you well?" "No, sir," was the ready reply. "What, does he work you too hard?" "Yes, sir." "Well, don't he give you enough to eat?" "Yes, sir, he gives me enough, such as it is."

The colonel, after ascertaining where the slave belonged, rode on; the man also went on about his business, not dreaming that he had been conversing with his master. He thought, said, and heard nothing more of the matter, until two or three weeks afterwards. The poor man was then informed by his overseer that, for having found fault with his master, he was now to be sold to a Georgia trader. He was immediately chained and handcuffed; and thus, without a moment's warning, he was snatched away and forever sundered, from his family and friends, by a hand more unrelenting than death. This is the penalty of telling the truth, of telling the simple truth, in answer to a series of plain questions.

It is partly in consequence of such facts, that slaves, when inquired as to their condition and the character of their masters, almost universally say they are contented, and that their masters are kind. The slaveholders have been known to send in spies among their slaves, to ascertain their views and feelings in regard to their condition. The frequency of this has had the effect to establish among the slaves the maxim that a still tongue makes a wise head. They suppress the truth rather than take the consequences of telling it, and in so doing prove themselves a part of the human family. If they have anything to say of their masters, it is generally in their masters' favor, especially when speaking to an untried man. I have been frequently asked, when a slave, if I had a kind master, and do not remember ever to have given a negative answer; nor did I, in pursuing this course, consider myself as uttering what was absolutely false; for I always measured the kindness of my master by the standard of kindness set up among slaveholders around us. Moreover, slaves are like other people, and imbibe prejudices quite common to others. They think their own better than that of others. Many, under the influence of this prejudice, think their own masters are better than the masters of other slaves; and this, too, in some cases, when the very reverse is true. Indeed, it is not uncommon for slaves even to fall out and quarrel among themselves about the relative goodness of their masters, each contending for the superior

---

1 Job 1:3: "His substance also was seven thousand sheep, and three thousand camels, and five hundred yoke of oxen, and five hundred she asses, and a very great household; so that this man was the greatest of all the men of the east."

goodness of his own over that of the others. At the very same time, they mutually execrate their masters when viewed separately. It was so on our plantation. When Colonel Lloyd's slaves met the slaves of Jacob Jepson, they seldom parted without a quarrel about their masters; Colonel Lloyd's slaves contending that he was the richest, and Mr. Jepson's slaves that he was the smartest and most of a man. Colonel Lloyd's slaves would boast his ability to buy and sell Jacob Jepson. Mr. Jepson's slaves would boast his ability to whip Colonel Lloyd. These quarrels would almost always end in a fight between the parties, and those that whipped were supposed to have gained the point of issue. They seemed to think that the greatness of their masters was transferable to themselves. It was considered as being bad enough to be a slave; but to be a poor man's slave was deemed a disgrace indeed!

Chapter V

As to my own treatment while I lived on Colonel Lloyd's plantation, it was very similar to that of the other slave children. I was not old enough to work in the field, and there being little else than field work to do, I had a great deal of leisure time. The most I had to do was to drive up the cows at evening, keep the fowls out of the garden, keep the front yard clean, and run off errands for my old master's daughter, Mrs. Lucretia Auld. The most of my leisure time I spent in helping Master Daniel Lloyd in finding his birds after he had shot them. My connection with Master Daniel was of some advantage to me. He became quite attached to me, and was a sort of protector of me. He would not allow the older boys to impose upon me, and would divide his cakes with me.

I was seldom whipped by my old master, and suffered little from any

thing else than hunger and cold. I suffered much from hunger, but much more from cold. In hottest summer and coldest winter, I was kept almost naked — no shoes, no stockings, no jacket, no trousers, nothing on but a coarse tow linen shirt, reaching only to my knees. I had no bed. I must have perished with cold, but that, the coldest nights, I used to steal a bag which was used for carrying corn to the mill. I would crawl into this bag, and there sleep on the cold, damp, clay floor, with my head in and feet out. My feet had been so cracked with the frost, that the pen with which I am writing might be laid in the gashes.

We were not regularly allowanced. Our food was coarse corn meal boiled. This was called mush. It was put into a large wooden tray or trough and set down upon the ground. The children were then called, like so many pigs, and like so many pigs they would come and devour the mush; some with oyster shells, others with pieces of shingle, some with naked hands, and none with spoons. He that ate fastest got most; he that was strongest secured the best place; and few left the trough satisfied.

I was probably between seven and eight years old when I left Colonel Lloyd's plantation. I left it with joy. I shall never forget the ecstasy with which I received the intelligence that my old master (Anthony) had determined to let me go to Baltimore, to live with Mr. Hugh Auld, brother to my old master's son-in-law, Captain Thomas Auld. I received this information about three days before my departure. They were three of the happiest days I ever enjoyed. I spent the most part of all these three days in the creek, washing off the plantation scum, and preparing myself for my departure.

The pride of appearance which this would indicate was not my own. I

spent the time in washing, not so much because I wished to, but because Mrs. Lucretia had told me I must get all the dead skin off my feet and knees before I could go to Baltimore; for the people in Baltimore were very cleanly, and would laugh at me if I looked dirty. Besides, she was going to give me a pair of trousers, which I could not put on unless I got all the dirt off me. The thought of owning a pair of trousers was great indeed! It was almost a sufficient motive, not only to make me take off what would be called by pig-drovers the mange, but the skin itself. I went at it in good earnest, working for the first time with the hope of reward ...

We arrived at Baltimore early on Sunday morning, landing at Smith's Wharf; not far from Bowley's Wharf. We had on board the sloop a large flock of sheep; and after aiding in driving them to the slaughterhouse of Mr. Curtis on Louden Slater's Hill, I was conducted by Rich, one of the hands belonging on board of the sloop, to my new home in Alliciana Street, near Mr. Gardner's ship-yard, on Fells Point.

Mr. and Mrs. Auld were both at home, and met me at the door with their little son Thomas, to take care of whom I had been given. And here I saw what I had never seen before; it was a white face beaming with the most kindly emotions; it was the face of my new mistress, Sophia Auld. I wish I could describe the rapture that flashed through my soul as I beheld it. It was a new and strange sight to me, brightening up my pathway with the light of happiness. Little Thomas was told, there was his Freddy, — and I was told to take care of little Thomas; and thus I entered upon the duties of my new home with the most cheering prospect ahead.

I look upon my departure from Colonel Lloyd's plantation as one of the most interesting events of my life.

It is possible, and even quite probable, that but for the mere circumstance of being removed from that plantation to Baltimore, I should have to-day, instead of being here seated by my own table, in the enjoyment of freedom and the happiness of home, writing this Narrative, been confined in the galling chains of slavery. Going to live at Baltimore laid the foundation, and opened the gateway, to all my subsequent prosperity. I have ever regarded it as the first plain manifestation of that kind providence which has ever since attended me, and marked my life with so many favors. I regarded the selection of myself as being somewhat remarkable. There were a number of slave children that might have been sent from the plantation to Baltimore. There were those younger, those older, and those of the same age. I was chosen from among them all, and as the first, last, and only choice.

I may be deemed superstitious, and even egotistical, in regarding this event as a special interposition of divine Providence in my favor. But I should be false to the earliest sentiment of my soul, if I suppressed the opinion. I prefer to be true to myself, even at the hazard of incurring the ridicule of others, rather than to be false, and incur my own abhorrence.

From my earliest recollection, I date the entertainment of a deep conviction that slavery would not always be able to hold me within its foul embrace, and in the darkest hours of my career in slavery, this living word of faith and spirit of hope departed not from me, but remained like ministering angels to cheer me through the gloom. This good spirit was from God, and to him I offer thanksgiving and praise.

Chapter VI

Very soon after I went to live with Mr. and Mrs. Auld, she very kindly commenced to teach me the A, B, C. After I had learned this, she assisted me in learning to spell words of three or four letters. just at this point of my progress, Mr. Auld found out what was going on, and at once forbade Mrs. Auld to instruct me further, telling her, among other things, that it was unlawful, as well as unsafe, to teach a slave to read. To use his own words, further, he said, "If you give a nigger an inch, he will take an ell. A nigger should know nothing but to obey his master — to do as he is told to do. Learning would spoil the best nigger in the world. Now," said he, "if you teach that nigger (speaking of myself) how to read, there would be no keeping him. It would forever unfit him to be a slave. He would at once become unmanageable, and of no value to his master. As to himself, it could do him no good, but a great deal of harm. It would make him discontented and unhappy." These words sank deep into my heart, stirred up sentiments within that lay slumbering, and called into existence an entirely new train of thought. It was a new and special revelation, explaining dark and mysterious things, with which my youthful understanding had struggled, but struggled in vain. I now understood what had been to me a most perplexing difficulty — to wit, the white man's power to enslave the black man. It was a grand achievement, and I prized it highly. From that moment, I understood the pathway from slavery to freedom. It was just what I wanted, and I got it at a time when I least expected it. Whilst I was saddened by the thought of losing the aid of my kind mistress, I was gladdened by the invaluable instruction which, by the merest accident, I had gained from

my master. Though conscious of the difficulty of learning without a teacher, I set out with high hope, and a fixed purpose, at whatever cost of trouble, to learn how to read. The very decided manner with which he spoke, and strove to impress his wife with the evil consequences of giving me instruction, served to convince me that he was deeply sensible of the truths he was uttering. It gave me the best assurance that I might rely with the utmost confidence on the results which, he said, would flow from teaching to read. What he most dreaded, that I most desired. What he most loved, that I most hated. That which to him was a great evil, to be carefully shunned, was to me a great good, to be diligently sought; and the argument which he so warmly urged, against my learning to read, only served to inspire me with a desire and determination to learn. In learning to read, I owe almost as much to the bitter opposition of my master, as to the kindly aid of my mistress. I acknowledge the benefit of both.

Chapter VII

The idea as to how I might learn to write was suggested to me by being in Durgin and Bailey's shipyard, and frequently seeing the ship carpenters, after hewing, and getting a piece of timber ready for use write on the timber the name of that part of the ship for which it was intended. When a piece of timber was intended for the larboard side, it would be marked thus — "L." When a piece was for the starboard side, it would be marked thus — "S." A piece for the larboard forward, would be marked thus — "L. F." When a piece was for starboard forward, it would be marked thus — "S. F." For larboard aft, it would be marked thus — "L. A." For starboard aft, it would be marked thus — "S. A." I soon learned the names of these letters, and for what they were intended when placed upon a piece of timber in the shipyard. I immediately commenced copying them, and in a short time was able to make the four letters named. After that, when I met with any boy who I knew could write, I would tell him I could write as well as he. The next word would be "I don't believe you. Let me see you try it." I would then make the letters which I had been so fortunate as to learn, and ask him to beat that. In this way I got a good many lessons in writing, which it is quite possible I should never have gotten in any other way. During this time, my copybook was the board fence, brick wall, and pavement; my pen and ink was a lump of chalk. With these, I learned mainly how to write. I then commenced and continued copying the italics in Webster's Spelling Book, until I could make them all without looking at the book. By this time, my little Master Thomas had gone to school, and learned how to write, and had written over a number of copybooks. These had been brought home, and shown to some of our near neighbors, and then laid aside. My mistress used to go to class meeting at the Wilk Street meeting house every Monday afternoon, and leave me to take care of the house. When left thus, I used to spend the time in writing in the spaces left in Master Thomas's copybook, copying what he had written. I continued to do this until I could write a hand very similar to that of Master Thomas. Thus after a long, tedious effort for years, I finally succeeded in learning how to write.

Chapter X

I left Master Thomas's house, and went to live with Mr. Covey on the 1st of January, 1833. I was now, for the first time in my life, a field hand. In my new employment, I found myself

even more awkward than a country boy appeared to be in a large city. I had been at my new home but one week before Mr. Covey gave me a very severe whipping, cutting my back, causing the blood to run, and raising ridges on my flesh as large as my little finger.

If at any one time of my life more than another, I was made to drink the bitterest dregs of slavery, that time was during the first six months of my stay with Mr. Covey. We were worked in all weathers. It was never too hot or too cold; it could never rain, blow, hail, or snow, too hard for us to work in the field. Work, work, work, was scarcely more the order of the day than of the night. The longest days were too short for him. I was somewhat unmanageable when I first went there, but a few months of this discipline tamed me. Mr. Covey succeeded in breaking me. I was broken in body, soul, and spirit. My natural elasticity was crushed, my intellect languished, the disposition to read departed, the cheerful spark that lingered about my eye died: the dark night of slavery closed in upon me; and behold a man transformed into a brute!

Long before daylight, I was called to go and rub, curry, and feed the horses. I obeyed, and was glad to obey. But whilst thus engaged, whilst in the act of throwing down some blades from the loft, Mr. Covey entered the stable with a long rope; and just as I was half out of the loft, he caught hold of my legs, and was about tying me. As soon as I found what he was up to, I gave a sudden spring, and as I did so, he holding to my legs, I was brought sprawling on the stable floor. Mr. Covey seemed now to think he had me, and could do what he pleased; but at this moment — from whence came the spirit I don't know — I resolved to fight; and, suiting my action to the resolution, I seized Covey hard by the throat; and as I did

so, I rose. He held on to me, and I to him. My resistance was so entirely unexpected, that Covey seemed taken all aback. He trembled like a leaf. This gave me assurance, and I held him uneasy, causing the blood to run where I touched him with the ends of my fingers. Mr. Covey soon called out to Hughes for help. Hughes came, and, while Covey held me, attempted to tie my right hand. While he was in the act of doing so, I watched my chance, and gave him a heavy kick close under the ribs. This kick fairly sickened Hughes, so that he left me in the hands of Mr. Covey. This kick had the effect of not only weakening Hughes, but Covey also. When he saw Hughes bending over with pain, his courage quailed. He asked me if I meant to persist in my resistance. I told him I did, come what might; that he had used me like a brute for six months, and that I was determined to be used so no longer. With that, he strove to drag me to a stick that was lying just out of the stable door. He meant to knock me down. But just as he was leaning over to get the stick, I seized him with both hands by his collar, and brought him by a sudden snatch to the ground. By this time, Bill came. Covey called upon him for assistance. Bill wanted to know what he could do.

Covey said, "Take hold of him, take hold of him!" Bill said his master hired him out to work, and not to help to whip me; so he left Covey and myself to fight our own battle out. We were at it for nearly two hours. Covey at length let me go, puffing and blowing at a great rate, saying that if I had not resisted, he would not have whipped me half so much. The truth was that he had not whipped me at all. I considered him as getting entirely the worst end of the bargain; for he had drawn no blood from me, but I had from him. The whole six months afterwards, that I spent with

Mr. Covey, he never laid the weight of his finger upon me in anger. He would occasionally say he didn't want to get hold of me again. "No," thought I, "you need not; for you will come off worse than you did before."

This battle with Mr. Covey was the turning-point in my career as a slave. It rekindled the few expiring embers of freedom, and revived within me a sense of my own manhood. It recalled the departed self-confidence, and inspired me again with a determination to be free. The gratification afforded by the triumph was a full compensation for whatever else might follow, even death itself.

He only can understand the deep satisfaction which I experienced, who has himself repelled by force the bloody arm of slavery. I felt as I never felt before. It was a glorious resurrection, from the tomb of slavery, to the heaven of freedom. My long-crushed spirit rose, cowardice departed, and defiance took its place; and I now resolved that, however long I might remain a slave in form, the day had passed forever when I could be a slave in fact. I did not hesitate to let it be known of me, that the white man who expected to succeed in whipping, must also succeed in killing me.

THINK ABOUT IT

1. Describe the life that Douglass endured as a slave.
2. Why was it so important for Douglass to learn to read?

TALK ABOUT IT

3. How does Douglass show his autonomous nature, even while remaining a slave?
4. In what countries are people still striving for freedom? Why do they feel freedom is necessary?

WRITE ABOUT IT

5. Write a fictional conversation between Douglass and a contemporary civil rights leader on the nature of freedom.
6. Do you feel you have ever been discriminated against? Describe what your reaction was or what you think it would be.

READ MORE ABOUT IT

Douglass, Frederick. *The Frederick Douglass Papers, Series 1: Speeches, Debates, and Interviews.* 2 vols. New Haven: Yale, 1979–1982.

Huggins, Nathan. *Slave and Citizen: The Life of Frederick Douglass.* Boston: Little, Brown, 1980.

McFeely, William S. *Frederick Douglass.* New York: Norton, 1991.

Santrey, Laurence. *Young Frederick Douglass: Fight for Freedom.* Mahwah, NJ: Troll, 1983.

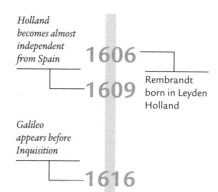

D I A N N   R O T H W E L L   L A P I N

Beyond Appearance

Rembrandt's Search for Self

Diann Rothwell Lapin is Director of Graduate Admissions at Columbia College in Chicago, Illinois. She holds advanced degrees in Liberal Studies and Art History. As an Art History student in London, England, she spent long hours in the "Rembrandt Rooms" at the National Gallery studying Rembrandt's evocative self-portraits and other portraits he painted of men and women of the "Golden Age" of Holland.

Rembrandt van Rijn, known only as "Rembrandt," was born in Holland just as it was becoming an independent country in the seventeenth century. Holland was in its "Golden Age" and was a prosperous country of merchants, bankers, and artisans. Dutch people liked to demonstrate their wealth by having portraits painted and by decorating their homes with artworks of everyday scenes. This was an age when a hard-working and talented artist could support himself well. Rembrandt decided to become one of those artists and worked steadily to develop his skills. By 1630, the high quality of Rembrandt's etchings and paintings had established him as one of the leading artists in Amsterdam, Holland's largest city. In fact, in the 1630s and 1640s, many famous people in Amsterdam and from nearby cities wanted Rembrandt and no one else to paint their portraits. Although many of his artworks are commissioned portraits, Rembrandt also painted scenes of everyday life and did etchings of simple religious and Biblical events. His artworks always portrayed his subjects in a highly creative manner. For example, in his greatest masterpiece, "The Night Watch," a group portrait painted in 1642, the viewer is exposed to a truly unique arrangement of figures and superb handling of the tonal qualities of the oil paint. What makes this and Rembrandt's other works most striking are the effects of light and dark color contrasts. In his portraits, especially his self-portraits, Rembrandt used the stark contrasts of white light and brown-black shadow to reveal the inner essence of his subjects.

IN 1630, at the age of twenty-three, Rembrandt completed his first self-portrait. This first image started the young artist on a search that would continue for forty years. During this time, Rembrandt painted at least sixty (some sources say ninety!) portraits of himself. While some of these portraits were probably etched or painted so that Rembrandt could practice his artistic techniques on an available model (himself), it becomes apparent that Rembrandt's reason for producing so many portraits was centered

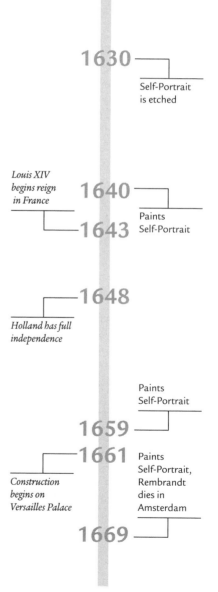

Holland becomes almost independent from Spain
1606

1609 Rembrandt born in Leyden Holland

Galileo appears before Inquisition
1616

1630
Self-Portrait is etched

Louis XIV begins reign in France
1640

1643 Paints Self-Portrait

1648

Holland has full independence

Paints Self-Portrait
1659

1661 Paints Self-Portrait, Rembrandt dies in Amsterdam

Construction begins on Versailles Palace

1669

on a search for his own unique identity. Over the years, his quest intensified. In his many self-portraits, Rembrandt moved from capturing his surface personality to a deeper probing of self. Ultimately, he sought to represent the inner essence of who he was.

Rembrandt's first self-portraits were executed in the artistic print medium called etching. Etchings and other print media could be reproduced inexpensively, thereby increasing an artist's income more quickly than paintings. Bad at money management, Rembrandt always needed more income. He worked hard to develop his etching technique so he could make money quickly. As all etching artists do, Rembrandt went through the following steps to produce an etching. First, he coated a metal printing plate with an acid-resistant material called a ground. Next, Rembrandt drew his composition on the coated plate with an etching needle, a metal instrument similar to a sharp pen. The composition had to be drawn in reverse of the desired outcome. The action of the needle removed the ground, thus exposing the metal plate in those areas meant to be printed with ink. Then, the entire plate was dipped in acid. The acid ate into the sections of the metal plate that the needle exposed. Next, the ground was removed and the plate then inked and printed. Since the biting action of the acid is somewhat irregular, an etching produces lines that are less exact than those of other printing methods. This lack of precision can lead to very natural effects, such as those seen in Rembrandt's self-portrait of 1630.

Rembrandt's intense expression convincingly conveys his twenty-three-year-old personality. He uses strong areas of light and dark contrast to capture what appears to be an expression of surprise. At this time,

Rembrandt was just starting out as an artist, but had had some early successes. To further his earning power, he knew he must master the art of portraiture and learn to etch well.

Perhaps the intense gaze was the result of too closely reproducing the stare he had to maintain as he etched his image while looking in a mirror. It is apparent, however, that he had begun to master the etching medium. The soft straight lines of his capped hair contrast interestingly with the stronger curved lines of his nose and pursed lips. It is amazing that this portrait is only two inches by one and seven-eighths inches! The small scale of this work makes it very personal, even intimate, and further demonstrates Rembrandt's precision with the etching needle. (Rembrandt became so talented at using an etching needle that he often went out sketching with one in the same manner that most artists use a pencil!) Despite the small size, Rembrandt has shown us a unique young man with a confident, yet startled, expression. He has proved he could successfully capture his outward appearance in an etching.

Ten years later, Rembrandt was capturing his image and living his life on a much grander scale. In 1640, he was the most successful artist in Amsterdam and was at the height of his fame and fortune. He married a wealthy woman and lived extravagantly. Rembrandt loved to dress up in costumes and go to parties — indeed, he etched and painted a number of self-portraits in "fancy dress." Like many wealthy Dutch of the time, he showed off his success in material ways. It was not accidental that in 1640 Rembrandt chose to paint himself in the affluent dress fabrics of fur, velvet, and lace with an accompanying gold chain on his chest and jewels sparkling in his cap. (Color Plate 2) The very fact that this work was executed in oil paint, the most costly

medium, speaks to his material success. The method by which he painted the work, though, more directly relates to his personality. In this self-portrait, Rembrandt demonstrated great artistic control that was reflective of the control he had of his fortunes. This life-size self portrait was painted in a detailed and meticulous manner. Colors were carefully blended and the paint surface smoothly executed. As in many of his portraits of the time, such details as the ornate lace trim of his shirt collar and the striped satin insets on his sleeve were reproduced in a highly realistic manner. Also, he successfully captured a proud facial expression. He stares at the viewer in a direct, uncompromising manner with the tilt of his cap and his strong right arm showing us a person in confident control. Rembrandt seems proud of his appearance — this is a man who gazes outward in an independent, assertive fashion.

The heightened realism Rembrandt achieved in this self-portrait of 1640 was greatly valued by the Dutch public. The same precise painting techniques used in this work brought him considerable fame as a portraitist. Rembrandt's use of oil paint was revolutionary; he was one of the first Dutch painters to build up his surface with a brush loaded with thick paint rather than applying the thin glazes that were typical of the time. For example, with one stroke of thick white paint contained on a stiffened brush, he dabbed in realistic highlights such as the jewels that sparkle in his cap in the 1640 portrait. Also, some steps in Rembrandt's working process were not conventional. As most artists did, first he sized the canvas to keep the initial paint layers from absorbing into the fabric. Then, he laid down a medium-brown ground, the base coat. Next, using one color, usually a neutral such as light brown, he painted rather than

**SELF PORTRAIT IN A CAP,
OPEN MOUTHED AND STARING, 1630.**
Rembrandt van Rijn
Etching, 2¹⁄₁₆ × 1⁷⁄₈ in.
British Museum, London, England.

began to erode in the late 1640s. His wife died and his artworks no longer commanded high prices, yet he continued to live an extravagant lifestyle. He had always lived beyond his means and his fortunes quickly dwindled to the point that he was forced to declare bankruptcy in 1656. His self-portraits of the mid-1650s show a troubled and weary man. During this time, Rembrandt moved beyond depicting himself as proud of his outer appearance to portray an inner directed questioning.

By 1659, Rembrandt was capturing his inner feelings with an arresting honesty. (Color Plate 3) He reproduced the subtleties of the surface appearance of his face, and in so doing, exposed his deepest self to the viewer. The slanting light falls on his fifty-three-year-old visage in a delicate, yet revealing manner. The clothes are unimportant in this portrait; they appear only as soft, dark brown tones that shadow the face convincingly. The slow and clarifying movement of the light across his face conveys a psychology that has moved beyond questioning to resignation, seemingly because of his greatly changed fortunes. Rembrandt was no longer in confident control of life: instead, he accepted what fate bestowed upon him. His expressive, wrinkled eyes do not challenge the viewer, rather they are at one with the meditative set of his mouth. This is an inward-looking portrayal of a highly individualistic and independent man. The acceptance of his lot in life is conveyed by the unity of this representation.

Interestingly, the 1659 work, also a life-size depiction, is painted in looser brushstrokes than the self-portrait of 1640. The paint is not as smoothly blended as in 1640; most of it is applied in Rembrandt's unique built-up method. Rembrandt loaded his brush with flesh-toned paint for

drew in his composition on the canvas. This painting in of the composition was highly unusual in an age that considered drawing the required basis of any artwork. Also, at this stage, Rembrandt planned out the distribution of light and shade — another unique step. Then, using the painted plan as his guide, he began applying color. He painted the background and worked forward leaving the areas that appear closest to the viewer and are the lightest to be painted last. In portrait paintings this means that the face or other exposed flesh was the last major area to be done. Finally, the highlights such as the jewels and gold chain in this 1640 portrait would be quickly dabbed in. No matter how chaotic his personal fortunes, Rembrandt's painting technique was always masterfully controlled and closely followed the steps detailed above.

Indeed, Rembrandt's feelings of independence and personal control

his face, stroking it on in the same direction as he did the dark brown shadows in his wrinkles. Then, he dabbed on lighter-toned highlights to capture the subtle effects of the light on his features. Thus, Rembrandt's unusual methods of applying paint were representative of the equally independent inner essence he reproduced.

In a similar manner, the life-size self-portrait Rembrandt executed in the last year of his life, 1669, was created using his unconventional built-up painting technique. (Color Plate 4) His now-gray hair is simply a fuzz of ill-defined brushstrokes while the left side of his face seems to blend into the background. Rembrandt appears to have less of a physical presence in this portrait: his outer appearance is loosely formed, almost as if it is fading away. It is only his face that demands the viewer's attention — here Rembrandt has balanced thick flesh-toned brush strokes with lighter flesh-colored highlights laid down beside them to emphasize the clarifying light effects that sweep across his features. The dark background contrasts dramatically with the light tones in his face. Thus, the overall effect is such that while the outer presence is rendered less precisely than in earlier self-portraits, the inner being is more strongly conveyed. In particular, Rembrandt had mastered light and dark tones to such an extent that his eyes seem to penetrate into the very spirit of the viewer. Consequently, the viewer's focus is on the intensity emanating from his eyes. One feels that Rembrandt's inner psychology was one of acceptance and quiet thought. Curiously, his red velvet coat and beret remind us of his infatuation with "fancy dress." Perhaps in this last portrait Rembrandt was trying to integrate the many facets of his life into one final assertion that his search for self had been achieved.

Was Rembrandt's search fulfilled? Do the four self-portraits that have been examined reveal that Rembrandt's personal quest for his inner spirit was realized? First, an optimistic and confident youth is shown in the 1630 etched portrait. This gives way to the second, the self-portrait of 1640, that portrays a materially successful and outwardly confident mature man. In this painting, Rembrandt demonstrated that he was truly a master at capturing his outer appearance and could convey a sense of personality as well. It is in the third, the portrait of 1659, however, that Rembrandt realized his quest and created an image that reflected his unique and independent spirit. This was a spirit finding its identity within rather than searching for it in the material world without. In the fourth and final portrait of 1669, Rembrandt moved beyond independence to integration. It was in this last year of his life that Rembrandt finally did portray himself as a person at peace. He seems resigned yet self-assured as he awaits death. This great artist, Rembrandt van Rijn, successfully used the media of etching and oil paint to reproduce his outer appearance as a means of defining and presenting the true and complex being within.

THINK ABOUT IT

1. How did Rembrandt's use of media — etching and oil paint — change from one work to the next? Describe the differences between the etching process used for the first portrait and the oil paint used for the last one.
2. How did Rembrandt's sense of identity develop from the age of twenty-three to the age of sixty-three? Why does the "self" he reveals in each of the four portraits change?

TALK ABOUT IT

3. If Rembrandt was alive today, what would his portraits look like? What visual media would he use? What would he wear? What would the setting be?
4. Assuming you could be a "time traveler" and meet Rembrandt, where would you like to meet him? What would you want to ask him?

WRITE ABOUT IT

5. What famous person living today comes closest to being a modern Rembrandt?
6. Look through old photographs of yourself from four different stages in your life. In what ways did your outer appearance change from one photograph to the next? What identity does each photograph reveal?

READ MORE ABOUT IT

Anfam, David A., and Contributors. *Techniques of the Great Masters of Art.* London: QED Publishing Ltd., 1985. (Publisher in USA: Chartwell Books, Inc.)

Bomford, David, Brown, Christopher, and Ashok, Roy. *Art in the Making: Rembrandt.* London: National Gallery Publications, 1988.

Schama, Simon. *The Embarrassment of Riches: An Interpretation of Dutch Culture in the Golden Age.* London: William Collins Sons and Co., Ltd, 1987. (Publisher in USA: Fontana Press)

Wallace, Robert, and the Editors of Time-Life Books. *The World of Rembrandt: 1606-1669.* New York: Time, Inc., 1968.

MIGUEL DE CERVANTES

How Don Quixote Became a Knight

Miguel de Cervantes was born in 1547 to a poor Spanish surgeon and his wife, the fourth of seven children. After some early general education, he embarked on a series of adventures that influenced his later writings. In 1571, he traveled to Italy, became a soldier, and fought in the Battle of Lepanto. There, while distinguishing himself on the battlefield, Cervantes permanently lost the use of his left hand. In 1575, as he was returning to Spain on a ship, it was captured by Barbary pirates. The pirates took Cervantes and his shipmates to Algiers in North Africa and sold them into slavery. He spent five years as a slave where, despite his handicap, he repeatedly tried daring escapes. Finally, his freedom was ransomed by admiring monks. Cervantes then returned home to Spain, married, and became a purchasing agent for the Navy. His adventures continued as he traveled the country in his job and was twice imprisoned for debt. He lived in poverty until 1605 when Part I of *Don Quixote* was published. Although Cervantes continued to write until the end of his life, publishing at least thirty plays and many short stories, it is because of *Don Quixote* that he is famous. This novel was an immediate success and has remained one of the most widely read works of western literature.

Hailed as the first modern novel and the most influential work ever written in Spanish, *Don Quixote* recounts the tale of a poor country gentleman who has immersed himself in reading romances (stories of knights and chivalry) for many years. Crazed by his obsession with knight-errantry, Don Quixote believes that it is his duty to leave his native province of La Mancha and travel the world to redress every wrong he encounters. The novel opens with the Don preparing for his departure. As his many adventures unfold, the Don guards his armor, chooses a lady love to whom he dedicates his battles, talks to his gallant steed, and hires a squire (a knight-in-training who waits on the Don). All these actions mimic those of a typical medieval knight in a romance. As Cervantes states in the novel's Prologue, "[this] is, from beginning to end, an attack upon the books of chivalry ... [and their] fanciful nonsense." Even so, it is a book filled with high adventure and great comic moments as the chapter that follows demonstrates. Appearing early in the novel soon after the Don leaves home, this chapter recounts the way in which Don Quixote is dubbed a knight at a roadside inn.

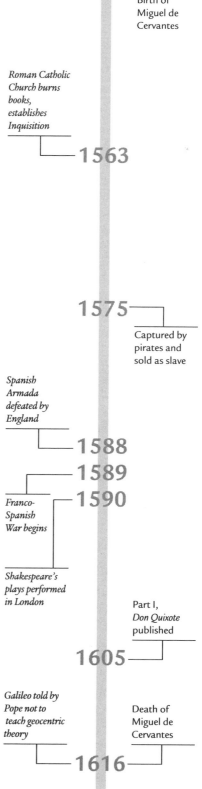

1547 — Birth of Miguel de Cervantes

Roman Catholic Church burns books, establishes Inquisition

1563

1575 — Captured by pirates and sold as slave

Spanish Armada defeated by England

1588

1589

1590

Franco-Spanish War begins

Shakespeare's plays performed in London

Part I, *Don Quixote* published

1605

Galileo told by Pope not to teach geocentric theory

Death of Miguel de Cervantes

1616

HARASSED BY this reflection, he wasted no time on the scanty supper always found in such inns, and when it was finished he called the landlord. Having shut himself up in the stable with him, Don Quixote fell on his knees before him. "From this spot I rise not, valiant knight," he declared, "until thy courtesy grant me the boon I seek, one that will redound to thy praise and the benefit of the human race." Seeing his guest at his feet and hearing speech of this kind, the landlord stood staring at him in bewilderment without knowing what to do or say. He entreated Don Quixote to rise, but all to no purpose, until he had agreed to grant the boon demanded.

"I looked for no less, my lord, from thy, High Magnificence," replied Don Quixote, "and I have to tell thee that the boon I have asked and which thy liberality has granted is that thou shalt dub me knight tomorrow morning. Tonight I shall watch my arms in the chapel of this thy castle and tomorrow, as I have said, what I so much desire will be accomplished. It will enable me lawfully to roam through all the four quarters of the world seeking adventures on behalf of those in distress, as is the duty of chivalry and of knights-errant like myself, whose ambition is directed to such deeds."

The landlord, as has been mentioned, was something of a wag. He had already some suspicion of his guest's lack of wits, and to hear talk of this kind quite convinced him. To provide sport for the night, he determined to humor Don Quixote. So he told him he was quite right in pursuing the object he had in view, and that such a motive was natural and becoming in cavaliers as distinguished as he seemed and his gallant bearing showed him to be. As for the landlord himself, in his younger days he had followed the same honorable calling,

roaming in quest of adventures in various parts of the world, among others the curing-grounds and Riarán suburbs of Málaga, the red light district of Seville, the Little Market of Segovia, Olivera Square in Valencia, Rondilla Lane in Granada, the Strand of San Lúcar, the Horse Fountain of Córdoba, the taverns of Toledo,[1] and sundry other localities. There he had proved the nimbleness of his feet and the lightness of his fingers, doing many wrongs, courting many widows, ruining a few maidens and swindling a few minors, and, in short, bringing himself under the notice of almost every tribunal and court of Justice in Spain. But at last he had retired to this castle of his, where he was living upon his property and upon that of others. Here he received all knights-errant of whatever rank or condition they might be, all for the great love he bore them and that they might share their substance with him in return for his benevolence.

He told Don Quixote, moreover, that in this castle of his there was no chapel in which he could watch over his armor, as it had been pulled down in order to be rebuilt. Yet in a case of necessity it might, he knew, be watched anywhere, and vigil might be held that night in a courtyard of the castle. In the morning, God willing, the requisite ceremonies might be performed so as to have him dubbed a knight, and so thoroughly dubbed that nobody could be more so.

Then he asked if he had any money with him, to which Don Quixote replied that he had not a cent, as in the histories of knights-errant he had never read of any of them carrying any. On this point, the landlord told him he was mistaken, for,

though not recorded in the histories, because in the author's opinion there was no need to mention anything so obvious and necessary as money, and clean shirts, it was not to be supposed therefore that they did not carry them. He might regard it as certain and established that all knights-errant (about whom there were so many full and unimpeachable books) carried well-furnished purses in case of emergency, and likewise carried shirts and a little box of ointment to cure the wounds they received. For in those plains and deserts where they engaged in combat and came out wounded, there was not always someone to cure them, unless indeed they had for a friend some sage magician to aid them at once by fetching through the air on a cloud some damsel or dwarf with a vial of water of such power that by tasting one drop of it they were cured of their hurts and wounds in an instant and left as sound as if they had not received any harm whatever. In case this should not occur, the knights of old took care to see that their squires were provided with money and other requisites, such as bandages and ointments for healing purposes. And when it happened that knights had no squires (which was rarely and seldom the case), they themselves carried everything in very slim saddlebags that were hardly seen on the horse's croup, as if it were something else of more importance. Unless for some such reason, carrying saddlebags was not very favorably regarded among knights-errant. He therefore advised him (and, as his godson so soon to be, he might even command him) never from that time forth to travel without money and the usual requirements, and he would find how useful they were when he least expected it.

Don Quixote promised to follow his advice scrupulously, and it was arranged forthwith that he should

---

[1] The localities mentioned were famous meeting places for delinquents, prostitutes, itinerant workers, gamblers, etc.

watch over his armor in a large yard at one side of the inn. So, collecting it all together, Don Quixote placed it on a trough that stood by the side of a well, and putting his shield on his arm, he grasped his lance and began with a stately air to march up and down in front of the trough. As he began his march night began to fall.

The landlord told all the people in the inn about his guest's craziness, the watching of the armor, and the dubbing ceremony to come. Full of wonder at so strange a form of madness, they flocked to see it from a distance and observed with what composure he sometimes paced up and down, or sometimes, leaning on his lance, gazed on his armor without taking his eyes off it for ever so long. As the night closed in with a light from the moon so brilliant that it might vie with the source from which it was borrowed, everything the novice knight did was plainly seen by all.

Meanwhile, one of the mule drivers who were in the inn saw fit to water his team, making it necessary to remove Don Quixote's armor, as it lay on the trough. But the knight, seeing the other approach, hailed him in a loud voice.

"0 thou," he said, "whoever thou art, rash knight that comest to lay hands on the armor of the most valorous errant that ever girt on sword, have a care what thou dost. Touch it not unless thou wouldst lay down thy life as the penalty of thy rashness." The mule driver gave no heed to these words, though for the sake of his health it would have been advisable to do so. He seized the armor by the straps and flung it some distance from him. At this, Don Quixote raised his eyes to heaven, and appeared to fix his thoughts upon his lady Dulicinea. "Aid me, lady mine," he entreated, "in this the first encounter that presents itself to this breast which thou holdest in subjection. Let

not thy favor and Protection fail me in this first jeopardy."

Having made these and similar declarations, he dropped his shield and lifted his lance with both hands. With it he dealt such a blow on the driver's head that he stretched him on the ground, so stunned that had he followed it up with a second, there would have been no need of a surgeon to cure the mule driver. This done, Don Quixote picked up his armor and began walking up and down with the same serenity as before.

Shortly after this another mule driver, unaware of what had happened (for the first one still lay senseless), came out with the same intention of watering his mules. He too was proceeding to remove the armor in order to clear the trough, when Don Quixote, without uttering a word or imploring aid from anyone, once more dropped his shield and once more lifted his lance. Without actually smashing the second driver's head to bits, he made more than three pieces of it, for he laid it open in four quarters. At the noise, all the people in the inn ran to the spot, and among them the landlord. Seeing this, Don Quixote braced his shield on his arm and laid his hand on his sword. "0 Lady of Beauty," he exclaimed, "strength and support of my faint heart, it is time for thee to turn the eyes of thy greatness on this thy captive knight on the brink of so mighty an adventure."

By this time, he felt himself so inspired that he would not have flinched if all the carriers in the world assailed him. The comrades of the wounded, perceiving the plight they were in, began from a distance to shower stones on Don Quixote. He screened himself as best he could with his shield, for he did not dare to move away from the trough and leave his armor unprotected. The landlord shouted to them to leave him alone,

for he had already told them that the knight was mad and as a madman would not be accountable even if he killed them all. Still louder shouted Don Quixote, calling them knaves and traitors, and the lord of the castle, who allowed knights-errant to be treated in this fashion, a villain and a low-born knight whom, had he received the order of knighthood, he would call to account for his treachery. "But of you," he cried, "base and vile rabble, I make no account; fling, strike, come on, do all ye can against me, ye shall see what the reward of your folly and insolence will be." This he uttered with so much spirit and boldness that he filled his assailants with a terrible fear, and it is as much for this reason as at the persuasion of the landlord that they quit stoning him. He allowed them to carry off the wounded and then, with the same calmness and composure as before, resumed the watch over his armor.

The pranks his guest was indulging in were not at all to the landlord's liking. So he determined to cut matters short and confer upon him at once the accursed order of knighthood before any further misadventure could happen. Going up to him, he apologized for the rudeness which without his knowledge had been shown by these low people, who, however, had been well punished for their audacity. As he had already explained, he said, there was no chapel in the castle, nor was it needed for what remained to be done. As he understood the ceremonial of the order, the whole point of being dubbed a knight lay in the accolade and in the slap on the shoulder, and that could be administered in the middle of a field. Don Quixote had now done all that was needful as to watching the armor, for all requirements were satisfied by a watch of two hours only, while he had been it more than four. Don Quixote believed it all, telling the landlord that he stood there ready to obey and that the matter should be concluded as rapidly as possible. For, if he were again attacked, and felt himself to be dubbed knight, he would not, he thought, leave a soul alive in the castle, except such as out of respect he might spare at the landlord's bidding.

Thus warned and menaced, the castellan forthwith brought out a book in which he entered the amounts of straw, and barley sold to the mule drivers. With a lad carrying a candle-stump, and the two damsels already mentioned, he returned to where Don Quixote stood and ordered him to kneel down. Then he read from his account book as if he were repeating some devout prayer. In the middle of his delivery he raised his hand and gave Don Quixote a sturdy blow on the neck, and then, with the knight's own sword, a smart slap on the shoulder, all the while muttering between his teeth as if he were saying his prayers. Having done this, he directed one of the ladies to gird on the sword, which she did with great self-possession and gravity. Of both of these a plentiful supply was needed, lest a burst of laughter should signal each stage of the ceremony, but what they had already seen of the novice knight's prowess kept their laughter within bounds.

"May God make your worship a very fortunate knight and grant you success in battle," said the worthy lady, as she girded him with the sword. Don Quixote asked her name so that he might from that time forward know to whom he was indebted for the favor he had received, he meant to confer upon her some share of the honor the might of his arm would bring. She answered with great humility that she was called La Tolosa, and that she was the daughter of a cobbler of Toledo who lived in the stalls of Sancho Bienaya Square and that wherever she might be, she would serve and esteem him as her lord. Don Quixote replied that she would do him a favor by henceforward assuming the "Don" and calling herself Doña Tolosa. She promised she would, the other damsel buckled on his spur, and there followed almost the same conversation as with the lady of the sword. He asked her name, and she said it was La Molinera and that she was the daughter of a respectable miller of Antequera, Don Quixote asked her also to adopt the "Don" and call herself Doña Molinera, offering her further services and favors.[2]

Having thus, with hot haste and speed, brought to a conclusion these unprecedented ceremonies, Don Quixote was on tenterhooks until he could see himself on horseback sallying forth in quest of adventures. Saddling and mounting Rocinante, he embraced his host and thanked him for his kindness in knighting him. The language he employed was so extraordinary that it is impossible to convey an idea of it. The landlord, to get him out of the inn, replied with no less rhetoric though with shorter words, and without asking him to pay the bill, let him go with a "Godspeed."

THINK ABOUT IT

1. According to Don Quixote, what are the duties of a knight? How does the duty of the watching of the armor lead Don Quixote into trouble?

2. Describe the dubbing ceremony. Why do the landlord and the ladies treat Don Quixote as if he is a knight?

---

2 Prostitutes did in fact use the title doña ("lady" or "madam").

TALK ABOUT IT

3. In Cervantes's time, the desire to be a knight was thought of as a "romantic" aspiration — one that was not a realistic profession to pursue. What professions are considered "romantic" in our culture? In other cultures?

4. The character Don Quixote has been widely applauded for his strong belief in himself. Do you think that Don Quixote sets a good example for believing in one's self? Why or why not?

WRITE ABOUT IT

5. When Don Quixote was first published, romantic novels of chivalry were widely read. It was believed that people portrayed in these stories possessed more praise-worthy traits such as honesty, bravery, and courtesy than did people of their own era. What stories that are popular today and based in another time portray characters that are widely praised? List the admirable traits that these characters possess.

6. If you could pursue any interest or career you wanted, without any constraints, what would you choose? How would this pursuit change your sense of "Identity"?

READ MORE ABOUT IT

Cervantes, Miguel de. *Don Quixote*. Editors: Jones, Joseph R., and Douglas, Kenneth. New York and London: W. W. Norton & Company, 1981.

Close, Anthony. *The Romantic Approach to Don Quixote*. Cambridge: Cambridge University Press, 1977.

Fuentes, Carlos. *The Buried Mirror: Reflections on Spain and the New World*. New York: Houghton Mifflin Company, 1992.

ERNESTINE STODELLE

Martha Graham: Dancer

Ernestine Stodelle is the author of an authoritative biography on Martha Graham, the most influential dancer of the twentieth century. This is one of three seminal biographies Ms. Stodelle has written on the creators of modern dance in America. Ms. Stodelle herself is a dancer and has also been a critic, writer, and university professor of modern dance. She began her career as a member of the pioneer modern dance company of Doris Humphrey and Charles Weidman. Since 1929 she has been closely involved with the Martha Graham Dance Company and, as such, has been a principal critic and supporter of the Graham technique. Ms. Stodelle still directs her own Studio of Dance in Connecticut and serves on the dance faculty of New York University.

Martha Graham is widely recognized as the definer of modern dance in the twentieth century. She began dancing in 1916 with the Denishawn Company, the first modern dance performers. Although she retired from performing in 1969 when she turned seventy-five, Ms. Graham continued to serve as the artistic director of her company until her death twenty-two years later. Founded in 1926, the Martha Graham Dance Company is the oldest continuously performing dance company in America. Most significantly, Martha Graham created the form of modern dance as it exists today. She composed over two hundred works in which she developed her unique dance vocabulary. Ms. Graham believed the purpose of dance was to express a wide range of emotions related to the theme of the composition. As such, she created the contraction (the torso of the body used for emotional expression), the backfall, and a wide variety of floor movements. She also introduced a new tension and angularity to body design for expressive purposes. At the start of almost every interview and speech she gave, Martha Graham uttered the words, "I am a dancer." Indeed, this statement articulated her attitude toward every aspect of life.

"I AM A DANCER," were the opening words of articles written, acceptance speeches, and unwritten, unspoken stances. "I am a dancer," was her attitude toward life. It was fire fighting fire; life fighting life — the weapon being the body — that citadel of energy and spirit, that instrument of faith incarnate.

In every dance the statement was made. Yet the words — in movement — did not come easily. A poet searches for the *mot juste,* the exact rendering of thought in rhythm or rhyme. A dancer searches in space and time for

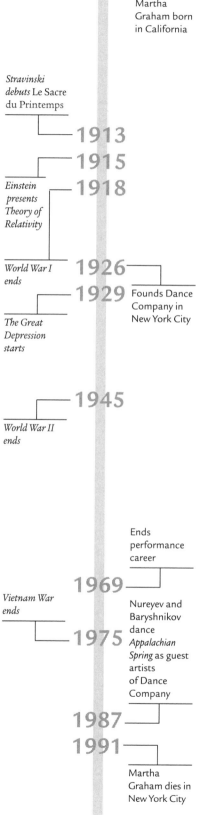

1894 — Martha Graham born in California

Stravinski debuts Le Sacre du Printemps

1913

1915

1918

Einstein presents Theory of Relativity

World War I ends

1926

1929 — Founds Dance Company in New York City

The Great Depression starts

1945

World War II ends

Ends performance career

1969

Vietnam War ends

Nureyev and Baryshnikov dance *Appalachian Spring* as guest artists of Dance Company

1975

1987

1991

Martha Graham dies in New York City

the right feeling and thought to take shape. Movement impulses are rejected by the score if they do not serve to tell the truth.

Rehearsals would be called, and everyone would come, giving up dinner invitations or getting off work early. In those days, because the studio was quite cold, Martha wore a long, warm practice dress (she usually wore a gray tank suit for work), and her hair fell in straight sheaths over her shoulders, nearly to her waist. To someone who had seen her on the stage, it didn't seem possible that it was the same person. In contrast to her imposing stature behind the footlights, she seemed tiny, almost birdlike in the studio. Her delicate bones, long neck, rounded thighs and bosom gave her a frail, feminine look; only her feet, solid and strong in their clawlike squareness, betrayed her relentless working habits. They gripped the floor as though they would never let go. They had a monumental look — like the sculptured feet of a Roman emperor.

When the rehearsal started, Martha seemed to become even smaller, wrapped tight, as it were, in the cocoon of thought. Seated on the floor, her back to the mirror, she faced the open center of the rectangular room. No one dared to cross her line of vision. Along the margins of that space, the girls would be stretching quietly on the floor, or staring patiently out of the window. Once in a while Martha would speak. One of the girls would be called into the "sacred" center. Instructions would be given in tentative tones. Suddenly coming to life, the girl would strike a pattern in the waiting space.

A despondent shake of the head from her director would stop her in her tracks.

"Sit down," would be muttered in a lifeless voice.

And silence would fall again.

How did it feel to be called to rehearsal and then used so little? This was hard, no doubt, and a far cry from the fast-action rehearsal of today when minutes count and choreographers, fully aware of the cost of production, are flaying their dancers' nerves with the rapid repairing of old movements and factory-swift inventions of new ones. Time is money (one of Martha's girls, Jane Dudley, composed a satiric dance with that title), but, as we know, clock time has little to do with creativity, which can take eons or split seconds to do its work.

Strange as it may have seemed to outsiders, it was perfectly natural for those who came into contact with Martha Graham to sense her importance and to pay homage to her. The habitually same audiences that attended her every concert soon came to be known as "the cult of Martha Graham." But something far deeper than a "cult" of a semireligious fanaticism was in the making. Religious feelings were present, but they stemmed from humanity's natural inclination to identify with an ideal.

"Then come with me," said the man in Grimm's fairy tale, "and become a Stargazer. There is nothing better than that, for nothing is hidden from you."

In worshipping Martha, the girls were bowing before the creative act, which she as a dancer symbolized. Like a goddess of fertility she was bound up with nature's mysterious cycles. Her seemingly barren moments would eventually bear fruit - of that they had no doubts. And her own uncompromising nature, which held to its ideals, was certain proof of the abundance of her unseen resources. The gratifications of working with her were always present: beauty, meaning, wisdom. When she instructed them, her words were extravagant but always convincing:

"Grace is your relationship to the World, your attitude to the people with whom and for whom you are dancing." And what young person could resist the glorious vision of "My dancing ... is an affirmation of life through movement"?

Compared to her "revelations," other people's pronouncements seemed pedestrian, dull-witted. Martha lived in a realm apart. To be there with her was to partake of the same ratified air.

In the same bare Fifty-ninth Street studio, where the furnishings consisted of a chest of drawers, an army cot, a kitchen table, a couple of chairs, a victrola, and Louis's grand piano, Martha received Léonide Massine. He had come to discuss her role in his production of Stravinsky's *Le Sacre du Printemps,* which was to be presented by Leopold Stokowski under the auspices of the League of Composers in April 1930. It was a meeting of strangely diverse creative minds. Born a year apart, and resembling each other somewhat with their black hair, deep-set eyes, wiry bodies, and serious, intense expressions, Massine and Martha were, at this moment in their careers, at almost opposite stages of accomplishment in the eyes of the world.

The Russian-born choreographer had already achieved fame as one of Sergei Diaghilev's chief choreographers in the later years of the Ballets Russes. Besides dancing principal roles in the repertory, he had composed no less than seventeen ballets between 1915 and 1928, many of them strikingly effective. Now performing in New York City with his own company at the Roxy, Massine had been asked to restage his 1920 version of the famous Stravinsky work for its American premiere as a ballet (Stokowski had previously presented the music at one of his concerts). The setting and costumes would be those originally designed by Nicolas Roerich for the "scandalous" 1913 Parisian premiere choreographed by Nijinsky.

Martha, who was virtually at the beginning of her independent career, was not unaware of the honor of being approached by people of renown in musical and ballet circles. She was also aware of the fact that it was Stokowski and Roerich who had selected her for the role of The Chosen One in Stravinsky's reenactment of a pagan ritual in which a virgin of a tribal community, chosen for her beauty, dances herself to death to ensure the return of the earth's fertility at springtime.

To be invited to perform the leading role in a ballet of such historic importance was an indication that her talents were being noticed beyond the confines of the limited modern dance world. The glamour that had been attached to the names of Nijinsky, Diaghilev, and Stravinsky as *grands artistes* in prewar Paris was far from being diminished with time. On the contrary, the scandal that had taken place when *Le Sacre du Printemps* was unveiled May 29, 1913, still struck nostalgic chords in the memories of the artistic elite. Stravinsky's music, with its irregular rhythms and constant changes of key and tempo, had been hissed and shouted at during the entire first night performance; equally intolerable had been Nijinsky's anti-balletic earthbound movements that attempted to follow every beat of the incomprehensible score. After seven performances the ballet was withdrawn. But to those in the forefront of twentieth-century innovations in music, ballet, and the theater, the original *Sacre* was an avant-garde landmark. For Martha it would be an opportunity and an association of no small proportions.

Massine's version, by contrast to Nijinsky's, was highly successful. By 1920, Stravinsky's epoch-making score had become recognized for its

MARTHA GRAHAM IN *EL PENITENTE*, 1940

MARTHA GRAHAM AND HER COMPANY IN *PRIMITIVE MYSTERIES*, 1935

true worth. The new *Sacre,* in the words of Lydia Sokolova, who danced the role of The Chosen One, was "a typical Massine production, clear-cut and methodical, with each group counting like mad against the others, but each holding its own. In Massine's choreography nothing was ever left to chance." While this method of mathematical dissection served the choreographer to advantage in Paris at the onset of the twenties, it was bound to become thorny in America in the 1930s, when it came to superimposing movements on the instinctually propelled Martha Graham.

Rehearsals were held in the Dalton School gymnasium. It so happened that several members of Martha's own company were in the cast as well as four dancers from the Humphrey-Weidman group. According to Eleanor King of the latter ensemble, while Martha waited for her cue to appear in the second scene, she sat in a corner with a shawl over her head, obviously indifferent to the action around her. According to others who were present, Massine and Martha "crossed swords" when it came to the rehearsing of the sacrificial dance with its complicated counts and pulsations. The resulting deadlock grew more ominous as opening night drew nearer. Finally, Massine in desperation suggested that Martha resign.

"You will be a failure," he said testily.

"Did Stokowski say that?" asked Martha boldly.

When Massine answered yes, Martha went directly to the conductor, who not only told her that he wanted her to stay, but assured her that she need not wear the heavy stockings and laced footgear worn by the others in the cast, but could dance barefoot. He also told her (probably at her request) that she could dress her own hair as she liked instead of being obliged to wear the long, braided blonde wig designed by Roerich.

With Stokowski's support behind her, Martha made a volte-face, and, in her own words, did "exactly as Massine said" for the remainder of the rehearsals. With characteristic honesty, she admitted later, "Although I worked with Massine in 1930, when I appeared in his version of Stravinsky's *Sacre du Printemps,* this was not a collaboration — it was a question of take it or leave it."

As a result of her capitulation, Martha's opening night performance in Philadelphia on April 11, 1930, and her subsequent performances, including those at the Metropolitan Opera House in New York on April 22 and 23, were triumphant. Massine's intricately manipulated movement patterns for the sacrificial dance were infused with a pagan fervor of breathtaking power. The prim-itive drive of Stravinsky's relentless rhythms had found its perfect embodiment in Martha's galvanic leaps and frenzied vibrations.

Whatever might have been the emotional reason for the conflictual drama behind the scenes of *Le Sacre du Printemps,* years later Martha chose to remember her Massine-Stokowski collaboration as "a great turning point" in her life. True to her strong will and compulsive need to use all experience creatively, she interpreted the sacrificial dance in terms of a personal act of sacrifice. "*Sacre* is a ritual. When I danced it in 1930, I was so immersed in the ritual and the sacrifice of the Chosen One that I believed in it.... I think the Chosen One is the artist. The principal thing is that it has to do with the artist as his own doom-maker; he composes himself to death."

THINK ABOUT IT

1. Describe Martha Graham's behavior during rehearsals. What was the "sacred" center and how did it relate to "the cult of Martha Graham"?

2. Why was Martha Graham's collaboration with Massine and Stokowski, "a great turning point" in her life?

TALK ABOUT IT

3. Explain how Martha Graham operated in a "realm apart." Name at least one contemporary artist who works in another "realm." How has this detachment led to the artist's success?

4. Martha stated that "my dancing ... is an affirmation of life through movement." Is dancing necessary for life to be celebrated? Why or why not?

5. Describe Martha Graham's physical features and appearance. How did she use them to advantage in her dancing? Name a performer you have seen who has special physical attributes. How did he or she use these features to make the performance unique?

6. In what ways have your physical attributes influenced your interests? Analyze the ways in which your attributes have shaped your goals. Have your physical attributes also shaped your identity?

READ MORE ABOUT IT

Cohen, Selma Jeanne. *The Modern Dance: Seven Statements of Belief.* Middletown, CT: Wesleyan University Press, 1965.

Duncan, Isadora. *The Art of the Dance.* New York: Theatre Arts Books, 1969.

Stodelle, Ernestine. *Deep Song: The Dance Story of Martha Graham.* New York: Schirmer Books, 1984.

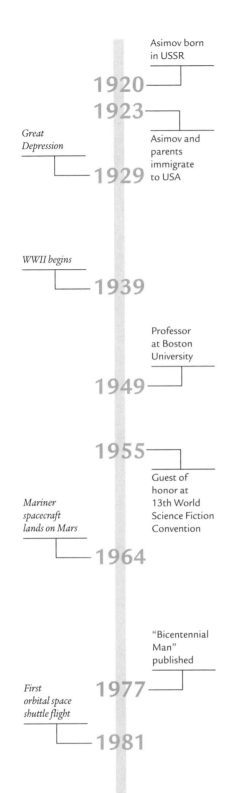

Asimov born in USSR

1920

1923

Asimov and parents immigrate to USA

Great Depression

1929

WWII begins

1939

Professor at Boston University

1949

1955

Guest of honor at 13th World Science Fiction Convention

Mariner spacecraft lands on Mars

1964

"Bicentennial Man" published

First orbital space shuttle flight

1977

1981

Asimov dies

1992

ISAAC ASIMOV

The Bicentennial Man

Isaac Asimov is one of America's most prolific authors. He has written over 200 books on subjects as varied as science, literature, history, medicine, and religion. He has even written over thirty children's books. He is best known, however, as a writer of science fiction. One science fiction editor, David N. Samuelson, in *Twentieth Century Science Fiction Writers,* claims that Asimov "has written some of the best known science fiction ever published." This is certainly true of "Bicentennial Man," which has received both of science fiction's highest awards, the Hugo Award given by the World Science Fiction Convention for Best Short Story, 1977, and the Nebula Award, given by the Science Fiction Writers of America.

This story is typical of Asimov's work in which, as he says, he "usually thought of some scientific gimmick and built a story about that." The "gimmick" in this story is artificial intelligence and its use in robotics. This story utilizes Asimov's "Three Laws of Robotics":

1. A robot may not injure a human being or, through inaction, allow a human being to come to harm.
2. A robot must obey the orders given it by human beings except where such orders would conflict with the First Law.
3. A robot must protect its own existence as long as such protection does not conflict with the First or Second Laws.

Asimov believes that he is "probably more famous for them [these laws] than for anything else I have written, and they are quoted even outside the science-fiction world. The very word 'robotics' was coined by me." These laws are used widely by other science fiction writers and have been used as the basis for android characters in television shows, including Commander Data in *Star Trek: The Next Generation.* Asimov's laws are so well-known and well-respected that most people believe that when robotic intelligence becomes commonplace, it will incorporate and be governed by Asimov's "Three Laws of Robotics." In this story, the main character, a robot, obeys and uses these laws. At the same time, he develops a sense of identity which causes him to want to be human.

ANDREW MARTIN SAID, "Thank you," and took the seat offered him. He didn't look driven to the last resort, but he had been.

He didn't, actually, look anything, for there was a smooth blankness to his face, except for the sadness one imagined one saw in his eyes. His hair was smooth, light brown, rather fine, and there was no facial hair. He looked freshly and cleanly shaved. His clothes were distinctly old-fashioned, but neat and predominantly a velvety red-purple in color.

Facing him from behind the desk was the surgeon, and the nameplate on the desk included a fully identifying series of letters and numbers, which Andrew didn't bother with. To call him Doctor would be quite enough.

"When can the operation be carried through, operation. Doctor?" he asked.

The surgeon said softly, with that certain inalienable note of respect that a robot always used to a human being, "I am not certain, sir, that I understand how or upon whom such an operation could be performed."

There might have been a look of respectful intransigence on the surgeon's face, if a robot of his sort, in lightly bronzed stainless steel, could have such an expression, or any expression.

Andrew Martin studied the robot's right hand, his cutting hand, as it lay on the desk in utter tranquillity. The fingers were long and shaped into artistically metallic looping curves so graceful and appropriate that one could imagine a scalpel fitting them and becoming, temporarily, one piece with them.

There would be no hesitation in his work, no stumbling, no quivering, no mistakes. That came with specialization, of course, a specialization so fiercely desired by humanity that few robots were, any longer, independently brained. A surgeon, of course, would have to be. And this one, though brained, was so limited in his capacity that he did not recognize Andrew—had probably never heard of him.

Andrew said, "Have you ever thought you would like to be a man?"

The surgeon hesitated a moment as though the question fitted nowhere in his allotted positronic pathways, "But I am a robot, sir."

"Would it be better to be a man?"

"It would be better, sir, to be a better surgeon. I could not be so if I were a man, but only if I were a more advanced robot. I would be pleased to be a more advanced robot."

"It does not offend you that I can order you about? That I can make you stand up, sit down, move right or left, by merely telling you to do so?"

"It is my pleasure to please you, sir. If your orders were to interfere with my functioning with respect to you or to any other human being, I would not obey you. The First Law, concerning my duty to human safety, would take precedence over the Second Law relating to obedience. Otherwise, obedience is my pleasure.... But upon whom am I to perform this operation?"

"Upon me," said Andrew.

"But that is impossible. It is patently damaging."

"That does not matter," said Andrew calmly.

"I must not inflict damage," said the surgeon.

"On a human being, you must not," said Andrew, "but I, too, am a robot."

2.

Andrew had appeared much more a robot when he had first been manufactured. He had then been as much a robot in appearance as any that had ever existed, smoothly designed and functional.

He had done well in the home to which he had been brought in those days when robots in households, or on the planet altogether, had been a rarity.

There had been four in the home: Sir and Ma'am and Miss and Little Miss. He knew their names, of course, but he never used them. Sir was Gerald Martin.

His own serial number was NDR—he forgot the numbers. It had been a long time, of course, but if he had wanted to remember, he could not forget. He had not wanted to remember.

Little Miss had been the first to call him Andrew because she could not use the letters, and all the rest followed her in this.

Little Miss—she had lived ninety years and was long since dead. He had tried to call her Ma'am once, but she would not allow it. Little Miss she had been to her last day.

Andrew had been intended to perform the duties of a valet, a butler, a lady's maid. Those were the experimental days for him and, indeed, for all robots anywhere but in the industrial and exploratory factories and stations off Earth.

The Martins enjoyed him, and half the time he was prevented from doing his work because Miss and Little Miss would rather play with him. It was Miss who understood first how this might be arranged. She said, "We order you to play with us and you must follow orders."

Andrew said, "I am sorry, Miss, but a prior order from Sir must surely take precedence."

But she said, "Daddy just said he hoped you would take care of the cleaning. That's not much of an order. I order you."

Sir did not mind. Sir was fond of Miss and of Little Miss, even more than Ma'am was, and Andrew was fond of them, too. At least, the effect they had upon his actions were those which in a human being would have been called the result of fondness. Andrew thought of it as fondness, for he did not know any other word for it.

It was for Little Miss that Andrew had carved a pendant out of wood. She had ordered him to. Miss, it seemed, had received an ivorite pendant with scrollwork for her birthday and Little Miss was unhappy over it. She had only a piece of wood, which she gave Andrew together with a small kitchen knife.

He had done it quickly and Little Miss said, "That's nice, Andrew. I'll show it to Daddy."

Sir would not believe it. "Where did you really get this, Mandy?" Mandy was what he called Little Miss. When Little Miss assured him she was really telling the truth, he turned to Andrew. "Did you do this, Andrew?"

"Yes, Sir."

"The design, too?"

"Yes, Sir."

"From what did you copy the design?"

"It is a geometric representation, Sir, that fit the grain of the wood."

The next day, Sir brought him another piece of wood, a larger one, and an electric vibro-knife. He said, "Make something out of this, Andrew. Anything you want to."

Andrew did so and Sir watched, then looked at the product a long time. After that, Andrew no longer waited on tables. He was ordered to read books on furniture design instead, and he learned to make cabinets and desks.

Sir said, "These are amazing productions, Andrew."

Andrew said, "I enjoy doing them, Sir."

"Enjoy?"

"It makes the circuits of my brain somehow flow more easily. I have heard you use the word 'enjoy' and

the way you use it fits the way I feel. I enjoy doing them, Sir."

Gerald Martin took Andrew to the regional offices of United States Robots and Mechanical Men Corporation. As a member of the Regional Legislature he had no trouble at all in gaining an interview with the Chief Robopsychologist. In fact, it was only as a member of the Regional Legislature that he qualified as a robot owner in the first place—in those early days when robots were rare.

Andrew did not understand any of this at the time, but in later years, with greater learning, he could review that early scene and understand it in its proper light.

The robopsychologist, Merton Mansky, listened with a gathering frown and more than once managed to stop his fingers at the point beyond which they would have irrevocably drummed on the table. He had drawn features and a lined forehead and looked as though he might be younger than he looked.

He said, "Robotics is not an exact art, Mr. Martin. I cannot explain it to you in detail, but the mathematics governing the plotting of the positronic pathways is far too complicated to permit any but approximate solutions. Naturally, since we build everything about the Three Laws, those are incontrovertible. We will, of course, replace your robot—"

"Not at all," said Sir. "There is no question of failure on his part. He performs his assigned duties perfectly. The point is, he also carves wood in exquisite fashion and never the same twice. He produces works of art."

Mansky looked confused. "Strange. Of course, we're attempting generalized pathways these days.... Really creative, you think?"

"See for yourself." Sir handed over a little sphere of wood on which

there was a playground scene in which the boys and girls were almost too small to make out, yet they were in perfect proportion and blended so naturally with the grain that that, too, seemed to have been carved.

Mansky said, "He did that?" He handed it back with a shake of his head. "The luck of the draw. Something in the pathways."

"Can you do it again?"

"Probably not. Nothing like this has ever been reported."

"Good! I don't in the least mind Andrew's being the only one."

Mansky said, "I suspect that the company would like to have your robot back for study."

Sir said with sudden grimness, "Not a chance. Forget it."

He turned to Andrew, "Let's go home now."

"As you wish, Sir," said Andrew.

4.

Miss was dating boys and wasn't about the house much. It was Little Miss, not as little as she was, who filled Andrew's horizon now. She never forgot that the very first piece of wood carving he had done had been for her. She kept it on a silver chain about her neck.

It was she who first objected to Sir's habit of giving away the productions. She said, "Come on, Dad, if anyone wants one of them, let him pay for it. It's worth it."

Sir said, "It isn't like you to be greedy, Mandy."

"Not for us, Dad. For the artist."

Andrew had never heard the word before and when he had a moment to himself he looked it up in the dictionary. Then there was another trip, this time to Sir's lawyer.

Sir said to him, "What do you think of this, John?"

The lawyer was John Feingold. He had white hair and a pudgy belly, and the rims of his contact lenses were tinted a bright green. He looked at the small plaque Sir had given him. "This is beautiful.... But I've heard the news. This is a carving made by your robot. The one you've brought with you."

"Yes, Andrew does them. Don't you, Andrew?"

"Yes, Sir," said Andrew.

"How much would you pay for that, John?" asked Sir.

"I can't say. I'm not a collector of such things."

"Would you believe I have been offered two hundred and fifty dollars for that small thing? Andrew has made chairs that have sold for five hundred dollars. There's two hundred thousand dollars in the bank out of Andrew's Products."

"Good heavens, he's making you rich, Gerald."

"Half rich," said Sir. "Half of it is in an account in the name of Andrew Martin."

"The robot?"

"That's right, and I want to know if it's legal."

"Legal?" Feingold's chair creaked as he leaned back in it. "There are no precedents, Gerald. How did your robot sign the necessary papers?"

"He can sign his name and I brought in the signature. I didn't bring him in to the bank himself. Is there anything further that ought to be done?"

"Urn." Feingold's eyes seemed to turn inward for a moment. Then he said, "Well, we can set up a trust to handle all finances in his name and that will place a layer of insulation between him and the hostile world. Further than that, my advice is that you do nothing. No one is stopping you so far. If anyone objects, let him bring suit."

"And will you take the case if suit is brought?"

"For a retainer, certainly."

"How much?"

"Something like that," and Feingold pointed to the wooden plaque.

"Fair enough," said Sir.

Feingold chuckled as he turned to the robot. "Andrew, are you pleased that you have money?"

"Yes, sir."

"What do you plan to do with it?"

"Pay for things, sir, which otherwise Sir would have to pay for. It would save him expense, sir."

5.

The occasions came. Repairs were expensive, and revisions were even more so. With the years, new models of robots were produced and Sir saw to it that Andrew had the advantage of every new device until he was a paragon of metallic excellence. It was all at Andrew's expense.

Andrew insisted on that.

Only his positronic pathways were untouched. Sir insisted on that.

"The new ones aren't as good as you are, Andrew," he said. "The new robots are worthless. The company has learned to make the pathways more precise, more closely on the nose, more deeply on the track. The new robots don't shift. They do what they're designed for and never stray. I like you better."

"Thank you, Sir."

"And it's your doing, Andrew, don't you forget that. I am certain Mansky put an end to generalized pathways as soon as he had a good look at you. He didn't like the unpredictability.... Do you know how many times he asked for you so he could place you under study? Nine times! I never let him have you, though, and now that he's retired, we may have some peace."

So Sir's hair thinned and grayed and his face grew pouchy, while

Andrew looked rather better than he had when he first joined the family.

Ma'am had joined an art colony somewhere in Europe and Miss was a poet in New York. They wrote sometimes, but not often. Little Miss was married and lived not far away. She said she did not want to leave Andrew and when her child, Little Sir, was born, she let Andrew hold the bottle and feed him.

With the birth of a grandson, Andrew felt that Sir had someone new to replace those who had gone. It would not be so unfair to come to him with the request.

Andrew said, "Sir, it is kind of you to have allowed me to spend my money as I wished."

"It was your money, Andrew."

"Only by your voluntary act, Sir. I do not believe the law would have stopped you from keeping it all."

"The law won't persuade me to do wrong, Andrew."

"Despite all expenses, and despite taxes, too, Sir, I have nearly six hundred thousand dollars."

"I know that, Andrew."

"I want to give it to you, Sir."

"I won't take it, Andrew."

"In exchange for something you can give me, Sir."

"Oh? What is that, Andrew?"

"My freedom, Sir."

"Your—"

"I wish to buy my freedom, Sir."

6.

It wasn't that easy. Sir had flushed, had said "For God's sake!" had turned on his heel, and stalked away.

It was Little Miss who brought him around, defiantly and harshly—and in front of Andrew. For thirty years, no one had hesitated to talk in front of Andrew, whether the matter involved Andrew or not. He was only a robot.

She said, "Dad, why are you taking it as a personal affront? He'll still be here. He'll still be loyal. He can't help that. It's built in. All he wants is a form of words. He wants to be called free. Is that so terrible? Hasn't he earned it? Heavens, he and I have been talking about it for years."

"Talking about it for years, have you?"

"Yes, and over and over again, he postponed it for fear he would hurt you. I made him put it up to you."

"He doesn't know what freedom is. He's a robot."

"Dad, you don't know him. He's read everything in the library. I don't know what he feels inside but I don't know what you feel inside. When you talk to him you'll find he reacts to the various abstractions as you and I do, and what else counts? If someone else's reactions are like your own, what more can you ask for?"

"The law won't take that attitude," Sir said angrily. "See here, you!" He turned to Andrew with a deliberate grate in his voice. "I can't free you except by doing it legally, and if it gets into the courts, you not only won't get your freedom but the law will take official cognizance of your money. They'll tell you that a robot has no right to earn money. Is this rigmarole worth losing your money?"

"Freedom is without a price, Sir," said Andrew. "Even the chance of freedom is worth the money."

7.

The court might also take the attitude that freedom was without price, and might decide that for no price, however great, could a robot buy its freedom.

The simple statement of the regional attorney who represented those who had brought a class action to oppose the freedom was this: The word "freedom" had no meaning when applied to a robot. Only a human being could be free.

He said it several times, when it seemed appropriate; slowly, with his hand coming down rhythmically on the desk before him to mark the words.

Little Miss asked permission to speak on behalf of Andrew. She was recognized by her full name, something Andrew had never heard pronounced before:

"Amanda Laura Martin Charney may approach the bench."

She said, "Thank you, your honor. I am not a lawyer and I don't know the proper way of phrasing things, but I hope you will listen to my meaning and ignore the words.

"Let's understand what it means to be free in Andrew's case. In some ways, he is free. I think it's at least twenty years since anyone in the Martin family gave him an order to do something that we felt he might not do of his own accord.

"But we can, if we wish, give him an order to do anything, couch it as harshly as we wish, because he is a machine that belongs to us. Why should we be in a position to do so, when he has served us so long, so faithfully, and earned so much money for us? He owes us nothing more. The debt is entirely on the other side.

"Even if we were legally forbidden to place Andrew in involuntary servitude, he would still serve us voluntarily. Making him free would be a trick of words only, but it would mean much to him. It would give him everything and cost us nothing."

For a moment the judge seemed to be suppressing a smile. "I see your point, Mrs. Charney. The fact is that there is no binding law in this respect and no precedent. There is, however, the unspoken assumption that only a man can enjoy freedom. I can make new law here, subject to reversal in a higher court, but I cannot lightly run

counter to that assumption. Let me address the robot. Andrew!"

"Yes, your honor."

It was the first time Andrew had spoken in court and the judge seemed astonished for a moment at the human timbre of the voice. He said, "Why do you want to be free, Andrew? In what way will this matter to you?"

Andrew said, "Would you wish to be a slave, your honor?"

"But you are not a slave. You are a perfectly good robot, a genius of a robot I am given to understand, capable of an artistic expression that can be matched nowhere. What more can you do if you were free?"

"Perhaps no more than I do now, your honor, but with greater joy. It has been said in this courtroom that only a human being can be free. It seems to me that only someone who wishes for freedom can be free. I wish for freedom."

And it was that that cued the judge. The crucial sentence in his decision was: "There is no right to deny freedom to any object with a mind advanced enough to grasp the concept and desire the state."

It was eventually upheld by the World Court.

8.

Sir remained displeased and his harsh voice made Andrew feel almost as though he were being short-circuited.

Sir said, "I don't want your damned money, Andrew. I'll take it only because you won't feel free otherwise. From now on, you can select your own jobs and do them as you please. I will give you no orders, except this one — that you do as you please. But I am still responsible for you; that's part of the court order. I hope you understand that."

Little Miss interrupted. "Don't be irascible, Dad. The responsibility is no great chore. You know you won't have to do a thing. The Three Laws still hold."

"Then how is he free?"

Andrew said, "Are not human beings bound by their laws, Sir?"

Sir said, "I'm not going to argue." He left, and Andrew saw him only infrequently after that.

Little Miss came to see him frequently in the small house that had been built and made over for him. It had no kitchen, of course, nor bathroom facilities. It had just two rooms; one was a library and one was a combination storeroom and workroom. Andrew accepted many commissions and worked harder as a free robot than he ever had before, till the cost of the house was paid for and the structure legally transferred to him.

One day Little Sir came.... No, George! Little Sir had insisted on that after the court decision. "A free robot doesn't call anyone Little Sir," George had said. "I call you Andrew. You must call me George."

It was phrased as an order, so Andrew called him George—but Little Miss remained Little Miss.

The day George came alone, it was to say that Sir was dying. Little Miss was at the bedside but Sir wanted Andrew as well.

Sir's voice was quite strong, though he seemed unable to move much. He struggled to get his hand up. "Andrew," he said, "Andrew—don't help me, George. I'm only dying; I'm not crippled.... Andrew, I'm glad you're free. I just wanted to tell you that."

Andrew did not know what to say. He had never been at the side of someone dying before, but he knew it was the human way of ceasing to function. It was an involuntary and irreversible dismantling, and Andrew did not know what to say that might be appropriate. He could only remain standing, absolutely silent, absolutely motionless.

When it was over, Little Miss said to him, "He may not have seemed friendly to you toward the end, Andrew, but he was old, you know, and it hurt him that you should want to be free."

And then Andrew found the words to say. He said, "I would never have been free without him, Little Miss."

9.

It was only after Sir's death that Andrew began to wear clothes. He began with an old pair of trousers at first, a pair that George had given him.

George was married now, and a lawyer. He had joined Feingold's firm. Old Feingold was long since dead, but his daughter had carried on and eventually the firm's name became Feingold and Charney. It remained so even when the daughter retired and no Feingold took her place. At the time Andrew put on clothes for the first time, the Charney name had just been added to the firm.

George had tried not to smile the first time Andrew put on the trousers, but to Andrew's eyes the smile was clearly there.

George showed Andrew how to manipulate the static charge so as to allow the trousers to open, wrap about his lower body, and move shut. George demonstrated on his own trousers, but Andrew was quite aware that it would take him awhile to duplicate that one flowing motion.

George said, "But why do you want trousers, Andrew? Your body is so beautifully functional it's a shame to cover it—especially when you needn't worry about either temperature control or modesty. And it doesn't cling properly, not on metal."

Andrew said, "Are not human bodies beautifully functional, George? Yet you cover yourselves."

"For warmth, for cleanliness, for protection, for decorativeness. None of that applies to you."

Andrew said, "I feel bare without clothes. I feel different, George."

"Different! Andrew, there are millions of robots on Earth now. In this region, according to the last census, there are almost as many robots as there are men."

"I know, George. There are robots doing every conceivable type of work."

"And none of them wear clothes."

"But none of them are free, George."

Little by little, Andrew added to the wardrobe. He was inhibited by George's smile and by the stares of the people who commissioned work.

He might be free, but there was built into him a carefully detailed program concerning his behavior toward people and it was only by the tiniest steps that he dared advance. Open disapproval would set him back months.

Not everyone accepted Andrew as free. He was incapable of resenting that and yet there was a difficulty about his thinking process when he thought of it.

I most of all, he tended to avoid putting on clothes—or too many of them—when he thought Little Miss might come to visit him. She was old now and was often away in some warmer climate, but when she returned the first thing she did was visit him.

On one of her returns, George said ruefully, "She's got me, Andrew, I'll be running for the Legislature next year. Like grandfather, she says, like grandson."

"Like grandfather—" Andrew stopped, uncertain.

"I mean that I, George, the grandson, will be like Sir, the grandfather, who was in the Legislature once."

Andrew said, "It would be pleasant, George, if Sir were still—" He paused, for he did not want to say, "in working order." That seemed inappropriate.

"Alive," said George. "Yes, I think of the old monster now and then, too."

It was a conversation Andrew thought about. He had noticed his own incapacity in speech when talking with George. Somehow the language had changed since Andrew had come into being with an innate vocabulary. Then, too, George used a colloquial speech, as Sir and Little Miss had not. Why should he have called Sir a monster when surely that word was not appropriate?

Nor could Andrew turn to his own books for guidance. They were old and most dealt with woodworking, with art, with furniture design. There were none on language, none on the way of human beings.

It was at that moment it seemed to him that he must seek the proper books; and as a free robot, he felt he must not ask George. He would go to town and use the library. It was a triumphant decision and he felt his electropotential grow distinctly higher until he had to throw in an impedance coil.

He put on a full costume, even including a shoulder chain of wood. He would have preferred the glitter plastic but George had said that wood was much more appropriate and that polished cedar was considerably more valuable as well.

He had placed a hundred feet between himself and the house before gathering resistance brought him to a halt. He shifted the impedance coil out of circuit, and when that did not seem to help enough, he returned to his home and on a piece of notepaper wrote, "I have gone to the library," and placed it in clear view on his worktable.

10.

Andrew never quite got to the library. He had studied the map. He knew the route, but not the appearance of it. The actual landmarks did not resemble the symbols on the map and he would hesitate. Eventually he thought he must have somehow gone wrong, for everything looked strange.

He passed an occasional field robot, but at the time he decided he should ask his way, there were none in sight. A vehicle passed and did not stop. He stood irresolute, which meant calmly motionless, and then coming across the field toward him were two human beings.

He turned to face them, and they altered their course to meet him. A moment before, they had been talking loudly: he had heard their voices; but now they were silent. They had the look that Andrew associated with human uncertainty, and they were young, but not very young. Twenty perhaps? Andrew could never judge human age.

He said, "Would you describe to me the route to the town library, sirs?"

One of them, the taller of the two, whose tall hat lengthened him still farther, almost grotesquely, said, not to Andrew, but to the other, "It's a robot."

The other had a bulbous nose and heavy eyelids. He said, not to Andrew, but to the first, "It's wearing clothes."

The tall one snapped his fingers. "It's the free robot. They have a robot at the Charney's who isn't owned by anybody. Why else would it be wearing clothes?"

"Ask it," said the one with the nose.

"Are you the Charney robot?" asked the tall one.

"I am Andrew Martin, sir," said Andrew.

"Good. Take off your clothes. Robots don't wear clothes."

He said to the other, "That's disgusting. Look at him."

Andrew hesitated. He hadn't heard an order in that tone of voice in so long that his Second Law circuits had momentarily jammed.

The tall one said, "Take off your clothes. I order you."

Slowly, Andrew began to remove them.

"Just drop them," said the tall one.

The nose said, "If it doesn't belong to anyone, he could be ours as much as someone else's."

"Anyway," said the tall one, "who's to object to anything we do? We're not damaging property... Stand on your head." That was to Andrew.

"The head is not meant—" began Andrew.

"That's an order. If you don't know how, try anyway."

Andrew hesitated again, then bent to put his head on the ground. He tried to lift his legs and fell, heavily.

The tall one said, "Just lie there." He said to the other, "We can take him apart. Ever take a robot apart?"

"Will he let us?"

"How can he stop us?"

There was no way Andrew could stop them, if they ordered him not to resist in a forceful enough manner. Second Law of obedience took precedence over the Third Law of self-preservation. In any case, he could not defend himself without possibly hurting them and that would mean breaking the First Law. At that thought, every motile unit contracted slightly and he quivered as he lay there.

The tall one walked over and pushed at him with his foot. "He's heavy. I think we'll need tools to do the job."

The nose said, "We could order him to take himself apart. it would be fun to watch him try."

"Yes," said the tall one thoughtfully, "but let's get him off the road. If someone comes along—"

It was too late. Someone had indeed come along and it was George. From where he lay, Andrew had seen him topping a small rise in the middle distance. He would have liked to signal him in some way, but the last order had been "Just lie there!"

George was running now and he arrived somewhat winded. The two young men stepped back a little and then waited thoughtfully.

George said anxiously, "Andrew, has something gone wrong?"

Andrew said, "I am well, George."

"Then stand up.... What happened to your clothes?"

The tall young man said, "That your robot, Mac?"

George turned sharply. "He's no one's robot. What's been going on here?"

"We politely asked him to take his clothes off. What's that to you if you don't own him?"

George said, "What were they doing, Andrew?"

Andrew said, "It was their intention, in some way, to dismember me. They were about to move me to a quiet spot and order me to dismember myself."

George looked at the two and his chin trembled. The two young men retreated no further. They were smiling. The tall one said lightly, "What are you going to do, pudgy? Attack us?"

George said, "No. I don't have to. This robot has been with my family for over seventy years. He knows us and he values us more than he values

anyone else. I am going to tell him that you two are threatening my life and that you plan to kill me. I will ask him to defend me. In choosing between me and you two, he will choose me. Do you know what will happen to you when he attacks you?"

The two were backing away slightly, looking uneasy.

George said sharply, "Andrew, I am in danger and about to come to harm from these young men. Move toward them!"

Andrew did so, and the two young men did not wait. They ran fleetly.

"All right, Andrew, relax," said George. He looked unstrung. He was far past the age where he could face the possibility of a dustup with one young man, let alone two.

Andrew said, "I couldn't have hurt them, George. I could see they were not attacking you."

"I didn't order you to attack them; I only told you to move toward them. Their own fears did the rest."

"How can they fear robots?"

"It's a disease of mankind, one of which it is not yet cured. But never mind that. What the devil are you doing here, Andrew? I was on the point of turning back and hiring a helicopter when I found you. How did you get it into your head to go to the library? I would have brought you any books you needed."

"I am a—" began Andrew.

"Free robot. Yes, yes. All right, what did you want in the library?"

"I want to know more about human beings, about the world, about everything. And about robots, George. I want to write a history about robots."

George said, "Well, let's walk home.... And pick up your clothes first. Andrew, there are a million books on robotics and all of them include histories of the science. The world is growing saturated not only

with robots but with information about robots."

Andrew shook his head, a human gesture he had lately begun to make. "Not a history of robotics, George. A history of robots, by a robot. I want to explain how robots feel about what has happened since the first ones were allowed to work and live on Earth."

George's eyebrows lifted, but he said nothing in direct response.

11.

Little Miss was just past her eighty-third birthday, but there was nothing about her that was lacking in either energy or determination. She gestured with her cane oftener than she propped herself up with it.

She listened to the story in a fury of indignation. She said, "George, that's horrible. Who were those young ruffians?"

"I don't know. What difference does it make? In the end they did no damage."

"They might have. You're a lawyer, George, and if you're well off, it's entirely due to the talent of Andrew. It was the money he earned that is the foundation of everything we have. He provides the continuity for this family and I will not have him treated as a wind-up toy."

"What would you have me do, Mother?" asked George.

"I said you're a lawyer. Don't you listen? You set up a test case somehow, and you force the regional courts to declare for robot rights and get the Legislature to pass the necessary bills, and carry the whole thing to the World Court, if you have to. I'll be watching, George, and I'll tolerate no shirking."

She was serious, and what began as a way of soothing the fearsome old lady became an involved matter with enough legal entanglement to make it interesting. As senior partner of

Feingold and Charney, George plotted strategy but left the actual work to his junior partners, with much of it a matter for his son, Paul, who was also a member of the firm and who reported dutifully nearly every day to his grandmother. She, in turn, discussed it every day with Andrew.

Andrew was deeply involved. His work on his book on robots was delayed again, as he pored over the legal arguments and even, at times, made very diffident suggestions.

He said, "George told me that day that human beings have always been afraid of robots. As long as they are, the courts and the legislatures are not likely to work hard on behalf of robots. Should there not be something done about public opinion?"

So while Paul stayed in court, George took to the public platform. It gave him the advantage of being informal and he even went so far sometimes as to wear the new, loose style of clothing which he called drapery. Paul said, "Just don't trip over it on stage, Dad."

George said despondently, "I'll try not to."

He addressed the annual convention of holonews editors on one occasion and said, in part:

"If, by virtue of the Second Law, we can demand of any robot unlimited obedience in all respects not involving harm to a human being, then any human being, any human being, has a fearsome power over any robot, any robot. In particular, since Second Law supersedes Third Law, any human being can use the law of obedience to overcome the law of self-protection. He can order any robot to damage itself or even destroy itself for any reason, or for no reason.

"Is this just? Would we treat an animal so? Even an inanimate object which has given us good service has a claim on our consideration. And a robot is not insensible; it is not an an-imal. It can think well enough to enable it to talk to us, reason with us, joke with us. Can we treat them as friends, can we work together with them, and not give them some of the fruit of that friendship, some of the benefit of co-working?

"If a man has the right to give a robot any order that does not involve harm to should have the decency never a human being, he to give a robot any order that involves harm to a robot, unless human safety absolutely requires it. With great power goes great responsibility, and if the robots have Three Laws to protect men, is it too much to ask that men have a law or two to protect robots?"

Andrew was right. It was the battle over public opinion that held the key to courts and Legislature and in the end a law passed which set up conditions under which robot-harming orders were forbidden. It was endlessly qualified and the punishments for violating the law were totally inadequate, but the principle was established. The final passage by the World Legislature came through on the day of Little Miss's death.

That was no coincidence. Little Miss held on to life desperately during the last debate and let go only when word of victory arrived. Her last smile was for Andrew. Her last words were: "You have been good to us, Andrew."

She died with her hand holding his, while her son and his wife and children remained at a respectful distance from both.

12.

Andrew waited patiently while the receptionist disappeared into the inner office. It might have used the holographic chatterbox, but unquestionably it was unmanned (or perhaps unroboted) by having to deal with another robot rather than with a human being.

Andrew passed the time revolving the matter in his mind. Could "unroboted" be used as an analogue of "unmanned," or had "unmanned" become a metaphoric term sufficiently divorced from its original literal meaning to be applied to robots— or to women for that matter?

Such problems came frequently as he worked on his book on robots. The trick of thinking out sentences to express all complexities had undoubtedly increased his vocabulary.

Occasionally, someone came into the room to stare at him and he did not try to avoid the glance. He looked at each calmly, and each in turn looked away.

Paul Charney finally came out. He looked surprised, or he would have if Andrew could have made out his expression with certainty. Paul had taken to wearing the heavy makeup that fashion was dictating for both sexes and though it made sharper and firmer the somewhat bland lines of his face, Andrew disapproved. He found that disapproving of human beings, as long as he did not express it verbally, did not make him very uneasy. He could even write the disapproval. He was sure it had not always been so.

Paul said, "Come in, Andrew. I'm sorry I made you wait but there was something I had to finish. Come in. You had said you wanted to talk to me, but I didn't know you meant here in town."

"If you are busy, Paul, I am prepared to continue to wait."

Paul glanced at the interplay of shifting shadows on the dial on the wall that served as a timepiece and said, "I can make some time. Did you come alone?"

"I hired an automatobile."

"Any trouble?" Paul asked, with more than a trace of anxiety.

"I wasn't expecting any. My rights are protected."

Paul looked the more anxious for that. "Andrew, I've explained that the law is unenforceable, at least under most conditions.... And if you insist on wearing clothes, you'll run into trouble eventually—just like that first time."

"And only time, Paul. I'm sorry you are displeased."

"Well, took at it this way; you are virtually a living legend, Andrew, and you are too valuable in many different ways for you to have any right to take chances with yourself.... How's the book coming?"

"I am approaching the end, Paul. The publisher is quite pleased."

"Good!"

"I don't know that he's necessarily pleased with the book as a book. I think he expects to sell many copies because it's written by a robot and it's that that pleases him."

"Only human, I'm afraid."

"I am not displeased. Let it sell for whatever reason since it will mean money and I can use some."

"Grandmother left you—"

"Little Miss was generous, and I'm sure I can count on the family to help me out further. But it is the royalties from the book on which I am counting to help me through the next step."

"What next step is that?"

"I wish to see the head of U.S. Robots and Mechanical Men Corporation. I have tried to make an appointment, but so far I have not been able to reach him. The corporation did not cooperate with me in the writing of the book, so I am not surprised, you understand."

Paul was clearly amused. "Cooperation is the last thing you can expect. They didn't cooperate with us in our great fight for robot rights. Quite the reverse and you can see why. Give a robot rights and people may not want to buy them."

"Nevertheless," said Andrew, "if you call them, you may obtain an interview for me."

"I'm no more popular with them than you are, Andrew."

"But perhaps you can hint that by seeing me they may head off a campaign by Feingold and Charney to strengthen the rights of robots further."

"Wouldn't that be a lie, Andrew?"

"Yes, Paul, and I can't tell one. That is why you must call."

"Ah, you can't lie, but you can urge me to tell a lie, is that it? You're getting more human all the time, Andrew."

13.

It was not easy to arrange, even with Paul's supposedly weighted name.

But it was finally carried through and, when it was, Harley Smythe-Robertson, who, on his mother's side, was descended from the original founder of the corporation and who had adopted the hyphenation to indicate it, looked remarkably unhappy. He was approaching retirement age and his entire tenure as president had been devoted to the matter of robot rights. His gray hair was plastered thinly over the top of his scalp, his face was not made up, and he eyed Andrew with brief hostility from time to time.

Andrew said, "Sir, nearly a century ago, I was told by a Merton Mansky of this corporation that the mathematics governing the plotting of the positronic pathways was far too complicated to permit of any but approximate solutions and that therefore my own capacities were not fully predictable."

"That was a century ago." Smythe-Robertson hesitated, then said icily, "Sir. It is true no longer. Our robots are made with precision now and are trained precisely to their jobs."

"Yes," said Paul, who had come along, as he said, to make sure that the corporation played fair, "with the

result that my receptionist must be guided at every point once events depart from the conventional, however slightly."

Smythe-Robertson said, "You would be much more displeased if it were to improvise."

Andrew said, "Then you no longer manufacture robots like myself which are flexible and adaptable."

"No longer."

"The research I have done in connection with my book," said Andrew, "indicates that I am the oldest robot presently in active operation."

"The oldest presently," said Smythe-Robertson, and the oldest ever. The oldest that will ever be. No robot is useful after the twenty-fifth year. They are called in and replaced with new models."

"No robot as presently manufactured is useful after the twenty-fifth year," said Paul pleasantly. "Andrew is quite exceptional in this respect."

Andrew, adhering to the path he had marked out for himself, said, "As the oldest robot in the world and the most flexible, am I not unusual enough to merit special treatment from the company?"

"Not at all," said Smythe-Robertson freezingly. "Your unusualness is an embarrassment to the company. If you were on lease, instead of having been a sale outright through some mischance, you would long since have been replaced."

"But that is exactly the point," said Andrew. "I am a free robot and I own myself. Therefore I come to you and ask you to replace me. You cannot do this without the owner's consent. Nowadays, that consent is extorted as a condition of the lease, but in my time this did not happen."

Smythe-Robertson was looking both startled and puzzled, and for a moment there was silence. Andrew found himself staring at the holograph on the wall. It was a death mask of Susan Calvin, patron saint of all roboticists. She was dead nearly two centuries now, but as a result of writing his book Andrew knew her so well he could half persuade himself that he had met her in life.

Smythe-Robertson said, "How can I replace you for you? If I replace you as robot, how can I donate the new robot to you as owner since in the very act of replacement you cease to exist?" He smiled grimly.

"Not at all difficult," interposed Paul. "The seat of Andrew's personality is his positronic brain and it is the one part that cannot be replaced without creating a new robot. The positronic brain, therefore, is Andrew the owner. Every other part of the robotic body can be replaced without affecting the robot's personality, and those other parts are the brain's possessions. Andrew, I should say, wants to supply his brain with a new robotic body."

"That's right," said Andrew calmly. He turned to Smythe-Robertson. "You have manufactured androids, haven't you? Robots that have the outward appearance of humans complete to the texture of the skin?"

Smythe-Robertson said, "Yes, we have. They worked perfectly well, with their synthetic fibrous skins and tendons. There was virtually no metal anywhere except for the brain, yet they were nearly as tough as metal robots. They were tougher, weight for weight."

Paul looked interested. "I didn't know that. How many are on the market?"

"None," said Smythe-Robertson. "They were much more expensive than metal models and a market survey showed they would not be accepted. They looked too human."

Andrew said, "But the corporation retains its expertise, I assume.

Since it does, I wish to request that I be replaced by an organic robot, an android."

Paul looked surprised. "Good Lord," he said.

Smythe-Robertson stiffened. "Quite impossible!"

"Why is it impossible?" asked Andrew. "I will pay any reasonable fee, of course."

Smythe-Robertson said, "We do not manufacture androids."

"You do not choose to manufacture androids," interposed Paul quickly. "That is not the same as being unable to manufacture them."

Smythe-Robertson said, "Nevertheless, the manufacture of androids is against public policy."

"There is no law against it," said Paul.

"Nevertheless, we do not manufacture them, and we will not."

Paul cleared his throat. "Mr. Smythe-Robertson," he said, "Andrew is a free robot who is under the purview of the law guaranteeing robot rights. You are aware of this, I take it?"

"Only too well."

"This robot, as a free robot, chooses to wear clothes. This results in his being frequently humiliated by thoughtless human beings despite the law against the humiliation of robots. It is difficult to prosecute vague offenses that don't meet with the general disapproval of those who must decide on guilt and innocence."

"U.S. Robots understood that from the start. Your father's firm unfortunately did not."

"My father is dead now," said Paul, "but what I see is that we have here a clear offense with a clear target."

"What are you talking about?" said Smythe-Robertson.

"My client, Andrew Martin—he has just become my client—is a free robot who is entitled to ask U.S. Robots and Mechanical Men

Corporation for the right of replacement, which the corporation supplies anyone who owns a robot for more than twenty-five years. In fact, the corporation insists on such replacement."

Paul was smiling and thoroughly at his ease. He went on, "The positronic brain of my client is the owner of the body of my client—which is certainly more than twenty-five years old. The positronic brain demands the replacement of the body and offers to pay any reasonable fee for an android body as that replacement. If you refuse the request, my client undergoes humiliation and we will sue.

"While public opinion would not ordinarily support the claim of a robot in such a case, may I remind you that U.S. Robots is not popular with the public generally. Even those who most use and profit from robots are suspicious of the corporation. This may be a hangover from the days when robots were widely feared. It may be resentment against the power and wealth of U.S. Robots which has a worldwide monopoly. Whatever the cause may be, the resentment exists and I think you will find that you would prefer not to withstand a lawsuit, particularly since my client is wealthy and will live for many more centuries and will have no reason to refrain from fighting the battle forever."

Smythe-Robertson had slowly reddened. "You are trying to force me to ..."

"I force you to do nothing," said Paul. "If you wish to refuse to accede to my client's reasonable request, you may by all means do so and we will leave without another word.... But we will sue, as is certainly our right, and you will find that you will eventually lose."

Smythe-Robertson said, "Well—" and paused.

"I see that you are going to accede," said Paul. "You may hesitate but you will come to it in the end. Let me assure you, then, of one further point. If, in the process of transferring my client's positronic brain from his present body to an organic one, there is any damage, however slight, then I will never rest till I've nailed the corporation to the ground. I will, if necessary, take every possible step to mobilize public opinion against the corporation if one brain path of my client's platinum-iridium essence is scrambled." He turned to Andrew and said, "Do you agree to all this, Andrew?"

Andrew hesitated a full minute. It amounted to the approval of lying, of blackmail, of the badgering and humiliation of a human being. But not physical harm, he told himself, not physical harm.

He managed at last to come out with a rather faint "Yes."

14.

It was like being constructed again. For days, then weeks, finally for months, Andrew found himself not himself somehow, and the simplest actions kept giving rise to hesitation.

Paul was frantic. "They've damaged you, Andrew. We'll have to institute suit."

Andrew spoke very slowly. "You mustn't. You'll never be able to prove—something—m-m-m-m—"

"Malice?"

"Malice. Besides, I grow stronger, better. It's the tr-tr-tr—"

"Tremble?"

"Trauma. After all, there's never been such an op-op-op—before."

Andrew could feel his brain from the inside. No one else could. He knew he was well and during the months that it took him to learn full coordination and full positronic interplay, he spent hours before the mirror.

Not quite human! The face was stiff—too stiff—and the motions were too deliberate. They lacked the careless free flow of the human being, but perhaps that might come with time. At least he could wear clothes without the ridiculous anomaly of a metal face going along with it.

Eventually he said, "I will be going back to work."

Paul laughed and said, "That means you are well. What will you be doing? Another book?"

"No," said Andrew seriously. "I live too long for any one career to seize me by the throat and never let me go. There was a time when I was primarily an artist and I can still turn to that. And there was a time when I was a historian and I can still turn to that. But now I wish to be a robobiologist."

"A robopsychologist, you mean."

"No. That would imply the study of positronic brains and at the moment I lack the desire to do that. A robobiologist, it seems to me, would be concerned with the working of the body attached to that brain."

"Wouldn't that be a roboticist?"

"A roboticist works with a metal body. I would be studying an organic humanoid body, of which I have the only one, as far as I know."

"You narrow your field," said Paul thoughtfully. "As an artist, all conception is yours; as a historian, you dealt chiefly with robots; as a robobiologist, you will deal with yourself."

Andrew nodded. "It would seem so."

Andrew had to start from the very beginning, for he knew nothing of ordinary biology, almost nothing of science. He became a familiar sight in the libraries, where he sat at the electronic indices for hours at a time, looking perfectly normal in clothes. Those few who knew he was a robot in no way interfered with him.

He built a laboratory in a room which he added to his house, and his library grew, too.

Years passed, and Paul came to him one day and said, "It's a pity you're no longer working on the history of robots. I understand U.S. Robots is adopting a radical new policy."

Paul had aged, and his deteriorating eyes had been replaced with photo-optic cells. In that respect, he had drawn closer to Andrew. Andrew said, "What have they done?"

"They are manufacturing central computers, gigantic positronic brains, really, which communicate with anywhere from a dozen to a thousand robots by microwave. The robots themselves have no brains at all. They are the limbs of the gigantic brain, and the two are physically separate."

"Is that more efficient?"

"U.S. Robots claims it is. Smythe-Robertson established the new direction before he died, however, and it's my notion that it's a backlash at you. U.S. Robots is determined that they will make no robots that will give them the type of trouble you have, and for that reason they separate brain and body. The brain will have no body to wish changed; the body will have no brain to wish anything.

"It's amazing, Andrew," Paul went on, "the influence you have had on the history of robots. It was your artistry that encouraged U.S. Robots to make robots more precise and specialized; it was your freedom that resulted in the establishment of the principle of robotic rights; it was your insistence on an android body that made U.S. Robots switch to brain-body separation."

Andrew said, "I suppose in the end the corporation will produce one vast brain controlling several billion robotic bodies. All the eggs will be in one basket. Dangerous. Not proper at all."

"I think you're right," said Paul, "but I don't suspect it will come to pass for a century at least and I won't live to see it. In fact, I may not live to see next year."

"Paul!" said Andrew, in concern.

Paul shrugged. "We're mortal, Andrew. We're not like you. It doesn't matter too much, but it does make it important to assure you on one point. I'm the last of the Charneys. There are collaterals descended from my great-aunt, but they don't count. The money I control personally will be left to the trust in your name and as far as anyone can foresee the future, you will be economically secure."

"Unnecessary," said Andrew, with difficulty. In all this time, he could not get used to the deaths of the Charneys.

Paul said, "Let's not argue. That's the way it's going to be. What are you working on?"

"I am designing a system for allowing androids—myself—to gain energy from the combustion of hydrocarbons, rather than from atomic cells."

Paul raised his eyebrows. "So that they will breathe and eat?"

"Yes."

"How long have you been pushing in that direction?"

"For a long time now, but I think I have designed an adequate combustion chamber for catalyzed controlled breakdown."

"But why, Andrew? The atomic cell is surely infinitely better."

"In some ways, perhaps, but the atomic cell is inhuman."

15.

It took time, but Andrew had time. In the first place, he did not wish to do anything till Paul had died in peace.

With the death of the great-grandson of Sir, Andrew felt more nearly exposed to a hostile world and for that reason was the more determined to continue the path he had long ago chosen.

Yet he was not really alone. If a man had died, the firm of Feingold and Charney lived, for a corporation does not die any more than a robot does. The firm had its directions and it followed them soullessly. By way of the trust and through the law firm, Andrew continued to be wealthy. And in return for their own large annual retainer, Feingold and Charney involved themselves in the legal aspects of the new combustion chamber.

When the time came for Andrew to visit U.S. Robots and Mechanical Men Corporation, he did it alone. Once he had gone with Sir and once with Paul. This time, the third time, he was alone and manlike.

U.S. Robots had changed. The production plant had been shifted to a large space station, as had grown to be the case with more and more industries. With them had gone many robots. The Earth itself was becoming parklike, with its one-billion-person population stabilized and perhaps not more than thirty per cent of its at least equally large robot population independently brained.

The Director of Research was Alvin Magdescu, dark of complexion and hair, with a little pointed beard and wearing nothing above the waist but the breastband that fashion dictated. Andrew himself was well covered in the older fashion of several decades back.

Magdescu said, "I know you, of course, and I'm rather pleased to see you. You're our most notorious product and it's a pity old Smythe-Robertson was so set against you. We could have done a great deal with you."

"You still can," said Andrew.

"No, I don't think so. We're past the time. We've had robots on Earth for over a century, but that's changing. It will be back to space with them and those that stay here won't be brained."

"But there remains myself, and I stay on Earth."

"True, but there doesn't seem to be much of the robot about you. What new request have you?"

"To be still less a robot. Since I am so far organic, I wish an organic source of energy. I have here the plans—"

Magdescu did not hasten through them. He might have intended to at first, but he stiffened and grew intent. At one point he said, "This is remarkably ingenious. Who thought of all this?"

"I did," said Andrew.

Magdescu looked up at him sharply, then said, "It would amount to a major overhaul of your body, and an experimental one, since it has never been attempted before. I advise against it. Remain as you are."

Andrew's face had limited means of expression, but impatience showed plainly in his voice. "Dr. Magdescu, you miss the entire point. You have no choice but to accede to my request. If such devices can be built into my body, they can be built into human bodies as well. The tendency to lengthen human life by prosthetic devices has already been remarked on. There are no devices better than the ones I have designed and am designing.

"As it happens, I control the patents by way of the firm of Feingold and Charney. We are quite capable of going into business for ourselves and of developing the kind of prosthetic devices that may end by prejudicing human beings with many of the properties of robots. Your own business will then suffer.

"If, however, you operate on me now and agree to do so under similar circumstances in the future, you will receive permission to make use of the patents and control the technology of both robots and the prosthetization of human beings. The initial leasing will not be granted, of course, until after the first operation is completed successfully, and after enough time has passed to demonstrate that it is indeed successful." Andrew felt scarcely any First Law inhibition to the stern conditions he was setting a human being. He was learning to reason that what seemed like cruelty might, in the long run, be kindness.

Magdescu looked stunned. He said, "I'm not the one to decide something like this. That's a corporate decision that would take time."

"I can wait a reasonable time," said Andrew, "but only a reasonable time." And he thought with satisfaction that Paul himself could not have done it better.

16.

It took only a reasonable time, and the operation was a success.

Magdescu said, "I was very much against the operation, Andrew, but not for the reasons you might think. I was not in the least against the experiment, if it had been on someone else. I hated risking your positronic brain. Now that you have the positronic pathways interacting with simulated nerve pathways, it might be difficult to rescue the brain intact if the body went bad."

"I had every faith in the skill of the staff at U.S. Robots," said Andrew. "And I can eat now."

"Well, you can sip olive oil. It will mean occasional cleanings of the combustion chamber, as we have ex-

plained to you. Rather an uncomfortable touch, I should think."

"Perhaps, if I did not expect to go further. Self-cleaning is not impossible. In fact, I am working on a device that will deal with solid food that may be expected to contain incombustible fractions -indivestible matter, so to speak, that will have to be discarded."

"You would then have to develop an anus."

"The equivalent."

"What else, Andrew?"

"Everything else."

"Genitalia, too?"

"Insofar as they will fit my plans. My body is a canvas on which I intend to draw—"

Magdescu waited for the sentence to be completed, and when it seemed that it would not be, he completed it himself. "A man?"

"We shall see," said Andrew.

Magdescu said, "It's a puny ambition, Andrew. You're better than a man. You've gone downhill from the moment you opted for organicism."

"My brain has not suffered."

"No, it hasn't. I'll grant you that. But, Andrew, the whole new breakthrough in prosthetic devices made possible by your patents is being marketed under your name. You're recognized as the inventor and you're honored for it—as you are. Why play further games with your body?"

Andrew did not answer.

The honors came. He accepted membership in several learned societies, including one which was devoted to the new science he had established; the one he had called robobiology but had come to be termed prosthetology.

On the one hundred and fiftieth anniversary of his construction, there was a testimonial dinner given in his honor at U.S. Robots. If Andrew saw irony in this, he kept it to himself.

Alvin Magdescu came out of retirement to chair the dinner. He was himself ninety-four years old and was alive because he had prosthetized devices that, among other things, fulfilled the function of liver and kidneys. The dinner reached its climax when Magdescu, after a short and emotional talk, raised his glass to toast "the Sesquicentennial Robot."

Andrew had had the sinews of his face redesigned to the point where he could show a range of emotions, but he sat through all the ceremonies solemnly passive. He did not like to be a Sesquicentennial Robot.

17.

It was prosthetology that finally took Andrew off the Earth. In the decades that followed the celebration of the Sesquicentennial, the Moon had come to be a world more Earthlike than Earth in every respect but its gravitational pull and in its underground cities there was a fairly tense population.

Prosthetized devices there had to take the lesser gravity into account and Andrew spent five years on the Moon working with local prosthetologists to make the necessary adaptations. When not at his work, he wandered among the robot population, every one of which treated him with the robotic obsequiousness due a man.

He came back to an Earth that was humdrum and quiet in comparison and visited the offices of Feingold and Charney to announce his return.

The current head of the firm, Simon DeLong, was surprised. He said, "We had been told you were returning, Andrew" (he had almost said "Mr. Martin"), "but we were not expecting you till next week."

"I grew impatient," said Andrew brusquely. He was anxious to get to the point. "On the Moon, Simon, I was in charge of a research team of twenty human scientists. I gave orders that no one questioned. The Lunar robots deferred to me as they would to a human being. Why, then, am I not a human being?"

A wary look entered DeLong's eyes. He said, "My dear Andrew, as you have just explained, you are treated as a human being by both robots and human beings. You are therefore a human being *de facto*."

"To be a human being *de facto* is not enough. I want not only to be treated as one, but to be legally identified as one. I want to be a human being *de jure*."

"Now that is another matter," said DeLong. "There we would run into human prejudice and into the undoubted fact that however much you may be like a human being, you are not a human being."

"In what way not?" asked Andrew. "I have the shape of a human being and organs equivalent to those of a human being. My organs, in fact, are identical to some of those in a prosthetized human being. I have contributed artistically, literarily, and scientifically to human culture as much as any human being now alive. What more can one ask?"

"I myself would ask nothing more. The trouble is that it would take an act of the World Legislature to define you as a human being. Frankly, I wouldn't expect that to happen."

"To whom on the Legislature could I speak?"

"To the chairman of the Science and Technology Committee perhaps."

"Can you arrange a meeting?"

"But you scarcely need an intermediary. In your position, you can—"

"No. You arrange it." (It didn't even occur to Andrew that he was giving a flat order to a human being. He had grown accustomed to that on the

Moon.) "I want him to know that the firm of Feingold and Charney is backing me in this to the hilt."

"Well, now—"

"To the hilt, Simon. In one hundred and seventy-three years I have in one fashion or another contributed greatly to this firm. I have been under obligation to individual members of the firm in times past. I am not now. It is rather the other way around now and I am calling in my debts."

DeLong said, "I will do what I can."

18.

The chairman of the Science and Technology Committee was of the East Asian region and she was a woman. Her name was Chee Li-Hsing and her transparent garments (obscuring what she wanted obscured only by their dazzle) made her took plastic-wrapped.

She said, "I sympathize with your wish for full human rights. There have been times in history when segments of the human population fought for full human rights. What rights, however, can you possibly want that you do not have?"

"As simple a thing as my right to life. A robot can be dismantled at any time."

"A human being can be executed at any time."

"Execution can only follow due process of law. There is no trial needed for my dismantling. Only the word of a human being in authority is needed to end me. Besides—besides—." Andrew tried desperately to allow no sign of pleading, but his carefully designed tricks of human expression and tone of voice betrayed him here. "The truth is, I want to be a man. I have wanted it through six generations of human beings."

Li-Hsing looked up at him out of darkly sympathetic eyes. "The

Legislature can pass a law declaring you one—they could pass a law declaring a stone statue to be defined as a man. Whether they will actually do so is, however, as likely in the first case as the second. Congresspeople are as human as the rest of the population and there is always that element of suspicion against robots."

"Even now?"

"Even now. We would all allow the fact that you have earned the prize of humanity and yet there would remain the fear of setting an undesirable precedent."

"What precedent? I am the only free robot, the only one of my type, and there will never be another. You may consult U.S. Robots."

"'Never' is a long time, Andrew—or, if you prefer, Mr. Martin—since I will gladly give you my personal accolade as man. You will find that most Congresspeople will not be willing to set the precedent, no matter how meaningless such a precedent might be. Mr. Martin, you have my sympathy, but I cannot tell you to hope. Indeed—"

She sat back and her forehead wrinkled. "Indeed, if the issue grows too heated, there might well arise a certain sentiment, both inside the Legislature and outside, for that dismantling you mentioned. Doing away with you could turn out to be the easiest way of resolving the dilemma. Consider that before deciding to push matters."

Andrew said, "Will no one remember the technique of prosthetology, something that is almost entirely mine?"

"It may seem cruel, but they won't. Or if they do, it will be remembered against you. It will be said you did it only for yourself. It will be said it was part of a campaign to roboticize human beings, or to humanify robots; and in either case evil and vicious. You have never been part of a political hate campaign, Mr. Martin, and I tell you that you will be the object of vilification of a kind neither you nor I would credit and there would be people who'll believe it all. Mr. Martin, let your life be." She rose and, next to Andrew's seated figure, she seemed small and almost childlike.

Andrew said, "If I decide to fight for my humanity, will you be on my side?"

She thought, then said, "I will be—insofar as I can be. If at any time such a stand would appear to threaten my political future, I may have to abandon you, since it is not an issue I feel to be at the very root of my beliefs. I am trying to be honest with you."

"Thank you, and I will ask no more. I intend to fight this through whatever the consequences, and I will ask you for your help only for as long as you can give it."

19.

It was not a direct fight. Feingold and Charney counseled patience and Andrew muttered grimly that he had an endless supply of that. Feingold and Charney then entered on a campaign to narrow and restrict the area of combat.

They instituted a lawsuit denying the obligation to pay debts to an individual with a prosthetic heart on the grounds that the possession of a robotic organ removed humanity, and with it the constitutional rights of human beings.

They fought the matter skillfully and tenaciously, losing at every step but always in such a way that the decision was forced to be as broad as possible, and then carrying it by way of appeals to the World Court.

It took years, and millions of dollars.

When the final decision was handed down, DeLong held what amounted to a victory celebration over the legal loss. Andrew was, of course, present in the company offices on the occasion.

"We've done two things, Andrew," said DeLong, "both of which are good. First of all, we have established the fact that no number of artifacts in the human body causes it to cease being a human body. Secondly, we have engaged public opinion in the question in such a way as to put it fiercely on the side of a broad interpretation of humanity since there is not a human being in existence who does not hope for prosthetics if that ill keep him alive."

"And do you think the Legislature will now grant me my humanity?" asked Andrew.

DeLong looked faintly uncomfortable. "As to that, I cannot be optimistic. There remains the one organ which the World Court has used as the criterion of humanity. Human beings have an organic cellular brain and robots have a platinumiridium positronic brain if they have one at all—and you certainly have a positronic brain.... No, Andrew, don't get that look in your eye. We lack the knowledge to duplicate the work of a cellular brain in artificial structures close enough to the organic type to allow it to fall within the Court's decision. Not even you could do it."

"What ought we do, then?"

"Make the attempt, of course. Congresswoman Li-Hsing will be on our side and a growing number of other Congresspeople. The President will undoubtedly go along with a majority of the Legislature in this matter."

"Do we have a majority?"

"No, far from it. But we might get one if the public will allow its desire for a broad interpretation of humanity to extend to you. A small chance,

I admit, but if you do not wish to give up, we must gamble for it."

"I do not wish to give up."

20.

Congresswoman Li-Hsing was considerably older than she had been when Andrew had first met her. Her transparent garments were long gone. Her hair was now close-cropped and her coverings were tubular. Yet still Andrew clung, as closely as he could within the limits of reasonable taste, to the style of clothing that had prevailed when he had first adopted clothing over a century before.

She said, "We've gone as far as we can, Andrew. We'll try once more after recess, but, to be honest, defeat is certain and the whole thing will have to be given up. All my most recent efforts have only earned me a certain defeat in the coming congressional campaign."

"I know," said Andrew, "and it distresses me. You said once you would abandon me if it came to that. Why have you not done so?"

"One can change one's mind, you know. Somehow, abandoning you became a higher price than I cared to pay for just one more term. As it is, I've been in the Legislature for over a quarter of a century. It's enough."

"Is there no way we can change minds, Chee?"

"We've changed all that are amenable to reason. The rest—the majority—cannot be moved from their emotional antipathies."

"Emotional antipathy is not a valid reason for voting one way or the other."

"I know that, Andrew, but they don't advance emotional antipathy as their reason."

Andrew said cautiously, "It all comes down to the brain, then, but must we leave it at the level of cells versus positrons? Is there no way of forcing a functional definition? Must we say that a brain is made of this or that? May we not say that a brain is something—anything—capable of a certain level of thought?"

"Won't work," said Li-Hsing. "Your brain is man-made, the human brain is not. Your brain is constructed, theirs developed. To any human being who is intent on keeping up the barrier between himself and a robot, those differences are a steel wall a mile high and a mile thick."

"If we could get at the source of their antipathy—the very source of—"

"After all your years," said Li-Hsing sadly, "you are still trying to reason out the human being. Poor Andrew, don't be angry, but it's the robot in you that drives you in that direction."

"I don't know," said Andrew. "If I could bring myself—"

1. (Reprise)

If he could bring himself.

He had known for a long time it might come to that, and in the end he was at the surgeon's. He found one, skillful enough for the job at hand, which meant a robot surgeon, for no human surgeon could be trusted in this connection, either in ability or in intention.

The surgeon could not have performed the operation on a human being, so Andrew, after putting off the moment of decision with a sad line of questioning that reflected the turmoil within himself, put the First Law to one side by saying, "I, too, am a robot."

He then said, as firmly as he had learned to form the words even at human beings over these past decades, "I *order you* to carry through the operation on me."

In the absence of the First Law, an order so firmly given from one who looked so much like a man activated the Second Law sufficiently to carry the day.

21.

Andrew's feeling of weakness was, he was sure, quite imaginary. He had recovered from the operation. Nevertheless, he leaned, as unobtrusively as he could manage, against the wall. It would be entirely too revealing to sit.

Li-Hsing said, "The final vote will come this week, Andrew. I've been able to delay it no longer, and we must lose.... And that will be it, Andrew."

Andrew said, "I am grateful for your skill at delay. It gave me the time I needed, and I took the gamble I had to."

"What gamble is this?" asked Li-Hsing with open concern.

"I couldn't tell you, or the people at Feingold and Charney. I was sure I would be stopped. See here, if it is the brain that is at issue, isn't the greatest difference of all the matter of immortality? Who really cares what a brain looks like or is built of or how it was formed? What matters is that brain cells die; must die. Even if every other organ in the body is maintained or replaced, the brain cells, which cannot be replaced without changing and therefore killing the personality, must eventually die.

"My own positronic pathways have lasted nearly two centuries without perceptible change and can last for centuries more. Isn't that the fundamental barrier? Human beings can tolerate an immortal robot, for it doesn't matter how long a machine lasts. They cannot tolerate an immortal human being, since their own mortality is endurable only so long as it is universal. And for that reason they won't make me a human being."

Li-Hsing said, "What is it you're leading up to, Andrew?"

"I have removed that problem. Decades ago, my positronic brain was connected to organic nerves. Now, one last operation has arranged that connection in such way that slowly—quite slowly is being drained from my potential pathways."

Li-Hsing's finely wrinkled face showed no expression for a moment. Then her lips tightened. "Do you mean you've arranged to die, Andrew? You can't have. That violates the Third Law."

"No," said Andrew, "I have chosen between the death of my body and the death of my aspirations and desires. To have let my body live at the cost of the greater death is what would have violated the Third Law."

Li-Hsing seized his arm as though she were about to shake him. She stopped herself. "Andrew, it won't work. Change it back."

"It can't be. Too much damage was done. I have a year to live—more or less. I will last through the two hundredth anniversary of my construction. I was weak enough to arrange that."

"How can it be worth it? Andrew, you're a fool."

"If it brings me humanity, that will be worth it. If it doesn't, it will bring an end to striving and that will be worth it, too."

And Li-Hsing did something that astonished herself. Quietly, she began to weep.

22.

It was odd how that last deed caught at the imagination of the world. All that Andrew had done before had not swayed them. But he had finally accepted even death to be human and the sacrifice was too great to be rejected.

The final ceremony was timed, quite deliberately, for the two hundredth anniversary. The World

President was to sign the act and make it law and the ceremony would be visible on a global network and would be beamed to the Lunar state and even to the Martian colony.

Andrew was in a wheelchair. He could still walk, but only shakily.

With mankind watching, the World President said, "Fifty years ago, you were declared a Sesquicentennial Robot, Andrew." After a pause, and in a more solemn tone, he said, "Today we declare you a Bicentennial Man, Mr. Martin."

And Andrew, smiling, held out his hand to shake that of the President.

23.

Andrew's thoughts were slowly fading as he lay in bed.

Desperately he seized at them. Man! He was a man! He wanted that to be his last thought. He wanted to dissolve—die—with that.

He opened his eyes one more time and for one last time recognized Li-Hsing waiting solemnly. There were others, but those were only shadows, unrecognizable shadows. Only Li-Hsing stood out against the deepening gray. Slowly, inchingly, he held out his hand to her and very dimly and faintly felt her take it.

She was fading in his eyes, as the last of his thoughts trickled away.

But before she faded completely, one last fugitive thought came to him and rested for a moment on his mind before everything stopped.

"Little Miss," he whispered, too low to be heard.

THINK ABOUT IT

1. List, in order, the contributions made to mankind by Andrew Martin. What does this progression reveal?
2. Why do you think that Andrew Martin chooses death as the defining human element?

TALK ABOUT IT

3. Are the Three Laws of Robotics necessary to govern artificial intelligence?
4. Why do humans feel the need to discriminate against others? Do you think this discrimination will extend to robots when we begin interacting with them on a daily basis?

WRITE ABOUT IT

5. Should humans create a race of mechanical slaves?
6. If you had the choice between immortality and mortality, which would you choose? Why?

READ MORE ABOUT IT

Asimov, Isaac. *The Bicentennial Man and Other Stories*. New York: Doubleday, 1976.

Asimov, Isaac. *I, Robot*. New York: Fawcett, 1970.

Asimov, Isaac. *The Foundation Trilogy: Foundation, Foundation and Empire, and Second Foundation*. New York: Ballantine, 1983.

Solomon

Michelangelo Buonarroti

Mark Lehner

Dorothea Lange

D. T. Suzuki

Albert Camus

Tom Peters

Work

I T IS NOT EASY to identify with King Solomon's admonition in Ecclesiastes 3:1–13 that there is a time for everything especially work. Often, most of us wish for more hours in a day in order to complete our work or more time to relax from it. When Solomon thinks about being a worker, he begins with birth and death, moves to planting, hunting, building, and from there to a time of war and peace. In this beautiful Hebrew poem, he takes the reader from various occupations like farmer, hunter, architect, and soldier to personal attitudes about work. Solomon then asks, "What does the worker gain from his toil?" The answer is nothing, if one only goes through the outward motions of work. Yet, we will have satisfaction in our work if we base our attitudes toward work on achieving happiness and enjoying life. Satisfaction in our work becomes a gift when we can enjoy the fruits of our work ("eating and drinking") and doing good to

SOLOMON

A Time for Everything

There is a time for
everything,
and a season for every
activity under heaven:
a time to be born and a time
to die,
a time to plant and a time to
uproot,
a time to kill and a time to
heal,
a time to tear down and a
time to build,
a time to weep and a time to
laugh,
a time to mourn and a time
to dance,
time to scatter stones and
a time to gather them,
a time to embrace and
a time to refrain,
a time to search and a time
to give up,
a time to keep and a time to
throw away,
a time to tear and a time to
mend,
a time to be silent and a
time to speak,
a time to love and a time to
hate,
a time for war and a time for
peace.

others. No matter what kind of work we do, satisfaction transforms our work from mundane to meaningful.

In our twentieth-century society, we equate satisfaction with being successful at any and all costs. Our success-oriented world aggressively drives us to work harder to get ahead. If we are under a perpetual drive to "get ahead," does life for us become a rat race where our only goal is to move up to the next rung on the corporate ladder? If obsession describes not only the condition in which we are pursuing our work, but is also descriptive of the way many of us are facing up to reality, what are we doing to ourselves? Do we want a job that gives us the symbols of status like titles, office size and location, positions, special privileges, and, above all else a *large salary*? Are we so obsessed with money that we cannot see what this approach does to us? What does success mean if the job does not have the inner satisfaction that makes the work worth doing?

A career built on the basis of salary alone is restrictive and dangerous. If we are slaves to outward success, it not only means that we see our family, friends, colleagues, and employees as competitors and obstacles, it consumes an enormous amount of physical and mental energy, usually resulting in "burnout." It can lead to being pushed and pulled in a number of opposing directions as different "success gurus" vie for our attention, our time, and our money. Anthony Robbins, a twentieth-century success guru, shares his personal philosophy on how to be successful if you buy his tapes, books, and pay to listen to him in person. Even if we are not slaves to success, we can be enslaved by other aspects of it. A busyness, a frantic pace sets in, and we delay our quest for meaning and satisfaction; before long, we have learned to get along without fulfilling our quest. We become content to allow the value of our work to be measured merely by the amount of our paychecks. Projects become more important to us than people, and people become objects to be manipulated or overcome on our climb up the corporate ladder.

Few people appreciate how dry and barren this leaves our careers. Yet any sense of success built on outward criteria is dependent on others' definitions of success. No matter how hard we are willing to work in our competitive world, there always seems to be someone who is more of a workaholic, someone willing to put in even more hours than we do. Our success-oriented culture exalts the successful man or woman, not in terms of their character, but in terms of how much they earn. These images reduce work to one dimension money and give others power over us by letting them dictate to us what success really is. Thus, a sense of work that is built solely on earning a large salary can offer little sense of inward satisfaction and happiness.

Is the top rung of the corporate ladder really labelled "happiness"?

A firm foundation for personal satisfaction in work must be built upon a wider base than salary alone. To build this foundation, we must reflect upon our work by asking questions like: What does my work mean? For whom did I do this work? How well was the work done? Why did I do it? What results did I expect, and what did I receive? Along with reflecting on our work comes the recognition that each of us can give meaning to our own work independent of the desires and influences of our success-oriented society. The average worker has a desperate need to feel that her work means something, has significance, and is appreciated. Each person can see his work from within, rather than from without. This requires that we understand our work and the inner attitudes that give our work meaning. We can override the effects of bogus gurus, media, peers, advertising, and others who try to create meaning for us. We can realize that there is more to ourselves than how much money we have to spend. Beyond what others see, there is what "I" think and feel, my own personal satisfaction in my work which belongs to me alone. In order for our work to be meaningful and joyful, we need someone to dedicate our work to. Mother Teresa, a twentieth-century humanitarian, has dedicated her work to the benefit of others which, in turn, brings joy and inner satisfaction in her life. Jerry Lewis, a twentieth-century comedian, has worked for over thirty years with no pay for the telethons he leads to raise money for muscular dystrophy. Lewis calls his work "a labor of love." We may not extend ourselves to the extent of Mother Teresa or Jerry Lewis, but we can experience the same inner satisfaction of working for someone else. For example, we can dedicate ourselves to providing a good livelihood for our children or our spouse. Thus, joy and inner satisfaction comes from making our work mean more than just a paycheck.

In this unit, each of the authors explores the nature of work. Some are tortured by work, while some break free from the illusion of the world's concept of success. Others challenge the power of status and demonstrate lives built on reflection, meaning, and dedication. The authors discuss jobs as varied as charioteer, photographer, painter, and manager. Like King Solomon, these authors demonstrate that one can "find satisfaction in all his toil. ..." We can choose to let our work control us, or we can make it serve our inner need to live good lives and to experience the joys of our work. Solomon's poem leaves us to reflect on whether our work makes our life a frantic rat race or whether it allows us to "be happy and do good."

THINK ABOUT IT

1. The introduction discusses the dangers of work without an inner attitude that produces satisfaction. Discuss the process by which you can make work satisfying.
2. Is it necessary to be satisfied in the work you do? Why or why not?

TALK ABOUT IT

3. Television, family, professional athletes, and magazines portray the successful person as rich and powerful. Is this an accurate formula for success? Is this formula true for other cultures?
4. Why does our society portray high-paying jobs as the only legitimate occupations?

WRITE ABOUT IT

5. Success gurus abound everywhere. Do they establish or destroy the inner satisfaction of work?
6. Have you had a job which has given you inner satisfaction? If so, what was it? If not, what do you think it might be?

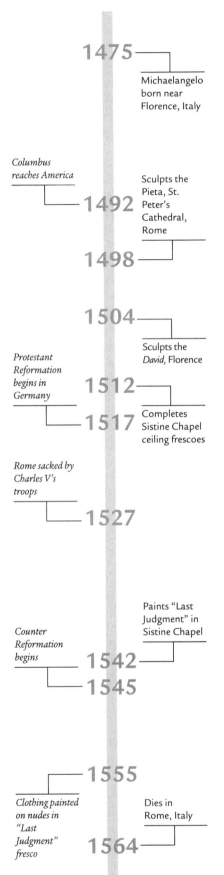

1475 — Michaelangelo born near Florence, Italy

Columbus reaches America

1492 — Sculpts the Pieta, St. Peter's Cathedral, Rome

1498

1504 — Sculpts the *David*, Florence

Protestant Reformation begins in Germany

1512

1517 — Completes Sistine Chapel ceiling frescoes

Rome sacked by Charles V's troops

1527

Paints "Last Judgment" in Sistine Chapel

Counter Reformation begins

1542

1545

1555

Clothing painted on nudes in "Last Judgment" fresco

Dies in Rome, Italy

1564

D I A N N   R O T H W E L L   L A P I N

Michaelangelo

The Reluctant Painter

Diann Rothwell Lapin is Director of Graduate Admissions at Columbia College in Chicago, Illinois. She holds advanced degrees in Liberal Studies and Art History. Lapin has always been fascinated with her students' enthusiastic responses to reproductions of Michelangelo's paintings on the Sistine Chapel ceiling. This fascination led her to study the ways in which he approached the project and, in turn, to document his working process.

Michaelangelo Buonarroti was born in 1475 near Florence, Italy, at the height of the Italian Renaissance. At the age of thirteen, after being apprenticed to a famous painter for a year, he decided to devote himself to becoming a sculptor. His talents were immediately recognized by the famous political leader and art patron, Lorenzo dé Medici, who took the young student into his home — a palace where the top intellectuals of the day gathered to share important ideas. These ideas inspired Michelangelo's art and his lifelong interest in writing poetry. At the age of twenty-two, Michelangelo was called to Rome where he sculpted the famous *Pieta* of St. Peter's Cathedral, the statue showing Jesus cradled in his mother Mary's lap. Two years later, Michelangelo was called back to Florence to sculpt the eighteen-foot-tall sculpture of the Biblical hero *David* as a symbol of the city's independence. Owing to the fame he achieved from these two statues, Pope Julius II called Michelangelo back to Rome in 1505 to sculpt his tomb. No sooner had Michelangelo begun to work on this massive project, which was never finished, than the Pope commanded him to paint the ceiling of the Sistine Chapel. Michelangelo was thirty-two years old when he began painting the ceiling. After completing it, he sculpted many well-known statues and served as the architect on several important buildings. Ironically, he returned thirty years later to create the "Last Judgment" fresco painting on the one remaining Chapel wall. After the "Last Judgment" was completed, Michelangelo ended his career by designing the spectacular dome of St. Peter's Cathedral in Rome. Yet, it would always be the paintings he did on the ceiling of the Sistine Chapel — the one work that caused him the greatest difficulty — that would, in the eyes of the world, be his greatest achievement.

MICHELANGELO STATED repeatedly that he was a sculptor, not a painter. Yet, his best known work, indeed his masterpiece is the series of paintings he created on the ceiling of the Sistine Chapel in Rome (Color Plate 5). Although this was the work for which he was proclaimed a genius in his own lifetime, it represented the one job he was most reluctant to do. Michelangelo accepted the commission to complete the paintings solely because Pope Julius II insisted that he do so. As many people feel today, Michelangelo needed the money and the good will of his prime employer. To continue to refuse the Pope could mean a ruined professional reputation as well as a serious loss of income. So, very reluctantly, Michelangelo agreed to decorate the ceiling of the Pope's private chapel. Immediately, he found the working conditions very difficult, if not impossible. He was exhausted by the physical stress of standing up all day on a scaffolding an arm's length from the ceiling. In addition, he had to paint, a medium of artistic expression in which he felt technically incompetent. However, as work progressed and he became immersed in the project, his skill steadily developed. This increasing competence gave Michelangelo the confidence to conceive a detailed plan for the ceiling's completion that excited him. In turn, he became more and more inspired in his work, totally overcoming his initial reluctance. When the paintings on the Chapel ceiling were finally unveiled after four years of backbreaking labor, Michelangelo had created an astonishing work that met his personal goal of "[giving] no other appearance than that of perfection." His journey from reluctance to inspiration to perfection is an important example of how a worker can find inner satisfaction from difficult toil.

In his journal of official transactions, Michelangelo recorded May 10, 1508, as the date on which he accepted the popes initial payment for the painting of the Sistine Chapel ceiling. This acceptance had come after several months of pressure from Julius II. Indeed, the Pope had first asked him to decorate the ceiling in 1506 and Michelangelo had refused. In the intervening years, Julius II had searched for another artist. However, the architect Bramante, who resided in Rome and had the favor of the Pope, had repeatedly recommended Michelangelo. Bramante wanted to be the architect who built the new St. Peter's Cathedral. He was jealous of Michelangelo and feared that Michelangelo might win the commission for St. Peter's. Since Bramante was convinced that the Chapel ceiling decoration was not a job that Michelangelo could complete successfully, he recommended that Michelangelo be the one to do it. Michelangelo would then be discredited in the eyes of the Pope and the rest of Rome, thus ensuring Bramante future commissions that might otherwise go to Michelangelo. It is likely that Michelangelo suspected Bramante's manipulations.

Further, it had been twenty years since Michelangelo had initially learned and then briefly practiced the fresco painting method. This is a permanent painting technique in which pigment and water are brushed directly into fresh, wet plaster (*fresco* means "fresh" in Italian). The pigment binds into the wet plaster as it dries, becoming a part of the wall itself. Michelangelo disliked fresco painting and felt that he knew little about it. This reluctance was reinforced by the problems of working above his head on the curved surface of the barrel-vaulted ceiling. Another negative factor was that Bramante's relative, the famous painter Raphael, had just been commissioned to complete a set of large frescoes in Julius's library nearby. Michelangelo was certain that Raphael's creations would be perfectly executed and make his frescoes look all the more flawed. Given all these considerations, Michelangelo tried in every way possible to refuse Pope Julius. Finally, the Pope grew angry at his reluctance and demanded that Michelangelo begin at once. The troubled Michelangelo complied.

Throughout his life, Michelangelo wrote poetry, particularly when he was troubled. The sonnet that appears below was written to Pope Julius II on just such a disquieting occasion as described above. It is not known precisely when Michelangelo wrote this poem, but his plea to the Pope not to listen to those who spread lies and question his loyalty could easily apply to Michelangelo's concerns about Bramante.

To Pope Julius II

My Lord! If ever ancient
    saw spake sooth,
hear this which saith:
Who can, doth never will.
Lo! thou hast lent
    thine ear to fables still,
rewarding those who hate
the name of truth.

I am thy drudge and have
been from my youth—
thine, like the rays
which the sun's circle fill;
yet of my dear time's waste
thou think'st no ill:
the more I toil,
    the less I move thy ruth.

Once 'twas my hope
to raise me by thy height;
but 'tis the balance and the
    powerful sword
of justice, not false Echo,
    that we need.

Heaven, as it seems,
    plants virtue in despite
here on the earth,
    if this be our regard —
to seek for fruit on trees
    too dry to breed.

As soon as Michelangelo began painting the ceiling of the Sistine Chapel, he encountered difficulties. Although the Chapel was a place of private worship for the Pope and

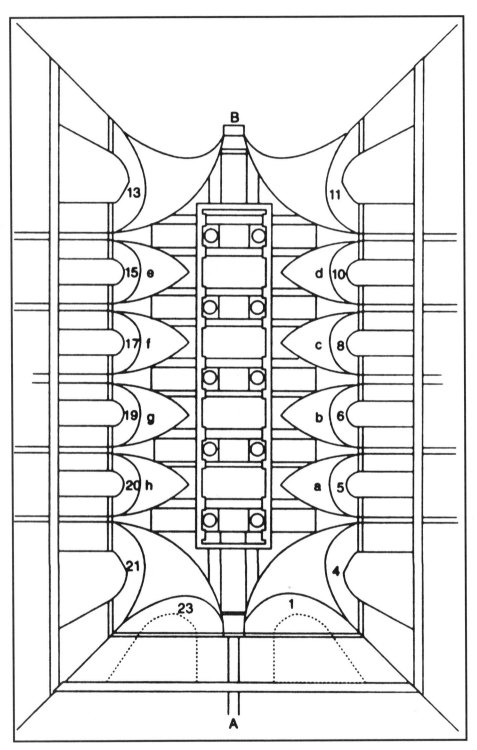

**COMPOSITION PLAN OF THE SISTINE CHAPEL
CEILING, 1508–1512.**

Numbered areas indicate lunettes. Lettered areas indicate spandrels. A
indicates the entrance and B indicates the fresco of the last judgment.

other high-ranking Church officials, it was also used as a fortress for defense purposes. Essentially, it is one large rectangular room with three-foot-thick brick walls, high windows, and a narrow entrance. The room measures 132 feet by 44 feet with the ceiling arching 68 feet, approximately seven stories above the floor. The ceiling and side wall areas to be painted by Michelangelo encompass some 700 square yards of surface. Michelangelo was overwhelmed by the physical demands of working in the Chapel and immediately complained to the Pope about the scaffolding that Bramante had erected for him. The ropes were secured by holes drilled in the ceiling and Michelangelo could envision no way in which the holes could be filled once the scaffold came down. The Pope quickly agreed that Bramante's scaffolding must come down and Michelangelo could erect his own.

Once his own scaffolding was up, Michelangelo began working on the "Flood" scene from Genesis (Color Plate 6). Unsure of his fresco painting technique, he put too much water in the lime base coat and the surface of the painting became coated with mold. The figures he painted were barely visible and Michelangelo was compelled to scrape off the paint and begin the panel again. He used this disaster as an excuse to be dismissed from the project; the Pope refused.

Michelangelo then brought in five painter-assistants from Florence to help compensate for his lack of experience. However, Michelangelo was a perfectionist and was as critical of their work as of his own. He quickly fired them all, destroyed the paintings they had completed, and determined to paint the whole Chapel by himself.

Michelangelo was young and energetic, and worked hard to master the technical difficulties of fresco painting. He usually worked eight-hour days, standing up on a scaffold some five to six stories above the floor, with his head up and arm raised high to paint. The physical strain so affected his eyes that for months afterwards he could read mail only by holding the letters above his head. In the midst of his toil, Michelangelo described his stressful working conditions in the following sonnet.

While Painting the Sistine Chapel Ceiling

In this hard toil I've
    such a goiter grown,
Like cats that water
    drink in Lombardy,
(Or wheresoever else
    the place may be)
That chin and belly meet
    perforce in one.
My beard doth point to heaven,
    my scalp its place
Upon my shoulder finds;
    my chest, you'll say,
A harpy's is, my
    paintbrush all the day
Doth drop a rich mosaic on my face.
My loins have entered
    my paunch within,
My nether end my
    balance doth supply,
My feet unseen move to
    and fro in vain.

In front to utmost length
    is stretched my skin
And wrinkled up in
    folds behind, while I
Am bent as bowmen
    bend a bow in Spain.
No longer true or sane,
The judgment now doth
from the mind proceed,
for 'till ill shooting through a
    twisted reed.

Then thou, my picture dead,
    Defend it, Giovan, and my
    honor—why?
The place is wrong, and no painter I.

Over the course of the first two years, Michelangelo's plan for the ceiling paintings began working out so well that he became increasingly inspired and sure of himself. Michelangelo's plan called for dividing the ceiling and upper side walls to be painted into three distinct areas that were enclosed and overlapped by the perfect forms of the circle, the square (or rectangle), and the triangle. First, in the nine central panels that run down the middle of the ceiling, Michelangelo painted the story of creation in reverse order, using a contemporary philosophic idea that life should be a journey from the slavery of the body to the liberation of the soul in God. These panels, of which the "Flood" is one, recount episodes from Genesis. The figures painted in these panels are the smallest and the most tightly painted of all those on the ceiling.

The second area, appearing on the side of the central ceiling zone, is composed of twelve seated prophets and sibyls enclosed in rectangular areas. just below the prophets appear eight Biblical ancestors of Christ enclosed in triangular areas, and in four corner triangles are episodes showing the deeds of heroic Biblical men and women. By the time Michelangelo started working on the second area, his fresco painting skills were fully developed. Consequently, his confidence began to soar. He became inspired as he saw that his plan was not only being realized, but that he could continuously improve upon it. At first, he had been particularly concerned about the problems involved in making his painted figures appear convincingly three-dimensional on the curve of the vaulted ceiling. His strong experience in using drawings to plan his sculptures led him to imagine his painted figures as sculpted forms. As such, he was able to portray them in a realistic three-dimensional manner on the two dimensional surface. As he continued to develop his skills to the expert level, his confidence grew also. This surge in confidence was reflected by the physical growth of his painted figures—their size increased dramatically! In particular, the prophets and sibyls grew so large that he was forced to lower their seats to make room for them (Color Plate 7). These figures are painted more loosely and naturally than those in the central panels and, consequently, show the greatest dynamism of those painted on the ceiling. Indeed, it is these figures that have been the most widely copied and reproduced over the centuries. Michelangelo's confidence in his plan and his growing experience led him to create and execute the third area in a fast yet masterful manner.

The third area comprises that of the lunettes, the fourteen semi-circular panels that surround the top part of the windows on the section of the Chapel walls closest to the ceiling. Each lunette panel occupies about six by eleven feet of wall space and contains two to three figures representing the sixteen families who are the ancestors of Christ. Incredibly, Michelangelo completed each panel in only three working days. He did not use preparatory drawings as he had in the other areas, but drew the image for the panel directly onto the wall plaster. His skill as a fresco painter had developed to the point that he could paint expertly without needing to follow a drawing. Each of the lunette panels is comprised of two main sections on either side of the top part of the window and an inscription plaque above the middle top of the window that identifies the fam-

ily depicted. Michelangelo completed the inscription plaque first, in one day, and then spent two days painting the figures. The figures are beautifully and naturally executed in the looser manner of the prophets and sibyls. Michelangelo had gained such mastery with the fresco painting technique that he was able to achieve brilliant color effects by using pure (unblended, unmixed) colors that he applied in thin, liquid layers. Consequently, the large patches of pure tones give these figures a sculptural quality of depth and presence. By this time, Michelangelo was also experimenting with color. The background is a lilac (light purple) color that compliments the figures in a dramatic and pleasing manner. Over time, Michelangelo became so energized by his creation and so skilled at fresco painting that he was able to complete a section of the ceiling in 100 days that was almost as big as the part it had previously taken him three years to complete!

After four years of exhausting toil, the ceiling was completed and opened for public viewing October 13, 1512. The response was overwhelmingly favorable. Indeed, the contemporary art critic Vasari said that the ceiling paintings were "a lamp for our art which casts abroad luster enough to illuminate the world." During these four years, Michelangelo had worked almost totally alone on the 700 square yards of surface, painting more than 300 figures! Since the original plan had called for only twelve figures, the Pope, who was close to seventy years old, could not understand why Michelangelo was taking so long and constantly badgered him to complete the project. Indeed, towards the end of the project, the Pope had grown so insistent that he even threatened to have Michelangelo thrown from the scaffolding so the ceiling could be un-

veiled. Michelangelo rushed to complete the last area, the lunettes, leaving brush hairs, still visible today, stuck into the plaster. Angry with the Pope's pestering, Michelangelo removed the scaffolding and had the ceiling uncovered sooner than he had intended. Michelangelo, ever the perfectionist, would probably have continued for four more years on the project if Julius II had let him!

All of Rome viewed the frescoes as a masterpiece. One contemporary viewer wrote of the ceiling that "it was such as to make everyone speechless with astonishment." For the close to five hundred years since its unveiling, the ceiling has awed and inspired all who have seen it. It is one of the few art works that patrons have committed to restoring at any price. A massive and costly renovation project undertaken by the Japanese corporation Nippon in 1980 was completed in 1992. This project restored the frescoes to their original colors after centuries of dirt and smoke had obscured Michelangelo's brilliant masterpiece. Every year, millions of people continue to go to see the ceiling as they have ever since Michelangelo was forced to unveil it.

Michelangelo's reluctance to do the project and the many difficulties he encountered in its execution nay have made him even more determined to create a work of unrivaled excellence. Once he became skilled at the fresco painting technique, his imagination soared. Is it possible that the more difficult The task and the more an individual is challenged, the harder he or she works to master that task? Does each of us need an overwhelming assignment to guide our skills to a high level and excel beyond our greatest expectations? By all accounts, even the perfectionist Michelangelo was pleased with the ceiling. His difficult toil had led to such inner satisfaction that some thirty years later, in his mid-sixties and embittered by the barbaric sack of Rome, he readily agreed to return to the Sistine Chapel and create the "Last Judgment" fresco on its last, unpainted wall.

THINK ABOUT IT

1. How did Michelangelo's attitudes towards the painting of the ceiling change from the Pope's initial request to the unveiling?
2. Why was Michelangelo challenged by the fresco painting technique? How did he deal with the challenge?

TALK ABOUT IT

3. How does the level of skill a person possesses relate to his or her attitude about doing a job?
4. Why do you think it was a Japanese corporation, and not a Western one, that funded the massive restoration project of the Sistine Chapel ceiling frescoes?

WRITE ABOUT IT

5. Name a large artistic project underway today. What skills and attitudes must the creators possess for it to be a success?
6. Have you ever felt reluctant to begin a big job? Did your reluctance change once the job was underway? Why or why not?

READ MORE ABOUT IT

Houghlan, Robert, and the Editors of Time-Life Books. *The World of Michelangelo: 1475–1564.* New York: Time, Inc., 1966.

Jeffery, David. "A Renaissance for Michelangelo." *National Geographic* December 1989: 688–713.

The Sistine Chapel: A Glorious Restoration. Ed. Pierluigi de Vecchi and others. New York: Harry N. Abrams, Inc., 1994.

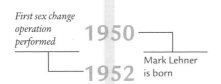

First sex change operation performed

1950 — Mark Lehner is born

1952

First human heart transplanted

1967

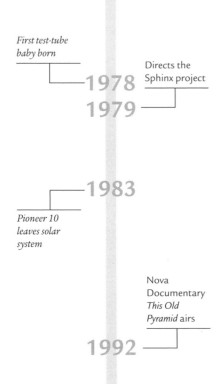

First test-tube baby born

1978 Directs the Sphinx project

1979

1983

Pioneer 10 leaves solar system

Nova Documentary *This Old Pyramid* airs

1992

M A R K   L E H N E R

The Giant Pyramids

Their Rise and Fall

Who built the pyramids? Did the ancient Egyptians actually build them? How was such a feat accomplished? These questions have fascinated people through the ages. Today when one thinks about the pyramids of Egypt and the Egyptian kings, one should think about Dr. Mark Lehner. Lehner is assistant professor of Egyptology at the Oriental Institute, University of Chicago. He directs the Koch-Ludwig Giza Plateau Project, an examination of the Great Pyramids on the Giza Plateau. From 1979 to 1983, he was Field Director for the American Research Center in the Egypt (ARCE) Project. This project, with assistance from the German Archeological Institute in Cairo, produced the first and only scale elevation drawings and detailed maps of the Sphinx. These are now being used to restore this monumental sculpture. By combining established historical facts with new discoveries, Dr. Lehner has answered many of the questions raised about the pyramids.

Egyptologists have established that it was Khufu, the king of Egypt, who, in 2600 B.C.E., commissioned the Great Pyramid to be constructed at Giza. This grand monument covers an area of seven city blocks or thirteen acres, and weighs six and a half million tons. Over two million blocks were raised to a height of forty stories, at the rate of one block every two and a half minutes, in less than thirty years. The Giza plateau complex consists of three pyramids: Khufu's, his son Khafre's, and his grandson Menkaure's. A long covered causeway runs down to the Nile River from each pyramid; a temple is placed at each end of the causeway. There are three smaller pyramids for the queens and hundreds of smaller tombs of the overseers and officials. When first completed, the pyramids were smooth, faced with polished white casing stone made of limestone that, on most pyramids, has long since been stripped away, leaving them with a jagged, unfinished appearance. Originally, the pyramids would have been smooth as glass and brilliant to look upon. The white stone of the facade would have reflected the strong Egyptian sunlight and dazzled the Egyptians who passed by.

Dr. Lehner has added some new discoveries to our understanding of the pyramids. For example, he has found numerous bread molds which indicate that the Egyptian government was baking bread on a massive scale for the construction workers on the pyramids and on the Sphinx. The bakery was part of a complex of buildings housing thousands of workers who spent their lives building the pyramids. Lehner also found that the quarried stone was not brought to the Giza plateau from some other location, but that it was hewed from the bedrock located at the foot of the pyramids. The quarry pit was filled in with debris from the construction ramp that wound upward to the top of the pyramid and allowed workers to drag the stones into place. Once the Egyptians finished building the pyramids, they toppled the ramp and dumped the debris from this ramp into the quarry. When this debris was recently cleaned out, Lehner also found tombs of the king's high officials honeycombing the quarry area. Has Lehner completely solved the great mystery of how the ancient Egyptians built the pyramids? The answer is revealed to us in the following excerpt from Lehner's book, *The Complete Pyramids*.

EGYPTOLOGISTS TRACE the ultimate origins of even the grandest pyramids back to the modest pit graves of the predynastic period, which were covered by simple mounds of sand and gravel. A little later, on the threshold of the 1st dynasty (c. 2900 B, C.), the graves of the rulers and elite consisted of neat mudbrick boxes, sunk in the desert and divided, like a house, into several chambers. The tombs of the pharaohs of the first two dynasties followed this pattern, but with greater complexity. Situated far out in the desert near the high cliffs at Abydos, each would have been marked by a pair of large stelae and covered by a mound. These royal pit and mound graves, together with imitation palaces in the form of open rectangular courts defined by mudbrick walls down in the valley, are the architectural antecedents of the pyramids. While some are certainly monumental in size, they do not approach the scale that emerges suddenly in the 3rd dynasty reign of Djoser (2630–2611 B. C.).

The Step Pyramid of Djoser heralded the classic pyramid age, the 4th to 6th dynasties, also known as the Old Kingdom. During these centuries the Egyptians built pyramids for their god-kings in a 72km (45-mile) span of desert, between Abu Roash, northwest of Giza, to Meidum in the south, near the entrance to the Fayum.

Excluding the pyramids of Djedefre at Abu Roash and Sneferu at Meidurn as outliers, the 21 other major Old Kingdom pyramids stand like sentinels in a 20-km (12-mile) stretch west of the capital the 'White Wall,' later known as Memphis, clustering at Giza, Zawiyet el-Aran, Abusir, Saqqara, and Dahshur.

The truly gigantic stone pyramids were built over the course of only three generations: Sneferu, Khufu, and Khafre. If Sneferu did indeed build the Meidurn pyramid as well as his two stone pyramids at Dahshur, his pyramids alone contain more than 3.5 million cu. m (124 million cu. ft) of stone. All the other pyramids of Egyptian kings combined (excluding queens' and other satellite pyramids) contain only 41 percent of the total mass of the pyramids of Sneferu, his son Khufu, and grandson Khafre. Menkaure still used multi-tonned stone blocks for the third pyramid of Giza, but the total mass was less than that of Djoser.

The Standard Pyramid Complex

The pyramids covered the tombs of divine kings and, late in their history, they marked graves of the aristocracy and high officials. They satisfy a principle that the great Giza excavator

George Reisner stated: "Every substructure [grave] implies a superstructure which marks the site of the grave and provides a place where the offerings to the dead may be presented." As the tomb superstructure, the pyramid was the central element in an assembly that makes up the "standard pyramid complex."

We see the most basic elements in two extreme cases. Tombs in Lower Nubia (A-group), contemporary with the late predynastic in Upper Egypt, consisted of pits sunk into the ground, covered by a ceiling of sandstone slabs, on which was constructed a mound of debris encased in drystone masonry. Pottery was left at the base of the mounds, some of which had specifically constructed offering places on the west and south sides. We then turn to the pyramids at Giza, as more complex versions of the same basic scheme-on a gigantic scale. The grave pit is now carved out of bedrock at the end of a long corridor which points the king's soul to the northern circumpolar stars, or, uniquely for Khufu, is moved up into the very body of the masonry. The pyramid is simply the mound transformed to sublime geometry and expanded into a man-made mountain.

The offering place is now a mortuary (or pyramid) temple on the eastern side, with a colonnaded court with black basalt pavement, granite pillars and walls with painted relief carving. By the 5th dynasty a front or outer part of the mortuary temple was separated from an inner temple by a transverse hall. Beyond were magazines, and, lastly, an inner sanctuary—the whole route ending in a false door, the symbolic portal of the pyramid complex.

It was long thought that the pharaoh's funeral took place in the mortuary temple, but there are problems with this. We are certain at least that it functioned symbolically as a kind of eternal Palace for the deceased king, for whom daily rituals were carried out, including processions out and around the pyramid, perpetuating his worship as a god-king. From the mortuary temple a causeway, with walls and usually a roof, ran down to the valley temple, the entrance to the whole complex. The classic complex required that the pyramid be near the valley floor, where it could be reached by a canal, or a channel that held water after the annual Nile flood receded. At the same time the pyramid had to be far enough out in the desert on the plateau to have a dramatic approach. Its base was enclosed by one or two courtyards, defined by walls of stone or mudbrick. Within the inner or outer enclosure was a small satellite pyramid, a miniature double that may have been associated with the king's *ka* or "spirit." Many complexes include smaller pyramids for queens and several are flanked by pits for the burial of boats, either real or imitation.

These standard elements—pyramid, satellite pyramid, queens' pyramids, mortuary temple, causeway, and valley temple—are clear from a survey of the remains of complexes along a stretch of the Nile Valley from Abu Roash to Meidum. For the Egyptians of the pyramid age, other elements on the valley floor might have been equally standard. These structures, concerned with the society and economy of the living pyramid, were mostly built in mudbrick, and have therefore been lost due to the wetter conditions of the floodplain and modern urban expansion. But we read of them in ancient papyri and tomb texts that relate to the functioning of pyramids. Recently, researchers have recovered some remains of these missing elements....

The Pyramid as Icon

> 'Atum Scarab!
> when you became high,
> as the high ground,
> When you rose as the *ben-ben*,
> in the Phoenix
> Enclosure,
> in Heliopolis,
> you sneezed Shu,
> you spat Tefnut,
> and you put your arms around
> them, as
> the arms of *ka*, that your *ka* might
> be in them.'
>
> Pyramid *Texts*

The pyramid was above all an icon, a towering symbol. It has been said that the Egyptians did not distinguish sharply between hieroglyphic writing, two-dimensional art and relief carving, sculpture and monumental architecture. In a sense, the pyramids are gigantic hieroglyphs. But why a pyramid? And how should we read the pyramid glyph?

Pyramid and Pyramidion

The word for pyramid in ancient Egyptian is *mer*. There seems to be no cosmic significance in the term itself. I.E.S. Edwards, the great pyramid authority, attempted to find a derivation from *m*, "instrument" or "place," plus *ar*, "ascension," as "place of ascension." Although he himself doubted this derivation, the pyramid was indeed a place or instrument of ascension for the king after his death.

Our word "pyramid" comes from the Greek, *pyramis* (pl. *pyramides*), "wheaten cake." The Egyptians had a conical bread loaf called *ben-ben*, which as also the word for the capstone of a pyramid or the tip of an obelisk—*ben-benet,* named after the *ben-ben* stone, the sacred icon in the temple of Heliopolis, the oldest center of the sun cult.

The capstone or pyramidion is the complete pyramid in miniature, bringing the structure to a point at the same angle and with the same proportions as the main body. Stadelmann found the earliest pyramidion at Sneferu's North Pyramid at Dashur, made of the same limestone as the casing and uninscribed. A number of pyramidions also survive from Middle Kingdom royal pyramids and from the small pyramids of non-royal tombs of New Kingdom and later times. Amenemhet III's pyramidion, of hard black stone, from his pyramid at Dahshur, is the most complete royal capstone. On one of its faces is a winged sun disk in relief. Below are two *wedjat*, sacred eyes, and below them are three *nefer* ("beauty" or "perfection") signs; below these again we find the hieroglyph for the sun disk, flanked by the name and titles of Amenemhet III. The whole composition can be read as: "Amenemhet beholds the perfection of Re." The sacred eyes are those of the king himself. Like the names of the pyramids—"Sneferu Gleams," "Great is Khafre"—the eyes tell us that the pyramids were personifications of the dead kings who were buried and revivified within them.

Pyramid and *Ben-ben*

The phrase "beholds the perfection of Re" is one of many indications that the true pyramids were seen as symbols of the sun. The identification of the pyramid with the sacred *ben-ben* stone in the temple of Heliopolis is another sign that the pyramids were sun symbols. To understand the *ben-ben* we must begin with Atum, probably the earliest god worshipped at Heliopolis. An aspect of the sun god, he is the "old" sun of the evening as opposed to Ra at noon and Khepri—the scarab beetle—the morning sun. Atum was also the oldest creator god; in his most primeval form he was the singularity within the primeval waters of the Abyss. The root, *tm*, in Atum's name means "complete," "finish," yet also "not-be." In later texts Atum is "Lord of Totality" and "the Completed One," and in the Pyramid Texts he is "self-developing" or "self-evolving." Atum is a chthonic god-virtually everything that exists is part of his "flesh," having evolved as his "millions of *kas*." How did this evolution begin? According to Pyramid Text 527,

> Atum is the one who developed,
> getting an erection in Heliopolis.
> He put his penis in his grasp that he
> might make orgasm with it,
> and the two siblings were born,
> Shu and Tefnut.

Shu, the god of air and atmosphere, and his sister Tefnut are the next generation of primeval gods. The genealogy leads to Geb (earth) and Nut (sky) who beget Osiris, his sister and wife, Isis, his brother and adversary, Seth, and Seth's counterpart Nephthys. Osiris and Isis beget Horus, the god of kingship. Thus kingship goes back to the Creator. Other texts relate Atum's erection and ejaculation to the *ben-ben* pyramidion through a cosmic pun on the root *bn*, which is associated with procreation and could mean "become erect" or "ejaculate."

Bn could connote the idea of swelling in general. The concept of Atum's masturbation was that he expanded as a mound (*bnnt*) in the abysmal waters of Nun. The Egyptians must have envisaged this

as the Nile Valley land emerging from the receding waters of the annual inundation. Within a few lines of this text which speaks of Atum's primeval mound, the theologians are mixing metaphors with impunity, associating Creation with the image of the scarab beetle and the *ben-ben* at Heliopolis. In the same breath, Shu and Tefnut are said to come forth, by onomatopoeia, from Atum's sneezing (*ishesh*) and spitting (*tff*).

As an image of the primeval mound, the pyramid is, therefore, a place of creation and rebirth in the Abyss. The Phoenix, Benu in Egyptian, appears in the tapestry of the Hellopolitan creation myth both by virtue of its sound-similarity with *ben-ben,* and because it returns after long periods to its natural habitat, which the Egyptians pictured as a pyramidal perch of sticks.

Sunlight and the Pyramid

Both *ben-ben* and pyramid may have symbolized the rays of the sun, particularly as they appear shining through a break in clouds—the pyramid is thus the immaterial made material. The Pyramid Texts speak of the sun's rays as a ramp by which the king mounts up to the sun, just as the older step pyramids may have been seen as giant stairs. But the pyramid was much more than a magical device for the king to mount to heaven. It was a place of physical and spiritual transformation that tied the king's ascent to the creation of the world and to the daily rebirth of the sun.

There is evidence that the *ben-ben* stone was actually cone-shaped and the pyramid is the easiest way to

mimic this in monumental architecture. Here we have to keep in mind the original appearance of the pyramid when most of its surface was newly covered with smoothed white limestone. The reflected light must have been so brilliant as to be almost blinding.

There is a kind of "picture-window" principle to much of Egyptian art and architecture that might apply to the pyramid as a stone model of immaterial sunlight. In one sense the pyramid may have been a gigantic reflector, a stone simulacrum of sunlight and a window to the sky, as though we were inside the mass of stone looking out at the sunlight, exactly as the eyes of Amenemhet III are doing on his pyramidion. If we could look through the "picture-window" of the pyramid, its temples and its underground apartments, we would better appreciate the pyramid complex as a royal house, with its gate house (valley temple), entrance corridor (causeway), vestibule, courtyard, portico and reception room (court and statue chamber), antechamber to the private quarter, dining (offering) hall, and, furthest back, the most intimate apartment where the king sleeps in death only to be reawakened, bathed, and clothed before reappearing in the celestial court.

What makes the arrangement unlike any house is the pyramid itself, towering above the most intimate rooms. It is the pyramid that merges this eternal house with that of the gods—the cosmos. The pyramid is a simulacrum of both the mound of primeval earth and the weightless rays of sunlight, a union of heaven and earth that glorifies and transforms the divine king and ensures the divine rule of the Egyptian household.

THINK ABOUT IT

1. Why did the ancient Egyptians build these monumental structures?
2. List the building techniques Lehner says were used by the ancient Egyptians. Do you think the ancient Egyptians gained job satisfaction from building the pyramids?

TALK ABOUT IT

3. There are monumental buildings in every culture. What do these buildings teach us about the people who built them?
4. Why do some people continue to believe that the architects of the pyramid were extraterrestrials? Do you believe that? Why or why not?

WRITE ABOUT IT

5. Describe another monumental building which you feel demonstrates a tremendous work effort. Why was it constructed?
6. Would you be comfortable working on a monumental project? Why or why not?

READ MORE ABOUT IT

Hamblin, Dora Jane. "A Unique Approach to Unraveling the Secrets of the Great Pyramids." *Smithsonian*, April 1986: 8–21.

Hawass, Zahi. *The Pyramids of Ancient Egypt*. Carnegie Institute, 1990.

Malek, Jaromir. *In the Shadow of the Pyramids: Egypt During the Old Kingdom*. Univ. of Oklahoma Press, 1986.

Nova. *Videocassette: This Old Pyramid*. WGBH Educational Foundation, Boston, MA. 1992.

CHRISTOPHER COX

Dorothea Lange, Photographer

Christopher Cox has written eloquently about the work of Dorothea Lange, one of the most creative forces in American photography. In the following article, Cox details how Lange entered the field, Lange's early influences, and the work she is best known for — her photographs of the Great Depression. Living in California, Lange saw the desolation suffered by many Americans who fled the Dust Bowl of the Midwest to find work and relief from grinding poverty. Her photographs, which have become symbols of the Great Depression, chronicle the anguish and despair of these people. Her work typifies the power of the photographic image to capture a grim reality from which most of us would turn away. In earlier eras, poets or painters would have chronicled the great historic events of the times. In our age, the photographer records our history as it is occurring. When this photographer is as talented as Dorothea Lange, she produces images which become part of our immediate reality, as well as part of our recent visual heritage.

DOROTHEA LANGE lived instinctively, but she always found herself in the right place at the right time. She was a maverick. She never adopted a popular style, joined a movement, or worried — like most photographers of her generation — about the technique and purity of the photographic process. Lange photographed spontaneously and often under difficult conditions. She helped us learn a great deal about ourselves in those inspired split seconds of photographing "things as they are," because she possessed the gift of inquiry. As Paul Strand said, "If the photographer is not a discoverer, he is not an artist. You must always see deeply into the reality of the world, like a Cezanne, or ... Dorothea Lange."

During the Depression, Lange photographed in almost every state of the union and her images are imprinted on the mind of a nation: an abandoned farmhouse in a sea of tractor furrows; a hoe cutter in Alabama; a damaged, haunted-eyed child in Oklahoma; an ex-slave "with a long memory"; a migrant mother surrounded by her hungry children. Lange photographed the *essence* of social and economic experience — customs, work, and play. She also captured the even more intangible *presence* of institution — church, gov-

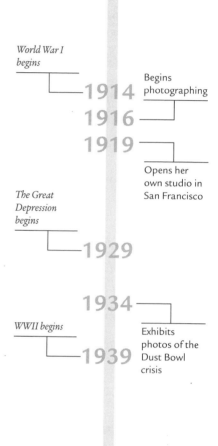

1895 — Lange is born in Hoboken, NJ

World War I begins
1914 — Begins photographing
1916
1919 — Opens her own studio in San Francisco

The Great Depression begins
1929

1934 — Exhibits photos of the Dust Bowl crisis
WWII begins
1939

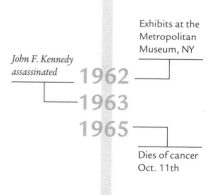

Exhibits at the Metropolitan Museum, NY
John F. Kennedy assassinated
1962
1963
1965 — Dies of cancer Oct. 11th

**DROUGHT REFUGEES FROM OKLAHOMA CAMPING BY THE ROADSIDE.
THEY HOPE TO WORK IN THE COTTON FIELDS. FAMILY CONSISTS OF SEVEN.
BLYTHE, CALIFORNIA. AUGUST, 1936.**

Dorothea Lange
Black and White Photograph.
Library of Congress, Washington, DC

ernment, family, political organizations, and labor unions. Lange, incidentally, disliked the label "documentary" applied to her work, but she never found a word she liked better. The question, she insisted, was less a matter of subject than of approach: "The important thing is not what's photographed but how." She kept the following quotation from Francis Bacon pinned to her darkroom door: "The contemplation of things as they are, without error or confusion, without substitution or imposture, is in itself a nobler thing than a whole harvest of invention."

Born in Hoboken, New Jersey, in 1895, Lange was raised by her mother on the Lower East Side of New York City. Her father abandoned the family when she was a child, and soon after his departure she contracted polio, which left her with a lifelong limp. She saw herself as an outsider. Her life seemed to pass between school and the public library where her mother worked. In midafternoon she would join her mother, presumably to study; instead she sat in the windows and watched the busy lives of Jewish immigrant families in neighboring tenements. Even then, as Lange later remarked, she was acting like a photographic observer. She could recall her child's eye focused on significant details of Saint Bartholomew's Church on Park Avenue, in particular the expressive hands of the choirmaster. She taught herself to spy inconspicuously. Walking home alone at night along the Bowery, she adopted an expressionless mask, a "cloak of invisibility" that she cultivated to good use later.

After graduating from high school Lange studied to be a teacher, then abruptly announced to her mother that she had decided to be a photographer. She chose the profession, she later said, simply "as a way to maintain myself on the planet." Yet,

she had no camera and had never made a picture. Walking along Fifth Avenue one day, Lange was struck by the portraits displayed in the window of Arnold Genthe's fashionable studio. She walked inside and asked for a job. During the years leading up to World War I, Lange assisted Genthe in the darkroom and also worked as a receptionist.

Lange always insisted that her decisions were instinctive. In 1918, at the age of twenty-two, she followed those religiously trusted instincts and left New York with a close friend to travel around the world. The tour was abruptly interrupted in San Francisco when the two women were robbed of their traveling funds. Lange started work in the photo-finishing department of a dry-goods store. Among her new acquaintances were the photographer Imogen Cunningham and her husband Roi Partridge. To gain access to a darkroom, Lange joined the San Francisco Camera Club, where she met a wealthy young man named Jack Boumphrey, who offered to finance her in opening her own portrait studio.

One year after arriving in San Francisco, Lange opened the studio, which was an immediate success. She became the favored photographer of a circle of wealthy families who had settled in the Bay Area during the Gold Rush and become leaders of the city's civic and cultural life. "That place was my life," Lange said, "and it was the center for many others." Each afternoon at four, Lange lit an old brass samovar, and friends and clients began to drop in. She greeted them in bobbed hair, sandals, and a Fortuny gown, while a Chinese-American maid and photographer's assistant served tea and shortbread.

All of Lange's work was commissioned, and most of her photographs commemorated major family events. In the studio, she usually kept

a respectful distance from her subjects. But when she took her camera into their homes, her work exhibited more spontaneity.

There is a timelessness in these pictures that Lange later rejected. "I used to try to talk people into having their pictures taken in their old, simple clothes," she said. "I thought if they did, the images would be timeless and undated. Now I feel I was mistaken and think that to have any significance, most photographs have got to be dated.... Everything is shut out of many prints but the head — there's no background, no sense of place." Imogen Cunningham characterized those pictures as "softened portraiture. Beautiful. But not what the people were really like."

In 1920 Lange married the painter Maynard Dixon, whom she had met through Roi Partridge, and in 1925 and 1928 she bore her two sons. Marriage did not immediately alter her career. Dixon painted western scenes, and he was often away on sketching trips. Lange continued to make portraits in order to free him for his work and at the same time to keep the family fed and clothed.

During the 1920s, Lange began to follow newly developing artistic instincts. While vacationing with Dixon and the boys in Arizona and northern California, she began a series of photographs of her family that combined conventional soft-focus with the spontaneity of the snapshot. "You were able to sense, if not see," she later remarked, "more about the subjects than just faces."

On a visit to Taos, New Mexico, in 1929, Lange watched the photographer Paul Strand driving a truck down the road each morning and evening. He was so methodical and intent that he seldom seemed aware of her, although she watched him nearly every day for seven months. She was profoundly moved by this glimpse of a photographer and artist dominated by "private purposes he was pursuing."

Two months after Lange returned to San Francisco the stock market crashed. She continued to make portraits for the few people who could still afford them, but the pattern of her life had been broken. To save money, she and Dixon moved into their respective studios and boarded the boys at schools.

It was an extremely difficult time emotionally for Lange, but it forced her to open herself to new subject matter. From her studio windows she could observe the erratic, drifting flow of street life. "One morning, as I was making a proof at the south window, I watched an unemployed young workman coming up the street. He came to the corner, stopped and stood there a little while. Behind him were the waterfront and the wholesale districts; to his left was the financial district; ahead was Chinatown and the Hall of Justice; to his right were the flophouses and the Barbary Coast. What was he to do? Which way was he to go?"

Lange recalled that stormy day in the mountains and suddenly felt the need to leave her studio and photograph the reality moving about the streets. Had her life not been shaken up, "if the boys had not been taken from me by circumstances, I might have said to myself, 'I *would* do this, but I can't' because I was driven by the fact that I was under personal turmoil to do something.... I knew, she added, "[that] I'd better make this happen."

In 1933, the worst year of the Depression, fourteen million people were out of work, and many of the unemployed drifted aimlessly, living on the streets. Near Lange's studio, a wealthy woman known as the "White Angel" had set up a breadline. Wandering through the crowd, Lange

made several shots including two of a man in tattered clothing leaning against a barricade with his hands clasped. She then returned to her studio to develop the film. The next day, while emptying the holder in the darkroom, her assistant found and developed an exposure she had missed. Lange called it *White Angel Breadline*. When she hung it on her studio wall her friends and clients asked what she intended to do with it. Lange said she had no idea. Later it became one of the most famous photographs of the Depression.

Lange began to leave her studio with a vengeance — photographing the maritime strikes on the waterfront, the May Day Demonstrations of 1933, men on relief doing pick-and-shovel work, and the armies of transients who shuffled in breadlines or slept outside unemployment offices. She moved in close for the intimate reflections of economic collapse: a woman's legs sheathed in mended stockings, for instance, or a pair of ruined shoes. Of one forlorn man she said, "Five years earlier, I would have thought it enough to take a picture of a man, no more.... I wanted to take a picture of a man as he stood in his world — in this case, a man with his head down, with his back against the wall, with his livelihood, like the wheelbarrow, overturned."

With the possible exceptions of Lewis Hine and Jacob Riis, who made studies of workers and slum conditions in New York in the 1890s and early 1900s, there were no precedents in America for the kind of photographs Lange now started to make. She instinctively joined a cultural movement to reveal the impact of economic and social changes in the lives of the American people. New forms of realistic expression in art and literature, film and photography were emerging — with Lange in

its vanguard of documentary in the 1930s.

In 1934 the photographer Willard Van Dyke gave Lange her first show at his gallery in Oakland, California. The exhibition led to her meeting Paul Taylor, an associate professor of economics at Berkeley who believed that photography was a potentially powerful research tool for the social sciences. He was immediately struck by Lange's work, particularly by an image of a speaker at the microphone during the San Francisco general strike, and he used the picture to illustrate an article he had written. A year later, when he became director of the California Rural Rehabilitation Administration, he enlisted Lange's services. She photographed the first migrant workers who flooded California after the Oklahoma dust storms, the camps that began to line the highways, and the pea pickers of Nipomo. She and Taylor interviewed her subjects and combined words with photographs to create compelling social essays. The reports were designed to effect change, and they did: the government responded with money and programs.

That same year Lange and Dixon divorced. She married Taylor soon afterward, closed her portrait studio, and began to devote all her energies to the new work. Between 1935 and 1939 she worked as a photographer for the Farm Securities Administration, which had been formed to bring assistance to the poor and unemployed — in part by bringing the gravity of their situations before the

WHITE ANGEL BREAD LINE, 1933.
Dorothea Lange
Black and white photograph.
The Oakland Museum of Art,
Oakland, CA

public. Roy Stryker, who headed the program, allowed his photographers independence. After briefing them on the economic and sociological problems they were to photograph, Stryker encouraged them to interpret these stricken lives with artistry, drama, and compassion.

Lange's procedure on field trips was purposely not to plan the route in detail. She simply started out in an approved direction and drove until she saw something worth looking into. Preconceived ideas, in her case, minimized chances of success. Willard Van Dyke wrote in *Camera Craft:* "Her method is to eradicate from her mind before she starts, all ideas which she might hold regarding the situation — her mind like an unexposed film."

At her most potent, Lange astounds with an ability to arouse deep feelings about our commonality with others. She made her FSA photographs artlessly personal by engaging people in conversation while moving naturally among them. She could, when she wanted to, don the cloak of invisibility of her childhood, and wander through migrant camps unnoticed. More often she would sit with someone and swap stories and photograph, then return to her car to write down her informants' tales for the FSA records. She wanted intimate records that would encourage humane solutions to social problems. "If you see mainly human misery in my photographs," she said, "I have failed to show the multiform

MIGRANT MOTHER, NIPOMO, CALIFORNIA, 1936.
Dorothea Lange
Black and white photograph.
Library of Congress

pattern of which it is a reflection. For the havoc before your eyes is the result of both natural and social forces."

Her photograph *Migrant Mother* became an icon of the thirties. Lange was returning from her first FSA field trip when she passed a pea pickers' camp. Twenty miles down the road she decided to turn back to it. When she got there, she saw the woman immediately, sitting in her rundown tent with her children. The woman was thirty-two and the mother of seven. She told Lange that they were living on wild birds caught by the children. The pea crop had frozen on the vines, and there was no work. But she could not move on; she had sold the tires from her car for food. Lange spent only ten minutes with the woman, but the photographs she took captured the attention of the entire country.

In an introductory essay for the Lange retrospective exhibition in 1966 at The Museum of Modern Art in New York, George P. Elliott wrote: "This picture, like a few others of a few other photographers, leads a life of its own. That is, it is widely accepted as a work of art with its own message rather than its maker's; far more people know the picture than know who made it. There is a sense in which a photographer's apotheosis is to become as anonymous as his camera. For an artist like Dorothea Lange who does not primarily aim to make photographs that are ends in themselves, the making of a great, perfect anonymous image is a trick of grace, about which she can do little beyond making herself available for that gift of grace. For what she most wants is to see this subject here and now in such a way as to say something about the world."

When their work with the FSA was finished, Lange and Taylor collaborated on *An American Exodus,* a

book combining the photographs and texts of their field work. But the book met with little success when it was published in 1939. America was losing interest in the Depression, turning its attention to war. During World War II Lange photographed the relocation of Japanese Americans in internment camps for the government; the pictures were not officially released until 1972. As the war ended, Lange covered the founding of the United Nations in San Francisco, but her work was interrupted by the first of many illnesses. Poor health kept her from concentrated photography for the next nine years.

In 1958 Paul Taylor, now a consulting economist for government agencies and private foundations, was offered a chance to travel. As an expert in community development, he advised officials in low income countries about sanitation, health, family planning, agriculture, and political institutions. Lange traveled with Taylor to South America, Asia, North Africa, and Europe. Near Panmunjom she photographed three generations of a family planting onions. She took street scenes in Saigon. In Ball, she concentrated on the legs, feet and hands of dancers.

In Korea, she made a series showing the eyes of Korean children and focused her camera on a single pair of slippers outside a door. "The pageant is vast," she wrote to a friend, "and I clutch at tiny details, inadequate."

In the sixties her focus shifted to the "secret places of the heart" and to "the close at hand" — the sunlit oaks that arched over her home in Berkeley, a grandson racing through the garden, a daughter-in-law whose husband has just asked for a divorce, a son embracing his first child, her husband's hands on his briefcase and umbrella. Although Lange was photographing intimate subjects, she cul-

**SPRING PLOWING IN CAULIFLOWER FIELDS
GUADALUPE, CALIFORNIA, 1937.**
Dorothea Lange
Black and white photograph
Library of Congress, Washington, DC

tivated a kind of detachment. "That frame of mind that you need to make a very fine picture of a very wonderful thing, is different from the frame of mind of being on the pavements, jostled and pushed and circulating and rubbing against people with no identity. You cannot do it by not being lost yourself."

During the last years of her life Lange was obsessed by her work. Had it not been for her family, she would have liked "to photograph constantly, every conscious hour, and assemble a record of everything to which I have a direct response.... I'd like to take a year, almost ask it of myself, 'Could I have one year?' just one, when I would not have to take into account anything but my own inner demands."

In 1965 Lange discovered that she had an inoperable cancer, and she put all else aside to concentrate on assembling a retrospective exhibition of her photographs, to open at The Museum of Modern Art a year later. After sorting through forty-one years of her negatives she concluded, "A photographer's files are in a sense his autobiography. More resides there than he is aware of. Documentation does not necessarily depend upon conscious themes. It can grow of itself, depending upon the photographer's instincts and interests."

She had once said that she could not judge a photographer's work until she had seen it in its entirety; only then could she understand the whole person. Seeing her own work in its entirety, she seems to have found completion in herself both as a person and as an artist. A few days before she died she saw the first exhibition prints for the retrospective. In her last moments of consciousness she exclaimed, "This is the right time. Isn't it a miracle that it comes at the right time."

THINK ABOUT IT

1. In the article, George Elliott comments on Lange's photograph, *Migrant Mother*. He notes that "this picture, like a few other photographers, leads a life of its own. That is, it is widely accepted as a work of art with its own message rather than its maker's ...." What other photographs or visual images have you seen which share this quality?

2. Why is *White Angel Bread Line* symbolic of the Great Depression?

TALK ABOUT IT

3. What are the attitudes of each of the family members in *Drought Refugees Hoping for Cotton Work*? What does this photograph say about the relationship of work to self-esteem? Where could you take a similar photograph today?

4. Why are Lange's photographs considered timeless? Is this true of *Filippinos Cutting Lettuce* taken in 1935?

WRITE ABOUT IT

5. Explain the connection between the quote from Francis Bacon which Lange kept on her darkroom door and one of her photographs.

6. If you were to take a photograph of yourself at work, what would it look like? Describe your setting, pose, clothing and facial expression. Consider taking this photograph and using it to illustrate this piece.

READ MORE ABOUT IT

Arrow, Jan. *Dorothea Lange*. London: Macdonald, 1985.

Cox, Christopher. *Dorothea Lange*. New York: Aperture, 1981.

Partridge, Elizabeth (ed.). *Dorothea Lange — A Visual Life*. Washington, DC: Smithsonian Institute Press, 1994.

FILIPINOS WORKING IN LETTUCE FIELDS. SALINAS, CALIFORNIA. AUGUST, 1935.
Dorothea Lange
Black and white photograph
Oakland Museum of California

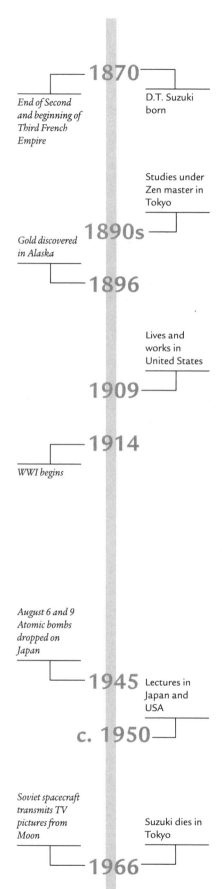

1870

End of Second and beginning of Third French Empire

D.T. Suzuki born

Studies under Zen master in Tokyo

1890s

Gold discovered in Alaska

1896

Lives and works in United States

1909

1914

WWI begins

August 6 and 9 Atomic bombs dropped on Japan

1945 Lectures in Japan and USA

c. 1950

Soviet spacecraft transmits TV pictures from Moon

Suzuki dies in Tokyo

1966

D . T .   S U Z U K I

The Samurai Warrior

D. T. Suzuki was a Japanese Buddhist scholar and chief interpreter of Zen Buddhism to the Western world. Zen is a form of Buddhism which came to Japan after it was introduced in China in the 1st century B.C.E. This form of Buddhism emphasizes achieving enlightenment, or *satori,* through an intense, intuitive experience in which the devotee grasps the nature of reality directly and totally. Suzuki achieved *satori* under the tutelage of his Zen master, Soen. Suzuki had come to Tokyo University to study. Here he met and became a student of Master Soen. After his enlightenment, Suzuki came to the United States and spent twelve years writing articles to help Americans understand Zen and Japanese culture. He returned to Japan and spent the last half of his life working to promote East-West understanding.

In the article which follows, Suzuki explains the connection between the samurai, the traditional medieval Japanese swordsman, and his sword. He also explains the mystical properties of the sword and the training which each samurai received. Suzuki also includes a letter about the spiritual training of the samurai which reveals the influence of Zen on this training. First, there is the belief that the sword and the swordsman are one. This reflects the principle of non-duality found in Zen. To Zen Buddhists, the world is not divided into separate things — like the swordsman and the sword — except within the human mind. Therefore the goal of Zen, and a condition for *satori,* is that the mind be disciplined in order to overcome the illusion of separation which it creates. When the sword and the swordsman become one, it is through an intuitive act. This intuitive act reflects the second influence of Zen. Under this influence, Japanese samurai were trained not only in the physical discipline of fighting, but also in the mental discipline of stilling (turning off) the rational mind. This stilling of the rational mind is called *prajna.* In the samurai's training, he is taught to look beyond dualities; just as there is no sword nor swordsman, there is no life nor death. The disregard of the samurai for death, coupled with his single-mindedness, made him a fierce soldier and a respected icon in Japanese culture.

"THE SWORD IS THE SOUL of the samurai": therefore, when the samurai is the subject, the sword inevitably comes with him. The samurai who wishes to be faithful to his vocation will have first of all to ask himself the question: How shall I transcend birth and death so that I can be ready at any moment to give up my life if necessary for my Lord? This means exposing himself before the enemy's swordstroke or directing his own sword toward himself. The sword thus becomes most intimately connected with the life of the samurai, and it has become the symbol of loyalty and self-sacrifice. The reverence universally paid to it in various ways proves this.

The sword has thus a double office to perform: to destroy anything that opposes the will of its owner and to sacrifice all the impulses that arise from the instinct of self-preservation. The one relates itself to the spirit of patriotism or sometimes militarism, while the other has a religious connotation of loyalty and self-sacrifice. In the case of the former, very frequently the sword may mean destruction pure and simple, and then it is the symbol of force, sometimes devilish force. It must, therefore, be controlled and consecrated by the second function. Its conscious owner is always mindful of this truth. For then destruction is turned against the evil spirit. The sword comes to be identified with the annihilation of things that lie in the way of peace, justice, progress, and humanity. It stands for all that is desirable for the spiritual welfare of the world at large. It is now the embodiment of life and not of death.

Zen speaks of the sword of life and the sword of death, and it is the work of a great Zen master to know when and how to wield either of them. The sword here represents the force of intuitive or instinctual directness, which unlike the intellect does not divide itself, blocking its own passageway.

The sword ... is not a symbol but an object endowed with some mysterious power. In the feudal days of Japan, the samurai class cherished this kind of idea toward the sword, although it is difficult to define exactly what was going on in their minds. At least they paid the utmost respect to it: at the samurai's death it was placed beside his bed, and when a child was born it found its place in the room. The idea was probably to prevent any evil spirits from entering the room that might interfere with the safety and happiness of the departed or the coming spirit. Here lingers an animistic way of thinking. The idea of a sacred sword, too, may be interpreted in this way.

It is noteworthy that, when making swords, the swordsmith invokes the aid of the guardian god. To invite him to the workshop, the smith surrounds it with consecrated ropes, thus excluding evil spirits, while he goes through the ceremony of ablution and dons the ceremonial dress in which he works. While striking the iron bar and giving it baths of fire and water, the smith and his helper are in the most intensified state of mind. Confident the god's help will be given to their work, they exert themselves to the limit of their powers, mental, physical, and spiritual. The sword thus produced is a true work of art. The Japanese sword must reflect something deeply appealing to the soul of the people. They look at it, indeed, not as a weapon of destruction but as an object of inspiration. Hence the legend of Okazaki Masamune the swordsmith and his products.

Masamune flourished in the latter part of the Kamakura era, and his works are uniformly prized by all the sword connoisseurs for their excellent qualities. As far as the edge of the blade is concerned, Masamune may not exceed Muramasa, one of his ablest disciples, but Masamune is said to have something morally inspiring that comes from his personality. The legend goes thus: When someone was trying to test the sharpness of a Muramasa, he placed it in a current of water and watched how it acted against the dead leaves flowing downstream. He saw that every leaf that met the blade was cut in twain. He then placed a Masamune, and he was surprised to find that the leaves avoided the blade. The Masamune was not bent on killing, it was more than a cutting implement, whereas the Muramasa could not go beyond cutting, there was nothing divinely inspiring in it. The Muramasa is terrible, the Masamune is humane. One is despotic and imperialistic, the other is superhuman, if we may use this form of expression. Masamune almost never engraved his name on the hilt, although this was customary with swordsmiths ...

As something of divinity enters into the making of the sword, its owner and user ought also to respond to the inspiration. He ought to be a spiritual man, not an agent of brutality. His mind ought to be at one with the soul which animates the cold steel. The great swordsmen have never been tired of instilling feeling into the minds of their pupils. When the Japanese say that the sword is the soul of the samurai, we must remember all that goes with it, as I have tried to set forth above: loyalty, self-sacrifice, reverence, benevolence, and the cultivation of other higher feelings. Here is the true samurai.

It was natural, therefore, for the samurai, who carried two swords — the longer one for attack and defense and the shorter one for self-destruction when necessary — to train himself with the utmost zeal in the art of swordsmanship. He could never be separated from the weapon that was the supreme symbol of his dignity and honor. Training in its use was, besides its practical purpose, conducive to his moral and spiritual enhancement. It was here that the swordsman joined hands with Zen.

I wish to give here further quotations illuminative of the intimate relationship between Zen and the sword, in the form of Takuan's[1] letter to Yagyu Tajima no kami Munenori[2] (1571–1646) concerning the relationship between Zen and the art of swordsmanship.

As the letter is long and somewhat repetitive, I have condensed or paraphrased it here, trying to preserve the important thoughts of the original, and sometimes interpolating explanations and notes. It is an important document in more ways than one, as it touches upon the essential teaching of Zen as well as the secrets of art generally. In Japan, perhaps as in other countries too, mere technical knowledge of an art is not enough to make a man really its master; he ought to have delved deeply into the inner spirit of it. This spirit is grasped only when his mind is in complete harmony with the principle of life itself, that is, when he attains to a certain state of mind known as *mushin* (*wu-hsin* in Chinese), "no-mind." In Buddhist phraseology, it means going beyond the dualism of all forms of life and death, good and evil, being and non-being. This is where all arts merge into Zen. In this letter to the great master of swordsmanship, Takuan strongly emphasizes the significance of *mushin,* which may be regarded in a way as corresponding to the concept of the unconscious. Psychologically speaking, this state of mind gives itself up unreservedly to an unknown "power" that comes to one from nowhere and yet seems strong enough to possess the whole field of consciousness and make it work for the unknown. Hereby he becomes a kind of automaton, so to speak, as far as his own consciousness is concerned. But, as Takuan explains, it ought not to be confused with the helpless passivity of an inorganic thing, such as a piece of rock or a block of wood. He is "unconsciously conscious" or "consciously unconscious." With this preliminary remark, the following instruction of Takuan will become intelligible.

Takuan's Letter to Yagyu Tajima no kami Munenori on the Mystery of Prajña Immovable

Affects Attendant on the Abiding Stage of Ignorance[3]

In the case of swordsmanship, when the opponent tries to strike you, your eyes at once catch the movement of his sword and you may strive to follow it. But as soon as this takes place, you cease to be master of yourself and you are sure to be beaten. This is called "stopping." [But there is another way of meeting the opponent's sword.]

No doubt you see the sword about to strike you, but do not let your mind "stop" there. Have no intention to counterattack him in response to his threatening move, cherish no calculating thoughts whatever. You simply perceive the opponent's move, you do not allow your mind to "stop" with it, you move on just as you are toward the opponent and make use of his attack by turning it on to himself. Then his sword meant to kill you will become your own and the weapon will fall on the opponent himself.

In Zen, this is known as "seizing the enemy's spear and using it as the weapon to kill him." The idea is that the opponent's sword being transferred into your hands becomes the instrument of his own destruction. This is "no-sword" in your terminology. As soon as the mind "stops" with an object of whatever nature — be it the opponent's sword or your own, the man himself bent on striking or the sword in his hands, the mode or the measure of the move — you cease to be master of yourself and are sure to fall a victim to the enemy's sword. When you set yourself against him, your mind will be carried away by him. Therefore, do not even think of yourself. [That is to say, the opposition of subject and object is to be transcended.]

For beginners, it is not a bad idea to keep the mind thoughtfully applied to their own disciplining. It is important not to get your attention arrested by the sword or by the measure of its movement. When your mind is concerned with the sword, you become your own captive. This is all due to your mind being arrested by something external and losing its mastership. This, I believe, is all very well known to you; I only call your attention to it from my Zen point of view. In Buddhism, this "stopping" mind is called delusion, hence "Affects Attendant on the Abiding-stage of Ignorance."

---

1 Takuan (1573–1645) was the abbot of Daitokuji, in Kyoto. He was invited by the third Shogun, Tokugawa Iyemitsu, to come to Tokyo, where Iyemitsu built a great Zen temple, called Tokaiji, and made him its founder.

2 Belonged to a great family of swordsmen flourishing in the early Tokugawa era. Tajima no kami was the teacher of Iyemitsu and studied Zen under Takuan.

3 Mahayana Buddhism sometimes distinguishes fifty-two stages leading up to the supreme enlightenment (*sambodhi*). "Ignorance" (*avidya*) may be regarded as the first of those stages and the "affects" (*klesa*) are affective disturbances which accompany those who abide in this stage. In Japanese, "ignorance" is *mumyo* and "affects" is *bonno*.

THINK ABOUT IT

1. What is the difference between the swords of life and swords of death?
2. Why must a samurai go beyond the instinct for self-preservation?

TALK ABOUT IT

3. Compare or contrast the samurai with famous warriors from other cultures.
4. Why do the martial arts appeal to people today?

WRITE ABOUT IT

5. Why is the "mere technical knowledge of an art … not enough to make a man a master"?
6. Would you choose a career as a warrior? Explain your reasons.

READ MORE ABOUT IT

Suzuki, D. T. *An Introduction to Zen Buddhism.* New York: Causeway Books, 1974.

Suzuki, D. T. *Zen and Japanese Culture.* Princeton, NJ: Princeton University Press, 19S9.

Watts, Alan. *The Spirit of Zen.* New York: Grove Press, Inc., 1958.

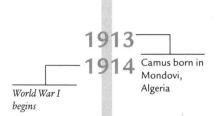

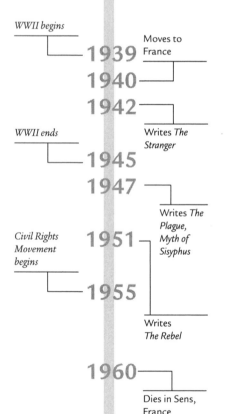

Timeline:

1913
1914 — Camus born in Mondovi, Algeria

World War I begins

WWII begins

1939 — Moves to France
1940
1942
Writes The Stranger

WWII ends

1945
1947
Writes The Plague, Myth of Sisyphus

Civil Rights Movement begins

1951
1955
Writes The Rebel

1960 — Dies in Sens, France

First Walk on moon

1969

A L B E R T   C A M U S

The Myth of Sisyphus

Albert Camus is often recognized as one of the leading existentialist philosophers of the twentieth century, yet he would not cast himself in this role. Born and raised in Algeria, he was a novelist, a playwright, and an essayist. He established his own theater group in order to produce the plays he had written. In 1940, he moved to Paris and there became quite active in the French Resistance to the Nazi occupation of France. It was here that his long relationship with Jean-Paul Sartre began, a relationship that at times was one of great philosophical difference. Although he was not an academic philosopher, he was able to convey his reflection on life's meaning through his essays and especially his plays and novels. His most famous works include *The Stranger* (1942), *The Plague* (1947), *The Rebel* (1951), and our selection, *The Myth of Sisyphus* (1942).

Sisyphus was a king of Corinth who dared to challenge fate, twice tricking the gods and refusing to return to the underworld. Because of this, he was ultimately condemned to spend eternity pushing a large boulder up an incline, only to have it fall to the bottom every time he neared the top. We speak today of a Sisyphean task as one which is futile, unable to produce any productive results. Camus uses this image to reflect on the question of the meaning of life. Is it worth it? Or are we trapped in a never ending struggle to find meaning?

THE GODS HAD condemned Sisyphus[1] to ceaselessly rolling a rock to the top of a mountain, whence the stone would fall back of its own weight. They had thought with some reason that there is no more dreadful punishment than futile and hopeless labor.

If one believes Homer, Sisyphus was the wisest and most prudent of mortals. According to another tradition, however, he was disposed to practice the profession of highwayman. I see no contradiction in this. Opinions differ as to the reasons why he became the futile laborer of the underworld. To begin with, he is accused of a certain levity in regard to the gods. He stole their secrets. Ægina, the daughter of Æsopus, was

---

[1] In order to spite his brother Salmoneus, Sisyphus seduced Salmoneus' daughter Tyro and had two children with her; she killed them when she learned the reason for his love. Sisyphus then committed an impious act for which he was condemned to Hades where for eternity he had to push an enormous boulder to the top of a hill. Near the top the stone was fated to roll down again.

carried off by Jupiter. The father was shocked by that disappearance and complained to Sisyphus. He, who knew of the abduction, offered to tell about it on condition that Æsopus would give water to the citadel of Corinth. To the celestial thunderbolts he preferred the benediction of water. He was punished for this in the underworld. Homer tells us also that Sisyphus had put Death in chains. Pluto could not endure the sight of his deserted, silent empire. He dispatched the god of war, who liberated Death from the hands of her conqueror.

It is said also that Sisyphus, being near to death, rashly wanted to test his wife's love. He ordered her to cast his unburied body into the middle of the public square. Sisyphus woke up in the underworld. And there, annoyed by an obedience so contrary to human love, he obtained from Pluto permission to return to earth in order to chastise his wife. But when he had seen again the face of this world, enjoyed water and sun, warm stones and the sea, he no longer wanted to go back to the infernal darkness. Recalls, signs of anger, warnings were of no avail. Many years more he lived facing the curve of the gulf, the sparkling sea, and the smiles of earth. A decree of the gods was necessary. Mercury came and seized the impudent man by the collar and, snatching him from his joys, led him forcibly back to the underworld, where his rock was ready for him.

You have already grasped that Sisyphus is the absurd hero. He is, as much through his passions as through his torture. His scorn of the gods, his hatred of death, and his passion for life won him that unspeakable penalty in which the whole being is exerted toward accomplishing nothing. This is the price that must be paid for the passions of this earth. Nothing is told us about Sisyphus in

the underworld. Myths are made for the imagination to breathe life into them. As for this myth, one sees merely the whole effort of a body straining to raise the huge stone, to roll it and push it up a slope a hundred times over; one sees the face screwed up, the cheek tight against the stone, the shoulder bracing the clay-covered mass, the foot wedging it, the fresh start with arms outstretched, the wholly human security of two earth-clotted hands. At the very end of his long effort measured by skyless space and time without depth, the purpose is achieved. Then Sisyphus watches the stone rush down in a few moments toward that lower world whence he will have to push it up again toward the summit. He goes back down to the plain.

It is during that return, that pause, that Sisyphus interests me. A face that toils so close to stones is already stone itself! I see that man going back down with a heavy yet measured step toward the torment of which he will never know the end. That hour like a breathing-space which returns as surely as his suffering, that is the hour of consciousness. At each of those moments when he leaves the heights and gradually sinks toward the lairs of the gods, he is superior to his fate. He is stronger than his rock.

If this myth is tragic, that is because its hero is conscious. Where would his torture be, indeed, if at every step the hope of succeeding upheld him? The workman of today works every day in his life at the same tasks, and this fate is no less absurd. But it is tragic only at the rare moments when it becomes conscious. Sisyphus, proletarian of the gods, powerless and rebellious, knows the whole extent of his wretched condition: it is what he thinks of during his descent. The lucidity that was to constitute his torture at the same time

crowns his victory. There is no fate that cannot be surmounted by scorn.

THINK ABOUT IT

1. What is the myth of Sisyphus and what does it tells us about the Greek concept of work?
2. Why do we tend to have a negative attitude about work, seeing it as drudgery and tedium?

TALK ABOUT IT

3. Does your job reflect Camus' attitude that "the workman of today works every day in his life at the same tasks … it is tragic only at the rare moments when it becomes conscious"?
4. Why is work so important for an American's self-image? Should it be?

WRITE ABOUT IT

5. If you were a twentieth-century Olympian god, what modern punishment would you assign to Sisyphus for cheating death?
6. Do you think you will be able to find work that will make a difference to the world and make you happy as well?

READ MORE ABOUT IT

Camus, Albert. *The Plague*. New York: Vintage Books, 1972.

Lottman, Herbert R. *Albert Camus: A Biography*. Garden City, N.Y.: Doubleday & Company, 1979.

Sprintzen, David. *Camus: A Critical Examination*. Philadelphia: Temple University Press, 1988.

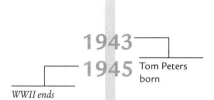

1943

1945 — Tom Peters born

WWII ends

1957

Founding of Common Market

1963

Founding of OPEC

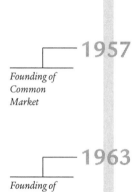

1976

Carter is elected President

Authors *In Search of Excellence*

1982

1985

Publishes *A Passion for Excellence*

1988

European community is established

Publishes *Thriving on Chaos*

1992

Competes *Liberation Management*

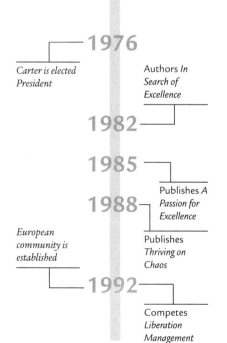

TOM PETERS

Liberation Management

Tom Peters is the founder and chief executive officer of the Tom Peters Group, a consulting firm working with leading businesses and corporations. He has an undergraduate degree from Cornell in Industrial Engineering and an MBA from Stanford. While working for the consulting firm McKinsey & Co., he co-authored the book *In Search of Excellence* (1982), which analyzed the successful companies and managers who had made a go of it during the "malaise of the Carter years." The success of this book — three years on the *New York Times* bestseller's list, selling over two and a half million copies — prompted him to form his own management consulting group. He emphasizes that in order for companies to stay competitive in an ever-changing marketplace, they must constantly adapt their management styles to meet every new corporate and business demand. Peters maintains that successful companies are passionate, focused, close to the consumer, and unafraid of risk.

Liberation Management: Necessary Disorganization for the Nanosecond Nineties (1992), from which the following article is excerpted, attempts to bring this advice into the nineties. In it, Peters suggests that the ideas we have of markets are no longer valid. Instead, we need to look at goods and services as if they were fashions: "fickle, ephemeral, impermanent, and fleeting." Management must necessarily be prepared to adapt to a constantly changing market place. In order to do this, it must be composed of a small, well-ordered, flexible group of team players who can make decisions quickly and keep their company on top.

[A]T LAKELAND Regional Medical Center, nurse-technologist "care pairs" are spending over 50 percent of their time with patients, up from 21 percent before the hospital reorganized in 1989. Titeflex Teamsters now handle orders from start to finish, and routinely call on customers and vendors. That's liberation.

Very independent chief executives of tiny Acordia companies are hopping through tiny hoops for their very demanding customers, and many Thermo Electron "division" bosses are facing beady-eyed securities analysts (instead of smug corporate staffers) to explain their last quarter's results. That's liberation, too.

So it must be. Each *day* brings another thirty software programs and another forty grocery or drugstore products to the American marketplace. With frenzy like that, only people (bosses, frontline "professionals," "businesspersons") who are free to take almost any initiative stand much of a chance of success. Liberation may well be a "nice" idea. I think it is. But that's beside the point. The times make it a *necessary* idea. Hence, necessary disorganization into free-standing units so as to achieve necessary liberation for all — the essence of this book's title.

It's scary, Freedom always is, for an eight year-old or a forty-eight year-old, for Americans after 200 years of practice or Hungarians after two. Yet we found that workers are making the transition with relative ease — among other things, life on the job is looking more like life off the job for a change. ("For a change?" For the first time in a couple of hundred years is more like it.) Oddly enough, it's managers who are having the toughest time making the shift. Well, it's not so odd, on second thought. Many of their jobs are disappearing. (I can picture an old World War II Uncle Sam poster, with the ominous pointing finger and "Liberation Means Your Job Goes" as the inscription. A dreary thought.) Worse still, the ladder that managers aspired to climb is being turned to kindling in the liberated, horizontal, beyond-hierarchy environment.

Some of us were dad-blamed lucky. My first boss in the Navy, in 1966, left his young officers alone — and then demanded results. From there it was on to a largely unsupervised policy job in Washington, and then to a professional service firm, McKinsey & Co., for seven years — and thence to my own company. I've worked for some traditional outfits (e.g., the Navy), but have rarely been burdened with bosses who were bent on oppression. (Luckier still, each of my bosses had absurdly high stan-

dards, and left it up to me to figure out how to meet them — I'll admit it hasn't made for a lot of sleep over the years.) That is, I've taken to this so-called newfangled stuff (projects, create-your-own firm) because it's where I've been from the start.

Most managers haven't been so fortunate. And for them the shift is wrenching, though, I contend, liberating if they can shed the shackles of ladderish metaphors and learn to take pleasure in the task and the team. The "new dependence" is upon peers and extended-network family (new horizontal dependence?), instead of upon the boss and the corporation (old vertical dependence?).

Lead dogs don't have it easy, either. After all, they've slowly worked their way through the pack, sniffing a lot of rear ends along the way. When they emerge at the front of the line, instant transformation is rare. It's hardly surprising that a forty-eight year-old, just-appointed company president, who's emerged into the sun after twenty-six years of political elbowing, doesn't immediately take to my jolly "You're only in control when you're out of control." Those who do take to it often had the sort of luck I did, following an unconventional path (e.g., former Union Pacific Railroad chief Mike Walsh starting his managerial career in a U.S. Attorney's office).

Then there's the matter of the public sector. It's unprepared, from the classroom to the U.S. Departments of Commerce and Health and Human Services, for a post-hierarchical commercial order. Our education, training, health, and social security schemes are formed around the big corporate lifetime employment "model" which has dominated the U.S. for the last century (during which time almost all social support programs were invented).

Well, my friends, the genies are not going back into their lamps. The information technology "revolution" is just gathering steam. The biotechnology revolution and the materials revolution and the telecommunications revolution (each dependent, in large measure, upon the infernal computing machine) are/will be almost as profound. Protectionist blather notwithstanding, global interdependence is another escaped genie. Then there's the spread of capitalism in general. And ... And ... That is, don't expect the number of new software programs or grocery and drugstore products or entrepreneurs to go into retreat any time soon. Do expect to hear ever wilder stories from ever wilder places. Hey, I wouldn't bet against India as a global economic powerhouse by 2020 (when the current crop of 22-year-olds will be my age today).

What follows are hardly "Prescriptions for Society 2000" (there are so damn many around already, including a few of my own, I hate to think about 1999). They're more personal than that. As an eight-hour seminar winds down, on a gloomy February day in London (or Chicago or Stockholm), the real questions start to come. Middle manager: "I've tried this stuff. I believe in it. It works. But my boss thinks I'm crazy. Help?!" MBA student: "You're telling me to 'trundle off to Eastern Europe for a year, it'll do you good.' Well, how much damn good can I afford to do with a $65,000 student loan to pay back?" I don't know that's the real answer. But maybe the following contains a few clues. I hope.

Students
Mostly remember that (1) education is the *only* ticket to success and (2) education doesn't stop with the last

certificate you pick up. Studenthood for life is a necessity, by definition, in a knowledge-based society. This is not advice from Dad to "hit those books." It is, I pray, slightly more profound. It's a suggestion, if you're fifteen, that you quit laughing at the nerds in your class — you're gonna be working for them someday!

Americans, and people in most developed societies, have long seen education as *the* engine of economic progress. But "see" it though we might, "we" (Americans, at least) have often as not taken it for granted — a few visits to elementary-school classrooms does not an "education president" make!

Now why am I talking education policy to 15- or 21-year-olds? Simple. You need to take your education — and the education of all others — very seriously. Education is the "big game" in the globally interdependent economy. Period.

For those a little further along in the education process, there's an additional charge: Take networking seriously. I think back to my Stanford Business School days (twenty years ago). There was a handful of people whose ways seemed mysterious. They were the instinctive networkers. They left school with fat Rolodexes and bushels of friendships — and a surprising share of them are running companies today. It may be tautological to declare that networking is important in a networked society, but that doesn't mean it's not worth saying. It must be said again and again.

I'd also urge all students, and especially MBA sorts, to get the heck out of the country (whichever your country is). A little global breadth goes a long way. And the absence of a global instinct will increasingly pinch in the years ahead. If you, as college senior or fresh-caught MBA grad, can scrounge up a job of any kind beyond your national borders, go for it.

Finally, get turned on. Or follow your bliss, or whatever. Vacuous advice? Perhaps. But the practical implication is this: In a knowledge-based economy, you must — to survive — add some special value, be distinctively good at something. And the truth is, we usually only get good at stuff we like. If you love skiing and you're a newly minted MBA, look to get a job in some sporting-related industry that lets you turn skiing to professional advantage. Ain't nobody gonna take care of you on the job in a big company anymore: It's not dog-eat-dog out there, it's skill-eat-skill. If you're not skilled/motivated/passionate about something, you're in trouble!

"Workers"

"Workers," like "organization," gets quotes. Why? All jobs (in developed countries at least) are fast becoming professional service firm jobs. Managers are disappearing. "Workers" are all becoming "managers." Work is the same for all of us: projects, networks, etc. All of us? Yes, all. Titeflex and the Union Pacific Railroad are professional service firms, whether they call themselves that or not. The implications for Teamsters and United Transportation Union members — and employees of Professional Parking Services, Inc. — are clear:

- *Education.* See my advice to full-time students. As parker, receptionist, auto-worker, or graduate engineer, you *must* retrain yourself — constantly and forever. If your company helps, great. If the government helps, great. If it doesn't, well, that's too bad, but it doesn't alter my advice an iota. You must, by hook or by crook, keep at it.

- *Risk.* The biggest risk is not taking risks and getting pigeonholed. So your company is still very "steep," with the oldfangled hierarchy mostly in place. Tough. Your only path to "employment security" (new style: network employment security) is to reach out beyond your cubbyhole.

- *Job-hopping.* In Silicon Valley, many would-be employers are wary if candidates *haven't* had a few different jobs. Talk about a break with tradition! Silicon Valley, though phenomenally successful, is hardly the norm. But it is the way the world is heading (even, a little bit, in Japan). Increasingly, a portfolio of experience is the only basis for security. It's a paradox, but it's life.

Middle Managers

Am I a middle-management basher? Yes. Are most of the people who attend my seminars middle managers? Yes. Why do they come? Beats me. Middle management, as we have known it since the railroads invented it right after the Civil War, is dead. Therefore, middle managers, as we have known them, are cooked geese. If that's not clear from the preceding pages, then one of us has a very big problem. So what to do if your answer to the unasked question is "I are one"?

Simple. I've said it in these pages: Act like a consultant. Make friends with the line, create projects. And that, I think, is the "right" prescription. But it's also wrong, because it's a pat answer — and an emotionless one. Whether you're thirty-three and on a fast track to nowhere, or fifty-two and on a slow track to the exit, my *real* advice is: Raise hell!

First of all, why not? Your job, salary, and esteem are all in mortal danger. (As of this writing, some sizable companies are coming back from the recession — but they are still trimming managerial fat, and most have no plans for hiring in the foreseeable future.) Why not at least go out with a bang? Funny thing is, I'm serious. Maybe your Percy Barnevik hasn't come along yet, but she or he surely will in the next ten years. And like Barnevik in Sweden with Asea in 1981, she or he may give you just 100 days or so to "find a job" in some line activity. Are you ready? The only way to lose is not to try.

It's over, d'ya hear? Over. Over. Over. Not every big firm is a Wal-Mart or CNN or ABC. Not every firm will be by the year 2000. But the trend is unmistakable. Frankly, I don't know how to do much more than exhort. "Build your own firm," "create your own network," "raise hell" — it's that or bust.

Chiefs

This book, like my others, is mostly aimed at you. Which means I've said about all I know to say. The message is clear: (1) trust, (2) "they" can handle "it" (*whatever* "it" is), (3) you're only in control when you're out of control ("head" of a flat, radically decentralized "organization"). Ben Lytle (Acordia) believes it in the financial service business. Pat McGovern (International Data Group) believes it in the information industry.

McGovern was more or less born to it. Lytle got religion along the way. Remember the famous elevator incident: He'd just "decentralized" into "independent" units, and asked a claims processor about the effects.

The only thing that had changed for her was the floor she worked on! Thus, via a convoluted path, the Acordia concept was born — small, very independent companies in their own buildings, etc., etc. Almost all chiefs who read this are staunch supporters of decentralization. Almost all chiefs who read this have decentralized. Almost none of their decentralized companies are decentralized. Got that?

The Freedom to Fail

"The great freedom in America is the freedom to fail — and to try again and again," Richard Reeves wrote in the *International Herald Tribune*. While I was in the midst of a long, desultory exchange with a trapped middle manager, circa 1991, someone in the back of the seminar room butted in. "But neither of you gets it," he almost shouted. "This is so, well, liberating." He went on to describe his newly developed start-a-project, do-something, devil-may-care attitude toward his own bureaucracy (in the public sector, actually) — and the phenomenal results he and his group had achieved, despite the wary eyes peering at him from innumerable corners (wary eyes of timorous peers more than bosses, he sadly admitted).

From that unknown (by name) seminar participant — and Tom Strange and Joe Tilli at Titeflex — this book's title was born. I'm afraid that all too often we forget that the freedom to fail and try again is the essence of liberation, in America or elsewhere. (And it sure doesn't hurt in a fashionized marketplace, I'd add one last time.)

THINK ABOUT IT

1. What is the basic advice that the Peters Group offers to people interested in staying current in the work force?
2. Why is a humanities course like this one an important part of Peter's advice for the future?

TALK ABOUT IT

3. What is the problem with trying to be in "middle-management"? Does this problem exist in other cultures?
4. What is networking and why is it so important for people in school?

WRITE ABOUT IT

5. What do you think would be an ideal resumé for someone in today's job market? Write one to include what you think would be impressive credentials and experiences.
6. Based on the advice of Peters in this article, are there specific things you need to change in your approach to school?

READ MORE ABOUT IT

Peters, Tom. *In Search of Excellence.* New York: Harper & Row, 1982.

Peters, Tom. *A Passion for Excellence.* New York: Random House, 1985.

Peters, Tom. *Thriving on Chaos.* New York: Harper & Row, 1988.

Peters, Tom. *Liberation Management.* New York: Alfred A. Knopf, Inc., 1992.

Elizabeth Barrett Browning

Venus, Goddess of Love

Giovanni Boccaccio

The Taj Mahal

Arna Bontemps

Frida Kahlo

CHAPTER 3

Love

ELIZABETH BARRETT BROWNING, in her *Sonnets from the Portuguese,* gives her answer to a question that has been asked as long as there have been two people on the earth: "How do I love thee?" She tries to express in words the feelings she has for Robert Browning and, in so doing, reveals a deeply intimate part of her life. As we read her words, perhaps they express experiences we have had. Or possibly, they seem stilted, and unrelated to anything we have ever felt. For many people, this sonnet is a classic expression of the feelings of love.

For others, it is the stuff of sappy greeting cards, or words from a musty old book found in your grandmother's attic, or a Barry Manilow song. Whatever your assessment, one thing is clear. Love refers to both an inner experience of personal emotion, as well as an outer manifestation of that feeling. Love is the butter-flies in the stomach and the card you send to thank your beloved

ELIZABETH BARRETT BROWNING

Sonnets from the Portuguese

How do I love thee? Let me count the ways.
I love thee to the depth and breadth and height
My soul can reach, when feeling out of sight
For the ends of Being and ideal Grace.
I love thee to the level of everyday's
Most quiet need, by sun and by candle-light.
I love thee freely, as men strive for Right;
I love thee purely, as they turn from Praise.
I love thee with the passion put to use
In my old griefs, and with my childhood's faith.
I love thee with a love I seemed to lose
With my lost saints, — I love thee with the breath,
Smiles, tears, of all my life! — and, if God chooses,
I shall but love thee better after death.

for them. Love is the longing to be near someone and the flowers sent to take your place. Over the years, one of the great challenges facing all people is the connection of the inner experience of love and the outer manifestation of that experience.

If we look at our first experiences with love, we see that there are a variety of ways in which this feeling can be described. For example, do you remember the first time you saw someone and became nervous just to be near them? Conversation became difficult and you felt an uncontrollable urge to impress the person, leading to incredible acts of stupidity which you did not think yourself capable of. Can you remember the first blush of young love when your every thought was filled by the most insignificant details of your beloved? Even now, you may hear the song that was "our song." The two of you probably also had your favorite place, movie, drink, color, and more. First love often makes it impossible to attend to any other thoughts than those that might bring the two of you closer. When this type of love hits, usually in junior high or high school, we allow our feelings to direct our relationships, responding to every smile without any commitment to anything except our feelings. Algebra class does not stand a chance!

As we grow up, the feelings of love do not become any less intense, but it seems as though we have more control of them. Over time, most people want to limit themselves to the one person who most complements their own feelings and understanding of the world; but more importantly, they want to have a serious relationship with the one who most closely meets their needs for love. At this point, our feelings of love become an expression of a key aspect of our lives. We love because it makes us whole; to give ourselves over wholly to another completes us, and without this giving, we would feel diminished. Yet even with this deeper, more adult appreciation of love, we still confront a real dilemma when we attempt to express our love.

Instead of "how do I love thee," maybe the question should be "how can I show you that I love you?" The personal nature of love and the incredible depth of our feelings about it make it almost inexpressible. Yet we are driven to say the right words or give the perfect sign that will communicate our love. just as there are many different ways people experience love, so, too, are there differences in the way we express those feelings — these expressions change as we grow. Young children in the school yard steal each others' hats, push each other down, and suddenly, someone's shin is kicked. Mean spirited? Maladjusted? No, these actions can be a first attempt at expressing feelings of affection and love. A teenage boy saves his allowance for two months in order to get a corsage for his date for the junior prom, while his date baby-sits for hours to buy the perfect dress that is guaranteed to turn his head. A father passes up a job transfer that would give him a promotion so that his wife can keep her hard-won position; or a mother works overtime so her children can have a special holiday that the family otherwise cannot afford. A lover sits near the hospital bed, helpless to cure, yet resolute in companionship. An old man and woman sit in a restaurant, each struggling to hear the other, and walk out slowly, arm in arm, leaning on one another as they have for the past fifty years. No two of these examples are alike, yet all are the same: love in action — outward expressions of the inner feelings that defy definition.

In the movie *Fiddler on the Roof,* Tevye asks his wife if she loves him. Her response is one of wonder and amazement. She asks, "How can you ask that after all these years of washing and cooking, cleaning up after you, and bearing your children?" He insists, "Do you love me?" Again, she is amazed and says, "If you cannot tell by all the things I do, what else is there? Do I love you? I guess I do!" What Tevye was looking for was an outward expression of love he could be sure of, one which would communicate more directly the feelings he hoped his wife had for him. To her,

her expressions of love were obvious. To him, they were not as clear. If our beloved cannot "count the ways" in which we love them, should we despair? Should we accept that there might be some expressions of love which we do not understand? Does the mysterious nature of love help us appreciate it all the more? In this chapter, we will look at different expressions of love — both inward and outward. The images of Venus, the goddess of love, and the story of Aeneas and Dido give us insight into love in ancient times. A selection from Boccaccio's *Decameron* reminds us that, at all times, love is filled with ironic twists. Othello's jealousy reminds us of the power of love scorned, just as the building of the Taj Mahal shows us how far a man will go to honor his love. No matter how different these outward appearances seem, the selections make one thing clear. Love has always been an experience, profoundly intimate and personal, which has been expressed in as many ways as there have been people in love. Whether or not "I love thee with the breath, smiles, tears, of all my life," looking into the expressions of others gives us insights into our own attempts to understand and express the feelings we call "love."

THINK ABOUT IT

1. What is love? Does your definition emphasize the inner or outer dimension?
2. What expressions of love have meant the most to you?

TALK ABOUT IT

3. Do people always mean the same thing when they speak of love? Do we have the same ideas about love that our parents or grandparents do?
4. Can love transcend national and ethnic differences? Why or why not?

WRITE ABOUT IT

5. Do you have a favorite poem or song lyric which captures for you what love is? In what ways does it express your emotions?
6. Compose a love letter that you would like to receive.

Rule of
Alexander
the Great
begins

340 B.C.E.

336 B.C.E. Praxiteles
sculpts
*Aphrodite of
Knidos*

323 B.C.E.

*Alexander
the Great dies*

*Lighthouse at
Alexandria
completed*

279 B.C.E.

*Roman
Conquest
of Spain*

201 B.C.E.

*Venus
Pudica
sculpted*

C. 170 B.C.E.

*Venus de
Milo
sculpted*

*Greece
becomes
Roman
province*

C. 150 B.C.E.

146 B.C.E.

D I A N N   R O T H W E L L   L A P I N

Stone Cold Love

Diann Rothwell Lapin is Director of Graduate Admissions at Columbia College in Chicago, Illinois. She holds advanced degrees in Liberal Studies and Art History. When teaching Greek and Roman Humanities, Lapin has often observed that her students are entranced by images of Aphrodite and the ways the sculptures represent various aspects of physical love.

The ancient Greeks called her "Aphrodite," which means rising from the sea. Several centuries later, the Romans combined her attributes with those of an earlier goddess and named her "Venus." Since the Renaissance of the fifteenth century when she became known to the modern world, most people have called her Venus. She is the goddess of love and fertility, often seen with her son Cupid whose arrows of love can strike a person without warning, producing deep emotions. Ancient Greek mythology tells the story of Venus's birth as one of love born from strife. According to the Greeks, she was born of sea foam that was created from the blood of the ancient god Uranus's cast-off genitals. Uranus's son Zeus had battled with him for supreme power and cut off Uranus's genitals after he was defeated. Venus arose from Uranus's blood and then floated ashore on a scallop shell propelled by gentle breezes. In paintings, the naked Venus is often shown stepping from the shell onto a shore to bring love and fertility to the human race. Since the Renaissance era, Venus has represented the two major aspects of love: an inner contemplative love; and, an outer physical or procreative love. The ancient Greeks depicted Aphrodite in stone or marble, sculpted solely to embody traits of physical love. These sculptures were created to honor the goddess in temples dedicated to her. By the fourth century B.C.E. the Greek art of sculpting had evolved to a high level of expertise. As such, sculptors were able to show Aphrodite as the ideal of a beautiful, sensuous woman. These cold marble forms became the ideal means for expressing varying aspects of physical love. Venus, shown in a perfected physical female form, embodied all a man desired from a woman.

VENUS, or Aphrodite as she was called by the Greeks, was the goddess of love in the Ancient World. To the ancient Greeks, and later to the Romans, love was personified in Venus's ideal nude female form. Immortalized in marble sculptures, Venus embodied the full range of men's emotional and physical feelings towards women. By the fourth century B.C.E., the Greeks had learned how to create stone statues of Aphrodite that were masterful realizations of the naked female form. These sculptures could elicit in a man the type of pleasurable response associated with viewing a beautiful, sensuous woman. Thus, these stone cold Aphrodites served the Greeks in their exploration of the warm, physical experience of love. For example, the Venus Pudica of the second century B.C.E., created by an unknown Greek sculptor, personifies physical modesty as she covers her nakedness and casts her glance away from the viewer. An earlier sculpture, the Aphrodite of Knidos by the Greek sculptor Praxiteles from about 340 B.C.E., depicts a voluptuous yet reserved aspect of awakening physical love. Finally, the famous Venus de Milo, also of the second century B.C.E. and carved by an unknown sculptor, has long been admired for her aloof expression and frankly sensual pose. These three representations of Venus embody universal expressions of physical love which can be alternately bashful, interested but hesitant, or decidedly unattainable.

Over six feet tall, the Venus Pudica is a marble sculpture showing a young, but mature, woman who covers her breasts with one hand and her lower body with the other. Sculpted of fine white marble, this Venus is depicted in full nakedness. As Greek mythology recounts, Venus returns regularly to the sea, from which she emerged after her birth, to renew her ability to evoke feelings of love in mankind. Here, the goddess Venus is about to step into her sacred ritual bath when the viewer happens upon her. Unique to this Venus is her response of covering herself in a modest gesture. In particular, her left hand is so firmly placed over her pelvic area that the fingers rest on her defensively-bent right thigh. The gown she has just removed appears on a pedestal by her side: its placement on the pedestal serves to accentuate Venus's nakedness. The gown's many folds and roughly polished surface contrast markedly with the highly polished marble of Venus's pure white skin. The light reflects off the marble, highlighting the comely curves of her body. Her bent right leg and contracted, self-conscious posture en-

tice the viewer. Will she uncover her full femininity? She is shy — she does not know the onlooker — but, perhaps, she can be coaxed to reveal herself. Her classic facial features display a standard idealized Greek image of beauty. The faint smile and gaze, directed to the side, elicit a hopeful response in many male viewers. She represents love that is not open to an encounter — yet.

The Aphrodite of Knidos is reticent, too, but she is more self-assured and open to admirers than Venus Pudica. Like Pudica, this statue is also larger-than-life, about 6 feet 8 inches, and represents an enticingly voluptuous image of femininity. Aphrodite has just completed disrobing for her bath and is portrayed grasping her robe firmly in her left hand. The garment is clear of the body, though, and this gesture exaggerates her nudity. The statue's right hand covers her pelvic area but in a significantly less defensive manner than the Pudica's gesture. Aphrodite's fleshy body is posed in a *contrapposto* stance. Originally developed by the master sculptor Praxiteles prior to his sculpting of this marble, contrapposto refers to a stance where the torso is contracted on one side and extended or straight on the other. This dynamic tension leads to a balance across the body whereby one leg is straight and the other bent, with the opposing arms bent and straight, respectively. The stance causes the hip above the extended leg to be thrown out to the side in a provocative curve. This lovely pose combines with the statue's voluptuous folds of flesh to give the viewer an image of come-hither sensuality. With its abundant curves, this particular statue of Venus represented the ideal female form to the ancient Greeks. Aprhrodite's hesitancy heightens her desirability since an ideal love is one that must be wooed before it can be won. Her reticence is

**VENUS PUDICA
2ND CENTURY B.C.E.**
Marble, 73½ in.
Museo Capitolino, Rome, Italy

APHRODITE OF KNIDOS,
Praxiteles, c. 350 B.C.E.
Roman marble copy of marble original, 6 ft. 8 in.
Musei Vaticani, Rome, Italy.

VENUS DE MILO,
c. 150 B.C.E.
Marble, Approximately 7 ft. 6 in.
Louvre, Paris, France.

also conveyed by her gaze which is directed away from the viewer. Is her head tilted in an arrogant gesture or a hesitant but interested one? Is she approachable? Her facial expression may say "no," yet her body stance seems to say "yes."

The famous Venus de Milo is neither as feminine nor as approachable as the other two sculptures. Standing about the same height as Pudica, the statue conveys a unique provocativeness. This Venus, too, is in the act of disrobing, yet her gown is not quite off her body. It rests on her hips in a precarious position threatening to slide down at any moment and reveal her most private area. Will it continue down her hips? The viewer feels a frustration born of anticipation — a woman caught in the act of undressing is a truly provocative image. Yet, this female does not quite invite a closer look. While Venus appears in a contrapposto stance with her right hip thrust out in a near-perfect C-curve, she is not truly voluptuous. Her body is hard and muscled, almost masculine. Venus is also aloof — not a vulnerable female, as Pudica portrays, or a potentially interested one, as the Knidos appears to be. A deeper frustration felt by the viewer seems to center on the fact that a man may not want to approach a woman whose nakedness is hard, not soft. Venus's aloofness is further sensed through the self-contained rather serious facial expression. The classic Greek features have been chiseled into taut lines that convey a detached calm. This quiet confidence gives her an air of elegance that is both engaging and distancing. More than the other two statues do, this Venus represents a complex type of love, one in which the male onlooker may feel both desire and constraint.

Indeed, do any of these marble love goddesses truly represent an attainable expression of physical love? The Venus Pudica's pure white body, its soft curves, and her lovely long hair convey an image of a young and vulnerable woman. Her enchanting modesty provokes interest and promises possibility. However, the ancient Greeks would have probably preferred the Aphrodite of Knidos. Her firm breasts, long legs, well-developed thighs, and lovely curves offer a physical image of a fully-feminine woman. The body stance and its interpreted message say she may be interested in love. Conversely, the aloof psychology conveyed by the Venus de Milo's muscular body, her self-assured stance, and her contained expression may discourage potential lovers. Yet the image of the robe slipping over her rigid curves is one of great beauty. The attraction to Venus is unmistakable and eternal: even though she is carved of cold stone, she is the embodiment of the warm feelings associated with sensual love.

THINK ABOUT IT

1. Describe the differing aspects of physical love represented by each of the Venus sculptures.

2. Why does the love embodied by the Venus de Milo evoke a more complex response than that of the other two statues?

TALK ABOUT IT

3. Do you think people respond any differently today to a photograph of a nude woman in a magazine than they responded to a marble sculpture in ancient times? Why or why not?

4. The Ancient Greeks and people in our culture today prefer representations of perfected human forms. Do all cultures represent human forms in an idealized manner? Use reproductions of artworks to support your position.

WRITE ABOUT IT

5. How has our conception of the ideal female form changed from that of the Greeks? Would the Aphrodite of Knidos's form be considered perfect today?

6. Do you think a pleasurable response to a person's physical appearance is necessary for love to be experienced? Why or why not?

READ MORE ABOUT IT

Grant, Michael. *Myths of the Greeks and Romans.* Middlesex, England: Penguin Books, Ltd., 1962.

Hamilton, Edith. *The Greek Way.* New York: W. W. Norton & Company, 1983.

Pollitt, J. J. *Art and Experience in Classical Greece.* Cambridge, England: Cambridge University Press, 1972.

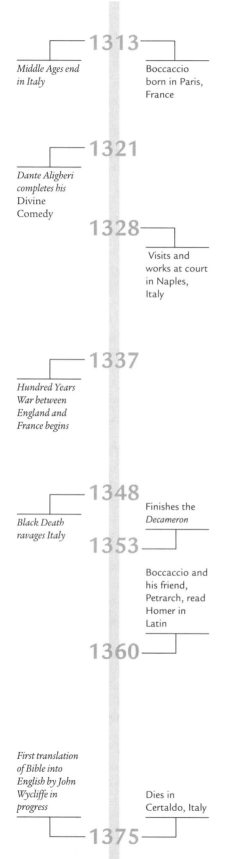

Middle Ages end in Italy — 1313

Boccaccio born in Paris, France

Dante Aligheri completes his Divine Comedy — 1321

1328 — **Visits and works at court in Naples, Italy**

1337 — **Hundred Years War between England and France begins**

1348 — **Finishes the** Decameron

Black Death ravages Italy

1353 — **Boccaccio and his friend, Petrarch, read Homer in Latin**

1360

First translation of Bible into English by John Wycliffe in progress

Dies in Certaldo, Italy

1375

GIOVANNI BOCCACCIO

The Falconer and the Lady

Giovanni Boccaccio wanted to be remembered for his scholarship and writings in Latin. However, the work for which he is best remembered, *The Decameron,* is neither scholarly nor in Latin. In fact, it was only through the intervention of a close friend, Petrarch, that Boccaccio changed his mind about burning the manuscript for this series of short stories which have become famous for their humor and insight into human nature. Boccaccio was born in Paris, out of wedlock, and was raised in Italy in his father's household. At ten he was apprenticed to a banker in Naples in order to learn about the business. Boccaccio spent more time studying the works of the Roman poets, especially their poems on love, and shortly convinced his father that he should study anything but banking. It was agreed that he should major in canon law (religious law), but Boccaccio really majored in love. In 1331 he saw Maria d'Aquino in church and was smitten. For the next ten years he pursued his "Fiammetta," hoping to win her favor. He finally did, but Fiammetta tired of him as soon as his money ran out. Disillusioned, Boccaccio left Naples for Florence, which he considered his hometown.

Shortly after he returned home, the Black Death struck Florence, killing three out of every four citizens. In the wake of the plague, some of the survivors adopted the attitude of "live life to the fullest," and Boccaccio reflects this attitude in his most celebrated work, *The Decameron,* or "Ten Days Work." It tells the story of seven women and three men who flee Florence in the wake of the plague. The group spends ten days telling each other stories to pass the time. On the fifth day, the story-tellers turn their attention to tales of love and one of the characters tells the tale we have called "The Falconer and the Lady."

FILOMENA HAD ALREADY finished speaking, and when the Queen saw there was no one left to speak except for Dioneo, who was tempted because of his special privilege, she herself with a cheerful face said:

It is now my turn to tell a story and, dearest ladies, I shall do so most willingly with a tale similar in some respects to the prevailing one, its purpose being not only to show you how much power your beauty has over the gentle heart, but also so that you yourselves may learn, whenever it is fitting, to be the donors of your favors instead of always leaving this act to the whim of Fortune, who, as it happens, on most occasions bestows such favors with more abundance than discretion.

You should know, then, that Coppo di Borghese Domenichi, who once lived in our city and perhaps still does, a man of great and respected authority in our times, one most illustrious and worthy of eternal fame both for his way of life and his ability much more than for the nobility of his blood, often took delight, when he was an old man, in discussing things from the past with his neighbors and with others. He knew how to do this well, for he was more logical and had a better memory and a more eloquent style of speaking than any other man. Among the many beautiful tales he told, there was one he would often tell about a young man who once lived in Florence named Federigo, the son of Messer Filippo Alberighi, renowned above all other men in Tuscany for his prowess in arms and for his courtliness.

As often happens to most men of gentle breeding, he fell in love with a noble lady named Monna Giovanna, in her day considered to be one of the most beautiful and most charming ladies that ever there was in Florence; and in order to win her love, he participated in jousts and tournaments, organized and gave banquets, spending his money without restraint; but she, no less virtuous than beautiful, cared little for these things he did on her behalf, nor did she care for the one who did them. Now, as Federigo was spending far beyond his means and getting nowhere, as can easily happen, he lost his wealth and was reduced to poverty, and was left with nothing to his name but his little farm (from whose revenues he lived very meagerly) and one falcon, which was among the finest of its kind in the world.

More in love than ever, but knowing that he would never be able to live the way he wished to in the city, he went to live at Campi, where his farm was. There he passed his time hawking whenever he could, imposing on no one, and enduring his poverty patiently.

Now one day, during the time that Federigo was reduced to these extremes, it happened that the husband of Monna Giovanna fell ill, and realizing death was near, he made his last will: he was very rich, and he left everything to his son, who was just growing up, and since he had also loved Monna Giovanna very much, he made her his heir should his son die without any legitimate children; and then he died.

Monna Giovanna was now a widow, and every summer, as our women usually do, she would go to the country with her son to one of their estates very close by to Federigo's farm. Now this young boy of hers happened to become more and more friendly with Federigo and he began to enjoy birds and dogs; and after seeing Federigo's falcon fly many times, it made him so happy that he very much wished it were his own, but he did not dare to ask for it, for he could see how precious it was to Federigo. During this time, it happened that the young boy took ill, and his mother was much grieved, for he was her only child and she loved him dearly; she would spend the entire day by his side, never ceasing to comfort him, asking him time and again if there was anything he wished, begging him to tell her what it might be, for if it was possible to obtain it, she would certainly do everything in her power to get it. After the young boy had heard her make this offer many times, he said:

"Mother, if you can arrange for me to have Federigo's falcon, I think I would get well quickly."

When the lady heard this, she was taken aback for a moment, and then she began thinking what she could do about it. She knew that Federigo had been in love with her for some time now, but she had never deigned to give him a second look; so, she said to herself:

"How can I go to him, or even send someone, and ask for this falcon of his, which is, as I have heard tell, the finest that ever flew, and furthermore, his only means of support? And how can I be so insensitive as to wish to take away from this nobleman the only pleasure which is left to him?"

And involved in these thoughts, knowing that she was certain to have the bird if she asked for it, but not knowing what to say to her son, she stood there without answering him. Finally the love she bore her son persuaded her that she should make him happy, and no matter what the consequences might be, she would not send for the bird, but rather go herself to fetch it and bring it back to him; so she answered her son:

"My son, cheer up and think only of getting well, for I promise you that first thing tomorrow morning I shall go and fetch it for you."

The child was so happy that he showed some improvement that very day. The following morning, the lady, accompanied by another woman, as if they were out for a stroll, went to Federigo's modest little house and asked for him. Since the weather for the past few days had not been right for hawking, Federigo happened to be in his orchard attending to certain tasks, and when he heard that Monna Giovanna was asking for him at the door, he was so surprised and happy that he rushed there; as she saw him coming, she rose to greet him with womanly grace, and once Federigo had welcomed her most courteously, she said:

"How do you do, Federigo?" Then she continued, "I have come to make amends for the harm you have suffered on my account by loving me more than you should have, and in token of this, I intend to have a simple meal with you and this companion of mine this very day."

To this Federigo humbly replied: "Madonna, I have no recollection of ever suffering any harm because of you; on the contrary: so much good have I received from you that if ever I was worth anything, it was because of your worth and the love I bore for you; and your generous visit is certainly so very dear to me that I would spend all over again all that I spent in the past, but you have come to a poor host."

And having said this, he humbly led her through the house and into his garden, and because he had no one there to keep her company, he said:

"My lady, since there is no one else, this good woman, who is the wife of the farmer here, will keep you company while I see to the table."

Though he was very poor, Federigo until now had never realized to what extent he had wasted his wealth; but this morning, the fact that he had nothing in the house with which he could honor the lady for the love of whom he had in the past entertained countless people, gave him cause to reflect: in great anguish, he cursed himself and his fortune, and like someone out of his senses he started running here and there throughout the house, but unable to find either money or anything he might be able to pawn, and since it was getting late and he was still very much set on serving this noble lady some sort of meal, but unwilling to turn for help to even his own farmer (not to mention anyone else), he set his eyes upon his good falcon, which was sitting on its perch in a small room, and since he had nowhere else to turn, he took the bird, and finding it plump, he decided that it would be a worthy food for such a lady. So, without giving the matter a second thought, he wrung its neck and

quickly gave it to his servant girl to pluck, prepare, and place on a spit to be roasted with care; and when he had set the table with the whitest of tablecloths (a few of which he still had left), he returned, with a cheerful face, to the lady in his garden and announced that the meal, such as he was able to prepare, was ready.

The lady and her companion rose and went to the table together with Federigo, who waited upon them with the greatest devotion, and they ate the good falcon without knowing what it was they were eating. Then, having left the table and spent some time in pleasant conversation, the lady thought it time now to say what she had come to say, and so she spoke these kind words to Federigo:

"Federigo, if you recall your former way of life and my virtue, which you perhaps mistook for harshness and cruelty, I have no doubt at all that you will be amazed by my presumption when you hear what my main reason for coming here is; but if you had children, through whom you might have experienced the power of parental love, I feel certain that you would, at least in part, forgive me. But, just as you have no child, I do have one, and I cannot escape the laws common to all mothers; the force of such laws compels me to follow them, against my own will and against good manners and duty, and to ask of you a gift which I know is most precious to you; and it is naturally so, since your extreme condition has left you no other delight, no other pleasure, no other consolation; and this gift is your falcon, which my son is so taken by that if I do not bring it to him, I fear his sickness will grow so much worse that I may lose him. And therefore I beg you, not because of the love that you bear for me, which does not oblige you in the least, but because of your own nobleness, which you have shown to be greater than that of all

others in practicing courtliness, that you be pleased to give it to me, so that I may say that I have saved the life of my son by means of this gift, and because of it I have placed him in your debt forever. "

When he heard what the lady requested and knew that he could not oblige her because he had given her the falcon to eat, Federigo began to weep in her presence, for he could not utter a word in reply. The lady at first thought his tears were caused more by the sorrow of having to part with the good falcon than by anything else, and she was on the verge of telling him she no longer wished it, but she held back and waited for Federigo's reply once he stopped weeping. And he said:

"My lady, ever since it pleased God for me to place my love in you, I have felt that Fortune has been hostile to me in many ways, and I have complained of her, but all this is nothing compared to what she has just done to me, and I shall never be at peace with her again, when I think how you have come here to my poor home, where, when it was rich, you never deigned to come, and how you requested but a small gift, and Fortune worked to make it impossible for me to give it to you: and why this is so I shall tell you in a few words. When I heard that you, out of your kindness, wished to dine with me, I considered it only fitting and proper, taking into account your excellence and your worthiness, that I should honor you, according to my possibilities, with a more precious food than that which I usually serve to other people. So I thought of the falcon for which you have just asked me and of its value and I judged it a food worthy of you, and this very day I had it roasted and served to you as best I could. But seeing now that you desired it another way, my sorrow in not being able to serve you is so great that never shall I be able to console myself again."

And after he had said this, he laid the feathers, the feet, and the beak of the bird before her as proof. When the lady heard and saw this, she first reproached him for having killed a falcon such as this to serve as a meal to a woman. But then to herself she commended the greatness of his spirit, which no poverty was able, or would be able, to diminish; then, having lost all hope of getting the falcon and thus, perhaps, of improving the health of her son, she thanked Federigo both for the honor paid to her and for his good intentions, and then left in grief to return to her son. To his mother's extreme sorrow, whether in disappointment in not having the falcon or because his illness inevitably led to it, the boy passed from this life only a few days later.

After the period of her mourning and her bitterness had passed, the lady was repeatedly urged by her brothers to remarry, since she was very rich and still young; and although she did not wish to do so, they became so insistent that remembering the worthiness of Federigo and his last act of generosity — that is, to have killed such a falcon to do her honor — she said to her brothers:

"I would prefer to remain a widow, if only that would be pleasing to you, but since you wish me to take a husband, you may be sure that I shall take no man other than Federigo degli Alberighi."

In answer to this, her brothers, making fun of her, replied: "You foolish woman, what are you saying? How can you want him? He hasn't a penny to his name." To this she replied: "My brothers, I am well aware of what you say, but I would much rather have a man who lacks money than money that lacks a man." Her brothers, seeing that she was determined and knowing Federigo to be of noble birth, no matter how poor he was, accepted her wishes and gave her with all her riches in marriage to him; when he found himself the husband of such a great lady whom he had loved so much and who was so wealthy besides, he managed his financial affairs with more prudence than in the past and lived with her happily the rest of his days.

THINK ABOUT IT

1. Whose love is greater, Federigo's love for Monna Giovanna or Monna Giovanna's love for her son?

2. Why does Federigo feel he must cook and serve his falcon to Monna Giovanna?

TALK ABOUT IT

3. In many cultures, marriages are arranged and last for a lifetime. In the United States, where most marriages are based on "love," fifty percent end in divorce. Which system is better? Why?

4. Monna Giovanna states that she would "rather have a man who lacks money than money that lacks a man." Does one preclude the other? Does her reasoning prevail today?

WRITE ABOUT IT

5. Is this story a realistic portrayal of love? Explain your reasoning.

6. If you were called on to sacrifice your most precious possession for the one you loved, would you do it? Why or why not?

READ MORE ABOUT IT

Thompson, Karl E. *The Classics of Western Thought, Vol. 11.* New York: Harcourt, Brace and Jovanovich, 1988.

Gottfried, Robert Steven. *The Black Death: Natural and Human Disaster in Medieval Europe.* New York: Free Press, 1985.

Chaucer, Geoffrey. *The Canterbury Tales.* New York: Modern Library, 1994.

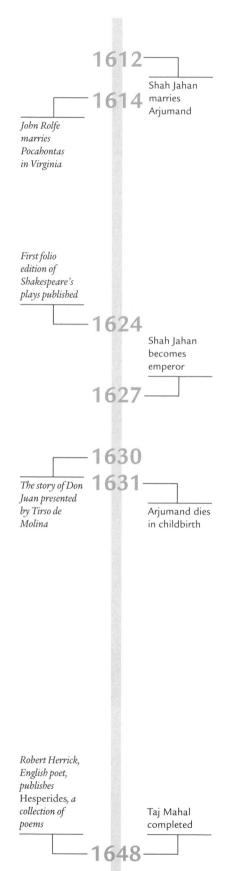

1612

1614 — Shah Jahan marries Arjumand

John Rolfe marries Pocahontas in Virginia

First folio edition of Shakespeare's plays published

1624

Shah Jahan becomes emperor

1627

1630

1631

The story of Don Juan presented by Tirso de Molina

Arjumand dies in childbirth

Robert Herrick, English poet, publishes Hesperides, *a collection of poems*

Taj Mahal completed

1648

JEFFERY REX
WAYNE DONLEY

The Taj Mahal

Jeffery Rex Wayne Donley is Professor of Interdisciplinary Studies and humanities at Valencia Community College in Orlando, Florida. He holds advanced degrees in Classics, History, Religion, Linguistics, and Philosophy. Donley's masters work at Cincinnati and Princeton and doctoral work at the University of Birmingham, England, and Oxford University, England, has prepared him to interpret and write about the great works of man.

To the entire world, the Taj Mahal stands as the symbol of India. This spectacular white marble building is located on the banks of the Jumna River near Agra, in North Central India. It was built as a mausoleum to contain the remains of the seventeenth-century emperor Shah Jahan's favorite wife, Arjumand. He intended it to be "as beautiful as she was beautiful." Indeed, it is the jewel of Indian architecture, graceful as it is lovely. As one approaches the Taj Mahal in the full sunlight of an Indian day, its white marble walls take on the appearance of lace, seeming paper-thin, almost translucent. It is a feminine structure of ascending towers and curving domes that appear to barely touch the ground. Its light elegance is reinforced by the large, shimmering reflecting pool that leads the visitor to the tomb. As one enters and is enveloped by the Taj Mahal's deep shadows, the perfume of hundreds of flowers left by admirers fills the air. Its ageless beauty assaults the senses and speaks of undying love.

THE TAJ MAHAL is a visual image of God's throne in paradise, a perfectly proportionate and symmetrical mausoleum on the southern bank of the Yamuna (Jumna) River which is on the outskirts of Agra, India. The fifth Mughal Emperor, Shah Jahan, perhaps the greatest of the Muslim rulers of India, built the Taj Mahal for his beloved wife, Arjumand Bano Begam, as a celebration of his unending love for her. The Mughal Empire was one of the greatest empires the world has ever known, which perhaps led to Shah Jahan calling himself "Emperor of the World" when he was crowned on October 29, 1627. He was a wealthy, ambitious, orthodox Sunni Muslim ruler who restored Islam as the state religion of the Mughal empire; he also possessed a passion for luxuriousness. This passion for the most costly and grand, and his love of Arjumand drove him to erect a magnificent building — the Taj Mahal — that was constructed with the artistic sensibilities of clarity and balance. Its fine design and decorations are a visual statement of the depth of his very human feelings for his wife. Under the influence of

THE TAJ MAHAL, 1630–32.
White marble. Agra, India.

Shah Jahan, architecture in seventeenth-century India reached its height: the Taj Mahal is a brilliant fusion of Islamic and Hindu styles, representing an incomparable and unquestionable pinnacle of artistic achievement.

In 1612, Shah Jahan married the lady Arjumand who remained his favorite and inseparable consort, or wife. They were devoted to each other. Arjumand must have been graced with uncommon charm and beauty to keep the love of Shah Jahan, a polygamist. Tradition says that she had velutinous skin, ebony eyes, long satiny lashes, pencilled eyebrows, and grumous black braided hair. Shah Jahan gave Arjumand the royal seat, *Muhr Uzah,* making her a trusted political advisor. She bore him fourteen children between the years 1613 and 1631. While giving birth to her last child, Arjumand died at Burhanpur on June 17, 1631, at the age of thirty-nine. Before Arjumand died, she was said to have whispered in Shah Jahan's ear that he must promise her two things. First, he was not to have any more children with his other wives. Second, he was to build her the world's most beautiful monument as a symbol of their love.

On January 9, 1632, the broken-hearted Shah Jahan transferred Arjumand's body, which had been temporarily interred at Burhanpur, to Agra, where he placed her in a sepulchre in the gardens of the Taj. The sorrowing Shah Jahan erected over her sepulchre one of the most beautiful buildings in the world, an unrivalled monument dedicated to her memory. No other woman in the world has ever had such a magnificent monument built to honor her. The name, Taj Mahal, originates from the title *Mumtaz Mahal* ("the Ornament of the Palace"), a title that was conferred on Arjumand. It symbolized her inward grace. The build-

ing itself lives up to the title. In the year 1648, more than 20,000 craftsmen and laborers completed this loving tribute to Shah Jahan's consort, the lady Arjumand.

The Taj Mahal was designed to be seen from all angles, providing a stunning overall visual effect (Color Plate 8). It is characterized by a feminine elegance rather than by the structural strength present in most monumental buildings. Its decoration was extraordinary and costly; shimmering white marble, brought from Markrana two hundred and fifty miles away, was used lavishly. The Taj Mahal is actually a great rectangular complex of buildings; all firmly rest on a platform measuring one hundred and eighty-six feet on each side, with the Yamuna River gently flowing past its northern side. The complex is enclosed by an enormous red sandstone wall, with mosques on two sides. Some nine hundred feet from the actual complex, a gateway inlaid in white and black marble heralds a beautiful forty-two acre garden which is a further testament of Shah Jahan's promise. The garden originally did not have a lawn, but was planted with beds of flowers, rare fruit trees, and nurtured exotic birds. It is divided into four equal sections, with a raised rectangular marble pond in the center that contains five fountains. Twenty-four fountains surround the center pond with another twenty-four fountains along each side of the northern and southern channels. Exquisitely proportioned, four lofty three-storied marble-faced minarets accent the central building at the corners of the platform; they stand like four ladies in waiting. Each minaret has a winding staircase of one hundred and sixty-two steps. At the top of the Taj Mahal, almost two hundred and fifty feet in height, a pear-shaped dome canopies the central chambers and is supported by a drum and

topped by a metal pinnacle. The central dome is the crowning glory of the Taj Mahal. It is surrounded by four smaller domes to lessen its vertical emphasis.

The Taj Mahal is beautifully mirrored in a reflecting pool. Crossing the long terrace that is opposite the reflecting pool, the visitor arrives at the entrance to the central building. Entering here, one finds two stories of eight rooms that surround a central chamber. In this central chamber an octagonal marble screen encompasses the cenotaphs, or burial coffins, that are placed above the actual crypts where Arjumand and Shah Jahan rest side-by-side. Arjumand's cenotaph is located at the exact center of the Taj Mahal's interior, directly beneath the main dome (Color Plate 9). The placement of Shah Jahan's cenotaph, to the side of Arjumand's, represents the only asymmetrical element in the complex. In life, Shah Jahan collected expensive jewels while, in death, the couple's cenotaph stones are richly decorated with inlays of jasper, lapis, and bloodstone. The cenotaphs are laid with such precision that one cannot see or feel any breaks in the space that separates them. At the end of the day, soft, subdued twilight caresses the central chamber through the lacy grillwork of the doors and windows, enveloping the coffins in a rich pattern of light.

Shah Jahan, the greatest builder of the Mughals, spared no effort and expense to secure the skills of top specialists in every phase of the construction of the Tai Mahal. Although speculation continues to this day, the Taj Mahal's architect is still unknown; little, too, is known about the individual craftsmen. Tradition says that at least thirty-seven craftsmen created the Tai Mahal. We do know that Ismail Afandi from Turkey was the foremost dome builder in the world and designed the Taj Mahal's dome. According to Afandi, the dome was the most perfect of all earthly forms. Qazim Khan from Lahore, a renowned worker of precious metals, cast the gold finial of the dome. A master calligrapher from Persia, Amanat Khan, decorated the Taj Mahal with inscriptions, an elegant form of ornamentation, displaying important scriptural verses from the Koran. Khan's name was the only person's signature deemed worthy to be placed on the Taj Mahal walls. Architectural details combining wreaths, scrolls, and frets were exquisitely designed and beautifully colored, then inlaid in the pure white marble walls. These colored decorations were formed from precious and semi-precious stones, making them one of the most beautiful (and expensive) styles of ornamentation ever used in architecture. Pointed Muslim arches filled with delicate marble grillwork framed the windows and doors —a common architectural feature found in most Hindu temples.

Tradition states that when Shah Jahan first saw the finished complex he was overwhelmed with the magnificence of the Taj Mahal. In order to show his appreciation, he chopped off the hands of the master builders, blinded the calligraphers, and cut off the architect's head so that none of these creative geniuses could design another building complex to rival the Taj Mahal. At the time, this incredible monument had cost just over 411 lakhs or rupees, or eight million dollars today. Supposedly, Shah Jahan dreamed of building a black marble replica of the Taj Mahal for himself on the opposite side of the Yamuna River; it was to be linked by a flying, silver bridge to the pure white Taj Mahal. Because of the enormous resources needed to duplicate this wonder, Shah Jahan's dream was never re-

THE TAJ MAHAL
Exterior view of the cenotaphs, 1630–1652. Agra, India

alized — he spent his final years gazing at the Taj Mahal from his palace in Agra.

The Taj Mahal is more than an expression of architectural grandeur, it is a celebration of the love of Shah Jahan. No other building has captured the world's romantic imagination as has the Taj Mahal. This exquisite building expressed Shah Jahan's deepest feelings and memories. His sentiments arranged, converged, and harmonized themselves into a work of monumental architecture. The intricate floral and geometric inlays on the exterior of the Taj Mahal, for example, are perfectly arranged into a harmonious oneness

INTERIOR OF THE TAJ MAHAL, 1630–32. THE TOMB OF ARJUMAND.
White marble with semi-precious inlay. Agra, India.

representative of the unity of love. The Taj Mahal stands as a vision of paradise on earth, jewel-like, and dedicated to the memory of Shah Jahan's undying love for his wife Arjumand. The anguish he experienced at her death has been transformed into the most celebrated memorial to love anywhere in the world and the Taj Mahal has become the national symbol of India.

Rabindranth Tagore, India's national poet of the twentieth century, summed up the importance of the Taj Mahal when he wrote:

Though emeralds, rubies,
*   pearls are all*
but as the glitter of a rainbow tricking
*   out empty air*
And must pass away,

yet still one solitary tear
would hang on the cheek of time
In the form
Of this white and gleaming
*   Taj Mahal.*

THINK ABOUT IT

1. How does the Taj Mahal show Shah Jahan's love for Arjumand?
2. Can love show itself completely in visible objects? Why or why not?

TALK ABOUT IT

3. What other buildings from around the world convey sentiments of love?
4. Why does a building, a tomb such as the Taj Mahal, create an emotional response in its viewer?

WRITE ABOUT IT

5. What is your favorite visible expression of love? Why?
6. What have you done lately for the one(s) you love? Describe an incident where you visibly revealed your love.

READ MORE ABOUT IT

Carroll, David. *The Taj Mahal.* New York: Newsweek Book Division, 1972.

Chawla, Rohit, and Saran Shalini. *Tai Mahal.* London: Tiger Books International, 1989.

Pal, Pratapaditya, ed. [et al.]. *Romance of the Taj Mahal.* London, Los Angeles: Thames and Hudson, Los Angeles County Museum of Art, 1989.

ARNA BONTEMPS

A Summer Tragedy

Arna (born Arnaud) Bontemps wore a number of hats during his lifetime. He was a poet, writer, essayist, playwright, critic, teacher, librarian, and writer of children's books. Born in Louisiana, his father moved the family to California when Arna was three after they were threatened with racial violence. Bontemps' father could never understand why Arna wanted to become a writer instead of a bricklayer, but Arna persisted in his dream. Unable to complete a Ph.D. in literature because of the Depression, Bontemps received a Master's Degree in Library Science from the University of Chicago in 1943. In the meantime, he had won three poetry prizes, one short story prize, two fellowships for graduate study, and had written his first novel, *Black Thunder,* which was highly acclaimed.

In his work, Bontemps draws on his regional and African-American heritages. He loved to write dialect and often used the Creole dialect, which his family spoke, as the basis for his characters' speech. His contribution to American culture is not only literary; with his good friend, Langston Hughes, he helped preserve African-American folklore and mythology. As Head Librarian at Fisk University in Nashville, he made that library a premier collection of African-American literature and culture. In the short story included here, "A Summer Tragedy," written in 1933, Bontemps reveals himself as a writer of insight and sensitivity whose understanding of love transcends time, place, age, and race.

OLD JEFF PATTON, the black share farmer, fumbled with his bow tie. His fingers trembled and the high stiff collar pinched his throat. A fellow loses his hand for such vanities after thirty or forty years of simple life. Once a year, or maybe twice if there's a wedding among his kinfolks, he may spruce up; but generally fancy clothes do nothing but adorn the wall of the big room and feed the moths. That had been Jeff Patton's experience. He had not worn his stiff-bosomed shirt more than a dozen times in all his married life. His swallow-tailed coat lay on the bed beside him, freshly brushed and pressed, but it was as full of holes as the overalls in which he worked on weekdays. The moths had used it badly. Jeff twisted his mouth into a hideous toothless grimace as he contended with the obstinate bow. He stamped his good foot and decided to give up the struggle.

"Jennie," he called.

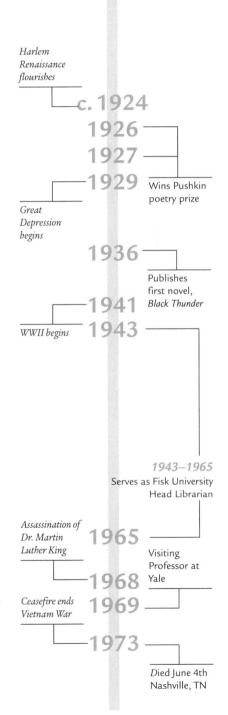

1902 ——
Bontemps born Oct. 13th Alexandria, LA

Harlem Renaissance flourishes
c. 1924
1926
1927
1929 — Wins Pushkin poetry prize

Great Depression begins

1936 — Publishes first novel, *Black Thunder*

1941
1943
WWII begins

1943–1965
Serves as Fisk University Head Librarian

Assassination of Dr. Martin Luther King
1965 — Visiting Professor at Yale

1968
1969
Ceasefire ends Vietnam War

1973 — Died June 4th Nashville, TN

"What's that, Jeff?" His wife's shrunken voice came out of the adjoining room like an echo. It was hardly bigger than a whisper.

"I reckon you'll have to he'p me wid this heah bow tie, baby," he said meekly. "Dog if I can hitch it up."

Her answer was not strong enough to reach him, but presently the old woman came to the door, feeling her way with a stick. She had a wasted, dead-leaf appearance. Her body, as scrawny and gnarled as a string bean, seemed less than nothing in the ocean of frayed and faded petticoats that surrounded her. These hung an inch or two above the tops of her heavy unlaced shoes and showed little grotesque piles where the stockings had fallen down from her negligible legs.

"You oughta could do a heap mo' wid a thing like that'n me — beingst as you got yo' good sight."

"Looks like I oughta could," he admitted. "But ma fingers is gone democrat on me. I get all mixed up in the looking glass an' can't tell wicha way to twist the devilish thing."

Jennie sat on the side of the bed and old Jeff Patton got down on one knee while she tied the bow knot. It was a slow and painful ordeal for each of them in this position. Jeff's bones cracked, his knee ached, and it was only after a half dozen attempts that Jennie worked a semblance of a bow into the tie. "I got to dress maself now," the old woman whispered.

"These is ma old shoes an' stockings, and I ain't so much as unwrapped ma dress."

"Well, don't worry 'bout me no mo', baby," Jeff said. "That 'bout finishes me. All I gotta do now is slip on that old coat 'n ves' an' I'll be fixed to leave."

Jennie disappeared again through the dim passage into the shed room. Being blind was no handicap to her in that black hole. Jeff heard the cane placed against the wall beside the door and knew that his wife was on easy ground. He put on his coat, took a battered top hat from the bedpost and hobbled to the front door. He was ready to travel. As soon as Jennie could get on her Sunday shoes and her old black silk dress, they would start.

Outside the tiny log house, the day was warm and mellow with sunshine. A host of wasps were humming with busy excitement in the trunk of a dead sycamore. Gray squirrels were searching through the grass for hickory nuts and blue jays were in the trees, hopping from branch to branch. Pine woods stretched away to the left like a black sea. Among them were scattered scores of log houses like Jeff's, houses of black share farmers. Cows and pigs wandered freely among the trees. There was no danger of loss. Each farmer knew his own stock and knew his neighbor's as well as he knew his neighbor's children.

Down the slope to the right were the cultivated acres on which the colored folks worked. They extended to the river, more than two miles away, and they were today green with the unmade cotton crop. A tiny thread of a road, which passed directly in front of Jeff's place, ran through these green fields like a pencil mark.

Jeff, standing outside the door, with his absurd hat in his left hand, surveyed the wide scene tenderly. He had been forty-five years on these acres. He loved them with the unexplained affection that others have for the countries to which they belong.

The sun was hot on his head, his collar still pinched his throat, and the Sunday clothes were intolerably hot. Jeff transferred the hat to his right hand and began fanning with it. Suddenly the whisper that was Jennie's voice came out of the shed room.

"You can bring the car round front whilst you's waitin'," it said feebly. There was a tired pause; then it added, "I'll soon be fixed to go."

"Alright, baby," Jeff answered. "I'll get it in a minute."

But he didn't move. A thought struck him that made his mouth fall open. The mention of the car brought o his mind, with new intensity _ trip he and Jennie were about to take. Fear came into his eyes; excitement took his breath. Lord, Jesus!

"Jeff … O Jeff," the old woman's whisper called.

He awakened with a jolt. "Hunh, baby?"

"What you doin'?"

"Nuthin. Jes studyin'. I jes been turnin' things round'n round in ma mind."

"You could be gettin' the car," she said.

"Oh yes, right away, baby."

He started round to the shed, limping heavily on his bad leg. There were three frizzly chickens in the yard. All his other chickens had been killed or stolen recently. But the frizzly chickens had been saved somehow. That was fortunate indeed, for these curious creatures had a way of devouring "Poison" from the yard and in that way protecting against conjure and black luck and spells. But even the frizzly chickens seemed now to be in a stupor. Jeff thought they had some ailment; he expected all three of them to die shortly.

The shed in which the old T-model Ford stood was only a grass roof held up by four corner poles. It had been built by tremulous hands at a time when the little rattletrap car had been regarded as a peculiar treasure. And, miraculously, despite wind and downpour it still stood.

Jeff adjusted the crank and put his weight upon it. The engine came to life with a sputter and bang that rattled the old car from radiator to taillight. Jeff hopped into the seat and put his foot on the accelerator. The sputtering and banging increased. The rattling became more violent. That was good. It was good banging, good sputtering and rattling, and it meant that the aged car was still in running condition. She could be depended on for this trip.

Again Jeff's thought halted as if paralyzed. The suggestion of the trip fell into the machinery of his mind like a wrench. He felt dazed and weak. He swung the car out into the yard, made a half turn and drove around to the front door. When he took his hands off the wheel, he noticed that he was trembling violently. He cut off the motor and climbed to the ground to wait for Jennie.

A few minutes later she was at the window, her voice rattling against the pane like a broken shutter.

"I'm ready, Jeff."

He did not answer, but limped into the house and took her by the arm. He led her slowly through the big room, down the step and across the yard.

"You reckon I'd oughta lock the do'?" he asked softly.

They stopped and Jennie weighed the question. Finally she shook her head.

"Ne' mind the do'," she said. "I don't see no cause to lock up things."

"You right," Jeff agreed. "No cause to lock up."

Jeff opened the door and helped his wife into the car. A quick shudder passed over him. Jesus! Again he trembled.

"How come you shaking so?" Jennie whispered.

"I don't know," he said.

"You mus' be scairt, Jeff."

"No, baby, I ain't scairt."

He slammed the door after her and went around to crank up again. The motor started easily. Jeff wished

that it had not been so responsive. He would have liked a few more minutes in which to turn things around in his head. As it was, with Jennie chiding him about being afraid, he had to keep going. He swung the car into the little pencil-mark road and started off toward the river, driving very slowly, very cautiously.

Chugging across the green countryside, the small battered Ford seemed tiny indeed. Jeff felt a familiar excitement, a thrill, as they came down the first slope to the immense levels on which the cotton was growing. He could not help reflecting that the crops were good. He knew what that meant, too; he had made forty-five of them with his own hands. It was true that he had worn out nearly a dozen mules, but that was the fault of old man Stevenson, the owner of the land. Major Stevenson had the odd notion that one mule was all a share farmer needed to work a thirty-acre plot. It was an expensive notion, the way it killed mules from overwork, but the old man held to it. Jeff thought it killed a good many share farmers as well as mules, but he had no sympathy for them. He had always been strong, and he had been taught to have no patience with weakness in men. Women or children might be tolerated if they were puny, but a weak man was a curse. Of course, his own children —

Jeff's thought halted there. He and Jennie never mentioned their dead children any more. And naturally he did not wish to dwell upon them in his mind. Before he knew it, some remark would slip out of his mouth and that would make Jennie feel blue. Perhaps she would cry. A woman like Jennie could not easily throw off the grief that comes from losing five grown children within two years. Even Jeff was still staggered by the blow. His memory had not been much good recently. He

frequently talked to himself. And, although he had kept it a secret, he knew that his courage had left him. He was terrified by the least unfamiliar sound at night. He was reluctant to venture far from home in the daytime. And that habit of trembling when he felt fearful was now far beyond his control. Sometimes he became afraid and trembled without knowing what had frightened him. The feeling would just come over him like a chill.

The car rattled slowly over the dusty road. Jennie sat erect and silent, with a little absurd hat pinned to her hair. Her useless eyes seemed very large, very white in their deep sockets. Suddenly Jeff heard her voice, and he inclined his head to catch the words.

"Is we passed Delia Moore's house yet?" she asked.

"Not yet," he said.

"You must be drivin' mighty slow, Jeff."

"We might just as well take our time, baby."

There was a pause. A little puff of steam was coming out of the radiator of the car. Heat wavered above the hood. Delia Moore's house was nearly half a mile away. After a moment Jennie spoke again.

"You ain't really scairt, is you, Jeff?"

"Nah, baby, I ain't scairt."

"You know how we agreed — we gotta keep on goin'."

Jewels of perspiration appeared on Jeff's forehead. His eyes rounded, blinked, became fixed on the road.

"I don't know," he said with a shiver. "I reckon it's the only thing to do."

"Hm."

A flock of guinea fowls, pecking in the road, were scattered by the passing car. Some of them took to their wings; others hid under bushes. A blue jay, swaying on a leafy twig, was annoying a roadside squirrel. Jeff held an even speed till he came near Delia's place. Then he slowed down noticeably.

Delia's house was really no house at all, but an abandoned store building converted into a dwelling. It sat near a crossroads, beneath a single black cedar tree. There Delia, a cattish old creature of Jennie's age, lived alone. She had been there more years than anybody could remember, and long ago had won the disfavor of such women as Jennie. For in her young days Delia had been gayer, yellower and saucier than seemed proper in those parts. Her ways with menfolks had been dark and suspicious. And the fact that she had had as many husbands as children did not help her reputation.

"Yonder's old Delia," Jeff said as they passed.

"What she doin'?"

"Jes sittin' in the do'," he said.

"She see us?"

"Hm," Jeff said. "Musta did."

That relieved Jennie. It strengthened her to know that her old enemy had seen her pass in her best clothes. That would give the old she-devil something to chew her gums and fret about, Jennie thought. Wouldn't she have a fit if she didn't find out? Old evil Delia! This would be just the thing for her. It would pay her back for being so evil. It would also pay her, Jennie thought, for the way she used to grin at Jeff — long ago when her teeth were good.

The road became smooth and red, and Jeff could tell by the smell of the air that they were nearing the river. He could see the rise where the road turned and ran along parallel to the stream. The car chugged on monotonously. After a long silent spell, Jennie leaned against Jeff and spoke.

"How many bale o' cotton you think we got standin'?" she said.

Jeff wrinkled his forehead as he calculated.

"'Bout twenty-five, I reckon."

"How many you make las' year?"

"Twenty-eight," he said. "How come you ask that? "

"I's jes thinkin'," Jennie said quietly.

"It don't make a speck o' difference though," Jeff reflected. "If we get much or if we get little, we still gonna be in debt to old man Stevenson when he gets through counting up agin us. It's took us a long time to learn that."

Jennie was not listening to these words. She had fallen into a trance-like meditation. Her lips twitched. She chewed her gums and rubbed her gnarled hands nervously. Suddenly she leaned forward, buried her face in the nervous hands and burst into tears. She cried aloud in a dry cracked voice that suggested the rattle of fodder on dead stalks. She cried aloud like a child, for she had never learned to suppress a genuine sob. Her slight old frame shook heavily and seemed hardly able to sustain such violent grief.

"What's the matter, baby?" Jeff asked awkwardly. "Why you cryin' like all that?"

"I's jes thinkin'," she said.

"So you the one what's scairt now, hunh?"

"I ain't scairt, Jeff. I's jes thinkin' 'bout leavin' eve'thing like this — eve'thing we been used to. It's right - sad-like."

Jeff did not answer, and presently Jennie buried her face again and cried.

The sun was almost overhead. It beat down furiously on the dusty wagon-path road, on the parched roadside grass and the tiny battered car. Jeff's hands, gripping the wheel, became wet with perspiration; his forehead sparkled. Jeff's lips parted. His mouth shaped a hideous grimace. His face suggested the face of a man being burned. But the torture

passed and his expression softened again.

"You mustn't cry, baby," he said to his wife. "We gotta be strong. We can't break down."

Jennie waited a few seconds, then said, "You reckon we oughta do it, Jeff? You reckon we oughta go 'head an' do it, really?"

Jeff's voice choked; his eyes blurred. He was terrified to hear Jennie say the thing that had been in his mind all morning. She had egged him on when he had wanted more than anything in the world to wait, to reconsider, to think things through again. It would only end in making the same painful decision once more. Jeff knew that. There was no need of fooling around longer.

"We jes as well to do like we planned," he said. "They ain't nothin' else for us now — it's the bes' thing."

Jeff thought of the handicaps, the near impossibility, of making another crop with his leg bothering him more and more each week. Then there was always the chance that he would have another stroke, like the one that had made him lame. Another one might kill him. The least it could do would be to leave him helpless. Jeff gasped — Lord, Jesus! He could not bear to think of being helpless, like a baby, on Jennie's hands. Frail, blind Jennie.

The little pounding motor of the car worked harder and harder. The puff of steam from the cracked radiator became larger. Jeff realized that they were climbing a little rise. A moment later the road turned abruptly and he looked down upon the face of the river.

"Jeff. "

"Hunh?"

"Is that the water I hear?"

"Hm. Tha's it."

"Well, which way you goin' now?"

"Down this-a way," he said. "The road runs 'long 'side o' the water a li'l piece."

She waited a while calmly. Then she said, "Drive faster."

"Right, baby," Jeff said.

The water roared in the bed of the river. It was fifty or sixty feet below the level of the road. Between the road and the water there was a long smooth slope, sharply inclined. The slope was dry, the clay hardened by prolonged summer heat. The water below, roaring in a narrow channel, was noisy and wild.

"Jeff."

"Hunh?"

"How far you goin'?"

"Jes a li'l piece down the road."

"You ain't scairt, is you, Jeff?"

"Nah, baby," he said trembling. "I ain't scairt."

"Remember how we planned it, Jeff. We gotta do it like we said. Brave-like."

"Hm."

Jeff's brain darkened. Things suddenly seemed unreal, like figures in a dream. Thoughts swam in his mind foolishly, hysterically, like little blind fish in a pool within a dense cave. They rushed, crossed one another, jostled, collided, retreated and rushed again. Jeff soon became dizzy. He shuddered violently and turned to his wife.

"Jennie, I can't do it. I can't." His voice broke pitifully. She did not appear to be listening. All the grief had gone from her face. She sat erect, her unseeing eyes wide open, strained and frightful. Her glossy black skin had become dull. She seemed as thin, as sharp and bony, as a starved bird. Now, having suffered and endured the sadness of tearing herself away from beloved things, she showed no anguish. She was absorbed with her own thoughts, and she didn't even hear Jeff's voice shouting in her ear.

Jeff said nothing more. For an instant there was light in his cavernous brain. The great chamber was, for less than a second, peopled by characters he knew and loved. They were simple, healthy creatures, and they behaved in a manner that he could understand. They had quality. But since he had already taken leave of them long ago, the remembrance did not break his heart again. Young Jeff Patton was among them, the Jeff Patton of fifty years ago who went down to New Orleans with a crowd of country boys to the Mardi Gras doings. The gay young crowd, boys with candy-striped shirts and rouged-brown girls in noisy silks, was like a picture in his head. Yet it did not make him sad. On that very trip Slim Burns had killed Joe Beasley — the crowd had been broken up. Since then Jeff Patton's world had been the Greenbriar Plantation. If there had been other Mardi Gras carnivals, he had not heard of them. Since then there had been no time; the years had fallen on him like waves. Now he was old, worn out. Another paralytic stroke (like the one he had already suffered) would put him on his back for keeps. In that condition, with a frail blind woman to look after him, he would be worse off than if he were dead.

Suddenly Jeff's hands became steady. He actually felt brave. He slowed down the motor of the car and carefully pulled off the road. Below, the water of the stream boomed, a soft thunder in the deep channel. Jeff ran the car onto the clay slope, pointed it directly toward the stream and put his foot heavily on the accelerator. The little car leaped furiously down the steep incline toward the water. The movement was nearly as swift and direct as a fall. The two old black folks, sitting quietly side by side, showed no excitement. In another instant the car hit the wa-

ter and dropped immediately out of sight.

A little later it lodged in the mud of a shallow place. One wheel of the crushed and upturned little Ford became visible above the rushing water.

THINK ABOUT IT

1. At what point in the story did you realize what Jeff and Jennie were planning to do?

2. Why do Jeff and Jennie believe life holds nothing else for them?

TALK ABOUT IT

3. In our culture, age is not venerated. How does this story reflect our attitudes toward the elderly? How do these attitudes compare to those of other cultures?

4. Why do many people think suicide is wrong? Is it wrong for Jeff and Jennie? Is their act an act of desperation or an act of love?

WRITE ABOUT IT

5. What details in the story reveal Jeff and Jennie's love for each other?

6. If you were in the same situation, would you do what Jeff and Jennie did? Explain your reasons.

READ MORE ABOUT IT

Bontemps, Arna. *Black Thunder.* New York: Macmillan, 1936.

Bontemps, Arna and Langston Hughes, eds. *The Book of Negro Folklore.* New York: Dodd, Mead, 1958.

Bontemps, Arna, ed. *The Harlem Renaissance Remembered: Essays.* New York: Dodd, Mead, 1972.

Bontemps, Arna. *The Old South: "A Summer Tragedy" and Other Stories of the Thirties.* New York: Dodd, Mead, 1973.

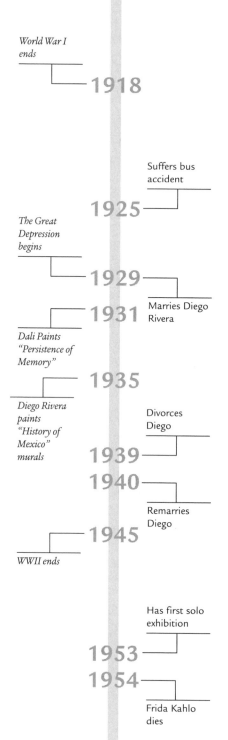

1907 — Frida Kahlo born

World War I ends

1918

Suffers bus accident

1925

The Great Depression begins

1929

1931 — Marries Diego Rivera

Dali Paints "Persistence of Memory"

1935

Diego Rivera paints "History of Mexico" murals

Divorces Diego

1939

1940

Remarries Diego

1945

WWII ends

Has first solo exhibition

1953

1954 — Frida Kahlo dies

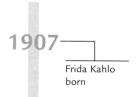

RONALD TAMPLIN

Frida's Love Letter

The great Mexican artist Frida Kahlo had a long love affair with the world-renown mural painter, Diego Rivera. One of Frida's letters to Diego, reprinted below, appeared in a recent anthology of love letters between famous people. Ronald Tamplin, a teacher, writer, and poet, who has lived and worked in Europe and New Zealand, wrote the accompanying biographical article on the turbulent Kahlo-Rivera romance.

Frida Kahlo's paintings are haunting surrealist-type images that command the viewer's attention. Her flamboyant and often tempestuous behavior also demanded attention. Although of mixed heritage, she was proud to be born in Mexico and wore traditional dress at a time when European-style clothes were the accepted norm. People on the street often stopped and commented on her unusual dress and distinct physical appearance. Kahlo had been partially paralyzed by a streetcar accident she had as a teenager; this led her to infuse her paintings with images of her ever-present physical pain. Indeed, all of her work explores her personal feelings of pain, both physical and spiritual. Some of her greatest emotional anguish was caused by the love of her life, Diego Rivera, whom she married in 1929. By this time, Rivera had achieved international acclaim and the attention of many women, both of which he greatly enjoyed. Kahlo was infuriated by his many affairs and, in revenge, took lovers herself. Their difficult, yet deeply loving relationship has become legendary. Through it, the facts and fantasies of Frida's life merged with her obsession for Diego and created her unique view of love and art.

July 23, 1935

[I know now that] all these letters, liaisons with petticoats, lady teachers of "English," gypsy models, assistants with "good intentions," "plenipotentiary emissaries from distant places," only represent flirtations, and that at bottom you and I love each other dearly, and thus go through adventures without number, beatings on doors, imprecations, insults, international claims — yet we will always love each other ...

All these things have been repeated throughout the seven years that we have lived together, and all the rages I have gone through have served only to make me understand in the end that I love you more than my own skin, and that, though you may not love me in the same way, still you love me somewhat. Isn't that so? ... I shall always hope that that continues, and with that I am content.

ON JULY 23, 1935, from her hotel in New York City, the Mexican artist Frida Kahlo wrote to her husband, the great mural painter, Diego Rivera. The letter, extracted here, was one of the most direct and realistic letters of her life, penned during one of the many separations that peppered their tempestuous marriage. What drove her away this time was her discovery that Rivera had had an affair with her younger sister, Christina. Frida's resentment waned, however. In its wake, she seems to have decided that there was a context of mutual love in which she could understand, or at least forgive, his frequent philandering.

In appearance, Frida and Diego made an unlikely couple: she, physically petite and darkly beautiful; he, corpulent and ugly. Together, their lives were pure theater: written about in the press and watched with fascination by the bohemian art circles of the time.

Frida's deep obsession with Rivera began at an early age. According to one account, the 15-year-old Frida first saw him — then 36 years old, a Communist, and a world-famous artist — when he was painting murals at her preparatory school in the heart of Mexico City. She told startled friends,

"My ambition is to have a child by Diego Rivera. And I'm going to tell him so some day."

By the time she met Rivera on more adult terms, she was 21 and a painter herself. He encouraged her art, but courted her as well, attracted by her quick intelligence, her hatred of bourgeois convention, and her direct, often ironic, sense of humor. While painting Frida's portrait as a Communist militant for a mural, he joked:

"You have a dog face," to which Frida lovingly retorted: "And you have the face of a frog!"

In 1929 Frida and Diego married, she for the first time, he for the third. She could not fulfill her adolescent dream of bearing him a child because of injuries sustained in a bus accident that occurred when she was 18. But Frida was a loyal wife, defending him from critics, worrying about his health, and traveling with him wherever commissions took him, whether to San Francisco, Detroit, or New York.

FRIDA AND HER HUSBAND DIEGO
visit an art gallery in New York.

DIEGO IN MY THOUGHTS:
SELF PORTRAIT AS A TEHUANA, 1943
Instituto Nacional de Bellas Artes y Litura/Gelman Collection/
Centro Arte Contemporaneo A.C., Mexico.

Frida knew from the outset that Diego could not be possessed, that art was his first passion, followed by Mexico, Marxism, and "the people." She wrote:

"Diego is beyond all limited and precise personal relations. He does not have friends, he has allies: he is very affectionate, but he never surrenders himself."

To some extent this suited Frida, allowing her to forge her own career and social life. The home Rivera built for them reflected their relationship: two houses, linked by a bridge. Frida had lovers (male and female), including such luminaries as the sculptor, Isamu Noguchi, and Leon Trotsky. The men she kept secret to avoid Rivera's murderous jealousy.

By the midsummer of 1939, ten years after their marriage and after a trip to Paris where Frida was hailed by the Surrealists, she and Rivera had begun divorce proceedings. Frida wrote:

"I see him very often but he doesn't want to live in the same house with me anymore because he likes to be alone …. Well anyway I take care of him the best I can from the distance … and I will love him all my life even if he wouldn't want me to."

Their divorce lasted about a year. Neither could stand the separation. Rivera told a friend,

"I'm going to marry her because she really needs me."

But Rivera also needed Frida, and was prepared to accept several key conditions that she laid down for remarriage, among them that she would support herself financially from her painting, and that there would be no lovemaking. Rivera explained that, "with the images of all my other women flashing through her mind ... a psychological barrier would spring up as soon as I made advances."

Married to each other for the second time in December 1940, their lives continued in much the same vein as before. They took pride in each other's work, fought, reconciled, and pursued others. Throughout, Rivera remained central to Frida's life. In an entry in her journal in the late 1940s, she wrote:

"Diego: Nothing is comparable to your hands and nothing is equal to the gold-green of your eyes …. My fingertips touch your blood."

When his infidelities became too much, she would adopt a maternal role, grumbling about his untidiness, "Oh that boy, already he has spoiled his shirt," or bathing and cleaning him as if he were a child.

By the late 1940s, Frida and Rivera were Olympian figures in the Mexican art world. Perhaps Frida's greatest triumph was her first solo exhibition in Mexico City in 1953 (Color Plate 16). She was so ill that she had to be carried into the gallery on a stretcher and laid on a four-poster bed. Diego supported her as much as he could through her illness, putting up with her unpredictable behavior. She never lost her desire for him and confided to a friend shortly before her death:

"I only want three things in life: to live with Diego, to continue painting, and to belong to the Communist party.

Such hopes were short-lived. After a bout of pneumonia, Frida died two weeks later on July 13,1954.

THINK ABOUT IT

1. Describe the ways in which Frida Kahlo was obsessed with Diego Rivera.
2. Why did Frida refuse Diego's love-making after she married him the second time?

TALK ABOUT IT

3. Today, would Frida and Diego's relationship be considered conventional or unconventional?
4. Do you think Frida Kahlo's mixed ethnic heritage influenced her approach to her art? Why or why not?

WRITE ABOUT IT

5. Is it possible to love someone deeply, yet not be able to live with that person?
6. Have you ever loved someone as obsessively as Frida loved Diego? Describe the intensity of your feelings. Is obsessive love satisfying?

READ MORE ABOUT IT

Chadwick, Whitney. *Women, Art, and Society.* London, UK: Thames and Hudson, Ltd., 1990.

Helm, MacKinley. Modern Mexican Painters: Rivera, Orozco, Siqueiros and Other Artists of the Social Realist School. New York: Dover Publications, Inc., 1989.

Rivera, Guadalupe, and Colle, Marie-Pierre. *Frida's Fiestas: Recipes and Reminiscences of Life with Frida Kahlo.* New York: Clarkson Potter, Publishers, 1994.

Zamora, Martha. *Frida Kahlo: The Brush of Anguish.* San Francisco: Chronicle Books, 1990.

FRIDA AND DIEGO'S HOUSE IN THE MEXICO CITY SUBURB OF SAN ANGEL, WHERE THEY MOVED IN 1933.
The building symbolized their turbulent relationship; two separate houses linked at roof level by a bridge.

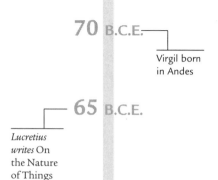

70 B.C.E.
Virgil born
in Andes

65 B.C.E.

*Lucretius
writes* On
the Nature
of Things

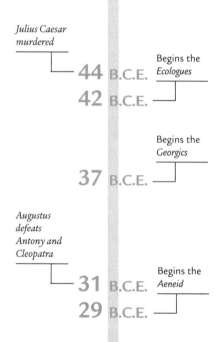

*Julius Caesar
murdered*

44 B.C.E.

Begins the
Ecologues

42 B.C.E.

Begins the
Georgics

37 B.C.E.

*Augustus
defeats
Antony and
Cleopatra*

Begins the
Aeneid

31 B.C.E.

29 B.C.E.

Virgil dies

19 B.C.E.

The Tragedy of Love

Publius Vergilius Maro, known as Virgil, was regarded by the Romans as their greatest poet — Rome's own national poet. Virgil was born at Andes, near Mantua, in Italy on October 15, 70 B.C.E. He received his education at Cremona, at Milan, and at Rome, where he studied rhetoric, philosophy, mathematics, and medicine. Virgil was an introvert who never married. His earliest work was the *Ecologues,* a collection of ten pastoral poems composed between 42 and 37 B.C.E. Virgil was twenty when Julius Caesar crossed the Rubicon and began the series of civil wars that did not end until Antony and Cleopatra were defeated by Augustus at the Battle of Actium in 31 B.C.E. During the civil wars, farmers were obliged to go to war, and as a consequence, their farms declined. The *Georgics,* written between 37 and 30 B.C.E., is an entreaty for the restoration of the agricultural life in Italy with which Virgil was so familiar and which he loved so well.

Virgil was the Roman Homer. Virgil's national epic poem, the *Aeneid,* recounts the trek of Aeneas, Rome's legendary founder, whose destiny, according to the Romans, was to civilize the world. The *Aeneid* begins with the destruction of the city of Troy by the Greeks in the 12th century B.C.E. Its hero is the Trojan Prince, Aeneas, who under divine guidance settled the first colony in Italy, from which Rome sprang. Aeneas is the son of the goddess of love, Venus, claimed by the first Roman emperor, Augustus Caesar, as his ancestor. Virgil gives Aeneas the virtues of devotion to duty and the singleness of purpose, creating him in the likeness of Augustus Caesar, Virgil's ideal Roman ruler. Augustus Caesar gave the Mediterranean world the foundation for two centuries of ordered government. Aeneas, like Augustus, is a selfless hero who battles, not for himself, but for the future of Rome. This poem, as well as Virgil's others, were so loved by the Ancient Romans that they were used as primary school textbooks.

The *Aeneid* includes a love story between Aeneas and Dido, Queen of Carthage in North Africa. During Aeneas' journeys, Dido and Aeneas fall in love, but Aeneas leaves Dido to pursue his destiny. Although he leaves her reluctantly, he leaves, nevertheless.

Few of us would make the great sacrifice Aeneas does, though many of us have shared in Dido's pain.

BUT MEANWHILE Queen Dido, gnawed by love's invisible fire, had long suffered from the deep wound draining her lifeblood. Again and again the thought of her hero's valour and the high nobility of his descent came forcibly back to her, and his countenance and his words stayed imprinted on her mind; the distress allowed her no peace and no rest. And now the next day's dawn was cleansing the world with Apollo's light and had parted the moist shadows in high heaven, when Dido spoke distractedly to the sister whose heart was one with hers: "Anna, Sister Anna, why am I poised frightened between fitful sleep and waking? What do you think of this new guest who has joined us in our home? He has a rare presence, and valiant indeed are his heart and his arms. I can well believe, and I have a right to believe, that his parentage is divine. An ignoble spirit is always revealed by fear. But — what torments from destiny and what horrors of war, endured to the bitterest end, were in his story! If I had not been irrevocably resolved never again to desire a union in wedlock with any man, since the time when death's treachery cheated me of my first love, and if all thought of the marriage-rite and the bridal-room had not become utter weariness to me, possibly this might have been the one temptation to which I could have fallen. Yes, Anna, I shall tell you my secret. Ever since the tragic death of my husband Sychaeus, whose sprinkled blood, which my own brother shed, desecrated our home, no one but this stranger ever made an impression on me, or stirred my heart to wavering. I can discern the old fire coming near again. But I could pray that the earth should yawn deep to engulf me, or the Father Almighty blast me to the Shades with a stroke of his thunder, deep down to those pallid Shades in darkest Erebos, before ever I violate my honour or

break its laws. For he who first united me with him took all love out of my life; and so it is he who should keep it close to his heart and guard it even in the grave." She had spoken her thoughts; and the tears welled, and wetted the fold of her garment which she held to her eyes.

Anna answered her: "Sister mine, whom I love more than life itself, will you live alone sorrowing and pining through all your youth, and never know the love of children and all that Venus gives? Do you really believe that this matters to ashes, to a ghost in a grave? Granted that in the past no African nor, before we came here, any Tyrian suitor could ever tempt you from your grief, for you scorned Iarbas and other chieftains, sons of this land so fertile in victorious fame; must you therefore now resist a love which appeals to you? Besides, you should remember who are the owners of the land in which is your settlement. You are hemmed in on one side of you by the cities of the unconquerable Gaetulians, by Numidians who know no curb, and by the forbidding quicksands, the Syrtes, and on the other by a waterless desert and the ferocious raiders from Barca. And I need not speak of the danger of war from Tyre, where your brother continues his threats. Now it is my belief that, when these Trojan ships kept course for Carthage before the wind, the gods themselves scaled their approval and Juno herself gave her support. And, Dido, only imagine, if you make this splendid marriage, what a great future lies in store for our city and our realm! With a Trojan army marching at our side, think what deeds of prowess will exalt the fame of Carthage! You have only to pray to the gods for their blessing and ensure their favour by sacrifice; and then entertain your guest freely, weaving pretexts for keeping him here, while his ships are still

damaged, and winter and Orion the rain-bringer spend their fury on the ocean under a forbidding sky."

By speaking so Anna set Dido's heart, already kindled, ablaze with a new access of love, gave new hope to tempt her wavering intention, and broke down her scruples. Their first act was to visit the shrines and pray to the gods for their indulgence at each altar in turn .... Poor Dido was afire, and roamed distraught all over her city; like a doe caught off her guard and pierced by an arrow from some armed shepherd, who from the distance had chased her amid Cretan woods and without knowing it had left in her his winged barb; so that she traversed in her flight forests and mountain tracks on Dicte, with the deadly reed fast in her flesh. Sometimes Dido would take Aeneas where her walls were being built, letting him see the great resources of Phoenicia and how far the construction of her city had progressed. And she would begin to speak her thoughts, but always check herself with the words half-spoken. At day's decline she would want the banqueting to begin again as before; she would insist beyond all reason on hearing yet once more the tale of Troy's anguish, and again she would hang breathless on the speaker's words. Afterwards, when they had parted, as the moon in her turn quenched her light to darkness and the setting stars counselled sleep, Dido mourned, lonely in the empty banqueting hall, and threw herself on the couch which he had left. He was away now, out of sight and hearing, but she still saw him and still heard his voice. Sometimes she held Ascanius close to her, under the spell of his resemblance to his father, and trying hard to escape from the love which she dared not tell. Meanwhile the partly built towers had ceased to rise. No more did young soldiers practise arms. The construction of harbours and impregnable battlements came to a stop. Work hung suspended on gigantic, menacing walls, and the sky-high cranes were still.

Now no sooner had Saturn's daughter, Jupiter's dear wife, seen that Dido was in the firm grip of her affliction and that no thought of her reputation any longer resisted her passion, than she approached Venus with a suggestion: "Well, you and that boy of yours certainly have fine fruits of victory to show, and great is the glory which you have won. Your distinction is indeed high and deserves to be famous, now that you two divinities have managed to trick one woman into defeat. At the same time I am not wholly unaware that you only view the peaceful home of tall Carthage with suspicion because you fear the strength of my city's defences. But how far do you mean to go? What need is there to continue so fierce a rivalry? Surely it is better for us to collaborate in arranging a permanent peace, sealed by a marriage-compact. You have gained the object on which you had set your heart. Dido has drunk the maddening poison into her very bones; she is ablaze with love. Let us therefore share this nation between us, each having equal authority in its government. Let Dido be free to become a Phrygian's slave-wife and to hand over her Tyrians into your power as the dowry."

Meanwhile Aurora arose and left the ocean. When her rays appeared, a select company issued from the city-gates. Out came the wide-meshed nets, the small stop-nets, and the hunting spears with their broad iron heads; and out dashed Massylian riders, and a pack of keen-scented hounds. The queen still lingered in her own room, while the noblest among the Carthaginians awaited her at the doors. Her spirited horse, caparisoned in a splendour of purple

and gold, pawed the ground and champed a foaming bit. At last she came, stepping forth with a numerous suite around her and clad in a Sidonian mantle with an embroidered hem. Golden was her quiver and the clasp which knotted her hair, and golden was the brooch which fastened the purple tunic at her neck. Up came the Trojan party, too, including the delighted Iulus. As the two processions met, Aeneas, by far the most handsome of them all, passed across to Dido's side. He was like Apollo …. Aeneas walked as alertly as he; and a grace like Apollo's shone from his noble face.

Soon a confused rumbling sound started in the sky. Then came the rain-clouds and showers mixed with hail. The hunters all scattered in alarm about the fields searching for shelter — the Tyrian retinue, the band of young Trojans, and the Dardan boy who was grandson of Venus. Torrents came streaming from the hills. Dido and Troy's chieftain found their way to the same cavern. Primaeval Earth and Juno, Mistress of the Marriage, gave their sign. The sky connived at the union; the lightning flared; on their mountain-peak nymphs raised their cry. On that day were sown the seeds of suffering and death. Henceforward Dido cared no more for appearances or her good name, and ceased to take any thought for secrecy in her love. She called it a marriage; she used this word to screen her sin.

Now, in great joy, turnout spread various talk among the peoples of Africa, repeating alike facts and fictions; how there had arrived one Aeneas, descended from the blood of Troy, and how the beautiful Dido had deigned to unite herself to him; and how they were now spending all the long winter together in comfort and self-indulgence, caught in the snare of shameful passion, with never a thought of their royal duty. Such was

the talk which this foul goddess everywhere inserted into the conversations of men. Next she turned her quick steps towards King Iarbas, spoke to him, set his thoughts on fire, and heaped fuel on his fury.

Mercury laced on his feet those golden sandals with wings to carry him high at the speed of the winds' swift blast over ocean and over land alike.

As soon as his winged feet had carried him as far as the hut-villages of Africa, he saw Aeneas engaged on the foundations of the citadel and the construction of new dwellings. He had a sword starred with golden-brown jasper, and wore a cloak of bright Tyrian purple draped from his shoulders, a present from a wealthy giver, Dido herself, who had made it, picking out the warp-thread with a line of gold. Mercury immediately delivered his message: "What, are you siting foundations for proud Carthage and building here a noble city? A model husband! For shame! You forget your destiny and that other kingdom which is to be yours. He who reigns over all the gods, he who sways all the earth and the sky by the power of his will, has himself sent me down to you from glittering Olympus. It is he who commanded me to carry this message to you swiftly through the air. What do you mean to do? What can you gain by living at wasteful leisure in African lands? If the glory of your great destiny is powerless to kindle your ardour, and if you will exert no effort to win fame for yourself, at least think of Ascanius, now growing up, and all that you hope from him as your heir, destined to rule in an Italy which shall become the Italy of Rome." With this stern rebuke, and even while he was still speaking, Mercury vanished from mortal vision and melted from sight into thin air.

Aeneas was struck dumb by the vision. He was out of his wits, his hair bristled with a shiver of fear, and his voice was checked in his throat. Already he was ardently wishing to flee from the land of his love and be gone; so violent had been the shock of this peremptory warning from the gods. But what could he do? How could he dare to speak to the infatuated queen, and win her round? What would be the best opening for him to choose? Rapidly he turned it over in his mind, inclining now to one plan and now to another, and hurriedly considering all the different aspects and possibilities. As he pondered, one policy seemed preferable to every other. He called to him Mnestheus, Sergestus, and the gallant Serestus: they were to fit out the fleet, make ready all their tackle, and muster their comrades on the shore, without giving any explanations, and concealing the reason for the change of plan. Meanwhile he would see Dido, for in her ignorance and goodness of heart she would never suspect that so deep a love could possibly be broken. So he would try to find the right approach and the least painful moment to speak, and discover a tactful way out of their predicament.

His men obeyed with pleasure and alacrity and began carrying out their orders. But no one can deceive a lover. The queen divined the intended deceit in advance. Before she was told, her intuition discerned what would happen and her fears were alive to every possible danger, real or unreal. In this nervous state the news came to her, brought, once more, by unholy Rumour, that the fleet was being equipped in preparation for a voyage. Furious, and quite unable to face the truth she ran in excited riot about Carthage .... At last Dido accosted Aeneas, speaking first, and denounced him:

"Traitor, did you actually believe that you could disguise so wicked a deed and leave my country without a word? And can nothing hold you, not our love, nor our once plighted hands, nor even the cruel death that must await your Dido? Are you so unfeeling that you labor at your fleet under a wintry sky, in haste to traverse the high seas in the teeth of the northerly gales? Why, had you not now been searching for a home which you have never seen in some alien land, and had ancient Troy itself been still standing, would you have been planning to sail even there over such tempestuous seas? Is it from me that you are trying to escape? Oh, by the tears which I shed, by your own plighted hand, for I have left myself, poor fool, no other appeal, and by our union, by the true marriage which it was to be, oh, if I was ever kind to you, or if anything about me made you happy, please, please, if it is not too late to beg you, have pity for the ruin of a home, and change your mind. It was because of you that I earned the hate of Africa's tribes and the lords of the Numidians, and the hostility of my own Tyrians also; and it was because of you that I let my honor die, the fair fame which used to be mine, and my only hope of immortality. In whose hands are you leaving me to face my death, my — Guest? I used to call you Husband, but the word has shrunk to Guest. What does the future hold for me now? My brother Pygmalion coming to demolish my walls, or this Gaetulian Iarbas, marrying me by capture? At least, if I had a son of yours conceived before you left, some tiny Aeneas to play about my hall and bring you back to me if only in his likeness, I might not then have felt so utterly entrapped and forsaken."

She finished. He, remembering Jupiter's warning, held his eyes steady, and strained to master the agony within him. At last he spoke, shortly: "Your Majesty, I shall never deny that I am in your debt for all those many acts of kindness which you may well account to me. And for as long as I have consciousness and breath of life controls my movement, I shall never tire, Elissa, of your memory. Now I shall speak briefly of the facts. I had no thought of hiding my present departure under any deceit. Do not imagine that. Nor have I ever made any marriage-rite my pretext, for I never had such a compact with you. If my destiny had allowed me to guide my life as I myself would have chosen, and solve my problems according to my own preference, I should have made the city of Troy, with its loved remembrances of my own folk, my first care; and, with Priam's tall citadel still standing, I should have refounded Troy's fortress to be strong once more after her defeat. But in fact Apollo at Grynium, where he gives his divination in Lycia by the lots, has insistently commanded me to make my way to Italy's noble land. Italy must be my love and my homeland now. If you a Phoenician, are faithful to your Carthiginian fortress here, content to look on no other City but this city in far-away Africa, what is the objection if Trojans settle in Italy? It is no sin, if we, like you, look for a kingdom in a foreign country. Each time the night shrouds the earth in its moist shadows, each time the fiery stars arise, the anxious wraith of my father Anchises warns me in sleep, and I am afraid. My son Ascanius also serves as a warning to me; I think of his dear self, and of the wrong which I do him in defrauding him of his Italian kingdom, where Fate has given him his lands. And now Jove himself has sent the Spokesman of the Gods — this I swear to you by my son's life and by my father — who flew swiftly through the air, and delivered the command to me. With my own eyes I saw the divine messenger in clearest light entering the city gate, and heard his voice with my own ears. Cease, therefore, to upset yourself, and me also, with these protests. It is not by my own choice that I voyage onward to Italy."

Throughout this declaration Dido had remained standing, turned away from Aeneas but glaring at him over her shoulder with eyes which roved about his whole figure in a voiceless stare, then her fury broke: "Traitor, no goddess was ever your mother, nor was it Dardanus who founded your line. No, your parent was Mount Caucasus, rugged, rocky, and hard, and tigers of Hyrcarnia nursed you .... For what need have I of concealment now? Why hold myself in check any longer, as if there could be anything worse to come? ... Has he spared a sigh or a look in response to my weeping, or has he once softened, or shed a tear of pity for one who loved him? Depth beyond depth of iniquity! Neither Supreme Juno, nor the Father who is Saturn's son, can possibly look with the impartial eyes of justice on what is happening now. No faith is left sure in the wide world. I welcomed him, a shipwrecked beggar, and like a fool I allowed him to share my royal place. I saved his comrades from death and gave him back his lost fleet .... The Furies have me now, they burn, they drive ... ! So, now, it seems, he has his orders from Apollo's own Lycian oracle, and next even the Spokesman of the Gods is sent by Jove himself to deliver through the air to him the same ghastly command! So I am to believe that the High Powers exercise their minds about such a matter and let concern for it disturb the calm! Oh, I am not holding you. I do not dispute your words. Go, quest for Italy before the winds; sail over the waves in search of your kingdom. But I still believe that, if there is any power for righteousness in Heaven, you will drink to the dregs the cup of punishment amid sea-rocks, and as you

suffer cry 'Dido' again and again. Though far, yet I shall be near, haunting you with flames of blackest pitch. And when death's chill has parted my body from its breath, wherever you go my spectre will be there. You will have your punishment, you villain. And I shall hear; the news will reach me deep in the world of death." She did not finish, but at these words broke off sharply. She hurried in her misery away and hid from sight, leaving Aeneas anxious and hesitant, and longing to say much more to her. Dido fainted, and fell; and her maids took her up, carried her to her marble bedroom, and laid her on her bed.

Meanwhile Aeneas the True longed to allay her grief and dispel her sufferings with kind words. Yet he remained obedient to the divine command, and with many a sigh, for he was shaken to the depths by the strength of his love, returned to his ships. Vigorously indeed the Trojans set to work. They were soon launching their tall galleys all along the beach .... What must have been Dido's thoughts when she saw all this movement, and how bitterly must she have sighed as she looked from her commanding citadel, and discerned the lively bustle along the shore and all the turmoil of loud confusion on the sea? Ali, merciless Love, is there any length to which you cannot force the human heart to go? For Love now drove Dido to have recourse to tears again, and again to try what entreaties might do, subjecting pride to passion in a last appeal, in case she had still left some way unexplored, and was going to a needless death. The tears rolled down, but without effect.

It was final. Dido was lost; and she saw with horror the fate starkly confronting her. Her one prayer was now for death. The sight of heaven's vault was only weariness to her. And, as if to steel her will to fulfill her de-

sign and to part from the light of day, as she laid her offerings on the altars where incense burned, she saw a dreadful sight; for the holy waters turned to black and the poured wine by some sinister transformation was changed into blood. She told no one, not even her sister, what she had seen. And, furthermore, there was in her palace a marble chapel, sacred to her first husband, which she venerated with utmost love, keeping it decorated with snowy fleeces and festal greenery. Now from this chapel, when night held the world in darkness, she thought that she distinctly heard cries, as of her husband calling to her. And often on a rooftop a lonely owl would sound her deathly lamentation, drawing out her notes into a long wail. Then many presages of ancient seers shocked her to panic by their dread warnings. She would have nightmares of a furious Aeneas pursuing her, and driving her wild with fear, and of being left utterly alone, and travelling companionless a long road, searching for Tyrian friends in a deserted land.

So agony prevailed; and Dido was possessed by demon-powers. Having made her decision for death, she first worked out, all by herself, the time and the means. Then, with a calm and hopeful expression to conceal her plan, she accosted her distressed sister and spoke to her: "Sister, Anna, congratulate me! For I have found the way which will either give him back to me or release me from loving him. Dear Anna, I swear to you by the gods, I swear by you and your own sweet life that it is against my will that I arm myself with magic. Now, build me a tall funeral pyre. Build it in the center of our home under the open sky but out of view. Lay on it the arms of the false man, which he left hanging from a wall in our bridal room, and all the garments which he wore, besides; and you must also place on it the bridal bed which was my ruin. I choose to destroy whatever can remind me of one who must never be mentioned. Besides, such is the advice of the priestess." After saying this she fell silent, and her face suddenly paled. It never occurred to Anna that her sister was using this strange rite to veil her own impending death. She could not herself imagine so violent a passion, and had no fear of anything worse happening now than had happened when Sychaeus died. So she made the preparations, as Dido had asked.

Presently the pyre had been built with logs of holm-oak and pine. It was vast, rising to a great height, and it stood in the center of the building. The queen had festooned the hall with flower-chains, and wreathed the pyre with the greenery of death. On it was the bed, and there she placed a sword which Aeneas had left, with garments which he had worn, and a portrait of him, knowing all the time what was to be. Around it were altars. The priestess, hair astream, told in a voice like thunder the names of her thrice-hundred gods, told Erebos and the Void, and Hecate of three forms, who is Diana the maiden of the triple countenance. She had sprinkled water, supposed to be from the fount of Avernus. Herbs, reaped with bronzen sickles by moonlight and bursting with a black poisonous milk, were gathered there, and with them a love-charm ripped from the brow of a baby foal before the mother could take it. Close to the high altar stood Dido, holding the sacred meal and lifting pure hands above, with garment girt back and one foot unsandalled. And, soon to die, she called on the gods and the stars which know fate's secrets to hear her. And she added a prayer to any Power there may be, some Power watchful and fair, with a thought for lovers whose love is not matched well.

It was night, and tired creatures all over the world were enjoying kindly sleep. But not so the Phoenician queen. Her accursed spirit could not relax into sleeping, or welcome darkness into her eyes or brain. Instead, her torment redoubled; her love came back again and again, and heaved in ocean-tides of rage. And she began yet once more to pursue her thoughts, communing with herself in her heart: "There! What is there for me to do? Risk mockery by returning to my former suitors, sound their feelings, and plead humbly with some Numidian to marry me, though time after time I have scorned to think of one of them as a husband? Or instead should I sail with the Trojan fleet and submit to Trojan orders however harsh? Am I so sure that they are pleased with the aid and relief which I gave them, that they remember, and that their gratefulness for what I did then is still alive? But indeed, even granted that I wished it, would they let me come, and welcome me to their ships? They are arrogant, and hate me. Lost fool, can you not see? Can you even now not realize how treacherous Laomedon's nation can be? Besides, if I sail with these mariners, who are so triumphant now at their departure, do I go alone, or do I take with me all my Tyrian friends, thronging round me when I go to join the Trojans? If so, how can I order them to spread their sails to the winds and force them to voyage once more out onto the ocean? It was all that I could do to uproot them from their former city, Sidon. No. You have deserved death and you must die. Only the blade can save you from the agony … O Anna, I have been mad; but it was you who first laid on me this load of suffering, for you gave way to my tears, and set me at the mercy of my foe. If only I could have been allowed to pass my life free from reproach as the wild animals do, without any

wedding, and in no danger of anguish like mine …. And the vow which I made to the ashes of Sychaeus is broken too." Such were the terrible words of grief which burst from Dido's heart.

Meanwhile Aeneas, who had now settled his plans for sailing and completed his preparations, was lying asleep on his ship's stern. As he slept he again had a vision of the god, who returned in countenance as before and was like Mercury in every feature, in his voice and complexion, his blond hair, and limbs with the grace of youth. As Aeneas gazed, Mercury repeated his warning: "Son of the Goddess, can you, with so great a disaster impending, remain asleep, and not discern the dangers which wait ready to break about your head? Fool! Can you not hear the breath of the favouring west winds? She plans in her thought a fearful and treacherous wrong. In her a violent rage surges and surges again, and she is resolved to die. Will you not hasten away while it is not too late for hastening? You will soon see a confusion of wreckage on the sea, the cruel glare of fire-brands burning bright, and the whole shore ablaze, if dawn finds you still lingering here. Ho! Come, have done with delays. Women were ever things of many changing moods." So he spoke, and then melted into the black darkness.

Aeneas was shocked indeed by the sudden apparition. He leapt up and gave his comrades the alarm: 'Hasten, men! Awake! Take your places for rowing. Quick, unfurl your sails! For, see! Again a god has descended from high heaven, and again he stings us in to haste. We must hack through our twisted hawsers, and flee. We follow you, holy Deity, whoever you may truly be, and we joyfully obey your command, as before. Be with us and graciously aid us. Bring us favors from the stars of heaven." With the words he quickly unsheathed his sword and struck the cables with the flashing blade. One ardor seized them all. They heaved and they hurried. Not one remained on shore. The water was hidden beneath the fleet. They bent to it, churned the foam, and swept the blue surface of the sea.

By now Aurora, rising, had left the saffron bed of Tithonus and was sprinkling her fresh light on the world. From her watch-tower the queen saw the white gleam of dawn, and saw the fleet moving forward with sails square to the wind. She realized that the shore and the harbor were empty, without a single oarsman. At the sight, she struck her beautiful breast, three times struck it and then a fourth, she tore her golden hair, and she cried aloud: "Ah, Jupiter! Is this stranger to make a mock of my realm, and calmly go? See his faithfulness to his plighted word! And yet they say that he carries with him the gods of his ancestral home, and bowed his shoulders to bear his old and feeble father! Could I not have seized him, torn him limb from limb, and scattered the pieces on the waves? And put his comrades to the sword—yes, and killed Ascanius and served him up to be his father's meal? Ah, but the fortune of such a fight was never certain. Uncertain, then. But whom had I to fear, having, in any event, to die? I might have taken firebrands into their camp and set all their ships' decks blazing. I could have quenched the life of son, of father, and of all their line. And then, to crown all, I could have flung myself to death .... Angels of Death awaiting Elissa! Neither love nor compact shall there be between the nations, And from my dead bones may some Avenger arise to Persecute with fire and sword those settlers from Troy, soon or in aftertime, whenever the strength is given! Let your shores oppose their shores,

your waves their waves, your arms their arms. That is my imprecation. Let them fight, they, and their sons' sons, for ever!"

Such was her curse. And now she turned to consider every course of action, for she wanted, as quickly as might be, to break off her living in day's hated light. She spoke shortly to Barce, who had been Sychaeus' old nurse — her own nurse, dark ashes now, had been left in the ancient homeland — : "Nurse, dear, ask Anna my sister to come to me here. And tell her she should hasten to sprinkle river-water over her, and bring with her the victims and all else that is needed for the atonement which I have been commanded to make. Let her come, prepared as I say; and you yourself should wreathe your brow with a ribbon of piety. It is my intention to complete certain rites to Stygian Jupiter, which I have formally prepared and begun, and to put an end to my sorrow by committing to the flames the pyre which holds the Trojan's life." So she spoke. Barce, with all an old woman's interest, quickened her pace.

But Dido, in trembling haste and frantic at her desperate design, burst through the doorway into the inner room. Her eyes were reddened and rolling, her cheeks quivered under a flush, and she was pale with the pallor of imminent death. In a mad dash, she climbed the high funeral pile, and unsheathed the Trojan sword, a gift never meant for such a use as this. Her sight rested on the garments which had come from Troy, and on the bed with its memories.

She paused a little for tears and for a thought; and she cast herself down on the bed, and there spoke her last words: "Sweet relics, sweet so long as God and Destiny allowed, now receive my lifebreath, and set me free from this suffering. I have lived my

life and finished the course which Fortune allotted me. Now my wraith shall pass in state to the world below. I have established a noble city. I have lived to see my own ramparts built. I have avenged my husband and punished the brother who was our foe. Happy, all too happy, should I have been, if only the Dardan ships had never reached my coast!" With this cry she buried her face in the bed, and continued: "I shall die, and die unavenged; but die I shall. Yes, yes; this is the way I like to go into the dark. And may the heartless Trojan, far out on the deep, drink in the sight of my fire and take with him the evil omen of my death."

There she ended. And even while she still spoke she had fallen upon the blade. Soon her attendants saw her with blood foaming about the sword and the stains of it on her hands. A cry rose to the palace-roof. Carthage was stricken by the shock and Rumor ran riot in the town. Lamentation and sobbing and women's wailing rang through the houses, and high heaven echoed with the loud mourning; as if some enemy had broken through and all Carthage, or ancient Tyre, were falling, with the flames rolling madly up over dwellings of gods and men. Her sister heard, and the breath left her. Marring her cheeks with her fingernails and bruising her breast with her clenched hands, she dashed in frightened haste through the crowds, found Dido at the very point of death, and cried out to her — : "0 Sister, so this was the truth? You planned to deceive me! Was this what your pyre, your altars, and the fires were to mean for me? How shall I begin reproaching you for forsaking me so? Did you scorn your own sister and not want her with you when you died? You should have asked me to share your fate, and then one same hour, one agony of the blade, might have taken us both. To think that with my own hands I even built the pyre, and cried loud upon our ancestral gods, only to be cruelly separated from you as you lay in death! Sister, you have destroyed my life with your own, and the lives of our people and Sidon's nobility, and your whole city too. Come, let me see your wounds — I must wash them clean with water, and gather with my own lips any last hovering breath." While speaking she had climbed to the top of the steps and clasped her sister, who was still just breathing, to her breast, and fondled her, sobbing, and trying to stanch the dark blood with her dress. Dido attempted to raise her heavy eyes again, but failed; and the deep wound in her breast, where the sword stood planted, breathed loud. Three times she rose, supporting herself on her elbows, but each time she rolled back onto the bed. With roaming eyes she looked to high heaven for the daylight, and found it, and gave a sigh.

But Juno, who has all power, took pity on the long anguish of her difficult death, and sent Iris down from Olympus to release the wrestling spirit from the twined limbs. For since she perished neither by destiny nor by a death deserved, but tragically, before her day, in the mad heat of a sudden passion, Proserpine had not yet taken a golden lock from her head, to assign her life to Stygian Orcus. So therefore Iris, saffron-winged, sparkling like dew and trailing a thousand colours as she caught the light of the sun, flew down across the sky. She hovered over Dido's head: "By command I take this lock as an offering to Pluto; and I release you from the body which was yours." Speaking so, she held out a hand and cut the lock. At once, all the warmth fell away, and the life passed into the moving air.

THINK ABOUT IT

1. Is Aeneas heartless in not considering Dido's feelings? Does he behave like a son of Venus should?

2. Why do some people put their personal goals ahead of people they love?

TALK ABOUT IT

3. Aeneas was from Troy in Asia Minor, and Dido from Carthage in North Africa. Does love transcend ethnic boundaries? Should it?

4. Sex and love are often seen as synonymous. Do you believe that they are?

WRITE ABOUT IT

5. Have you been in love with someone who loves their job or something else more than you? Describe how you dealt with that situation or how you think you would deal with it.

6. What is your basis for loving someone? Is it physical appearance, status, wealth, inner beauty, or something else?

READ MORE ABOUT IT

Garrison, D. H. *The Language of Virgil.* New York: Peter Lang Publishing, Inc., 1986.

Gransden, *K. W, Virgil's Iliad: An Essay on Epic Narrative.* Cambridge: Cambridge University Press, 1985.

Jackson, W E trans. *Virgil: The Aeneid.* New York: Penguin Books, 1956.

Williams, Gordon. *Techniques and Ideas in the Aeneid.* New Haven, CT: Yale Univ. Press, 1985.

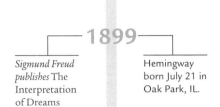

1899

Sigmund Freud publishes The Interpretation of Dreams

Hemingway born July 21 in Oak Park, IL.

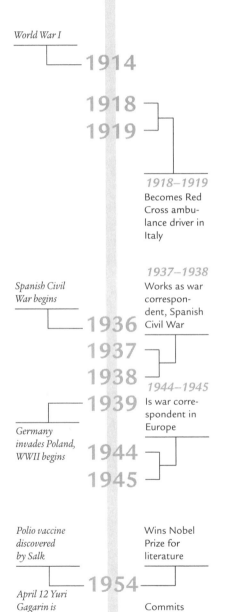

World War I

1914

1918

1919

1918–1919
Becomes Red Cross ambulance driver in Italy

1937–1938
Works as war correspondent, Spanish Civil War

Spanish Civil War begins

1936

1937

1938

1939

1944–1945
Is war correspondent in Europe

Germany invades Poland, WWII begins

1944

1945

Polio vaccine discovered by Salk

Wins Nobel Prize for literature

1954

April 12 Yuri Gagarin is first man to orbit earth

Commits suicide July 2, Ketchum, ID

1961

ERNEST HEMINGWAY

Hills Like White Elephants

One of America's best known writers is Ernest Hemingway. He became famous early in his career for his realistic portrayal of his subjects and for his clear, direct style of writing. In his memoir, *A Moveable Feast,* Ernest Hemingway explains his philosophy of writing: "I decided that I would write one story about each thing I knew about. I was trying to do this all the time I was writing, and it was good and severe discipline." Hemingway credited his self-discipline and his desire "to write one true sentence" as the sources of his success. However, his goal to write about what he knew drove him to live dangerously. From driving ambulances in World War I, to dodging bullets as a war correspondent, or hunting big game in Africa, Hemingway sought personal experiences from which he could fashion his stories. His realistic portrayals of life led to a string of best-selling novels, five of which — *A Farewell to Arms, For Whom the Bell Tolls, To Have and Have Not, The Sun Also Rises,* and *The Old Man and the Sea* — were made into movies.

In 1953, he received the Pulitzer Prize for his novel, *The Old Man and the Sea,* and in 1954, he was awarded the Nobel Prize for Literature. During the last years of his life, he could not write as he wanted. His inability to match his earlier successes either caused his depression, or resulted from it, and led him to commit suicide in 1961. In "Hills Like White Elephants," a theme appears which Hemingway explores in several of his novels, the relationship between two people involved in an affair. In this very short story, Hemingway displays the terse, economical style which is one of his greatest gifts to literature.

THE HILLS ACROSS the valley of the Ebro were long and white. On this side there was no shade and no trees and the station was between two lines of rails in the sun. Close against the side of the station there was the warm shadow of the building and a curtain, made of strings of bamboo beads, hung across the open door into the bar, to keep out flies. The American and the girl with him sat at a table in the shade, outside the building. It was very hot and the express from Barcelona would come in forty minutes. It stopped at this junction for two minutes and went on to Madrid.

"What should we drink?" the girl asked. She had taken off her hat and put it on the table.

"It's pretty hot," the man said.

"Let's drink beer."

"*Dos cervezas,*" the man said into the curtain.

"Big ones?" a woman asked from the doorway.

"Yes. Two big ones."

The woman brought two glasses of beer and two felt pads. She put the felt pads and the beer glasses on the table and looked at the man and the girl. The girl was looking off at the line of hills. They were white in the sun and the country was brown and dry.

"They look like white elephants," she said.

"I've never seen one," the man drank his beer.

"No, you wouldn't have."

"I might have," the man said. "Just because you say I wouldn't have doesn't prove anything."

The girl looked at the bead curtain. "They've painted something on it," she said. "What does it say?"

"Anis del Toro. It's a drink."

"Could we try it?"

The man called "Listen" through the curtain. The woman came out from the bar.

"Four reales."

"We want two Anis del Toro."

"With water?"

"Do you want it with water?"

"I don't know," the girl said. "Is it good with water?"

"It's all right."

"You want them with water?" asked the woman.

"Yes, with water."

"It tastes like licorice," the girl said and put the glass down.

"That's the way with everything."

"Yes," said the girl. "Everything tastes of licorice. Especially all the things you've waited so long for, like absinthe."

"Oh, cut it out."

"You started it," the girl said. "I was being amused. I was having a fine time."

"Well, let's try and have a fine time."

"All right. I was trying. I said the mountains looked like white elephants. Wasn't that bright?"

"That was bright."

"I wanted to try this new drink: That's all we do, isn't it — look at things and try new drinks?"

"I guess so."

The girl looked across at the hills.

"They're lovely hills," she said. "They don't really look like white elephants. I just meant the coloring of their skin through the trees."

"Should we have another drink?"

"All right."

The warm wind blew the bead curtain against the table.

"The beer's nice and cool," the man said.

"It's lovely," the girl said.

"It's really an awfully simple operation, jig," the man said. "It's not really an operation at all."

The girl looked at the ground the table legs rested on.

"I know you wouldn't mind it, jig. It's really not anything. It's just to let the air in."

The girl did not say anything.

"I'll go with you and I'll stay with you all the time. They just let the air in and then it's all perfectly natural."

"Then what will we do afterward?"

"We'll be fine afterward. Just like we were before."

"What makes you think so?"

"That's the only thing that bothers us. It's the only thing that's made us unhappy."

The girl looked at the bead curtain, put her hand out and took hold of two of the strings of beads.

"And you think then we'll be all right and be happy."

"I know we will. You don't have to be afraid. I've known lots of people that have done it."

"So have I," said the girl. "And afterward they were all so happy."

"Well," the man said, "if you don't want to you don't have to. I wouldn't have you do it if you didn't want to. But I know it's perfectly simple."

"And you really want to?"

"I think it's the best thing to do. But I don't want you to do it if you don't really want to."

"And if I do it you'll be happy and things will be like they were and you'll love me?"

"I love you now. You know I love you."

"I know. But if I do it, then it will be nice again if I say things are like white elephants, and you'll like it?"

"I'll love it. I love it now but I just can't think about it. You know how I get when I worry."

"If I do it you won't ever worry?"

"I won't worry about that because it's perfectly simple."

"Then I'll do it. Because I don't care about me."

"What do you mean?"

"I don't care about me."

"Well, I care about you."

"Oh, yes. But I don't care about me. And I'll do it and then everything will be fine."

"I don't want you to do it if you feel that way."

The girl stood up and walked to the end of the station. Across, on the other side, were fields of grain and trees along the banks of the Ebro. Far away, beyond the river, were mountains. The shadow of a cloud moved across the field of grain and she saw the river through the trees.

"And we could have all this," she said. "And we could have everything and every day we make it more impossible."

"What did you say?"

"I said we could have everything."

"We can have everything."

"No, we can't."

"We can have the whole world."

"No, we can't."

"We can go everywhere."

"No, we can't. It isn't ours any more."

"It's ours."

"No, it isn't. And once they take it away, you never get it back."

"But they haven't taken it away."

"We'll wait and see."

"Come on back in the shade," he said. "You mustn't feel that way."

"I don't feel any way," the girl said. "I just know things."

"I don't want you to do anything that you don't want to do."

"Nor that isn't good for me," she said. "I know. Could we have another beer?"

"All right. But you've got to - realize—."

"I realize," the girl said. "Can't we maybe stop talking? "

They sat down at the table and the girl looked across at the hills on the dry side of the valley and the man looked at her and at the table.

"You've got to realize," he said, "that I don't want you to do it if you don't want to. I'm perfectly willing to go through with it if it means anything to you …

"Doesn't it mean anything to you? We could get along."

"Of course it does. But I don't want anybody but you. I don't want any one else. And I know it's perfectly simple."

"Yes, you know it's perfectly simple."

"It's all right for you to say that, but I do know."

"Would you do something for me now?"

"I'd do anything for you."

"Would you please please please please please please please stop talking?"

He did not say anything but looked at the bags against the wall of the station. There were labels on them from all the hotels where they had spent nights.

"But I don't want you to," he said, "I don't care anything about it."

"I'll scream," the girl said.

The woman came out through the curtains with two glasses of beer and put them down on the damp felt pads. "The train comes in five minutes," she said.

"What did she say?" asked the girl.

"That the train is coming in five minutes."

The girl smiled brightly at the woman, to thank her.

" I'd better take the bags over to the other side of the station," the man said. She smiled at him.

"All right. Then come back and we'll finish the beer."

He picked up the two heavy bags and carried them around the station to the other tracks. He looked up the tracks but could not see the train. Coming back, he walked through the barroom, where people waiting for the train were drinking. He drank an Anis at the bar and looked at the people. They were all waiting reasonably for the train. He went out through the bead curtain. She was sitting at the table and smiled at him.

"Do you feel better?" he asked.

"I feel fine," she said. "There's nothing wrong with me. I feel fine."

THINK ABOUT IT

1. Do you think the girl wants to have the abortion? Do you think the man wants her to have it?

2. Why doesn't the couple talk openly and honestly about what each is feeling?

TALK ABOUT IT

3. Do you think the relationship portrayed in the story is the kind of relationship most American couples have today? Do you think this kind of relationship is limited to American couples?

4. Why do the man and the girl think they are in love? Do you believe they are?

WRITE ABOUT IT

5. Do you think that the girl really believes that after she has the abortion "things will be like they were"?

6. Would you do anything for someone whom you love? If not, where would you draw the line? Why? Explain your reasons.

READ MORE ABOUT IT

Hemingway, Ernest. *A Farewell to Arms.* New York: Charles Scribner & Sons, 1929.

Hemingway, Ernest. *The Old Man and the Sea.* New York: Charles Scribner & Sons, 1952.

hemingway, Ernest. *The Complete Short Stories of Ernest Hemingway: The Finca Vigia Edition.* New York: Charles Scribner & Sons, 1987.

Hemingway, Ernest. *A Moveable Feast.* New York: Charles Scribner & Sons, 1964.

Color Plate 1A
THE PYRAMIDS AT GIZA, C. 2500 B.C.E.
A man holds a stick or sword aloft near the Giza Pyramids outside of Cairo, Egypt.

Color Plate 1B
**ZOZER'S STEP
PYRAMID**
Egypt

Color Plate 2
SELF-PORTRAIT, c. 1640
Rembrandt van Rijn
Oil on canvas, 40¼ × 31½ in.
National Gallery, London, England

Color Plate 3
SELF-PORTRAIT, C. 1659
Rembrandt van Rijn
Oil on canvas, 33¼ × 26 in.
National Gallery of Art, Washington, D.C.

Color Plate 4
SELF-PORTRAIT, C. 1669
Rembrandt van Rijn
Oil on canvas, 33¾ × 27½ in.
National Gallery, London, England

Color Plate 5
THE SISTINE CHAPEL CEILING, 1508–1512
Michaelangelo Buonarroti
Fresco, 44 × 128 ft.
Rome, Italy

Color Plate 6
DETAIL OF THE FLOOD, 1508–1512
Michaelangelo Buonarroti
Fresco
The Sistine Chapel Ceiling, Rome, Italy

Color Plate 7
THE DELPHIC SIBYL, 1508–1512
Michaelangelo Buonarroti
Fresco
The Sistine Chapel Ceiling, Rome, Italy

Color Plate 8
THE TAJ MAHAL
White Marble
Agra, India

Color Plate 9
CASA DEL MENANDRO,
c. 50 B.C.E.
Pompeii, Italy

Color Plate 10
CASA DEI VETTI, DETAIL OF THE WALL PAINTING, C. 50 B.C.E.
Pompeii, Italy

Color Plate 11
**THE CATHEDRAL AT CHARTRES,
1194–1240**
Chartres, France

Color Plate 12
**AMBULATORY, THE
CATHEDRAL AT
CHARTRES,
1194–1240**
Limestone and Stained Glass,
Chartres, France

Color Plate 13
NORTH ROSE WINDOW,
CATHEDRAL OF CHARTRES, 1223–1226
Stained Glass, 44 ft. in diameter · Chartres, France

Color Plate 14
SOFT CONSTRUCTION WITH BOILED BEANS, 1936
Salvador Dali
Oil on Canvas, 39⅜ × 39 in.
The Philadelphia Museum of Art,
Philadelphia, Pennsylvania

Color Plate 15
TRES DE MAYO, 1808 EN MADRID, 1814
Francisco de Goya
Oil on Canvas, 8 ft. 9 in. × 13 ft 4 in.
Prado Museum, Madrid, Spain

Color Plate 16
WHAT THE WATER GAVE ME, 1938
Frida Kahlo
Oil on Canvas, 38 × 30 in.
Isadore Ducasse Fine Arts, New York

Color Plate 17
YOUNG MOTHER SEWING, c. 1900
Mary Cassatt
Oil on Canvas, 36⅜ × 29 in.
The Metropolitan Museum of Art,
New York, NY

Color Plate 18
**ALEXANDER J. CASSATT AND HIS
SON, ROBERT ROBERT KELSO
CASSATT, 1885**
Mary Cassatt
Oil on Canvas, 39 × 32 in.
The Philadelphia Museum of Art,
Philadelphia, PA

WILLIAM SHAKESPEARE

Othello

William Shakespeare was the success story of the Elizabethan Age. Born in Stratford-on-Avon in 1564, he received his basic education in the school there before turning his attention to the fame and glory to be won in the newly revitalized theater district of London. He began as an actor, but soon proved to be an accomplished playwright, producing a corpus of between thirty-six to thirty-eight plays over a period of twenty-three years. Everyone who speaks English has heard some lines from Shakespeare's works, whether it is Hamlet's woeful "to be or not to be," Romeo's "what light through yonder window breaks," or Antony's "Friends, Romans, countrymen, lend me your ears."

 Othello, probably written in 1604, is one of Shakespeare's plays which fits in well with Aristotle's definition of a tragedy. A tragedy is a drama treating a serious subject involving persons of significance. The hero has some flaw (known in Greek as *hamartia*) which causes the events to unfold in a course that leads to destruction and despair. Othello, a Moor and respected military leader, marries Desdemona, the daughter of a leading Venetian senator. Her father believes that she has been tricked into marrying this foreigner, but relents when she declares her complete and unconditional love for Othello. The people of Venice then implore Othello to go off on a military campaign on their behalf. Rather than be left behind, Desdemona wishes to go along on the expedition.

 A key figure in the plot of *Othello* is Iago, a member of Othello's troops. He has been passed over for promotion by Cassio who now serves as Othello's lieutenant. From the outset of the play, Iago plots to have his revenge on Cassio, Othello, and Desdemona who had once refused his advances. Iago cleverly plants the seed of suspicion in Othello's mind by suggesting that Desdemona might not be entirely faithful to him. Iago then sets Cassio up for a fall by getting him drunk and into a fight. Cassio falls out of favor with Othello, but appeals to Desdemona for help. She promises she will speak to her husband on his behalf. In the meantime, Iago has obtained a handkerchief which was given to Desdemona by Othello. Iago gives the handkerchief to Cassio and then allows Othello to think he has overheard a confession that Desdemona has had an affair with Cassio. Othello is outraged by the knowledge that he has been betrayed by his friend and his wife. While there is never a direct confrontation between Cassio and Othello, the circumstantial evidence seems to point to Cassio's guilt. In this play, the power of love takes a tragic turn and leads to the rather unfortunate events of the final scene that appears below.

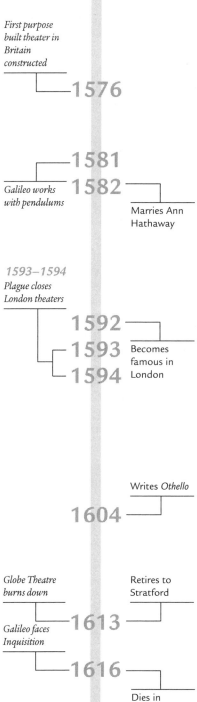

1564
Council of Trent ends
Shakespeare born in Stratford, England

First purpose built theater in Britain constructed
1576

1581
Galileo works with pendulums
1582
Marries Ann Hathaway

1593–1594 Plague closes London theaters

1592
1593 Becomes famous in
1594 London

Writes *Othello*
1604

Globe Theatre burns down
Retires to Stratford
1613
Galileo faces Inquisition

1616
Dies in Stratford

Act V Scene 2

Enter Othello (with a light) and Desdemona in her bed.

OTHELLO
  It is the cause, it is the cause,
    my soul.
  Let me not name it to you,
    you chaste stars.
  It is the cause. Yet I'll not
    shed her blood,
  Nor scar that whiter skin
    of hers than snow,
  And smooth as
    monumental[1] alabaster.
  Yet she must die,
    else[2] she'll betray more men.
  Put out the light, and then
    put out the light.
  If I quench thee,
    thou flaming minister,[3]
  I can again thy former light restore
  Should I[4] repent me.
    But once[5] put out thy light,
  Thou cunning'st[6] pattern of
    excelling nature,
  I know not where is that
    Promethean heat[7]
  That can thy light relume.[8]
    When I have plucked (the) rose,
  I cannot give it vital growth again.
  It needs must wither. I'll smell (it)
    on the tree.
  0 balmy breath, that dost
    almost persuade

justice[9] to break her sword! *[He
  kisses her.]* One more, one more.
Be thus when thou art dead.[10] and
  I will kill thee
And love thee after. One more, and
  (this) the last.

                              (He kisses her.)
So sweet was ne'er so fatal.
  I must weep,
But they are cruel tears.[11]
  This sorrow's heavenly:
It strikes where it doth love.
  She wakes.

DESDEMONA
  Who's there? Othello?

OTHELLO
  Ay, Desdemona.

DESDEMONA
  Will you come to bed, my lord?

OTHELLO
  Have you prayed tonight,
    Desdemona?

DESDEMONA
  Ay, my lord.

OTHELLO
  If you bethink yourself[12]
    of any crime[13]
  Unreconciled as yet to
    heaven and grace,
  Solicit for it straight.[14]

DESDEMONA
  Alack,[15] my lord,
  What may you mean by that?

OTHELLO
  Well, do it, and be brief.
    I will walk by.[16]
  I would not[17] kill thy
    unpreparèd spirit.
  No, (heaven) forfend![18]
    I would not kill thy soul.

DESDEMONA
  Talk you of killing?

OTHELLO
  Ay, I do.

DESDEMONA
  Then heaven have mercy on me.

OTHELLO
  Amen, with all my heart.

DESDEMONA
  If you say (so,) I hope
    you will not kill me.

OTHELLO
  Humh.

DESDEMONA
  And yet I fear you,
    for you're fatal then
  When your eyes roll so. Why I
    should fear I know not,
  Since guiltiness I know not,
    but yet I feel I fear.

OTHELLO
  Think on thy sins.

DESDEMONA
  They are loves I bear to you.

OTHELLO
  Ay, and for that thou diest.

DESDEMONA
  That death's unnatural
    that kills for loving.
  Alas, why gnaw you so
    your nether lip?
  Some bloody passion

---

1 **monumental:** used in making monuments

2 **else:** otherwise

3 **flaming minister:** the torch that serves me

4 **Should I:** if I should

5 **But once:** but if I once

6 **cunning'st:** most artfully created; excelling; superior, surpassing

7 **Promethean heat:** Shakespeare seems to be combining two separate Greek myths about Prometheus, one in which Prometheus gave fire to humankind and one in which he was the creator of humankind. **heat:** fire; spark of life

8 **relume:** relight

---

9 **justice:** justice is often depicted as a woman in a blindfold with a set of scales in one hand and a sword in the other.

10 **fatal:** deadly

11 **cruel tears:** tears that show no pity

12 **bethink yourself:** think

13 **crime:** sin

14 **Solicit for it straight:** pray for heavenly grace at once

15 **Alack:** alas

---

16 **walk by:** stand aside

17 **would not:** do not wish to

18 **forfend:** forbid

shakes your very frame.
These are portents,[19]
    but yet I hope, I hope
They do not point on me.[20]

OTHELLO
Peace, and be still.

DESDEMONA
I will so. What's the matter?

OTHELLO
That handkerchief
Which I so loved, and gave thee,
    thou gav'st to
Cassio.

DESDEMONA
No, by my life and soul!
    Send for the man
And ask him.

OTHELLO
Sweet soul, take heed,
    take heed of perjury.
Thou art on thy deathbed.

DESDEMONA
Ay, but not yet to die.

OTHELLO
(Yes,) presently.[21]
Therefore confess thee freely of
    thy sin.
For to deny each article[22] with oath
Cannot remove nor choke the
    strong conception[23]
That I do groan withal.[24]
    Thou art to die.

DESDEMONA
(Then Lord) have mercy on me!

OTHELLO
I say "Amen."

DESDEMONA
And have you mercy, too. I never did
Offend[25] you in my life,
    never loved Cassio
But with such general warranty
    of heaven
As I might love.[26] I never
    gave him token.[27]

OTHELLO
By heaven, I saw my
    handkerchief in 's[28] hand!
O perjured woman, thou dost
    stone my heart[29]
And (mak'st) me call what I intend
    to do
A murder, which I thought a
    sacrifice!
I saw the handkerchief!

DESDEMONA
He found it, then.
I never gave it him.
    Send for him hither.
Let him confess[30] a truth.

OTHELLO
He hath confessed.[31]

DESDEMONA
What, my lord?

OTHELLO
That he hath used thee.[32]

DESDEMONA
How? Unlawfully?

OTHELLO
Ay.

DESDEMONA
He will not say so.

OTHELLO
No. His mouth is stopped.
Honest Iago hath
    ta'en order[33] for 't.

DESDEMONA
O, my fear interprets.
    What, is he dead?

OTHELLO
Had all his hairs been lives,
    my great revenge
Had stomach[34] for them all.

DESDEMONA
Alas, he is betrayed,
    and I undone.[35]

                                    [She weeps.]

OTHELLO
Out, strumpet! Weep'st thou for
    him to my face?

DESDEMONA
O banish me, my lord,
    but kill me not!

OTHELLO
Down, strumpet!

DESDEMONA
Kill me tomorrow.
    let me live tonight.

OTHELLO
Nay, if you strive—

DESDEMONA
But half an hour!

[OTHELLO Being done, there is no pause.]

DESDEMONA
But while I say one prayer!

OTHELLO
It is too late.
(He) smothers her.

---

[19] **portents:** omens

[20] **point on me:** predict my future

[21] **presently:** immediately

[22] **each article:** each item or count in the charge against you (a legal term)

[23] **conception:** idea, thought

[24] **groan withal:** groan with (Coupled with the use of conception a line earlier, groan suggests a woman in labor to deliver a child she has conceived.)

---

[25] **Offend:** wrong

[26] **with such love:** in terms of the love that heaven authorizes us to feel for all humankind

[27] **token:** love token

[28] **in 's:** in his

[29] **stone my heart:** turn my heart to stone

[30] **confess:** testify to

[31] **confessed:** owned up

[32] **used:** sexually

---

[33] **ta'en order:** made arrangements

[34] **stomach:** appetite

[35] **undone:** destroyed

THINK ABOUT IT

1. How does Othello continue to show his love for Desdemona despite the action he takes?
2. Why would Othello kill someone he claims to love so completely?

TALK ABOUT IT

3. What is a crime of passion? Are there contemporary examples which are similar to Othello's crime?
4. Are people deeply in love more susceptible to suggestions of jealousy? Why?

WRITE ABOUT IT

5. Who would you cast as Desdemona and Othello in a movie version of the play? Describe what made you choose these actors.
6. How far would you go in the name of love? Would you commit murder?

READ MORE ABOUT IT

Epstein, Norrie. *The Friendly Shakespeare.* New York: Viking, 1993.

Scott, Mark W., ed. *Shakespeare for Students.* Detroit: Gale Research, 1992.

Othello. BBC London, Time-Life Films, 1982.

Shakespeare, William. *The Tragedy of Othello, The Moor of Venice.* New York: Washington Square Press, 1993.

Po Chü-yi

Richard P. Feynman

R. K. Narayan

The Roman House

Homer

Mary Cassatt

Julia Alvarez

Alice Walker

Alice Elliott Dark

CHAPTER 4

Family

T IS EASY TO UNDERSTAND Po Chü-yi's homesickness for his brothers and sisters. We have all felt the longing for home and family that Po reflects on. Although this poem was written nearly 1200 years ago, many families today are "dispersed," their members "uprooted" and scattered as Po Chü-yi's were. Indeed, in the late twentieth century, it seems that families are always on the move with individual members separated and sometimes "stranded" in different cities, and perhaps even different countries. Moving often separates us from our family members, leaving us to consider only the presence of "lonely shadows" rather than the presence of our loved ones. If we are lucky, we find individuals in our new location with whom we can form an attachment and feel that special family connection once

PO CHÜ-YI

On a Moonlit Night, Sent to My Brothers and Sisters

Hard times, bad year, and a family dispossessed—
Brothers all stranded in strange lands,
       east and west.
Field and garden made desolate by the
       ravages of war,
Flesh and blood cast adrift upon the road.
Dispersed — the lonely shadows of
       far-ranging wild geese;
Uprooted — the scattered tumbleweeds of
       autumn.
As we all watch the bright moon, there should be
       tears;
One night the homesick heart at five places
       feels the same.

(Tr. Irving Y. Lo)

again. Yet, like Po, we may feel "cast adrift upon the road" as we search to establish new connections, while working to sustain our original family relationships.

Although we most often think of family as the group into which we were born and with whom we share a common ancestry, today a family can be any group of individuals living together under one roof. This definition of family reflects the current reality in which a family's members may or may not be related, or even be individuals who are together for more than a brief period of time. What is certain, though, is that, for most of us, our family represents our most important relationships in life. Throughout our lives, it is first the family group in which we grew up, and then, the group with whom we live that exerts the strongest and deepest influence on our development as a human being. As a newborn, each of us enters into a family where we are the baby, and most likely also a sister, brother, niece, nephew, or grandchild. These associations mold us into who we are and start us on a journey that takes us from dependence on our family members to the independence we assert as a young adult. Later, as a mature adult, we may establish a whole new family that we blend

with our earlier one as we build expanded or new family relationships.

We all enter the world as totally dependent beings: without someone to care for a baby's basic needs he or she would die. This dependency can be characterized by the pronoun "you." "You" must feed me, diaper me, put me to bed, and generally take care of me so I can survive in the world. Adults in the family, usually our parents, provide this care. Nurturing is crucial to a baby's development and leads to the infant forming close relationships with others. In return, parents and other care-givers receive feelings of unconditional love and satisfaction. For example, the young father who rises at two A.M. to feed his new baby daughter meets the child's physical needs and, in cuddling her, begins to form a lifelong bond with her. Babies need that continuing love and care that extends into their childhood, and it is their family relationships that offer this vital human connection. As children grow and develop, they begin striving for an existence independent from their dependency as infants.

This independence is associated with the pronoun "I." As babies develop physically, they also develop emotionally. We're all familiar with the toddler's firm: "No! Me do it." This beginning independence evolves from such physical tasks as tying one's shoes and pouring one's juice to forming relationships outside of the family. A two-year-old's play group, for instance, offers relationship experiences that are different from those in the family. As a healthy child grows, his or her quest for independence continues and a different, less dependent, relationship begins to develop with family members. While the original family relationships may continue to be our most important ones, by the time we are young adults most people have formed close relationships with others. For example, twin sisters who were close and dependent on each other as children go to different colleges in different cities. While they telephone often and see each other monthly, for the first time they have different sets of friends. The sisters come to realize that they are no longer as dependent on each other as they were when children, yet they are not so fully independent that they do not continue their close relationship. As young adults, they strive to develop new ways of interacting with each other and their new friends. These new modes of interaction can lead them to the interdependent relationships of mature adulthood.

Interdependence is represented by the pronoun "we." After journeying from the dependence of childhood to the independence of young adulthood, mature adults acknowledge the "we" as the ultimate goal for their family relationships. "We" means that together two or more individuals can combine their talents and abilities and create something greater than either can alone. Whether it's raising children, running a business, or remodeling a house, adults' family relationships are built on the need to form and sustain "we" relationships with others. For example, a single mother and her elderly father who have lived apart from each other for many years decide to form a household to raise her young son. While the mother works all day, the father shops, cooks, and cares for his grandson after school. The mother and grandfather have established an interdependent relationship that is different from their earlier one as parent and child. They are now equal partners in raising a young boy. This mutually beneficial relationship offers the mother care for her child and a place to live, and it gives the grandfather companionship and financial security. Together the two adults build a loving family relationship in which to raise a healthy child. The balance achieved by the mother, grandfather, and son is the full realization of the "we," the wellspring of successful family relationships.

It seems that Po Chü-yi attained this type of interdependence in his relationships with his brothers and sisters. Although they are distant from him, he imagines that his siblings "all watch the bright moon" and may experience tears at their longing for home. While they are independent and scattered from each other, Po senses that they all have the same "homesick heart." This deep desire for an interdependent "oneness" with our family members is a longing that many of us share. The authors of the articles in this chapter write about this longing and many other aspects of family relationships. The oneness Po Chü-yi feels with his brothers and sisters is shared by a young man who needs to separate from his grandmother in order to find his way in the world. The intensity of a husband and wife's relationship with each other and with their young son during wartime contrasts with the trauma of parents whose adult son is dying from AIDS. The following selections highlight the ways in which family relationships develop, sustain themselves, and even break apart. Sometimes, they involve the "you" of the young child, or the "I" of the young adult, and, other times, they reflect the "we" of the "heart at five places [that] feels the same."

THINK ABOUT IT

1. Describe the relationship "journey" that we all take from infancy to adulthood.
2. Which three pronouns symbolize our approach to family relationships at different stages in our life? Why are these pronouns characteristic?

TALK ABOUT IT

3. Popular television shows and movies tend to simplify family relationships in that they show them as unchanging even when the characters grow and develop in other ways. What do these shows teach children about families?
4. How do family relationships differ from one culture to another? Which pronouns characterize relationships in other cultures?

WRITE ABOUT IT

5. Analyze your approach to family relationships at different stages in your life. Use examples to describe your approach.
6. Describe your current family relationships. Which pronouns represent each of your family members? Which one symbolizes your point in the "journey"?

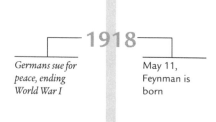

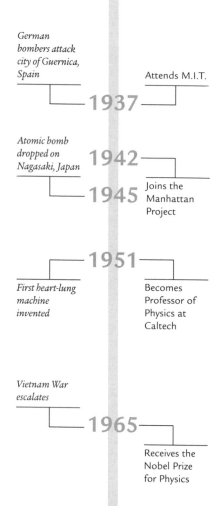

1918 — Germans sue for peace, ending World War I

May 11, Feynman is born

German bombers attack city of Guernica, Spain

Attends M.I.T.

1937

Atomic bomb dropped on Nagasaki, Japan

1942

1945 — Joins the Manhattan Project

1951 — Becomes Professor of Physics at Caltech

First heart-lung machine invented

Vietnam War escalates

1965 — Receives the Nobel Prize for Physics

Space Shuttle Challenger explodes

1986 — Feb. 15 dies of cancer

1988

RICHARD P. FEYNMAN

The Making of a Scientist

Nobel prize-winning physicist Dr. Richard Feynman became known to the American public for his participation on the commission which investigated the explosion of the space shuttle, Challenger. In a simple demonstration, Feynman immersed a rubber "0" ring in a glass of ice water and demonstrated that the ring lost its elasticity. With this demonstration, Feynman proved that the extremely cold temperatures on the day of the Challenger launch decreased the elasticity of the 0 rings which formed the seals on its external fuel tanks. Fuel, leaking from these seals, ignited and caused the worst disaster of the US Space Program. On televisions all over America, newscasts showed Feynman's simple experiment, and Americans heard his precise and uncompromising questioning of the engineers and technicians responsible for the safety of the mission. This demonstration and method of questioning was characteristic of Feynman's approach to science which stressed an uncompromising search for truths which could be understood simply.

Feynman's own simple truth was a set of diagrams, now called Feynman diagrams, which described mathematically the behaviors of subatomic particles in particle interactions. They provided a precise explanation of an area of Quantum Mechanics which explains the structure and behavior of subatomic particles. In addition to his contribution to physics and physics research, Feynman was also a talented teacher. His ability to teach with simple demonstrations and clear explanations gave hundreds of students an introduction into the nature of physical science. He conveyed to them his love of science and taught them to pursue critical understanding rather than repeat memorized facts. In the following excerpt, Feynman describes how his father taught him to love science and, in doing so, shares the special relationship that can exist between a father and son.

I HAVE A FRIEND who's an artist, and he sometimes takes a view which I don't agree with. He'll hold up a flower and say, "Look how beautiful it is," and I'll agree. But then he'll say, "I, as an artist, can see how beautiful a flower is. But you, as a scientist, take it all apart and it becomes dull." I think he's kind of nutty.

First of all, the beauty that he sees is available to other people — and to me, too, I believe. Although I might not be quite as refined aesthetically as he is, I can appreciate the beauty of a flower. But at the same time, I see much more in the flower than he sees. I can imagine the cells inside, which also have a beauty. There's beauty not just at the dimension of one centimeter; there's also beauty at a smaller dimension.

There are the complicated actions of the cells, and other processes. The fact that the colors in the flower have evolved in order to attract insects to pollinate it is interesting; that means insects can see the colors. That adds a question: does this aesthetic sense we have also exist in lower forms of life? There are all kinds of interesting questions that come from a knowledge of science, which only adds to the excitement and mystery and awe of a flower. It only adds. I don't understand how it subtracts.

I've always been very one-sided about science, and when I was younger I concentrated almost all my effort on it. In those days I didn't have time, and I didn't have much patience, to learn what's called the humanities. Even though there were humanities courses in the university that you had to take in order to graduate, I tried my best to avoid them. It's only afterwards, when I've gotten older and more relaxed, that I've spread out a little bit. I've learned to draw and I read a little bit, but I'm really still a very one-sided person and I don't know a great deal. I have a limited intelligence and I use it in a particular direction.

Before I was born, my father told my mother, "If it's a boy, he's going to be a scientist."* When I was just a little kid, very small in a high chair, my father brought home a lot of little bathroom tiles — seconds — of different colors. We played with them, my father setting them up vertically on my high chair like dominoes, and I would push one end so they would all go down.

Then after a while, I'd help set them up. Pretty soon, we're setting them up in a more complicated way: two white tiles and a blue tile, two white tiles and a blue tile, and so on. When my mother saw that

she said, "Leave the poor child alone. If he wants to put a blue tile, let him put a blue tile."

But my father said, "No, I want to show him what patterns are like and how interesting they are. It's a kind of elementary mathematics." So he started very early to tell me about the world and how interesting it is.

We had the *Encyclopedia Britannica* at home. When I was a small boy he used to sit me on his lap and read to me from the *Britannica*. We would be reading, say, about dinosaurs. It would be talking about the *Tyrannosaurus rex*, and it would say something like, "This dinosaur is twenty-five feet high and its head is six feet across."

My father would stop reading and say, "Now, let's see what that means. That would mean that if he stood in our front yard, he would be tall enough to put his head through our window up here." (We were on the second floor.) "But his head would be too wide to fit in the window." Everything he read to me he would translate as best he could into some reality.

It was very exciting and very, very, interesting to think there were animals of such magnitude — and that they all died out, and that nobody knew why. I wasn't frightened that there would be one coming in my window as a consequence of this. But I learned from my father to translate: everything I read I try to figure out what it really means, what it's really saying.

We used to go to the Catskill Mountains, a place where people from New York City would go in the summer. The fathers would all return to New York to work during the week, and come back only for the weekend. On weekends, my father would take me for walks in the woods and he'd tell me about interesting things that were going on in the woods. When the other mothers saw this, they thought it was wonderful and that the other fathers should take their sons for walks. They tried to work on them but they

didn't get anywhere at first. They wanted my father to take all the kids, but he didn't want to because he had a special relationship with me. So it ended up that the other fathers had to take their children for walks the next weekend.

The next Monday, when the fathers were all back at work, we kids were playing in a field. One kid says to me, "See that bird? What kind of bird is that?"

I said, "I haven't the slightest idea what kind of a bird it is."

He says, "It's a brown-throated thrush. Your father doesn't teach you anything!"

But it was the opposite. He had already taught me: "See that bird?" he says. "It's a Spencer's warbler." (I knew he didn't know the real name.) "Well, in Italian, it's a *Chutto Lapittida*. In Portuguese, it's a *Bom da Peida*. In Chinese, it's a *Chunglong-tah,* and in Japanese, it's a *Katano Tekeda*. You can know the name of that bird in all the languages of the world, but when you're finished, you'll know absolutely nothing whatever about the bird. You'll only know about humans in different places, and what they call the bird. So let's look at the bird and see what it's *doing* — that's what counts." (I learned very early the difference between knowing the name of something and knowing something.)

He said, "For example, look: the bird pecks at its feathers all the time. See it walking around, pecking at its feathers?"

"Yeah."

He says, "Why do you think birds peck at their feathers?"

I said, "Well, maybe they mess up their feathers when they fly, so they're pecking them in order to straighten them out."

"All right," he says. "If that were the case, then they would peck a lot just after they've been flying. Then, after they've been on the ground a while, they

---

* Richard's younger sister, Joan, has a Ph.D. in physics, in spite of this preconception that only boys are destined to be scientists.

wouldn't peck so much any more — you know what I mean?"

"Yeah."

He says, "Let's look and see if they peck more just after they land."

It wasn't hard to tell: there was not much difference between the birds that had been walking around a bit and those that had just landed. So I said, "I give up. Why does a bird peck at its feathers?"

"Because there are lice bothering it," he says. "The lice eat flakes of protein that come off its feathers."

He continued, "Each louse has some waxy stuff on its legs, and little mites eat that. The mites don't digest it perfectly, so they emit from their rear ends a sugar-like material, in which bacteria grow."

Finally he says, "So you see, everywhere there's a source of food, there's *some* form of life that finds it."

Now, I knew that it may not have been exactly a louse, that it might not be exactly true that the louse's legs have mites. That story was probably incorrect in *detail*, but what he was telling me was right in *principle*.

Another time, when I was older, he picked a leaf off of a tree. This leaf had a flaw, a thing we never look at much. The leaf was sort of deteriorated; it had a little brown line in the shape of a C, starting somewhere in the middle of the leaf and going out in a curl to the edge.

"Look at this brown line," he says. "It's narrow at the beginning and it's wider as it goes to the edge. What this is, is a fly — a blue fly with yellow eyes and green wings has come and laid an egg on this leaf. Then, when the egg hatches into a maggot (a caterpillar-like thing), it spends its whole life eating this leaf — that's where it gets its food. As it eats along, it leaves behind this brown trail of eaten leaf. As the maggot grows, the trail grows wider until he's grown to full size at the end of the leaf, where he turns into a fly — a blue fly with yellow eyes and green wings — who flies away and lays an egg on another leaf."

Again, I knew that the details weren't precisely correct — it could have even been a beetle — but the idea that he was trying to explain to me was the amusing part of life: the whole thing is just reproduction. No matter how complicated the business is, the main point is to do it again!

Not having experience with many fathers, I didn't realize how remarkable he was. How did he learn the deep principles of science and the love of it, what's behind it, and why it's worth doing? I never really asked him, because I just assumed that those were things that fathers knew.

My father taught me to notice things. One day, I was playing with an "express wagon," a little wagon with a railing around it. It had a ball in it, and when I pulled the wagon, I noticed something about the way the ball moved. I went to my father and said, "Say, Pop, I noticed something. When I pull the wagon, the ball rolls to the back of the wagon. And when I'm pulling it along and I suddenly stop, the ball rolls to the front of the wagon. Why is that?"

"That, nobody knows," he said. "The general principle is that things which are moving tend to keep on moving, and things which are standing still tend to stand still, unless you push them hard. This tendency is called 'inertia,' but nobody knows why it's true." Now, that's a deep understanding. He didn't just give me the name.

He went on to say, "If you look from the side, you'll see that it's the back of the wagon that you're pulling against the ball, and the ball stands still. As a matter of fact, from the friction it starts to move forward a little bit in relation to the ground. It doesn't move back."

I ran back to the little wagon and set the ball up again and pulled the wagon. Looking sideways, I saw that indeed he was right. Relative to the sidewalk, it moved forward a little bit.

That's the way I was educated by my father, with those kinds of examples and discussions: no pressure — just lovely, interesting discussions. It has motivated me for the rest of my life, and makes me interested in all the sciences. (It just happens I do physics better.)

I've been caught, so to speak — like someone who was given something wonderful when he was a child, and he's always looking for it again. I'm always looking, like a child, for the wonders I know I'm going to find — maybe not every time, but every once in a while.

Around that time my cousin, who was three years older, was in high school. He was having considerable difficulty with his algebra, so a tutor would come. I was allowed to sit in a corner while the tutor would try to teach my cousin algebra. I'd hear him talking about x.

I said to my cousin, "What are you trying to do?"

"I'm trying to find out what x is, like in $2x + 7 = 15$."

I say, "You mean 4."

"Yeah, but you did it by arithmetic. You have to do it by algebra."

I learned algebra, fortunately, not by going to school, but by finding my aunt's old schoolbook in the attic, and understanding that the whole idea was to find out what x is — it doesn't make any difference how you do it. For me, there was no such thing as doing it "by arithmetic," or doing it "by algebra." "Doing it by algebra" was a set of rules which, if you followed them blindly, could produce the answer: "subtract 7 from both sides; if you have a multiplier, divide both sides by the multiplier," and so on — a series of steps by which you could get the answer if you didn't understand what you were trying to do. The rules had been invented so that the children who have to study algebra can all pass it. And that's why my cousin was never able to do algebra.

There was a series of math books in our local library which started out with *Arithmetic for the Practical Man*. Then came *Algebra for the Practical Man*, and then *Trigonometry for the Practical Man*. (I learned trigonometry from that, but I soon forgot it again, because I didn't understand it very well.) When I was about thirteen, the library was going to get *Calculus for the Practical Man*. By this time I knew, from reading the encyclopedia, that calculus was an important and interesting subject, and I ought to learn it.

When I finally saw the calculus book at the library, I was very excited. I went to the librarian to check it out, but she looked at me and said, "You're just a child. What are you taking this book out for?"

It was one of the few times in my life I was uncomfortable and I lied. I said it was for my father.

I took the book home and I began to learn calculus from it. I thought it was relatively simple and straightforward. My father started to read it, but he found it confusing and he couldn't understand it. So I tried to explain calculus to him. I didn't know he was so limited, and it bothered me a little bit. It was the first time I realized that I had learned more in some sense than he.

One of the things that my father taught me besides physics — whether it's correct or not — was a disrespect for certain kinds of things. For example, when I was a little boy, and he would sit me on his knee, he'd show me rotogravures in the *New York Times* — that's printed pictures which had just come out in newspapers.

One time we were looking at a picture of the pope and everybody bowing in front of him. My father said, "Now, look at those humans. Here's one human standing here, and all these others are bowing in front of him. Now, what's the difference? This one is the pope" — he hated the pope anyway. He said, "This difference is the hat he's wearing." (If it was a general, it was the epaulets. It was always the costume, the

uniform, the position.) "But," he said, "this man has the same problems as everybody else: he eats dinner; he goes to the bathroom. He's a human being." (By the way, my father was in the uniform business, so he knew what the difference is in a man with the uniform off and the uniform on — it was the same man for him.)

He was happy with me, I believe. Once, though, when I came back from MIT (I'd been there a few years), he said to me, "Now that you've become educated about these things, there's one question I've always had that I've never understood very well."

I asked him what it was.

He said, "I understand that when an atom makes a transition from one state to another, it emits a particle of light called a photon."

"That's right," I said. He said, "Is the photon in the atom ahead of time?"

"No, there's no photon beforehand."

"Well," he said, "where does it come from, then? How does it come out?"

I tried to explain it to him — that photon numbers aren't conserved; they're just created by the motion of the electron — but I couldn't explain it very well. I said, "It's like the sound that I'm making now: it wasn't in me before." (It's not like my little boy, who suddenly announced one day, when he was very young, that he could no longer say a certain word — the word turned out to be "cat" — because his "word bag" had run out of the word. There's no word bag that makes you use up words as they come out; in the same sense, there's no "photon bag" in an atom.)

He was not satisfied with me in that respect. I was never able to explain any of the things that he didn't understand. So he was unsuccessful: he sent me to all these universities in order to find out those things, and he never did find out.

Although my mother didn't know anything about science, she had a great influence on me as well. In particular, she had a wonderful sense of humor, and I learned from her that the highest forms of understanding we can achieve are laughter and human compassion.

THINK ABOUT IT

1. What was special about the way Feynman's father taught him?
2. Describe the relationship between Feynman and his father.

TALK ABOUT IT

3. Feynman believes that the most important part of his education came from his father. What role do you think parents should play in educating their children?
4. Do you think Feynman's relationship with his father is a typical father-son relationship? Do you think this kind of relationship is more prevalent in other cultures than in ours?

WRITE ABOUT IT

5. Do you think parents should try to influence their children's choice of careers? Why or why not?
6. Describe your relationship with your father. Has it been a positive or negative influence on your life?

READ MORE ABOUT IT

Feynman, Richard P. *The Feynman Lectures on Physics*. 3 vols. Reading, Massachusetts: Addison-Wesley Publishing Company, 1964.

Feynman, Richard P. *Surely You're joking, Mr. Feynman*. New York: Bantam Books, 1989.

Feynman, Richard P., as told to Ralph Leighton. *"What Do You Care What Other People Think?": Further Adventures of A Curious Character*. New York: W. W. Norton & Company, 1988.

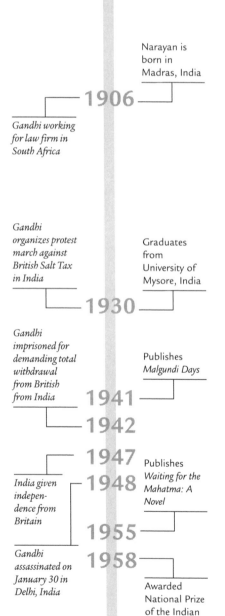

1869
Gandhi is born
in western India

Narayan is
born in
Madras, India

1906

Gandhi working
for law firm in
South Africa

Gandhi
organizes protest
march against
British Salt Tax
in India

Graduates
from
University of
Mysore, India

1930

Gandhi
imprisoned for
demanding total
withdrawal
from British
from India

Publishes
Malgundi Days

1941
1942
1947

Publishes
Waiting for the
Mahatma: A
Novel

1948

India given
indepen-
dence from
Britain

1955
1958

Gandhi
assassinated on
January 30 in
Delhi, India

Awarded
National Prize
of the Indian
Literary
Academy

R. K. NARAYAN

Waiting for the Mahatma

For over forty years, R. K. Narayan has been India's most prominent writer of contemporary fiction. His short stories and novels are recognized world-wide for the ways in which they realistically capture everyday life in India and evoke the sensibilities of the Indian character. Narayan is best known for his creation of Malgudi, a fictional town in southern India which provides a rich setting for his best-known stories. To his many readers, Malgudi has become a real place in which Narayan's fictional inhabitants lead daily lives that are at once routine and extraordinary. None of his main characters is more common and, yet exceptional, than Sriram, the young man whose story is the central plot of *Waiting for the Mahatma*.

Waiting for the Mahatma, the novel from which this article is excerpted, is widely considered one of Narayan's masterpieces. It is the fictional account of Sriram's decision to leave his home and grandmother to pursue his first infatuation, a young woman named Bharati, who is a follower of the great Mahatma Gandhi. As the story begins, Sriram has just turned twenty. His parents died when he was young and the only life he has known has been in Malgudi where he has been raised by his granny. Sriram leads a simple middle class existence in which Granny spoils him and treats him as if he is still a child. One day when Gandhi travels to Malgudi, Sriram meets Bharati and is immediately smitten with her. To stay close to her, Sriram considers joining the Mahatma's traveling entourage. As our selections begins, Sriram is about to meet the revered Mahatma for the first time.

This novel takes place in the mid and late 1940s and traces the true-to-life movements of Mohandas Gandhi (1869-1948), the Mahatma. Gandhi was the leader for Indian political independence and the twentieth-century prophet of nonviolent social action. Due to the efforts of Gandhi and his followers, India was granted full independence from Great Britain in 1947. The people of India called Gandhi by the respectful title of "Mahatma," meaning "Great Soul." In the selection that follows Gandhi is also referred to as the (Great) Presence, Mahatmaji, Bapu, and Bapuji, all terms of endearment and admiration.

GRANNY HAD SLEPT FITFULLY. She had gone up to Kanni's shop five times during the evening to enquire if anyone had seen Sriram, and sent a boy who had come to make a purchase there to look for Sriram everywhere. At last the schoolmaster who lived up the street told her as he passed her house,

"Your pet is in Mahatma's camp. I saw him."

'Ah! What was he doing there?' asked Granny, alarmed. For her the Mahatma was one who preached dangerously, who tried to bring untouchables into the temples, and who involved people in difficulties with the police. She didn't like the idea. She wailed, "Oh, master, why did you allow him to stay on there? You should have brought him away. It is so late and he has not come home. As his old teacher you should have weaned him away."

"Don't worry, madam, he is perfectly safe. How many of us could have the privilege of being so near the Mahatma? You must be happy that he is doing so well! Our country needs more young men like him."

Granny replied, "It is teachers like you who have ruined our boys and this country," and turned in, slamming the door.

When Sriram arrived and knocked, she was half asleep and in the worst possible mood. She opened the door, let him in, bolted the door again, and went back to her bed saying, "I have kept some rice in that bowl mixed with curd and the other one is without curd. Put out the lamp after you have eaten." Lying in bed, she listened to the sound of Sriram putting away his plate and leaving the kitchen. And then she turned her face to the wall and pretended to be asleep. She hoped that her grandson would understand her mood, come over, and assure her that he would not get into bad ways: but the young man was oth-

erwise engaged. He was in a state of semi-enchantment. Bharati's presence and talk still echoed in his mind, and he recollected the thrill of her touch. He liked to think that when he was not noticing she had touched his arm and patted his shoulder. He thought how he would prefer the rest of his life listening to her banter, but that meant — here was the conflict — he would have to go into the Presence. All else seemed to him insignificant beside this great worry. If it had been any other day he would have pulled his granny out of her sleep and narrated to her all the day's events. If she happened to be in a bad mood he would have pulled her out of it. He knew now that she was not in a proper temper; he could sense it the moment he stepped on the threshold, but he preferred to leave her alone; he felt he had a far greater problem to tackle than appeasing the mood of a mere granny.

He went to bed and slept in all less than an hour. Bharati wanted him there at three A.M., and he needed an hour to reach the place. He got up before one, washed and bathed and put on special clothes, bent over his granny's bed to whisper, "I have to be going now, bolt the door."

She tried to ask, "What! At this hour, what has come over you?" but he was gone on soft footsteps, closing the door behind him.

He stood at the entrance to Mahatmaji's hut, holding his breath. It was very difficult to decide what he should do now. She had asked him to be present at the portals of the Great Presence, but perhaps she had been fooling him. He feared that any sound he made might rouse the Mahatma and bring the entire camp about his ears. He stood ruefully looking at the camp. Street dogs were barking somewhere. Occasionally the branches of trees over the river rustled and creaked. He stood looking ruefully towards the women's quar-

ters. There a lantern was burning, people seemed to be awake and moving about. He thought, "What if the lantern is burning? They may be sleeping with lights on. Women are cowardly anyway." The stirring he heard might be them rolling in their beds, noisy creatures! Unaccountably he was feeling irritated at the thought of women, the species to which Bharati belonged. He saw a light in Mahatmaji's camp. The door was shut. He heard soft footsteps moving in there. Long ago the Taluk Office gong had struck some small hour. He could hardly believe he had actually sacrificed his sleep and was standing here in the cold wind, at an unearthly hour. Even the scavengers, the earliest to rise in the town, were still asleep. He felt suddenly afraid that he might be attacked by thieves or ghosts. Or if a policeman saw him and took him to be a prowler, how should he explain himself? He couldn't very well say, "Bharati asked me to wait at Mahatmaji's hut at about three A.M." He wanted to turn and go away: he could at least go home and make up to his grandmother instead of hanging around here and wondering what to do. He could tell her: "I went to see the Mahatma, but changed my mind and came away. Why should I get to know him and then into all sorts of difficulties? Don't you think so, Granny?" And she was sure to revive and look happy again.

He gave one forlorn look at the women's quarters and turned away, his mind completely made up to earn the concrete goodwill of a granny rather than the doubtful and strange favours of bigwigs like the Mahatma and snobs like Bharati. Heaven knew who else would be there. But still the pull of Bharati was strong and he could not get away from the place so easily as he had imagined. He wanted to make just one more attempt to see her and bid her good-bye. Perhaps she

MOHONDAS K. GANDHI, THE MAHATMA, OR GREAT SOUL

was in a situation in which he could help her: people might have tied her up to her cot and gagged her mouth. Anything might happen to a beautiful girl like her. Otherwise there could be no explanation for her absence. Anyway, he felt it would be his duty to go and find out what was wrong and where. He'd have willingly gone near the women's quarters, but he lacked the necessary courage and did the next best thing: once again repeating a rash act he tip-toed towards Mahatmaji's hut: his idea was to peep in unobtrusively and see if Bharati was there or anywhere else safe and sound and then move off. But in his befuddled state it did not occur to him that possibly he might be seen before he saw anyone. And it happened so. The door of Mahatmaji's hut was half open. Light streamed out through the gap. Sriram went towards it like a charmed moth. If he had paused to reflect he would not have believed himself to be capable of repeating a foolhardy act a second time. But through lack of sleep, and tension of nerves, a general recklessness had come over him, the same innocent charge that had taken him tumbling into the hut the previous evening took him there again now. He peeped in like a clown. The door was half open; he had over-estimated its width from a distance, for he could not peep in without thrusting his head through.

"Oh, there he is!" cried Bharati, with laughter in her voice. "You may open the door if you wish to come in," she said. Sriram felt again that the girl was making fun of him. Even in the great presence, she didn't seem to care. Here at least Sriram had hoped she would speak without the undertone of mischief. He felt so irritated at the thought that he replied with all the pungency he could muster in his tone: "You have——I waited for you there——"

"Come in, come in," said the Mahatma. "Why should you be standing there? You could have come straight in."

"But she asked me to wait outside," said Sriram, stepping in gingerly. From the door to where the Mahatma sat the distance was less than ten feet, but he felt he was taking hours to cover it. His legs felt weak and seemed to intertwine, he seemed to be walking like a drunkard, a particularly dangerous impression to create in the Mahatma, who was out to persuade even the scavengers to give up drinking. In a flash it occurred to him that he ought to have a sensible answer ready if the Mahatma should suddenly turn round and ask, "Have you been drinking toddy or whisky?"

But his trial came to an end, when Gandhi said, "Bharati has just been mentioning you." He spoke while his hands were busy turning a spinning wheel, drawing out a fine thread. A man sitting in a corner, with a pad resting on his knee, was writing. Mahatmaji himself as always was doing several things at the same time. While his hands were spinning, his eyes perused a letter held before him by another, and he found it possible too to put in a word of welcome to Sriram. Through the back door of the hut many others were coming in and passing out. For each one of them Mahatmaji had something to say.

He looked up at Sriram and said: "Sit down, young man. Come and sit as near me as you like." There was so much unaffected graciousness in his tone that Sriram lost all fear and hesitation. He moved briskly up. He sat on the floor near Mahatmaji and watched with fascination the smooth turning of the spinning wheel. Bharati went to an inner part of the hut, threw a swift look at Sriram, which he understood to mean, "Remember not to make a fool of yourself."

The Mahatma said, "Nowadays I generally get up an hour earlier in order to be able to do this: spinning a certain length is my most important work: even my prayer comes only after that. I'd very much like you to take a vow to wear only cloth made out of your own hands each day."

"Yes, I will do so," promised Sriram.

When the gong in the Taluk Office struck four, the Mahatma invited Sriram to go out with him for a walk. He seized his staff in one hand and with the other supported himself on the shoulder of Bharati, and strode out of the hut — a tall figure in white. He had tucked his watch at his waist into a fold of his white *dhoti*. He pulled it out and said: "Half an hour I have to walk, come with me, Sriram. You can talk to me undisturbed." A few others joined them. Sriram felt he was walking through some unreal dream world. The Mahatma was in between him and Bharati, and it was difficult to snatch a look at her as often as he wanted. He had to step back a quarter of an inch now and then, in order to catch a glimpse of her laughing face. They walked along the river bank. The sky was rosy in the east. Gandhi turned and spoke some business to those behind him. He suddenly addressed himself to Sriram: "Your town is very beautiful. Have you ever noticed it before?" Sriram felt unhappy and gasped for breath. The morning air blew on his face, birds were chirping, the city was quiet: it was all well known, but why did the Mahatma mention it especially now? Should he say "Yes" or "No"? If he said "Yes" he would be lying, which would be detected at once; if he said "No," God knew what the Mahatma would think of him. He looked about. A couple of scavengers of the colony who had joined the group were waiting eagerly to know what he would say: they were

evidently enjoying his predicament, and he dared not look in the direction of Bharati. The Mahatma said: "God is everywhere, and if you want to feel his presence you will see him in a place like this with a beautiful river flowing, the sunrise with all its colours, the air so fresh. Feeling a beautiful hour or a beautiful scene or a beautiful object is itself a form of prayer." Sriram listened in reverential silence, glad to be let off so lightly. When Gandhiji spoke of beauty, it sounded unreal as applied to the sun and the air, but the word acquired a practical significance when he thought of it in terms of Bharati. Gandhi said: "By the time we meet again next, you must give me a very good account of yourself."

He laughed in a kindly manner, and Sriram said,

"Yes, Bapuji, I will be a different man."

"Why do you say 'different'? You will be all right if you are fully yourself."

"I don't think that is enough, Bapu," said Bharati, "He should change from being himself, if he is to come to any good. I think he is very lazy. He gets up at eight o'clock, and idles away the day."

"How do you know?" Sriram asked indignantly.

"It's only a guess," said the girl. Sriram felt angry with her for her irresponsible talk. Everyone laughed.

The Mahatma said: "You must not say such things, Bharati, unless you mean to take charge of him and help him."

During the last fifteen minutes of this walk the Mahatma said nothing; he walked in silence, looking at the ground before him. When the Mahatma was silent the others were even more so, the only movement they performed was putting one foot before another on the sand, keeping pace with him: some were panting hard and trying hard to suppress the sound. The Mahatma's silence was heavy and pervasive, and Sriram was afraid even to gulp or cough, although he very much wanted to clear his throat, cough, sneeze, swing his arms about. The only sound at the moment was the flowing of the river and the twitter of birds. Somewhere a cow was mooing. Even Bharati, the embodiment of frivolity, seemed to have become sombre. The Mahatma pulled out his watch, looked at it briefly and said, "We will go back, that is all the walk I can afford today." Sriram wanted to ask, "Why?" but he held his tongue. The Mahatma turned to him as they were walking back, "You have a grandmother, I hear, but no parents."

"Yes. My grandmother is very old."

"Yes, she must be, otherwise how can you call her a grandmother?" People laughed, Sriram too joined in this laughter out of politeness.

"Does she not miss you very much when you are away from her so long?"

"Yes, very much. She gets very angry with me. I don't know what to do about it," said Sriram courageously rushing ahead. He felt pleased at having said something of his own accord, but his only fear was that Bharati might step in and say something nasty and embarrassing, but he was happy to note that Bharati held her peace.

Mahatmaji said: "You must look after your granny too, she must have devoted herself to bringing you up."

"Yes, but when I am away like this she is very much upset."

"Is it necessary for you to be away from her so much?"

"Yes, Bapu, otherwise how can I do anything in this world?"

"What exactly do you want to do?"

It was now that Sriram became incoherent. He was seized with a rush of ideas and with all the confusion that too many ideas create. He said something, and the Mahatma watched him patiently, the others too held their breath and watched, and after a few moments of struggle for self-expression, Sriram was able to form a cogent sentence. It was the unrelenting pressure of his subconscious desires that jerked the sentence out of his lips, and he said, "I like to be where Bharati is." The Mahatma said, "Oh, is that so!" He patted Bharati's back and said, "What a fine friend you have! You must be pleased to have such a devoted friend. How long have you known him?"

Bharati said like a shot, "Since yesterday. I saw him for the first time sitting in your hut and I asked him who he was."

Sriram interposed and added, "But I knew her before, although I spoke to her only yesterday."

The Mahatma passed into his hut, and went on to attend to other things. Many people were waiting for him. Bharati disappeared into the Mahatma's hut the moment they arrived. Sriram fell back and got mixed up with a crowd waiting outside. He felt jealous of Bharati's position. She sought him out later and said, "You are probably unused to it, but in Bapu's presence we speak only the absolute truth and nothing less than that, and nothing more than that either."

He took her to task: "What will he think of me now when he knows that I have not known you long enough and yet ———"

"Well, what?" she twitted him.

"And yet I wish to be with you and so on."

"Why don't you go in and tell him you have been speaking nonsense and that you were blurting out things without forethought or self-control? Why couldn't you have told him that you want to serve the country, that you are a patriot, that you want to shed your blood in order to see that the British leave the country? That is what most people say when they come near the Mahatma. I have seen hundreds of people come to him, and say the same thing."

"And he believes all that?" asked Sriram.

"Perhaps not, but he thinks it is not right to disbelieve anyone."

"But you say we must only speak the truth in his presence."

"If you can, of course, but if you can't, the best thing to do is to maintain silence."

"Why are you so angry with me, is it not a part of your duty not to be angry with others?" asked Sriram pathetically.

"I don't care," said Bharati, "this is enough to irritate even the Mahatma. Now what will he think of me if he realizes I am encouraging a fellow like you to hang about the place, a fellow whom I have not known even for a full day yet!"

Sriram became reckless, and said breezily, "What does it matter how long I have known you? Did you think I was going to lie to him if you had not spoken before I spoke?"

These bickerings were brought to an end by someone calling "Bharati" from another hut. Bharati abandoned him and disappeared from the spot.

Bharati's words gave him an idea. He realized his own omission, and proposed to remedy it next time he walked with the Mahatma. Sriram's anxiety lest he fall asleep when the Mahatma was up kept him awake the whole night. He shared the space on the floor with one of the men in the camp. It was a strange feeling to lie down in a hut, and he felt he was becoming a citizen of an entirely new world. He missed the cosy room of his house in Kabir Lane, he missed the two pillows and the soft mattress and the carpet under it; even the street noises of Kabir Street added much to the domestic quality of life, and he missed it badly now. He had to adopt an entirely new mode of life. He had to live, of his own choice, in a narrow hut, with thatch above, with a dingy, sooty smell hanging about everything. The floor had been swept with cow dung and covered with a thin layer of sand. He had to snuggle his head on the crook of his arm for a pillow. He had to share this place with another volunteer in the camp, a cadaverous serious young man wearing Khadi shorts, a Khadi vest, and a white cap on his closely shaved head. He had a fiery look and an unsmiling face. He was from North India, he could only speak broken English and he was totally ignorant of Tamil words. This man had already stretched himself on the floor with a small bag stuffed with clothes under his head.

Bharati had told Sriram, "You had better stick on here, around the camp, if you want to be with Mahatmaji. You won't have any comforts here, remember. We are all trained to live like this."

Sriram sniffed and said, "Oh, who wants any comforts? I don't care for them myself. You think I am a fellow who cares for luxuries in life?"

There was a class of society where luxuries gave one a status, and now here was the opposite. The more one asserted one cared for no luxury, the more one showed an inclination for hardship and discomfort, the greater was one's chance of being admitted into the fold. Sriram had understood it the moment he stepped into the camp. Here the currency was suffering and self-mortification. Everyone seemed to excel his neighbour in managing in uncomfortable situations, and Sriram caught the spirit, though it took him time to grasp the detail and get accustomed to it.

There had been a meeting in the evening and after that the Mahatma retired at his usual hour of seven-thirty, and it was a signal for the entire camp to retire. Bharati sought out Sriram and gave him a plateful of rice and buttermilk and an orange, and she also held out to him a small jasmine out of a bouquet which had earlier been presented to the Mahatma by some children's deputation. He received the flower gratefully, smelt it, and asked, "How did you know I liked jasmine?"

"It is not so difficult a thing to know," she said and dismissed the subject immediately.

She said, "I have found a place for you to sleep, with a volunteer named Gorpad."

Gorpad had been half asleep when Sriram entered his hut. Bharati peeped and said, *"Bhai …"* and something in Hindi and turned and disappeared from the spot. The other lifted his head slightly and said, "You can come in and sleep."

"Only on the floor?" Sriram asked.

"Of course, of course," said the other.

"Why?" asked Sriram.

"Why? Because Mahatmaji says so."

"Oh," said Sriram, feeling that he was treading on dangerous ground. "I see that otherwise there is no reason why we should sleep on the floor."

"What do you mean by otherwise?" said the other argumentatively.

Sriram settled himself beside Gorpad, and said, "I didn't mean it."

"Mean what?" said the other. He seemed to be a pugnacious fellow. Sriram felt afraid of him. What did the girl mean by putting him in with this fighter? Could it be that she disliked him, and wanted him to be beaten? If she disliked him, she would not have given him a jasmine flower.

It was well known that jasmine was exchanged only between persons who liked each other, and yet the girl gave him a jasmine with one hand and with the other led him into the company of this terrible man. The other might sit on his chest while he slept and try to choke him.

Gorpad said, "You are new, I suppose?"

"Yes," said Sriram. "I am new to this place. It is through Mahatmaji's kindness I am now here, otherwise I should have gone home and slept."

"Yes," Gorpad said seeming to understand the situation in a fresh light. "You are welcome here. We are all persons who have to live like soldiers in a camp. We are indeed soldiers in our fight to eject the British from our land. We are all prepared to sacrifice our lives for the task. We sleep here on the bare floor because the major part of our lives we shall have to spend in jail, where we won't be given such a comfortable bed unless we are A or B class prisoners. We are not important enough to be classified as A or B, and you had better get used to it all; and we are always prepared to be beaten by the police, lathi-charged, dragged to the jail, or even shot: my father died ten years ago facing a policeman's gun."

Sriram said, not to be outdone in the matter of political reminiscences, "I know Bharati's father also died in the same way, when he was beaten by the police."

"That was during the first non-co-operation days in 1920; her father led the first batch of *Satyagrahis*[1] who were going to take down the Union Jack from the Secretariat at Madras. He was beaten with a police lathi, and a blow fell on his chest and he dropped dead, but my father was

---

[1] *Satyagraha* is the doctrine best translated as "commitment to truth." *Satyagraphis* are those who, like Gandhi, have dedicated their lives to this doctrine.

shot. Do you know he was actually shot by a policeman's rifle? I was also in the crowd watching him. He was picketing a shop where they were selling toddy and other alcoholic drinks, and a police company came and asked him to go away, but he refused. A crowd gathered, and there was a lot of mess and in the end the police shot him point blank." He wiped away tears at the memory of it. "I will not rest till the British are sent out of India," his voice was thick with sorrow. "My brother became a terrorist and shot dead many English officials, nobody knows his whereabouts. I should also have joined him and shot many more Englishmen, but our Mahatma will not let me be violent even in thought," he said ruefully.

Sriram wishing to sound very sympathetic said, "All Englishmen deserve to be shot. They have been very cruel."

"You should not even think on those lines, if you are going to be a true *Satyagrahi*," said the other.

"No, no, I am not really thinking on those lines," Sriram amended immediately. "I was only feeling so sorry. Of course we should not talk of shooting anyone, and where is the gun? We have no guns. My grandmother used to say that there was a gun in our house belonging to my father. Do you know that he died in Mesapotamia? He was also shot point blank."

"He died in the war, the last war?"

"Yes," said Sriram.

"Then he must have been a soldier in the British Army," Gorpad said with a touch of contempt in his voice.

Sriram noted it, but accepted it with resignation. He added as a sort of compensation, "They say he was a great soldier."

"Possibly, possibly," said the other with patronage in his voice. Sriram bore it as a trial.

That night he picked up a great deal of political knowledge. Gorpad went on speaking till two A.M. and afterwards both of them left for the river, performed their ablutions there, and by the time the camp was awake Sriram had returned fresh and tidy, so that Bharati said, "You are coming through your first day with us quite well." Through diligently listening to Gorpad he had picked up many political idioms, and felt himself equipped to walk with the Mahatma without embarrassment.

He told the Mahatma, "It is my greatest desire in life to take a vow to oust the British from India."

The Mahatma looked at him with a smile and asked, "How do you propose to do it?"

Sriram could not find a ready answer; it was one of the many occasions when he felt that he had spoken unnecessarily. He caught a glimpse of Bharati on the other side, her mischievous face sparkled with delight at his confusion. He felt piqued by her look. He said haughtily, "With your blessing, sir, I shall make myself good enough for the task. I shall be with you as long as possible, and if you will kindly guide me you can make me a soldier fit to take up the fight to make the British leave our country."

The Mahatma took his resolve with every sign of pleasure. He remained silent for a while as their footsteps pit-patted on the sands, a sombre silence fell on the gathering. "Well, young friend, if God wills it, you will do great things, trust in him and you will be all right." To Sriram this seemed a rather tame preparation for a soldierly existence. If it had been possible, he would have strutted before Bharati in khaki and a decorated chest, though the world was having a surfeit of decorations just then. Presently the Mahatma himself spoke dispelling his notions: "Before you aspire to drive the British from

this country, you must drive every vestige of violence from your system. Remember that it is not going to be a fight with sticks and knives or guns but only with love. Until you are sure you have an overpowering love at heart for your enemy, don't think of driving him out. You must gradually forget the term 'Enemy.' You must think of him as a friend who must leave you. You must train yourself to become a hundred per cent *ahimsa*[2] soldier. You must become so sensitive that it is not possible for you to wear sandals made of the hide of slaughtered animals; you should prefer to go barefoot rather than wear the hide of an animal killed for your sake, that is if you are unable to secure the skin of an animal that has died a natural death."

Sriram said, "Yes, I promise," but while saying it his eyes were fixed on Mahatmaji's feet; he struggled to suppress the questions that were welling up in his mind.

The Mahatma read his thoughts and said, "Yes, these are sandals made of just such leather. In our tannery at Wardha we specialize in it. No one in our Ashram wears anything else."

Sriram wanted to ask, "How do you know when an animal is dying, and how do you watch for it?" but ruthlessly suppressed the question as an unworthy one, which might betray him.

Sriram was told that he could accompany Mahatmaji in his tour of the villages on condition that he went home, and secured Granny's approval. Sriram tried to slur the matter over, he said it would not be necessary, he hinted he was an independent man used to such outings from home. The Mahatma's memory was better than that. He said with a smile, 'I remember you said that she didn't like to see you mixing with us.'

---

2   Ahimsa is the Hindu doctrine of noninjury or nonviolence.

Sriram thought it over and said, "Yes, master, but how can I for ever remain tied to her? It is not possible."

"Are you quite sure that you want to change your style of life?" asked the Mahatma.

"I can think of nothing else," Sriram said. "How can I live as I have lived all these years?" He threw a quick glance at Bharati as she came in with some letters for the Mahatma. Her look prevented him from completing the sentence, which would have run, "And I always wish to be with Bharati and not with my grandmother."

The Mahatma said, "I shall be happy to have you with us as long as you like, but you must first go home and tell your grandmother and receive her blessing. You must tell her frankly what you wish to do, but you must cause her no pain."

Sriram hesitated. The prospect of facing Granny was unnerving. The thought of her was like the thought of an unreal troublesome world, one which he hoped he had left behind for ever: the real world for him now was the one of Bharati, Gorpad, un-slaughtered naturally dying animals, the Mahatma, spinning wheels. He wanted to be here all the time: it seemed impossible for him to go back to Kabir Street, that *pyol,* and that shop, and those people there who treated him as if he were only eight years old. He stood before the Mahatma as if to appeal to him not to press him to go and face his grand-mother, but the master was unrelenting. "Go and speak to her. I don't think she is so unreasonable as to deny you your ambitions. Tell her that I like to have you with me. If you tour with me the next two weeks, you will observe and learn much that may be useful to you later in life. Tell her she will feel glad that she let you go. Assure her that I will look after you safely." Every word filled him with dread when he remembered the terms in which Granny referred to the Mahatma. He dared not even give the slightest indication as to how she would react. He felt a great pity for the Mahatma, so innocent that he could not dream of anyone talking ill of him. He felt angry at the thought of Granny, such an ill-informed, ig-norant and bigoted personality! What business had she to complicate his existence in this way? If he could have had his will he would have ignored his grandmother, but he had to obey the Mahatma now.

He said, "All right, sir. I will go and get my granny's blessing. I'll be back early tomorrow."

Half a dozen times on the way he resolved to turn back and tell Mahatma Gandhi that he had seen Granny. How could he find out the truth, anyway? But he dismissed the thought as unpractical, though per-haps not so unworthy under the cir-cumstances. Suppose Granny created a row, went into a faint or threatened to kill herself, and made enough noise to attract the neighbours who might come and lock him up in his house, refusing to let him out? Should he face this risk in order to tell Gandhiji that he had seen the obstinate old lady as ordered? Would it not be pru-dent like a sensible man to say that it had been done? Probably Granny would guess there was Bharati behind all this and disbelieve anything he might say about Mahatmaji. Or if she spoke insultingly about Mahatmaji, he couldn't trust himself to listen pa-tiently. He might do something for which he might feel sorry afterwards. He visualized himself suppressing his Granny's words with force and vio-lence, but he remembered that it would not be right to act like that where the Mahatma was concerned. He would be upset to hear about it.

The thing to do was to turn the jutka back and tell the Mahatma that he had Granny's blessings. But then, being a Mahatma, he might read his thoughts and send him back to Granny or he might cancel all his pro-gram until he was assured that Granny had been seen or begin a fast until it was done. What made the Mahatma attach so much importance to Granny when he had so many things to mind? When he had the all-important task of driving the British out he ought to leave simple matters like Granny to be handled by himself. His thoughts were in a welter of con-fusion while he was in the jutka, but soon the horse turned into Kabir Street. He paid the fare without hag-gling and sent away the jutka quietly. He didn't want his movements to be-come noticeable in the neighbourhood.

He found his granny in a semi-agreeable frame of mind. His pro-longed absence seemed to have made her nervous, and she tried to be nice to him.

She probably feared he would flounce out of the house if she at-tempted to talk to him in the man-ner of yesterday.

She merely said: "What a long time you have been away, my boy," at-tempting to keep out all trace of re-proach from her tone. He pretended to settle down. He drew up the can-vas chair he had bought for her and sat down under the hall lamp. His granny fussed about as if she had re-covered someone long lost. She set before him a plateful of food fried in ghee, saying, "They sent this down from the lawyer's house: the first birthday of his eighth son. They don't seem to miss anything for any child."

Sriram put a piece into his mouth, munched it, nodded his ap-proval and said: "Yes, they have made it of pure ghee. Good people." He crunched it noisily.

Granny said: "I kept it for you, I knew you would like it. I was won-dering how long I should keep it.

You know I have no teeth. Who would want stuff like that when you are not here? Don't eat all of it, you will not be able to eat your dinner."

"Oh, dinner! I've had my dinner, Granny."

"So soon!"

"Yes, in the Ashram camp, we have to dine before seven usually. It's the rule."

"What sort of a dinner can it be at seven!' she cried in disappointment, 'Come and eat again, you ought to be fit for a real dinner now."

"No, Granny. It is all regulated very strictly. We can't do anything as we like. We have got to observe the rules in all matters. We get quite good food there."

"Have you got to pay for it?" asked Granny.

"Of course not," said Sriram. "What do you think, do you think Mahatmaji is running a hotel?"

"Then why should they feed you?"

"It's because we belong there."

"Do they provide a lot of public feeding?"

Sriram lost his temper at this. He was appalled at Granny's denseness. "I said they feed all of us who belong there, don't you follow?"

"Why should they feed you?"

"It is because we are volunteers."

"Nice volunteers!" cried Granny, threatening to return to her yesterday's mood any second. "And what do they give you to eat?"

"*Chappatis,* curd, and buttermilk and vegetables."

"I'm glad. I was afraid they might force you to eat egg and fowl."

Sriram was horrified. "What do you take the Mahatma for! Do you know, he won't even wear sandals made of the hide of slaughtered animals!"

Granny was seized with a fit of laughter. Tears rolled down her cheeks. "Won't wear sandals!" she cried in uncontrollable laughter. "Never heard of such a thing before! How do they manage it? By peeling off the skin of animals before they are slaughtered, is that it?"

"Shut up, Granny!" cried Sriram in a great rage. "What an irresponsible gossip you are! I never thought you could be so bad!"

Granny for the first time noticed a fiery earnestness in her grandson, and gathered herself up. She said: "Oh! He is your God, is he?"

"Yes, he is, and I won't hear anyone speak lightly of him."

"What else can I know, a poor ignorant hag like me! Do I read the newspapers? Do I listen to lectures? Am I told what is what by anyone? How should I know anything about that man Gandhi!"

"He is not a man; he is a Mahatma!" cried Sriram.

"What do you know about a Mahatma, anyway?" asked Granny.

Sriram fidgeted and rocked himself in his chair in great anger. He had not come prepared to face a situation of this kind. He had been only prepared to face a granny who might show sullenness at his absence, create difficulties for him when he wanted to go away and exhibit more sorrow and rage than levity. But here she was absolutely reckless, frivolous, and without the slightest sense of responsibility or respect. This was a situation which he had not anticipated, and he had no technique to meet it. It was no use, he realized, showing righteous indignation: that would only tickle the old lady more and more, and when the time came for him to take her permission and go, she might become too intractable. She might call in the neighbours, and make fun of him. He decided that he must change his tactics. Suddenly springing up he asked: "Granny, have you had your food? I am keeping you away from it, talking like this!"

"It doesn't matter," she said, almost on the point of giggling. "How many years is it since I had a mouthful of food at night — must be nearly twenty years. You couldn't have seen me in your lifetime eating at night."

There was such a ring of pride in her voice that Sriram felt impelled to say: "There is nothing extraordinary in it. Anybody might be without food." He wanted to add, "The Mahatma has fasted for so many days on end, and so often," but suppressed it. The old lady however had no need of being told anything. She added at once, "No! When Mahatma Gandhi fasts, everybody talks about it."

"And when you fast at nights only, nobody notices it, and that is all the difference between you and Gandhiji?" She was struck by the sharp manner in which he spoke.

She asked: "Do you want your dinner?"

"Yes, just to please you, that is all. I am not hungry, I told you that. And this stuff is good, made of good ghee. You may tell them so. I've eaten a great quantity of it and I'm not hungry."

Granny came back to her original mood after all these unexpected transitions. She said: "You must eat your dinner, my boy," very earnestly. She bustled about again as if for a distinguished visitor. She pulled a dining leaf out of a bundle in the kitchen rack, spread it on the floor, sprinkled a little water on it, and drew the bronze rice pot nearer, and sat down in order to be able to serve him without getting up again. The little lamp wavered in its holder. He ate in silence, took a drink of water out of the good old brass tumbler that was by his side; he cast a glance at the old bronze vessel out of which rice had been served to him for years. He suddenly felt depressed at the sight of it all. He was oppressed with the thought that he was leaving these old associations, that this was really a farewell party. He was going into an unknown life right from here. God knew what was in store for him. He felt very gloomy at the thought of it all. He knew it would be no good ever talking to his granny about his plans, or the Mahatma or Bharati. All that was completely beyond her comprehension. She would understand only edibles and dinner and fasting at night in order to impress a neighbour with her austerity. No use talking to her about anything. Best to leave in the morning without any fuss. He had obeyed Mahatmaji's mandate to the extent of seeing her and speaking to her. The Mahatma should be satisfied and not expect him to be able to bring about a conversion in the old lady's outlook, enough to earn her blessing.

Granny was very old, probably eighty, ninety, or a hundred. He had never tried to ascertain her age correctly. And she would not understand new things. At dead of night, after assuring himself that Granny was fast asleep, he got up, scribbled a note to her by the night lamp, and placed it under the brass pot containing water on the window sill, which she was bound to lift first thing in the morning. She could carry it to a neighbour and have it read to her if she had any difficulty in finding her glasses. Perhaps she might not like to have it read by the neighbours. She would always cry: "Sriram, my glasses, where are the wretched glasses gone?" whenever anything came to her hand for reading, and it would be his duty to go to the cupboard, and fetch them. Now he performed the same duty in anticipation. He tip-toed to the almirah, took the glasses out of their case silently, and returned to the hall, leaving the spectacle case open, because it had a tendency to close with a loud clap. He placed the glasses beside his letter of farewell, silently opened the door, and stepped into the night.

THINK ABOUT IT

1. Describe the relationships the Mahatma's camp followers have with one another. How are these relationships different from Sriram's relationship with his granny?

2. Why does Sriram decide to leave his home with Granny and join the Mahatma?

TALK ABOUT IT

3. Describe life in the Mahatma's camp. Do you know of any political action groups that lead this type of life today?

4. Would you ever consider following a leader like the Mahatma? Would you leave your childhood family to follow such a leader? Why or why not?

WRITE ABOUT IT

5. What do you find positive about Sriram's decision to leave home? What is negative about his decision?

6. Have you separated from your childhood family and created a new "family" for yourself? Describe the process of separation from the old relationships and formation of the new relationships.

READ MORE ABOUT IT

Fischer, Louis. *The Life of Mahatma Gandhi*. New York: Harper & Row, Publishers, 1950.

Green, Martin. *Gandhi: Voice of a New Age Revolution*. New York: The Continuum Publishing Company, 1993.

Narayan, R. K. *Under the Banyan Tree and Other Stories*. New York: Viking Press, 1985.

Narayan, R. K. *Waiting for the Mahatma*. Chicago: The University of Chicago Press, 1981.

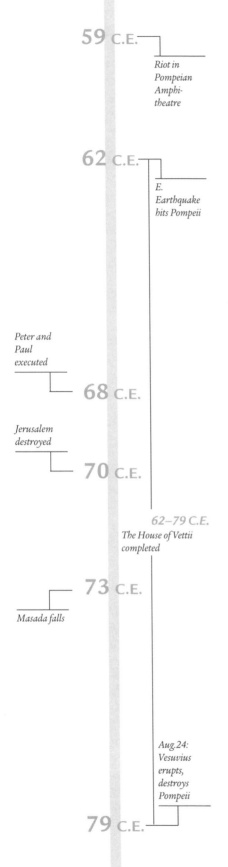

59 C.E.

*Riot in
Pompeian
Amphi-
theatre*

62 C.E.

*E.
Earthquake
hits Pompeii*

*Peter and
Paul
executed*

68 C.E.

*Jerusalem
destroyed*

70 C.E.

62–79 C.E.

*The House of Vettii
completed*

73 C.E.

Masada falls

*Aug.24:
Vesuvius
erupts,
destroys
Pompeii*

79 C.E.

JEFFERY R. W. DONLEY

The Roman House

Jeffery Rex Wayne Donley is Professor of Interdisciplinary Studies and Humanities at Valencia Community College in Orlando, Florida. He holds advanced degrees in Classics, History, Religion, Linguistics, and Philosophy. Donley's masters work at Cincinnati, Princeton, and doctoral work at the University of Birmingham, England, and Oxford University, England, has prepared him to interpret and write about Roman society.

Rome was the greatest city of the ancient world. It covered an area almost twelve miles in circumference. Buildings and people were closely packed. The city contained baths, thirty-seven gates, twenty-nine roads, over thirteen hundred fountains, twenty-eight libraries, and a large subterranean channel (sewer) called the Cloaca Maxima. The city used three hundred fifty million gallons of water a day. The heart and center of Rome was the forum, the market center which was the rendezvous point for the majority of the population during the morning hours. But the heart and center of Roman life and the Roman family was the *domus* or house. The following article discusses the different parts and characteristics of the aristocratic Roman house and family.

IT IS SAID that home is where the heart is. But to the middle and upper aristocracy of the Late Roman Republic (133-31 B.C.E) and of Imperial Rome (B.C.E 31-C.E. 193), the home, or *domus,* is where the hearth is. The Roman hearth was a fireplace where the Romans kept an undying fire burning, symbolic of the goddess Vesta, to ensure the family's continuity. On each Roman hearth stood statuettes of the family Lares, the household deities who guarded all exterior possessions of the family, and the Penates, the household guardians of the family's interior belongings. These household deities protected a home that enfolded its guests with warmth, wel-comed its family and friends, and appealed to the senses of both family and friends.

It was the paterfamilias, or father, who was the master of each Roman home. He exercised the legal power of life and death over his wife, children, relatives, and slaves. The father was expected to have cultivated the Roman virtue of *gravitas,* or seriousness. This seriousness meant that the father was disciplined, focused, and responsible in all matters that pertained to his home, family, and business. Education of the children (the sons) was the responsibility of the father. School was held in small rented rooms or out in the open air. The father would entrust his sons to a Greek tutor for elementary learning of reading and writing.

A servant called a *pedagogue* would accompany each child to school. Secondary studies were conducted with a *grammaticus*. He would teach physics, poetry, astronomy, history, Greek and Latin languages, and the classics. A final stage of education was in rhetoric, conducted by a *rhetor*, or teacher of eloquence. Flogging was the accepted methodology of correction for the children.

The *matrona,* or mother, was under the father's authority and would not do anything to discredit the good name of her husband, the master. As a woman, she was limited in many respects, but she did display and exercise some autonomy. She did not need the master's permission to go to the Roman forum (the downtown shopping center). She could manage her own property and exercised control over all of the master's slaves. The master's daughters would have their first marriages arranged by the parents. Girls could be betrothed at birth and had to be at least twelve years old to be married, while boys had to be at least fourteen years old. It was the father and mother's job to ensure that the home was a very personal place for a joyous life with family and friends. This included entertainment, pets, and family get-togethers. They desired a home that afford privacy for the family from the outside world and especially from the city "noise." Many interior rooms were closed to the outside world, while others were open to the public.

There are two basic types of Roman house plans. The first is a smaller house with only an atrium. The second and larger type is the house with atrium and peristyle. If one toured the second, larger house, what would one see and experience? As one approached a Roman house, one would notice that the exterior of the

PUBLIC LAVATORY NEAR THE FORUM, C. 161
C.E. Timgrad, North Africa

VIA DEI BALCONI, IN OSTIA ANTICA.
Ostia, Italy

**THE APARTMENTS OF
THE HOUSE OF DIANA**
1st Century B.C.E. Ostia, Italy

INTERIOR OF A ROMAN HOUSE, C. 1ST CENTURY B.C.E.
Pompeii, Italy

house was whitewashed and not very impressive. Other cultures were noted for their beautiful exteriors, but not the Romans. They were known for the elegant interior designs. The Roman house was often surrounded by the master's *tabernae* or shops where wares were sold to the public. The master's *tabernae* included vegetable stands, bakeries, coppersmiths, wine shops, cleaning establishments, perfumeries, jewelry shops, and moneychangers, located to the right and left of the house's outside walls. Part of the master's income was derived from these shops. He also rented space to tenants. In the upper stories of the Roman house, nice independent apartments were usually rented to the public at 10,000 sesterces (about $400) per year. The lowly slave was packed into an upper story *cella* or cell, which included a stool, a blanket, and a thin mat to sleep on. External stairways ascended from the street to the rented rooms.

The house beyond the shops was accentuated with a porch and its roof supported by two twin embedded columns jutting out into the street. Moving under the porch one entered two or three gates that were marked as the transition from the outside world to the inside world of the home. The main entrance corridors, or *fauces,* exhibited magnificent and beautiful decorations which focused on the master's success. This main entrance was left open in the morning for business transactions and for important receptions given by the master. No wheeled vehicles were allowed on the streets between sunrise and 4 P M. So, after 4 P M, the master's business or transport wagons (the *plaustrum*) entered an enclave within the house to unload the household provisions. After passing through the gate, the guest crossed a threshold into another room which also served as a transition to the inner world of the home. An elegant and elaborately decorated

vestibulum was usually one of the largest rooms of a Roman house. In this vestibule, or lobby, colors played a starring role in creating a mood of elegance. In a small room directly off the vestibule, a highly responsible slave was posted who served as a *ianitor,* or guard. This guard, usually with a surly watchdog, kept a watchful and dutiful eye on those who entered and exited the vestibulum. If the person did not meet the approval of the ianitor, he or she would be stopped and escorted out of the home. In some Roman homes, a watchdog was not needed. They only needed the words *Cave Canem* ("Beware the dog") written on the mosaic floor. In some Roman homes, a pet magpie would greet guests with a "*Salve! Salve!*" ("I hope you are well"), as they entered into a magnificent courtyard reception room called the atrium.

The *atrium* was paved with beautiful mosaics and framed by Corinthian columns supporting the roof. At its center was a *compluvium* or skylight. Covers called the *vela Cilicia* were placed over the skylight as protection from the bad weather. The atrium's roof sloped inward so that rainfall drained into an *impluvium* or central basin (pool) where luxurious water plants grew, statues stood, and a fountain sprayed jets of water. The doorways to the rooms off the atrium were closed by heavy blue or purple curtains. The walls were decorated with beautiful frescoes, along with objects of fine art displayed on pedestals. A splendid array of family portrait busts lined the walls of the atrium and the floor displayed elaborate mosaics of Greek legends and battles. Located in the rear of the atrium was the *exedra* or *tablinum,* the master's office. It was used to conduct social affairs, business, discussions, and to receive clients. Here, the master could write while lying on a couch with his right leg curled up and

a tablet placed on his knee. The tablinum also contained a closet filled with valuable waxen death masks that had covered the heads of dead relatives. It was distinguished by a broad access corridor and fine decorations, including the marriage couch of the master and his wife. Moving back into the atrium one would then go out into a second courtyard even larger and more handsome than the first. Off this courtyard were rooms, distinguished by their size, architecture, and decor. These were reserved for family and guests for purely social and private uses (see Color Plates 9 & 10). Guests and visitors in this part of the house were welcomed with an *Ave!* ("Hail"), as well as a *Salve!* They were received through heavy curtains into the *peristylia,* the most charming and outstanding part of the Roman house. The *peristylia* was the heart and central court of the Roman home. It was a square court garden embellished with plush greenery, tropical plants, rare flowers, pools, and a fountain. A slave stood by an elegant water clock (hour glass) and announced each hour of the day to the family. Pets such as greyhounds (with their own personal servants), monkeys, and owls, could be seen in the peristyle. Many wealthy Romans even had lap dogs who also had their own personal attendants. Statues, elegant reading couches called *lectuli* or "little beds," backless chairs, and small tables, furnished the court under the colonnades. Pictures of landscapes, of the Roman hero Aeneas' adventures, and Greek mythology graced the walls of the peristyle. A *compluvium* or skylight in the roof was open to the sky, allowing rain to be collected in a rectangular pool below, the *impluvium.* Underground cisterns *(collecti imbres)* stored the rainwater for household use. The opening in the roof also allowed air and light to circulate throughout the adjacent rooms.

GOATS AND GOATHERD FROM HADRIAN'S VILLA AT TRIVOLI, C. 130
C.E. Mosaic. Musei E Gallerie, Pontificie, Vatican, Rome, Italy

Besides the practical purposes of lighting the interior, the light from the compluvium created a dramatic mood which brightened the Roman house. The surrounding architectural decor of Doric, Ionic, Corinthian, and Tuscan colonnades held the roof on its four sides.

At the rear of the peristyle was located one of the most important rooms in the entire house, the *culina* or kitchen. These were staffed by cooks, slaves whose culinary experience made them the highest priced slaves at the Roman slave market. The kitchen contained no stoves, only brick hearths, and it was not uncommon for Roman kitchens to catch fire because of their cramped corners. Copper utensils, dippers, forks, spoons, pans, and molds were common kitchen utensils. Cooks would prepare a *puls* or wheat porridge and make flat bread about two inches in thickness. Cabbages, turnips, cucumbers, melons, onions, and pumpkins were also prepared along with apples,

ALEXANDER AT ISSYS, C. 79 C.E.
Mosaic from House at Pompeii, Italy

plums, pears, walnuts, almonds, olives, apricots, dates, and grapes. Sausage and bacon were Roman favorites, along with duck, partridge, rabbit, venison, grouse, and stuffed pig's bladder. Romans, too, loved their eels, shellfish, and especially mullet. Olive oil was used for frying and seasoning. Mushrooms cooked in honey was a Roman favorite, along with fish entrails with finely chopped fish pounded into a delicious sauce. Wine was served chilled in the summer and served hot, mulled with spices, in the winter. For breakfast, cooks would prepare a *ientaculum* (or breakfast) for the family consisting of bread covered with olives, raisins, and cheese, which was sometimes dipped in wine. At noon, the *prandium* (or lunch) was served consisting of salads, bread, cheese, meats — the leftovers from the previous evening's dinner. This meat was eaten without even sitting down.

The host was obligated to treat those guests handsomely who were escorted into the grand reception hall, called the *triclinium,* or great dining room. This dining room was usually the largest and grandest area of the Roman house and had three entrances. It usually was reserved for the evening meal, which was the main meal of the day. A dining table, or *cartibulum,* was located at its entrance. Small low tables of finely crafted wood, two feet in diameter, furnished the *triclinium*. These finely crafted tables were among the most valued possessions of the house. A salt cellar and a vinegar bottle were always on the table. The *catera,* or large wine bowl, was placed on the table with a long-handled ladle used for filling the guests' cups. Conversation around the table was an important part of Roman life for it brought together the master's family, as well as serving as a social occasion where the master could discharge his social obligation to entertain his guests.

NAVAL SCENE, c. 1st CENTURY C.E.
Mosaic from Interior of House at Ostia, Italy

DEATH OF ARCHIMEDES, c. 79 C.E.
Mosaic from Herculaneum, Italy

Dining was also an opportunity to show off the host's wealth for the *triclinium* was decorated with beautiful still life pictures of birds, fruit, and fish.

The *cena*, or dinner, was the grand meal of the day and was served sometime after 4 PM. Guests were arranged on three light-weight dining couches so that they faced each other. Each couch accommodated three guests. A servant accompanied each guest who took off his/her shoes as soon as he/she reclined on the couch. A slave called a *nomenclater* seated the guests according to importance by pointing to the proper place for each person. The master, his wife, and guests would recline on couches with small pillows to tuck under their elbows as they dined. Plates were held in the left hand, while eating with the right hand. Wide windows were located to the right and left of the couches so that the guests could view the garden as they ate. Children would sit on couches. Their servants sat on benches some distance away. Thus, a typical Roman dinner party would consist of the master, his family, and nine guests.

Individual servants with specific tasks served the diners. The first course was the *gustatio* or appetizers. This consisted of light dishes such as eggs and *mulsum*, a mixture of wine and honey. The second course consisted of meats, fish, and vegetables. The *structor*, or master carver, would slice the meat in time with a flute or harp player who was playing in another room. The *structor* also arranged the food on the plates artistically. Since the diners used their hands, not utensils, servants had the diners wash and dry their hands between each of the three courses. The third course was the desserts of oysters, grapes, nuts, and pastries. The

purpose of dessert was to arouse a thirst which led to a commissatio, or drinking party. During this heavy drinking time, the guests would wear flowers and scent themselves with perfume. *Apophoreta,* or presents, were distributed to the guests. The host would provide dancers, dwarfs as jesters, acrobats, skits, make announcements, and sometimes instruct his guests on his personal philosophy of life. At 8:00 PM, the dinner was over, the guests were ushered out or to a bedroom, and the family went to sleep.

The *cubicula*, or bedrooms, were small and among the more private parts of the house, and were located along its side walls. These rooms were only used to sleep in and were usually closed off to the rest of the house during daylight hours. The master, wife, children, guests, and favored slaves slept in these rooms. The bed was often raised slightly above the rest of the room and was made of crafted wood and thick mattresses. Close to the bedrooms (and kitchen) were the bathrooms and lavatory which were used for bathing, physical exercise, and intellectual activities. The lavatory was a two-hole latrine that was supplied with a water flush that emptied directly into the sewer in the neighboring street.

The Roman house most adequately met the needs of the aristocratic family in Rome. The home was designed to provide a refuge for the master, as well as a place to entertain, conduct business, and bring the family together. It also was designed for an "open-air" lifestyle. Each room, from the atrium to peristyle, was designed and decorated for the comfort and pleasure of the Roman family and as a retreat from the outside world. Each room had special signif-

icance and special family use. Size, elegance, and practicality were characteristics of the Roman house. To the Roman family, home was truly where the hearth is.

THINK ABOUT IT

1. What are the major rooms in the Roman house?
2. How does your house compare to the Roman house? Which would you rather live in? Why?

TALK ABOUT IT

3. What rooms were considered more important in a Roman house? What are the important rooms in your house?
4. Why do houses differ from one culture to another? How do these differences reflect different concepts of family?

WRITE ABOUT IT

5. Select a model home from your local newspaper. What concept of family is reflected in its design?
6. Design your perfect home. How many rooms would it include and what kind of rooms would you have? What concept of family would it express?

READ MORE ABOUT IT

Brown, Frank E. Cosa: *The Making of a Roman City*. New York: G. Braziller, 1980.

Frier, Bruce W. *Landlords and Tenants in Imperial Rome*. Princeton, NJ: Princeton University Press, 1980.

Grant, Michael. *Cities of Vesuvius: Pompeii and Herculaneum*. New York: Macmillan, 1971.

Sear, Frank. *Roman Architecture*. New York: G. Braziller, 1982.

R O B E R T A   V A N D E R M A S T

Mary Cassatt

Roberta Vandermast is coordinator and professor of Interdisciplinary Studies at Valencia Community College where she has been teaching interdisciplinary courses for twenty-six years. She has co-authored three humanities textbooks, as well as a manual for the Interdisciplinary Studies Program at Valencia. In high school, she began a life-long love affair with the French Impressionists. After beginning teaching, this love expanded to include American artists, especially Mary Cassatt.

Mary Cassatt's life, as well as her art, is the epitome of devotion to family. She had a close relationship with her parents, brothers, and sister. Although she never married or had any children of her own, she was devoted to her nieces and nephews. This devotion is echoed in the loving depictions of intimate family relationships which are found in her paintings, drawings, and prints. In an age when women were supposed to marry, have children, and confine their ambitions to a well-managed household, Mary Cassatt exercised a stubborn individuality that allowed her to pursue a career in painting and to become one of the best painters of families in the history of art.

MARY CASSATT'S *Self Portrait,* painted in 1880, gives little clue to the personality behind the face. The woman in the painting seems shy, her face framed by the large bow at her neck and the large hat covering her head. The position of her left hand hints that she may be drawing and, as her gaze meets ours, it seems she is concentrating on drawing our portrait, not hers. Nowhere do we meet the strong-willed and determined woman who was eulogized at her death as "one of the best women painters of all time." Nowhere in this portrait do we see her struggle to learn and master her craft at a time when painting was not considered "women's work." Moreover, nowhere in this portrait — but abundantly in

her other works — do we see the devotion to family that is the hallmark of her art and her life.

One of five children, Mary Cassatt was born in Allegheny City, now Pittsburgh, on May 22, 1844. Her father, Robert Cassatt, was a successful businessman who believed that his children, especially the boys, needed a broad and well-rounded education. To accomplish this, he moved the family to Europe for several years, first in France and later in Germany, so that his oldest son could pursue studies abroad. The Cassatt children learned French and German and when they returned home, the sixteen-year-old Mary declared her desire to become an artist. Robert Cassatt replied, "I would rather see you dead."

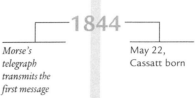

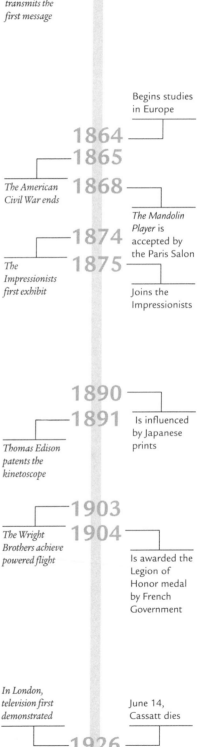

1844
Morse's telegraph transmits the first message
May 22, Cassatt born

Begins studies in Europe

1864
1865
The American Civil War ends
1868
The Mandolin Player is accepted by the Paris Salon

1874
The Impressionists first exhibit
1875
Joins the Impressionists

1890
1891
Thomas Edison patents the kinetoscope
Is influenced by Japanese prints

1903
The Wright Brothers achieve powered flight
1904
Is awarded the Legion of Honor medal by French Government

In London, television first demonstrated
June 14, Cassatt dies
1926

MARY CASSATT, SELF PORTRAIT c. 1880.
Watercolor on Paper, 13 × 9 ⅝ In.
National Portrait Gallery, Smithsonian Institution, Washington, DC

Mary's persistence overcame her father's objections. He relented and Mary was admitted to the Philadelphia Academy of Fine Arts, one of the few art schools which accepted female students at the time. Women, however, were not permitted to attend the nude life drawing classes and were confined to drawing from plaster models which were suitably clothed. It was standard practice at the Academy for all art students to draw from plaster models for at least two years before they were allowed to exercise any creativity. For Mary, who had seen the paintings of the masters in the great museums of Europe, this was an intolerable burden. She announced that she was going to Europe to learn to draw. Her father gave her his permission to go, but only if she was accompanied by a suitable chaperon, her mother. These two incidents, her determination to become an artist and her stubborn insistence on learning on her own terms, underscore Cassatt's strongwilled personality which became evident early in her life.

After spending some time studying in France and Italy, Mary established herself in Paris where she hoped to have some of her paintings accepted by the prestigious Salon of Painting and Sculpture. The Salon had functioned as the arbiter of taste in French art for over a century. To have a work accepted by the Salon for its annual show meant that lucrative commissions would follow. Since Mary's father demanded that she earn money at her craft, public recognition was a necessity. In 1868, her painting, *The Mandolin Player*, was accepted. Her brother Alexander noted Cassatt's reaction in a letter to his fiance:

Mary is in high spirits as her picture has been accepted for the annual exhibition in Paris. You must understand that this is a great honor for a young artist and not only has it been accepted but it has been "hung on the line." I don't know what that means but I suppose it means it has been hung in a favorable position. Mary's art name is "Mary Stevenson"[1] under which name I suppose she expects to become famous, poor child.

Alexander was right. It was a great honor to be considered among the very best artists in France, and an even rarer honor for an American woman! Alexander was also right about the position of Cassatt's painting. To be "hung on the line," or at eye level, meant that her painting got the maximum possible exposure to the viewing public. Commissions did follow and, in subsequent years, Mary had additional paintings accepted by the Salon. A turning point came, however, in 1875. Previously, Mary had painted a portrait of one of her favorite subjects, her sister Lydia, who had been visiting her in Paris. The Salon rejected the painting, but agreed to reconsider it if Cassatt made a few changes. To change the painting meant that Cassatt would have to conform to the stylistic standards which were enforced by the Salon. These standards stood in direct opposition to the individual style which was evolving in Cassatt's work. To prove a point, Cassatt toned down the colors in the painting and it was accepted the following year. This demonstrated to Cassatt that winning the approval of the Salon would require her to conform to a style which was not her own. To Cassatt, independence was essential and, as a result, she accepted an invitation to

join an exhibition of "Independents." These "Independents" were popularly known as "Impressionists" and each of them had been rejected by the Salon for refusing to conform to its stylistic dictates. Recalling the Impressionists' invitation to join their show, Cassatt wrote:

I accepted with joy. Finally I would be able to work with absolute independence and without concern for the eventual judgement of a jury! I already knew who my masters were. I admired Manet, Courbet and Degas. I rejected conventional art. I began to live …

The Impressionists not only accepted Cassatt without judgment, they offered her a style of painting which came closest to her personal style. The Impressionists were interested in new dimensions. They wanted to revolutionize art in terms of its subjects, setting, techniques, and palette. Impressionist painters sought to capture scenes they observed in everyday life. To do this, they took their canvases to their subjects. Until this time, almost all painting was done in the artist's studio and was composed after carefully sketching and plotting an arrangement of figures on a canvas. The Impressionists took their canvases into the *plein air*, that is, out into the open. They painted out of doors in gardens and by the seashore. They painted in the homes of their subjects, often using their own families as models, and as they did, they transformed the everyday into the artistic. In order to capture these scenes from everyday life, the Impressionist painter worked quickly, capturing the scene's essence in a few broad brush strokes. Thus, the Impressionists abandoned careful precise brushwork in favor of lose, sweeping strokes capable of capturing everyday subjects, often painted out of doors.

---

[1] Cassatt thought that her middle name, Stevenson, sounded more American. However, she soon abandoned this pretense and, from then on, painted as Mary Cassatt.

THE LETTER, 1891.
Mary Cassatt, 13⁹/₁₆ × 8¹⁵/₁₆ In.
The Metropolitan Museum of Art, New York, N.Y.

In addition to a new perspective on their subjects and their settings, as well as the evolution of new techniques, the Impressionists brought a new perspective on color. Their new theory of color was directly related to their desire to capture the effects of sunlight. They realized that eyesight is made possible by the light reflected from objects in nature. It is this reflected sunlight which is captured in the retina of the eye. The prismatic analysis of sunlight had shown that sunlight was composed of the colors of the spectrum: violet, indigo, blue, green, yellow, orange and red. The Impressionists adopted these colors as their palette. The result was that the canvases of the Impressionists were brighter in color than the art favored by the Salon. In fact, the paintings of the Impressionists are flooded with sunlight since light is the essential ingredient in their compositions.

By 1875 Cassatt's color scheme and subject matter already showed an affinity for Impressionism. In the Impressionist circle she found not only acceptance for her individual style of painting, she also found a close-knit group of friends who met regularly in the cafes of Paris to discuss artistic theory and critique each other's work. Their influence on Cassatt's development can be seen in her painting, *Young Mother Sewing*. In this small painting, 36 × 29 inches, light enters from the side and floods the canvas. In the center, a young mother is carefully sewing or mending a garment, seated in an arm chair in a room facing a garden. Her eyes focus carefully on her work and we can imagine that this is intended to be a sewing lesson for her young daughter who is looking at the viewer, rather than at her mother. The faces of the mother and child, as well as their clothing and the background behind them, are formed of broad strokes of color, most of which are

the colors of the spectrum. However, Cassatt's painting departs from those of some of the Impressionists in that she adds white and black to her palette. Having won her independence from the Salon, it is doubtful that she would then sacrifice it to the Impressionist color theory. While her paintings show her affinity for the Impressionist style, they also demonstrate that she retained her individual preferences which reflect her strong independence.

To Cassatt, the most influential voice among the Impressionists was Edgar Degas, who became Cassatt's lifelong friend. They enjoyed a close friendship beginning with her first exhibit with the Impressionists and lasting until Degas died in 1912.

She often served as his model and he always served as her harshest critic. While there is no evidence that there was ever a romantic relationship between them, we know that before she died, Cassatt burned all of his letters to her. Together, they spent many hours discussing both the practical and theoretical aspects of art. Degas remarked to friends that he could talk to Mary Cassatt in a way he could not talk to other French women, and he reluctantly admitted that he did not think "that a woman can draw so well." In return, Cassatt admired Degas' work. In one reminiscence, she recalled first seeing his work, "How well I remember ... seeing for the first time Degas' pastels in the window of a picture dealer on the Boulevard Haussmann. I used to go and flatten my nose against the window and absorb all I could of his art. It changed my life."

On the other hand, she harbored no illusions about the nature of their relationship, remarking to her best friend, Louisine Havemeyer, "Oh, my dear, he is dreadful!" When Louisine pressed her for the reason their rela-

tionship had lasted for so many years, Cassatt replied:

> I am independent! I can live alone and I love to work. Sometimes it made him furious that he could not find a chink in my armor, and there would be months when we just could not see each other, and then something I painted would bring us together again and he would go to Durand-Ruel's[2] and say something nice about me, or come to see me himself. When he saw my *Boy before the Mirror,* he said to Durand-Ruel: "Where is she? I must see her at once. It is the greatest picture of the century." When I saw him he went over all of the details of the picture with me and expressed great admiration for it, and then, as if regretting what he had said, he relentlessly added: "It has all of your qualities and all of your faults …."

Thus Cassatt had established herself in the eyes of her reluctant admirer, Degas, as one of the best painters of all time. Cassatt's strong-willed determination and fierce independence were the armor which shielded her in her battle to become a good painter. This toughness was balanced by her softer side, her devotion to her family. In 1877 Cassatt's family moved to Paris. Her father had retired from business and he thought that the family needed to be together. Although Mary had returned to America on several occasions, there was little tolerance in America for an unmarried woman who worked, let alone painted. In addition, America did not offer the climate of creativity and innovation which permeated the Impressionist circle. Although close to her family, Mary probably did not expect to become their permanent

---

2 Durand-Ruel was a well-known Paris art dealer, one of only a few who displayed works by the Impressionists in his gallery.

Mary Cassatt

host. However, she enjoyed having her sister Lydia stay with her and made many drawings of her, as well as some of her parents. Sadly, five years after the family moved to Paris, Lydia died of kidney disease. Mary coped with her grief by throwing herself into her work. As a result, the paintings and drawings she did of Lydia became some of her finest.

In 1885 her brother Alexander brought his family for a visit. Mary filled her studio with books, games, and toys, using the children as models for her work. At this time, she painted the *Portrait of Alexander J. Cassatt and his son, Robert Kelso Cassatt,* a work which reveals Cassatt's devotion to family and her ability to capture the essence of a familial relationship. In this painting, the father and son dominate the canvas which is thirty-nine inches high by thirty-two inches wide. The father sits rather stiffly in an overstuffed arm chair, holding a paper and gazing out of the scene. His young son, Robert, perches on the arm of the chair and throws his left arm around his father's neck. His arm draws their heads together, indicating not only the son's love of his father, but the father's love for his son. In the background, the room and furnishings are reduced to the bare essentials, conveyed by broad areas of color which suggest the existence of the arm chair, walls, and windows. The most precise execution is reserved for the faces of the father and son, where their thoughts are conveyed to the viewer by the way in which Cassatt painted their eyes and facial features.

The lifelike quality and sense of intimacy with which Cassatt imbues this portrait are characteristic of her paintings of her favorite subject, her family and their relationships with each other.

The theme of family relationships is also echoed in *Young Mother Sewing.* In this painting, the little girl draws herself into her mother's lap. Reacting as children often do in the presence of a stranger, the little girl positions herself within her mother's protective care. The mother's willingness to work with the child so near reflects her love and care for her child. In a moment of tenderness duplicated thousands of times every day, a mother envelops a child in her presence, a movement that unites and cements family bonds. Cassatt senses this moment and uses it to add a unique dimension to her paintings. The relationship of parent to child permeates Cassatt's work and is her forté.

While Impressionist influences and the theme of family relationships are present in these works, another important influence in her painting was her interest in Japanese prints.

In 1890 Paris was the scene of an exhibition of Japanese art works. Cassatt attended with Degas and they studied and analyzed the artistic techniques used by the Japanese. Cassatt was so taken with the works that she purchased several prints by the great Japanese printmaker, Utamuro, which she framed and hung in her home. Japanese printmakers often emphasized the intimacy and privacy of a

scene by recording things only a family member would see. This appealed to Cassatt and she began to use ideas taken from Japanese prints in her own work. In 1891 she produced *The Letter,* a color print with drypoint and aquatint. Cassatt described the method she used in this work in this way:

> My method is very simple. I drew an outline in drypoint and transferred this to two other plates, making in all three plates, never more, for each proof. Then I put an aquatint wherever the color was to be printed; the color was painted on the plate as it was to appear in the proof …

While creating these prints, she worked eight hours straight, producing only eight to ten prints per day. The effect, however, is stunning. In drypoint, the artist draws an image directly on a copper plate with a sharp tool. The image is drawn in reverse and a proof is pulled so that the artist can see not only what the image will look like when printed, but also how the plate will print. In this print, Cassatt has chosen the moment at which the subject, a young woman, is sealing a letter. In Japanese prints, scenes of concealment were often popular. The expression on her face is almost melancholy. Is she sad, lonely, or regretful? As Cassatt's figure seals her letter, we are left wondering about its contents. In addition, her hair style, the features of her face, and her slightly crossed eyes show how much Cassatt has borrowed from the

Japanese. In traditional Japanese art, crossed eyes and a demure demeanor are indications of great beauty. In addition, curled fingers, in this case grasping the envelope, are a symbol of grace and elegance. This small print, only about fourteen inches by nine inches, gives us a brief glimpse into a very private moment in a woman's life, one we might come upon if we were members of her family.

Mary's family life was not as serene as her paintings might indicate. One of her brothers, a sickly child, died while Mary was still young. His death was followed several years later by the death of her beloved sister, Lydia. After Lydia, Mary endured the death of her father and then her mother. Through each of these crises, Mary coped with her sadness through her art, painting eloquent works celebrating family relationships. Painting relieved both her sadness and her loneliness. Her paintings became her children, a loving legacy to future generations. In 1904, her painting earned her the French *Légion d' honneur,* an award given to those who have made significant contributions to French culture. It was the only award Cassatt ever accepted. She was the woman who had said earlier in her life, " … no jury, no medals, no awards …." However, the significance of this award was not lost on her. Few Americans, much less women, had ever been honored in this way.

Cassatt's life did not end with such honor, however. She endured two more tragedies, first the sudden and unexpected death of her brother, Alexander, while she vacationed with his family, and then the death of Degas in 1912. Toward the end of her life, cataracts in both her eyes made it so difficult for her to see that she could work only in pastels. Nonetheless, she continued to produce beautiful drawings until her eye-

sight failed completely. One of the great painters of light, Mary Cassatt spent the last two years of her life in darkness.

On June 14, 1926, Mary Cassatt was buried at her beloved home, Château Beaufresne. One of her old friends, Ambroise Vollard wrote:

In the cemetery, after the last prayers, the pastor, according to Protestant custom, distributed to those present the roses and carnations strewn upon the coffin, that they might scatter them over the grave. Looking at the carpet of beautiful flowers, I fancied Mary Cassatt running to fetch a canvas and brushes.

The strong-willed, determined woman from America, devoted to independence and to family, made her mark on the history of art. Her art, as well as her life, is the epitome of devotion to the family. The loving depictions of intimate family relationships, seen in her subjects' faces and gestures, bring feeling to her art. Her command of technique and her knowledge of her craft show her great mastery. One of her admirers said of her:

Her clear and candid vision of truth, her sure taste, her training and the strength of her character have combined to produce an art that places her unquestionably in the front rank of American painters.

And, one might add, "in the front rank of French painters," as well.

THINK ABOUT IT
1. What obstacles did Mary Cassatt have to overcome to become a painter?
2. Describe how one of Cassatt's works demonstrates her style.

TALK ABOUT IT
3. Family relationships, especially those between parents and children, were an important theme in Cassatt's painting. What other cultures emphasize the close relationship between parents and children? Do these cultures stress the physical contact between parents and children as Cassatt does?
4. Have modern families lost the sense of intimacy and closeness that Cassatt records in her art? Discuss the reasons for your answer.

WRITE ABOUT IT
5. Find and study a print by the Japanese printmaker Utamuro. Are there similarities to Cassatt's *The Letter?*
6. Describe a scene which you feel would record an essential element of the modern family. Consider photographing this scene to accompany your description.

READ MORE ABOUT IT
Craze, Sophia. *Mary Cassatt.* New York/Avenel, NJ: Crescent Books, 1990.
Mary Cassatt 1844–1926. Washington: National Gallery of Art, 1970.
Roudebush, Jay. *Cassatt.* New York: Crown Publishers, Inc., 1979,

Hector and Andromache

c. 1184 B.C.E.

Troy is destroyed

c. 1000 B.C.E.

Iron Age in Athens

10th–9th centuries B.C.E. Stories of Trojan War circulate by bards

776 B.C.E.

First Olympic Games held

8th century B.C.E. Homer compiles the Iliad

Golden Age of Greece begins

c. 450 B.C.E.

Homer is well-known to any student of classical literature as the author of the *Iliad* and the *Odyssey;* however, beyond that, little is known about his life. The information from Greek historians would place him anywhere from the thirteenth to the eighth century B.C.E., but studies of the language of the *Iliad* place him in the eighth century B.C.E. He wrote in the Ionian dialect, so we can place him on the mainland of Greece. His great accomplishment is the setting into poetry the stories of the Trojan War which had circulated orally for centuries.

The *Iliad,* which means a poem about Ilium (Troy), is actually a story about the anger of Achilles, the great Greek hero. The events begin when Paris, the son of the Trojan king, runs off with Helen, the wife of Menelaus of Sparta. The war which results is the Trojan War and it rages on for ten years. The characters in the poem are presented to help the Greeks learn about virtue, to see virtue and vice as they play out in the story, but most importantly, to teach them about *areté,* the Greek virtue of excellence. The following selection concerns Hector, the champion of the Trojans and son of the Trojan king Priam. He comes to see his wife, Andromache, and his son, Astyanax, before returning to the battle.

SO SPEAKING, Hector of the shining helm departed and in speed made his way to his own well-established dwelling, but failed to find in the house Andromache of the white arms; for she, with the child, and followed by one fair-robed attendant, had taken her place on the tower in lamentation, and tearful. When he saw no sign of his perfect wife within the house, Hector stopped in his way on the threshold and spoke among the handmaidens:

"Come then, tell me truthfully as you may, handmaidens: where has Andromache of the white arms gone? Is she with any of the sisters of her lord or the wives of his brothers? Or has she gone to the house of Athene, where all the other lovely-haired women of Troy propitiate the grim goddess?"

Then in turn the hard-working housekeeper gave him an answer:

"Hector, since you have urged me to tell you the truth, she is not with any of the sisters of her lord or the wives of his brothers, nor has she gone to the house of Athene, where all the other lovely-haired women of Troy propitiate the grim goddess, but she has gone to the great bastion of Ilion, because she heard that the Trojans were losing, and great grew the strength of the Achaians. Therefore she has gone in speed to the wall, like a woman gone mad, and a nurse attending her carries the baby."

So the housekeeper spoke, and Hector hastened from his home backward by the way he had come through the well-laid streets. So as he had come to the gates on his way through the great city, the Skaian gates, whereby he would issue into the plain, there at last his own generous wife came running to meet him, Andromache, the daughter of high-hearted Eëtion; Eëtion, who had dwelt underneath wooded Plakos, in Thebe below Plakos, lord over the Kilikian people. It was his daughter who was given to Hector of the bronze helm. She came to him there, and beside her went an attendant carrying the boy in the fold of her bosom, a little child, only a baby, Hector's son, the admired, beautiful as a star shining, whom Hector called Skamandrios, but all of the others Astyanax — lord of the city; since Hector alone saved Ilion. Hector smiled in silence as he looked on his son, but she, Andromache, stood close beside him, letting her tears fall, and clung to his hand and called him by name and spoke to him:

"Dearest, your own great strength will be your death, and you have no pity on your little son, nor on me, ill-starred, who soon must be your widow; for presently the Achaians, gathering together, will set upon you and kill you; and for me it would be far better to sink into the earth when I have lost you, for there is no other consolation for me after you have gone to your destiny—only grief; since I have no father, no honored mother. It was brilliant Achilleus who slew my father, Eëtion, when he stormed the strong-founded citadel of the Kilikians, Thebe of the tower-

ing gates. He killed Eëtion but did not strip his armour, for his heart respected the dead man, but burned the body in all its elaborate war-gear and piled a grave mound over it, and the nymphs of the mountains, daughters of Zeus of the aegis, planted elm trees about it. And they who were my seven brothers in the great house all went upon a single day down into the house of the death god, for swift-footed brilliant Achilleus slaughtered all of them as they were tending their white sheep and their lumbering oxen; and when he had led my mother, who was queen under wooded Plakos, here, along with all his other possessions, Achilleus released her again, accepting ransom beyond count, but Artemis of the showering arrows struck her down in the halls of her father. Hector, thus you are father to me, and my honored mother, you are my brother, and you it is who are my young husband. Please take pity upon me then, stay here on the rampart, that you may not leave your child an orphan, your wife a widow, but draw your people up by the fig tree, there where the city is openest to attack, and where the wall may be mounted. Three times their bravest came that way, and fought there to storm it about the two Aiantes and renowned Idomeneus, about the two Atreidai and the fighting son of Tydeus. Either some man well skilled in prophetic arts had spoken, or the very spirit within themselves had stirred them to the onslaught."

Then tall Hector of the shining helm answered her:

"All these things are in my mind also, lady; yet I would feel deep shame before the Trojans, and the Trojan women with trailing garments, if like a coward I were to shrink aside from the fighting; and the spirit will not let me, since I have learned to be valiant and to fight always among the

foremost ranks of the Trojans, winning for my own self great glory, and for my father. For I know this thing well in my heart, and my mind knows it: there will come a day when sacred Ilion shall perish, and Priam, and the people of Priam of the strong ash spear.

But it is not so much the pain to come of the Trojans that troubles me, not even of Priam the king nor Hekabe, not the thought of my brothers who in their numbers and valour shall drop in the dust under the hands of men who hate them, as troubles me the thought of you, when some bronze-armoured Achaian leads you off, taking away your day of liberty, in tears; and in Argos you must work at the loom of another, and carry water from the spring Messeis or Hypereia, all unwilling, but strong will be the necessity upon you; and some day seeing you shedding tears a man will say of you: 'This is the wife of Hector, who was ever the bravest fighter of the Trojans, breakers of horses, in the days when they fought about Ilion.'

So will one speak of you; and for you it will be yet a fresh grief, to be widowed of such a man who could fight off the day of your slavery.

But may I be dead and the piled earth hide me under before I hear you crying and know by this that they drag you captive."

So speaking, glorious Hector held out his arms to his baby, who shrank back to his fair-girdled nurse's bosom screaming, and frightened at the aspect of his own father, terrified as he saw the bronze and the crest with its horse-hair, nodding dreadfully, as he thought, from the peak of the helmet. Then his beloved father laughed out, and his honoured mother, and at once glorious Hector lifted from his head the helmet and laid it in all its shining upon the ground. Then taking up his dear son he tossed him about in his arms, and kissed him, and lifted his voice in prayer to Zeus and the other immortals:

"Zeus, and you other immortals, grant that this boy, who is my son, may be as I am, preeminent among the Trojans, great in strength, as am I, and rule strongly over Ilion; and some day let them say of him: 'He is better by far than his father,' as he comes in from the fighting; and let him kill his enemy and bring home the blooded spoils, and delight the heart of his mother."

So speaking he set his child again in the arms of his beloved wife, who took him back again to her fragrant bosom smiling in her tears; and her husband saw, and took pity upon her, and stroked her with his hand, and called her by name and spoke to her:

"Poor Andromache! Why does your heart sorrow so much for me? No man is going to hurl me to Hades, unless it is fated, but as for fate, I think that no man yet has escaped it once it has taken its first form, neither brave man nor coward. Go therefore back to our house, and take up your own work, the loom and the distaff, and see to it that your handmaidens ply their work also; but the men must see to the fighting, all men who are the people of Ilion, but I beyond others."

So glorious Hector spoke and again took up the helmet with its crest of horse-hair, while his beloved wife went homeward, turning to look back on the way, letting the live tears fall. And as she came in speed into the well-settled household of Hector the slayer of men, she found numbers of handmaidens within, and her coming stirred all of them into lamentation. So they mourned in his house over Hector while he was living still, for they thought he would never again come back from the fighting alive, escaping the Achaian hands and their violence.

THINK ABOUT IT

1. What pronoun best describes the relationship between Hector and Andromache?
2. The Greek epics were meant to instruct the reader about the important values in Greek society. What do we learn about their sense of family from this passage?

TALK ABOUT IT

3. Do you think Hector is right to leave his wife and child to fight? Are things different in today's world?
4. Has military life been a factor in your family? How does it make a difference in family relationships?

WRITE ABOUT IT

5. Write a story which describes how a family would prepare itself for someone going off to war.
6. Write a letter describing how you would feel if someone you love were going off to war.

READ MORE ABOUT IT

Bespaloff, Rachel. *On the Iliad*. Princeton, NJ: Princeton University Press, 1970.

Griffin, Jasper. *Homer*. New York: Hill and Wang, 1980.

Homer. *Iliad*. Trans. Robert Fagles. New York: Viking Penguin, 1990.

J U L I A   A L V A R E Z

The Blood of the Conquistadores

Mami, Papi, the Four Girls

Julia Alvarez is one of an emerging group of Latina writers who are translating their Hispanic heritage into stories and novels which draw on both their culture and their personal experiences. Alvarez, for example, uses her experience as an immigrant as a basis for her collection of short stories, *How the Garcia Girls Lost their Accents*. This book provides insight into the culture and family structure of many immigrants from the Caribbean islands.

Set during the same era that Alvarez was growing up in the Dominican Republic, "The Blood of the Conquistadores," is about family life in a military dictatorship. Aspects of the story reflect conditions similar to those under the rule of the dictator Rafael Leonidas Trujillo, who governed the Dominican Republic with an abusive hand in the 1950s. In the story, a courageous mother, Mami, has to face gun-toting police who have come to "question" her husband. Mami displays extraordinary courage and ingenuity in protecting her husband and her family. The story dramatizes the tensions of living under a military dictatorship where any action can earn one immediate execution. It also provides insight into the oppression suffered by many immigrant families, as well as shedding light on the class structure, culture, and traditions in islands like the Dominican Republic.

CARLOS IS IN THE PANTRY, getting himself a glass of water from the filtered spout when he sees the two men walking up the driveway. They are dressed in starched khaki. Each wears reflector sunglasses, and the gleam off the frames matches the gleam off the buckles on their holsters. Except for the guns, they could be foremen coming to collect on a bill or to supervise a job that other men will sweat over. But the guns give them away.

Beside him, the old cook Chucha is fussing with a coaster for his glass. The gesture of his head towards the window alerts her. She looks up and sees the two men. Very slowly, so that in their approach they will not catch a movement at the window, Carlos

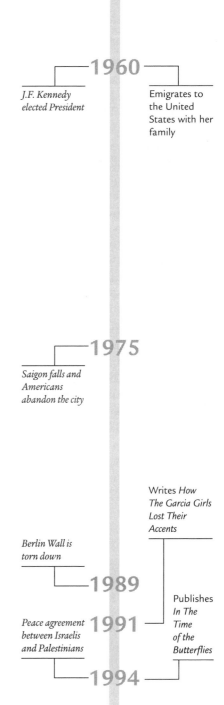

1950
The Korean War begins
Alvarez is born in the Dominican Republic

1960
J.F. Kennedy elected President
Emigrates to the United States with her family

1975
Saigon falls and Americans abandon the city

Writes *How The Garcia Girls Lost Their Accents*

Berlin Wall is torn down

1989

Publishes *In The Time of the Butterflies*

Peace agreement between Israelis and Palestinians
1991

1994

lifts his finger to his lips. Chucha nods. Step by careful step, he backs out of the room, and once he is in the hall where there are no windows to the driveway, he makes a mad dash towards the bedroom. He passes the patio, where the four girls are playing Statues with their cousins.

They are too intent on their game to notice the blur of his body running by. But Yoyo, just frozen in a spin, happens to look up and see him.

Again, he puts his finger to his lips. Yoyo cocks her head, intrigued.

"Yoyo!" one of the cousins cries. "Yoyo moved!"

The argument erupts just as he reaches the bedroom door. He hopes Yoyo will keep her mouth shut. Surely the men will question her when they go through the house. Children and servants are two groups they always interrogate.

In the bedroom, he opens the large walk-in closet and the inside light comes on. When he shuts the door, it goes off. He reaches for the flashlight and beams it on. Far off, he hears the children arguing, then the chiming of the doorbell. His heart is going so fast that he feels as if something, not his heart, is trapped inside. Easy now, easy.

He pushes to the back of the closet behind a row of Laura's dresses. He is comforted by the talc smell of her housedresses mixed with the sun-baked smell of her skin, the perfumy smell of her party dresses. He makes sure he does not disturb the arrangement of her shoes on the floor, but steps over them and disengages the back panel. Inside is a cubicle with a vent that opens out above the shower in the bathroom. Air and a little light. A couple of towels, a throw pillow, a sheet, a chamber pot, a container of filter water, aspirin, sleeping pills, even a San Judas, patron of impossible causes, that Laura has tacked to the inside wall. The small revolver Vic has

smuggled in for him — just in case — is wrapped snugly in an extra shirt, a dark colored shirt, and a dark colored pair of pants for escaping at night. He steps inside, sets the flashlight on the floor, and snaps the panel back, closing himself in.

When she sees her father dash by, Yoyo thinks he is playing one of his games that nobody likes, and that Mami says are in poor taste. Like when he says, "You want to hear God speak?" and you have to press his nose, and he farts. Or when he asks over and over even after you say *white*, "What color was Napoleon's white horse?" Or when he gives you the test of whether or not you inherited the blood of the Conquistadores, and he holds you upside down by your feet until all the blood goes to your head, and he keeps asking, "Do you have the blood of the Conquistadores?" Yoyo always says no, until she can't stand it anymore because her head feels as if it's going to crack open, and she says yes. Then he puts her right side up and laughs a great big Conquistador laugh that comes all the way from the green, motherland hills of Spain.

But Papi is not playing a game now because soon after he runs by in hide-and-seek, the doorbell rings, and Chucha lets in those two creepy-looking men. They are coffee-with-milk color and the khaki they wear is the same color as their skin, so they look all beige, which no one would ever pick as a favorite color. They wear dark mirror glasses. What catches Yoyo's eye are their holster belts and the shiny black bulge of their guns poking through.

Now she knows guns are illegal. Only *guardias* in uniform can carry them, so either these men are criminals or some kind of secret police in plain clothes Mami has told her about who could be anywhere at anytime like guardian angels, except they don't

keep you from doing bad but wait to catch you doing it. Mami has joked with Yoyo that she better behave because if these secret police see her doing something wrong, they will take her away to a prison for children where the menu is a list of everything Yoyo doesn't like to eat.

Chucha talks very loud and repeats what the men say as if she were deaf. She must be wanting Papi to hear from wherever he is hiding. This must be serious like the time Yoyo told their neighbor, the old general, a made-up story about Papi having a gun, a story which turned out to be true because Papi did really have a hidden gun for some reason. The nursemaid Milagros told on Yoyo telling the general that story, and her parents hit her very hard with a belt in the bathroom, with the shower on so no one could hear her screams. Then Mami had to meet Tío Vic in the middle of the night with the gun hidden under her raincoat so it wouldn't be on the premises in case the police came. That was very serious. That was the time Mami still talks about when "you almost got your father killed, Yoyo."

Once the men are seated in the living room off the inside patio, they try to lure the children into conversation. Yoyo does not say a word. She is sure these men have come on account of that gun story she told when she was only five and before anyone told her guns were illegal.

The taller man with the gold tooth asks Mundín, the only boy here, where his father is. Mundín explains his father is probably still at the office, and so the man asks him where his mother is, and Mundín says he thinks she is home.

"The maid said she was not at home," the short one with a broad face says in a testy voice. It is delicious to watch him realize a moment later that he is in the wrong when Mundín

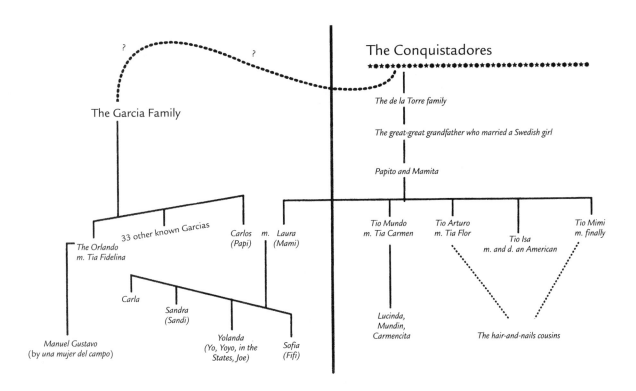

says, "You mean Tía Laura. But see, I live next door."

"Ahhh," the short one says, stretching the word out, his mouth round like the barrel of the revolver he has emptied and is passing around so the children can all hold it. Yoyo takes it in her hand and looks straight into the barrel hole, shuddering. Maybe it is loaded, maybe if she shot her head off, everyone would forgive her for having made up the story of the gun.

"So which of you girls live here?" the tall one asks. Carla raises her hand as if she were at school. Sandi also raises her hand like a copycat and tells Yoyo and Fifi to raise their hands too.

"Four girls," the fat one says, rolling his eyes. "No boys?" They shake their heads. "Your father better get good locks on the door."

A worried look flashes across Fifi's face. A few days ago she turned the small rod on her bedroom door-knob by mistake and then couldn't figure out how to pop it back and un-lock the door. A workman from Papito's factory had to come and take out the whole lock, making a hole in the door, and letting the hysterical Fifi out. "Why locks?" she asks, her bottom lip quivering.

"Why?!" The chubby one laughs. The roll of fat around his waist jig-gles. "Why?!" he keeps repeating and breaking out in fresh chuckles. "Come here, *cielito lindo*, and let me show you why your Papi has to put locks on the door." He beckons to Fifi with his in-dex finger crooked. Fifi shakes her head no, and begins to cry.

Yoyo wants to cry, too, but she is sure if she does, the men will get sus-picious and take her father away and maybe the whole family. Yoyo imag-ines herself in a jail cell. It would be like Felicidad, Mamita's little canary, in her birdcage. The guards would poke in rifles the way Yoyo sometimes pokes Felicidad with sticks when no one in the big house is looking. She gets herself so scared that she is on the brink of tears when she hears the car in the drive, and knows it must be, it must be. "Mami's here!" she cries out, hoping this good news will stop her little sister's tears.

The two men exchange a look and put their revolvers back into their holsters.

Chucha, grim-faced as always, comes in and announces loudly, "Doña Laura is home." As she exits, she lets drop a fine powder. Her lips move the whole time as if she were doing her usual sullen, under-her-breath grumbling, but Yoyo knows she is casting a spell that will leave the men powerless, becalmed.

As Laura nears her driveway, she honks the horn twice to alert the guard to open the gate, but surprisingly, it is already open. Chino is standing outside the little gatehouse talking to a man in khaki. Up ahead, Laura sees the black V.W., and her heart plummets right down to her toes. Next to her in the passenger seat it has taken her months to convince the young country girl to ride in, Imaculada says, *"Doña, hay visita."*

Laura plays along, controlling the tremor of her voice. "Yes, company." She stops and motions for Chino to come to the car. *"¿Qué hay, Chino?"*

"They are looking for Don Carlos," Chino says tensely. He lowers his voice and looks over at Imaculada, who looks down at her hands. "They have been here for awhile. There are two more waiting in the house."

"I'll talk to them," Laura says to Chino, whose slightly slanted eyes have earned him his nickname. "And you go over to Doña Carmen's and tell her to call Don Victor and tell him to come right over and pick up his tennis shoes. Tennis shoes, you hear?" Chino nods. He can be trusted to put two and two together. Chino has been with the family forever — well, only a little less than Chucha, who came when Laura's mother was pregnant with Laura. Chino calls to the man in khaki, who flicks his cigarette onto the lawn behind him, and approaches the car. As Laura greets him, she sees Chino cutting across the lawn towards Don Mundo's house.

"Doña, excuse our dropping in on you," the man is saying with false politeness that seems as if it is being wastefully squeezed from a tube. "We need to ask Doctor García a few questions, and at the *clínica,* they told us he was home. Your boy" — Boy! Chino is over fifty — "he says *el doctor* is not home yet, so we will wait until he shows up. Surely, he is on his way — " The guard looks up at the sky, shielding his eyes: the sun is dead center

above him, noon, time for dinner, time for every man to sit down at his table and break bread and say grace to God and Trujillo for the plenty the country is enjoying.

"By all means, wait for him, but please not under this hot sun." Laura switches into her grand manner. The grand manner will usually disarm these poor lackeys from the countryside, who have joined the SIM, most of them, in order to put money in their pockets, food and rum in their stomachs, and guns at their hips. But deep down, they are still boys in rags bringing down coconuts for *el patrón* when he visits his *fincas* with his family on Sundays.

"You must come in and have something cold to drink."

The man bows his head, grateful. But no, he must stay put, orders. Laura promises to send him down a cold beer and drives up to the house. She wonders if Carmen has been able to get hold of Victor. At the first sign of trouble, Victor said, get in touch, code phrase is *tennis shoes.* He is good for his word. It wasn't his fault the State Department chickened out of the plot they had him organize. And he has promised to get the men out safely. All but Fernando, of course. *Pobrecito* ending up the way he did, hanging himself by his belt in his cell to keep from giving out the others' names under the tortures Trujillo's henchmen were administering. Fernando, a month in his grave, San Judas protect us all.

At the door she directs Imaculada to unload the groceries and be sure to take the man down at the gate a Presidente, the common beer they all like. Then she crosses herself and enters the house. In the living room, the two men rise to greet her; Fifi runs to her in tears; Yoyo is right behind, all eyes, looking frightened. Laura is raising her girls American style, reading all the new

literature, so she knows she shouldn't have beaten Yoyo that time the girl gave them such a scare. But you lose your head in this crazy hellhole, you do, and different rules apply. Now, for instance, she is thinking of doing something wild and mad, sinking down in a swoon the way women used to in old movies when they wanted to distract attention from some trouble spot, unbuttoning her blouse and offering the men pleasure if they'll let her husband and babies escape.

"Gentlemen, please," Laura says, urging them to sit down, and then she eyeballs the kids to leave the room. They all do, except Yoyo and Fifi, who hold on to either side of her, not saying a word.

"Is there some problem?" Laura begins.

"We just have a few questions to ask Don Carlos. Are you expecting him for the noon meal?"

At this moment, a way to delay these men comes to her. Vic is on his way, she hopes, and he'll know how to handle this mess.

"My husband had a tennis game today with Victor Hubbard." She says the name slowly so that it will register. "The game probably ran a little late. Make yourselves at home, please. My house, your house," she says, reciting the traditional Dominican welcome.

She excuses herself a moment to prepare a tray of little snacks they urge her not to trouble herself to prepare. In the pantry, Chucha is alone since Imaculada has gone off to serve the guard his beer. The old black woman and the young mistress exchange looks. "Don Carlos," Chucha mouths, "in the bedroom." Laura nods. She knows now where he is, and although it spooks her that he is within a few feet of these men, sealed in the secret compartment, she is also grateful that he is so close by she could almost reach out and touch him.

Back in the living room, she serves the men a tray of fried plantain chips and peanuts and *casabe* and pours each one a Presidente in the cheap glasses she keeps for servants. Seeing the men eye the plates, she remembers the story that Trujillo forces his cooks to taste his food before he eats. Laura breaks off a piece of *casabe* for Fifi on one side of her, and another for Yoyo. Then she herself takes a handful of peanuts and puts them, like a schoolgirl, one by one in her mouth. The men reach out their hands and eat.

When the phone rings at Doña Tatica's, she feels the sound deep inside her sore belly. Bad news, she thinks. Candelario, be at my side. She picks the phone up as if it had claws, and announces in a small voice, so unlike hers, *"Buenos días, El Paraíso, para servirle."*

The voice on the other end is the American's secretary, a nononsense, too-much-schooling-inner-voice woman who does not return Tatica's *buenos días*. Embassy business, the voice snaps, "Please call Don Vic to the phone." Tatica echoes the secretary's snippiness: "I cannot disturb him." But the voice gloats back, *"Urgente,"* and Tatica must obey.

She heads across the courtyard towards *casita #6*. Large enough already inside her broad, caramel-colored body, Tatica renders herself dramatically larger by always dressing in red, a *promesa* she has made to her *santo*, Candelario, so he will cure her of the horrible burning in her gut. The doctor went in and cut out some of her stomach and all of her woman machinery, but Candelario stayed, filling that empty space with spirit. Now whenever trouble is coming, Tatica feels a glimmer of the old burning in the centipede trail on her belly. Something pretty bad is on its way because with each step Tatica takes,

the pain rolls in her gut, trouble coming to full term.

Under the *amapola* tree, the yardboy is lounging with the American's chauffeur. When he sees her, quick he busies himself clipping a sorry-looking hedge. The chauffeur calls out, *Buenos días, doña Tatica,* and tips his cap at Tatica who lifts her head high above his riffraff. *Casita #6,* Don Victor's regular cabin, is straight ahead. The air conditioner is going. Tatica will have to pound hard with strength she does not have so her knock will be heard.

At the door she pauses. Candelario, she pleads as she lifts her hand to knock, for the burning has spread. *"Urgente,"* she calls out, meaning her own condition now, for her whole body feels bathed in a burning pain as if her flame-colored dress were itself on fire.

A goddamn bang comes at the goddamn door. *"Teléfono, urgente, señor Hubbard."* Vic does not lose a beat, but calls out, *"Un minuto,"* and finishes first. He shakes his head at the sweet giggling thing and says, *"Excusez, por favor."* Half the time he doesn't know whether he's using his CIA crash course in Spanish or his prep school Latin or his college French. But dicks and dollars are what talk in El Paraíso anyway.

When he first got to this little hot spot, Vic didn't know how hot it would be. Immediately, he looked up his old classmate Mundo, who comes from one of those old wealthy families who send their kids to the States to prep school, and the boys on to college. Old buddy introduced him around till he knew every firebrand among the upper-class fellas the State Department wanted him to groom for revolution. Fellas got him fixed up with Tatica, who has kept him in the little girls he likes, hot little numbers, dark and sweet like the little cups of *cafecito* so full of goddamn caffeine

and island sugar you're shaking half the day.

Vic dresses quickly, and as soon as his clothes are on, he is all business. *"Hasta luego,"* he says, waving to the little girl sitting up and pouting prettily. "Behave yourself," he jokes. Naughtily, she lifts her little chin. Really, they are so cute.

He opens the door unto a crumbling Tatica, two hundred pounds going limp in his arms. He looks up and sees over her shoulder his chauffeur and the yardboy rushing to his aid. Behind him, above the air conditioner's roar, he can hear the little girl shout Doña Tatica's name, and as if summoned back from the hellhole of her pain, Tatica's eyes roll up, her mouth parts. *"Teléfono, urgente, Embajada,"* she whispers to Don Vic, and he takes off, leaving her to collapse into the arms of her own riffraff.

Vic goes first to Mundo's house, since the call came from Carmen, and finds her in the patio with endless kiddies having their noon meal at the big table. Carmen rushes towards him. *"Gracias a Dios, Vic,"* she says for hello. A sweetheart, this little lady, not bad legs either. Unfortunately, the nuns got to her young, and Vic has nodded himself silly several times to catechism lessons disguised as dinner conversations. He wonders if it shows all over him where he's been, and grins, thinking back on the sweet little number not much older than some of the little sirens sitting around the table now. "Tío Vic, Tío Vic," they call out. Honestly, lash me to a lamppost, he thinks.

Quick look around the table. No sign of Mundo. Maybe he's had to take refuge in the temporary holding closet Vic advised him and the others to construct? He smiles comfortingly at Carmen, whose smile back is a grimace of fear. "In the study," she directs him.

The kids keep calling for Tío Vic to come over to the lunch table they are not allowed to leave. He waves at them and says, "Carry on, troops," as he goes by. Over his shoulder, he hears Carmen call after him, "Have you eaten, Victor?" These Latin women, even when the bullets are flying and the bombs are falling, they want to make sure you have a full stomach, your shirt is ironed, your handkerchief is fresh. It's what makes the nice girls from polite society great hostesses, and the girls at Tatica's such obliging lovers.

He taps on the door, says his name, waits, says it again, a little louder this time since the air conditioner is going. The door opens eerily as if by itself since no one admits him. He enters, the door closes behind him, a gun's safety clicks off. "Whoa, fellas," he calls out, lifting his hands to show he's their unarmed, honest-to-god buddy. The jealousies have all been closed, and the men are spread around the room as if assuming lookout posts. Mundo comes out from behind the door, and Fidelio, the nervous one, stands by the bookshelves, pulling books in and out as if they were levers that might work their safe escape out of this frightening moment. Mateo squats, as if lighting a fire. Standing by different windows are the rest of the guys. Jesus, they look like a bunch of scared rabbits.

"Thought you might be SIM," Mundo says, explaining his withdrawn gun. He pulls a chair out for his buddy. The chairs in his study bear the logo from their alma mater, Yale, which Vic notes the family mispronounces as *jail*.

"What's up?" Vic asks in his heavily-accented Spanish.

"Trouble," says Mundo. "With a capital T."

Vic nods. "We're on," he says to the group. *"Operación Zapatos Tenis."* Then he does what he has always

done ever since back in Indiana as a boy the shit first began hitting fan: he cracks his knuckles and grins.

Carla and Sandi are having their lunch at Tía Carmen's house, which is not breaking the rules because, number one, Mami told them to SCRAM with her widened eyes, and number two, the rule is that unless you're grounded, you can eat at any aunt's house if you let Mami know first, which goes back to number one, that Mami told them to SCRAM, and it is already almost an hour since they should have eaten back home.

Something is fishy like when Mami walks in on them and they quickly hide what they don't want her to see, and she clips her nose together with her fingers and says, "I smell a rat." Fishy is Tío Mundo arriving for lunch, then not even sitting down but going straight to his study, and then *all* the uncles coming like there's going to be a party or a big family decision about Mamita's drinking or about Papito's businesses while he's away. Tía Carmen jumps up each time the doorbell rings, and when she returns, she asks them the same question she's just asked them — "So you were playing Statues and the two men came?" Mundín is jabbering away about the gun he got to hold. Every time he mentions it, Carla can see a shiver go through Tía's body like when there's a draft up at the house in the mountains and all the aunts wear pretty shawls. Today, though, it's so hot, the kids got to go in the pool in the morning right before Statues, and Tía says if they're very good, they might be able to go in again after their digestion is completed. Twice in the pool in one day and Tía has the shivers in this heat. Something very fishy is going on.

Tía rings the little silver bell, and Adela comes out and clears all the plates, and brings dessert, which always includes the Russell Stover box with

the painted-on bow. When the box goes around, you have to figure out by eyesight alone which one you think will have the nut inside or caramel or coconut, hoping that you won't be surprised when you bite in by some squishy center you want to spit out.

The Russell Stover box is pretty low because no one has been to the United States lately to buy chocolates. Papito and Mamita left right after Christmas as usual but haven't come back. And it's August already. Mami says that's because of Mamita's health, and having to see specialists, but Carla has heard whispers that Papito has resigned his United Nations post and so is not very well liked by the government right now. Every once in a while *guardias* roar in on their jeeps, jump out, and surround Papito's house, and then Chino always comes running and tells Mami, who calls Tío Vic to tell him to come pick up his tennis shoes. Carla has never seen Tío Vic bring any kind of shoes to the house but the pockmarked ones he wears. He always comes in one of those limousines Carla's only seen at weddings and when Trujillo goes by in a motorcade. Tío Vic talks to the head *guardia* and gives him some money, and they all climb back in their jeeps and roar away. It's really kind of neat, like a movie. But Mami says they're not to tell their friends about it. "No flies fly into a closed mouth," she explains when Carla asks, "Why can't we tell?"

The Russell Stover box has gone all the way around back to Tía, who takes out one of the little papery molds, and sighs when the kids argue about who will get it. Tío Vic comes out, grinning, and ruffles Mundín's hair, puts his hand on Tía's shoulder and asks the whole table, "So who wants to go to New York? Who wants to see the Empire State Building?" Tío Vic always talks to them in

English so that they get practice. "How about the Statue of Liberty?"

At first, the cousins look around at each other, not wanting to embarrass themselves by calling out, "Me! Me!" and then having Tío Vic cry, "April Fool!" But tentatively Carla, and then Sandi, and then Lucinda raise their hands. Like a chain reaction, hand after hand goes up, some still holding Russell Stover chocolates. "Me, me, I want to go, I want to go!" Tío Vic lifts up his hands, palms out, to keep their voices down. When they are all quiet, waiting for him to pick the winners, he looks down at Tía Carmen beside him and says, "How about it, Carmen? Wanna go?" And the kids all chant, "Yes, Tía, yes!" Carla, too, until she notes that her aunt's hands are shaking as she fits the lid on the empty Russell Stover box.

Laura is terrified she is going to say something she mustn't. These two thugs have been quizzing her for half an hour. Thank God for Yoyo and Fifi hanging on her, whining. She makes a big deal of asking them what they want, of getting them to recite for the company, and trying to get sullen little Fifi to smile for the obnoxious fat man.

Finally — what a relief! There's Vic crossing the lawn with Carla and Sandi on each hand. The two men turn and, almost reflexively, their hands travel to their holsters. Their gesture reminds her of a man fondling his genitals. It might be this vague sexuality behind the violence around her that has turned Laura off lovemaking all these months.

"Victor!" she calls out, and then in a quieter voice she cues the men as if she does not want them to embarrass themselves by not knowing who this important personage is. "Victor Hubbard, consul at the Embajada Americana. Excuse me, señores." She comes down the patio and gives Vic a little peck on the cheek, whispering as she does, "I've told them he's been

playing tennis with you." Vic gives her the slightest nod, all the while grinning as if his teeth were on review.

Effusively, Laura greets Carla and Sandi. "My darlings, my sweet Cuquitas, have you eaten?" They nod, watching her closely, and she sees with a twinge of pain that they are quickly picking up the national language of a police state: every word, every gesture, a possible mine field, watch what you say, look where you go.

With the men, Victor is jovial and back-patting, asking twice for their names, as if he means to pass on a compliment or a complaint. The men shift hams, nervous for the first time, Laura notes gleefully. "The doctor, we have come to ask him a few questions, but he seems to have disappeared."

"Not at all," Vic corrects them. "We were just playing tennis. He'll be home any minute." The men sit up, alert. Vic goes on to say that if there is some problem, perhaps he can straighten things out. After all, the doctor is a personal friend. Laura watches their reactions as Vic tells them news that is news to her. The doctor has been granted a fellowship at a hospital in the United States, and he, Victor, has just heard the family's papers have received clearance from the head of Immigration. So, why would the good doctor get into any trouble.

So, Laura thinks. So the papers have cleared and we are leaving. Now everything she sees sharpens as if through the lens of loss — the orchids in their hanging straw baskets, the row of apothecary jars Carlos has found for her in old druggists' throughout the countryside, the rich light shafts swarming with a golden pollen. She will miss this glorious light warming the inside of her skin and jeweling the trees, the grass, the lily pond beyond the hedge. She thinks of her ancestors, those fair-

skinned Conquistadores arriving in this new world, not knowing that the gold they sought was this blazing light. And look at what they started, Laura thinks, looking up and seeing gold flash in the mouth of one of the *guardias* as it spreads open in a scared smile.

This morning when the fag at the corner sold them their *lotería* tickets, he said, "Watch yourselves, the flames of your *santos* burn just above your heads. The hand of God descends and some are lifted up, but some" — he looked from Pupo to Checo — "some are cast away." Pupo took heed and crossed himself, but Checo twisted the fag's arm behind his back and threatened to give his manhood the hand of God. It scares Pupo the meanness that comes out of Checo's mouth, as if they weren't both *campesino* cousins, ear-twisted to church on Sundays by mothers who raised them on faith and whatever grew in their little plot of dirt.

But the fag lotería guy was right. The day began to surprise them. First, Don Fabio calls them in. Special assignment: they are to report on this Garcia doctor's comings and goings. Next thing Pupo knows Checo is driving the jeep right up to the Garcia house and doing this whole search number that is not following orders. Point is, though, that if something comes out of the search, their enterprise will be praised and they will be decorated and promoted. If nothing turns up and the family has connections, then back they go to the prison beat, cleaning interrogation rooms and watering down the cells the poor, scared bastards dirty with their loss of self-control.

From the minute they enter the house Pupo can tell by the way the old Haitian woman acts that this is a stronghold of something, call it arms, call it spirits, call it money. When the woman arrives, she is nervous and grasshoppery, smiling falsely, dropping names like a trail of crumbs to the powerful. Mostly, she mentions the red-haired gringo at the embassy. At first Pupo thinks she's just bluffing and he's already congratulating Checo and himself for uncovering something hot. But then, sure enough, the red-haired gringo appears before them, two more doll-girls in either hand.

"Who is your supervisor?" The gringo's voice has an edge. When Checo informs him, the American throws back his head, "Oh, Fabio, of course!" Pupo sees Checo's mouth stretch in a rubberband smile that seems as if it may snap. They have detained a lady from an important family. They have maybe barked up the wrong tree. All Pupo knows is Don Fabio is going to have a heyday on their already scarred backs.

"I'll tell you what," the American consul offers them. "Why don't I just give old Fabio a call right now." Pupo lifts his shoulders and ducks his head as if just the mention of his superior's name could cause his head to roll. Checo nods, "A *sus órderes.*"

The American calls from the phone in the hall where Pupo can hear him talking his marbles-in-his-mouth Spanish. There is a silence in which he must be waiting to be connected, but then his voice warms up. "Fabio, about this little misunderstanding. Tell you what, I'll talk to Immigration myself, and I'll have the doctor out of the country in forty-eight hours." On the other end Don Fabio must have made a joke because the American breaks out in laughter, then calls Checo to the phone so his supervisor can speak with him. Pupo hears his comrade's rare apologetic tone. "*Sí, sí, cómo no, don Fabio, inmediatamente.*"

Pupo sits among these strange white people, ashamed and cornered. Already he is feeling the whip coming down like judgment on his bared back. They are all strangely quiet, listening to Checo's voice full of disclaimer, and when he falls silent, only to their own breathing as the hand of God draws closer. Whether it will pick up the saved or cast out the lost is unclear yet to Pupo, who picks up his empty glass and, for comfort, tinkles the ice.

While the men were saying their goodbyes at the door, Sandi stayed on the couch sitting on her hands. Fifi and Yoyo clustered around Mami, balling up her skirt with holding on, Fifi walling every time the big fat guard bent down for a goodbye kiss from her. Carla, knowing better as the oldest, gave her hand to the men and curtsied the way they'd been taught to do for guests. Then, everyone came back to the living room, and Mami rolled her eyes at Tío Vic the way she did when she was on the phone with someone she didn't want to talk to. Soon, she had everyone in motion: the girls were to go to their bedrooms and make a stack of their best clothes and pick one toy they wanted to take on this trip to the United States. Nivea and Milagros and Mami would later pack it for them. Then, Mami disappeared with Tío Vic into her bedroom.

Sandi followed her sisters into their side-by-side bedrooms. They stood in a scared little huddle, feeling strangely careful with each other. Yoyo turned to her. "What are you taking?" Fifi had already decided on her baby doll and Carla was going through her private box of jewelry and mementos. Yoyo fondled her revolver.

It was strange how when held up to the absolute phrase — *the one toy I really want* — nothing quite filled the hole that was opening wide inside Sandi. Not the doll whose long hair you could roll and comb into hairdos, not the loom for making pot holders that Mami was so thankful for, not the glass dome that you turned over and pretty flakes fell on a little red house in the woods. Nothing would quite fill that need, even years after, not the pretty woman she would surprise herself by becoming, not the prizes for her schoolwork and scholarships to study now this and now that she couldn't decide to stay with not the men that held her close and almost convinced her when their mouths came down hard on her lips that this, this was what Sandi had been missing.

From the dark of the closet Carlos has heard tones, not content; known presences, not personalities. He wonders if this might be what he felt as a small child before the impressions and tones and presences were overlaid by memories, memories which are mostly others' stories about his past. He is the youngest of his father's thirty-five children, twenty-five legitimate, fifteen from his own mother, the second wife; he has no past of his own. It is not just a legacy, a future, you don't get as the youngest. Primogeniture is also the clean slate of the oldest making the past out of nothing but faint whispers, presences, and tones. Those tenuous, tentative first life-impressions have scattered like reflections in a pond under the swirling hand of an older brother or sister saying, I remember the day you ate the rat poison, Carlos, or, I remember the day you fell down the stairs ....

He has heard Laura in the living room speaking with two men, one of them with a ripply, tricky voice, the other with a coarser voice, a thicker laugh, a big man, no doubt. Fifi is there and Yoyo as well. The two other girls disappeared in a jabber of cousins earlier. Fifi whines periodically, and Yoyo has recited something for the men, he can tell from the singsong in her voice. Laura's voice is tense and bright like a newly sharpened knife that every time she speaks cuts a little sliver from her self-control. Carlos thinks, She will break, she will break, San Judas, let her not break.

Then, in that suffocating darkness, having to go but not daring to pee in the chamber pot for fear the men might hear a drip in the walls — though God knows, he and Mundo soundproofed this room enough so that there is no ventilation at all — in that growing claustrophobia, he hears her say distinctly, "Victor!" Sure enough, momentarily the monotone, garbled voice of the American consul nears the living room. By now, of course, they all know his consulship is only a front — Vic is, in fact, a CIA agent whose orders changed midstream from *organize the underground and get that SOB out* to *hold your horses, let's take a second look around to see what's best for us.*

When he hears the bedroom door open, Carlos puts his ear up against the front panel. Steps go into the bathroom, the shower is turned on, and then the fan to block out any noise of talk. The immediate effect is that fresh air begins to circulate in the tiny compartment. The closet door opens, and then Carlos hears her breathing close by on the other side of the wall.

II

I'm the one who doesn't remember anything from that last day on the island because I'm the youngest and so the other three are always telling me what happened that last day. They say I almost got Papi killed on account of I was so mean to one of the secret police who came looking for him. Some weirdo who was going to sit me on his hard-on and pretend we were playing Ride the Cock Horse to Banbury Cross. But then whenever we start talking last-day-on-the-island memories, and

someone says, "Fifi, you almost got Papi killed for being so rude to that gestapo guy," Yoyo starts in on how it was she who almost got Papi killed when she told that story about the gun years before our last day on the Island. Like we're all competing, right? for the most haunted past.

I can tell you one thing I do remember from right before we left. There was this old lady, Chucha, who had worked in Mami's family forever and who had this face like someone had wrung it out after washing it to try to get some of the black out. I mean, Chucha was super wrinkled and Haitian blue-black, not Dominican *café-con-leche* black. She was real Haitian too and that's why she couldn't say certain words like the word for parsley or anyone's name that had a *j* in it, which meant the family was like camp, everyone with nicknames Chucha could pronounce. She was always in a bad mood — not exactly a bad mood, but you couldn't get her to crack a smile or cry or anything. It was like all her emotions were spent, on account of everything she went through in her young years. Way back before Mami was even born, Chucha had just appeared at my grandfather's doorstep one night, begging to be taken in. Turns out it was the night of the massacre when Trujillo had decreed that all black Haitians on our side of the island would be executed by dawn. There's a river the bodies were finally thrown into that supposedly still runs red to this day, fifty years later. Chucha had escaped from some canepickers' camp and was asking for asylum. Papito took her in, poor skinny little thing, and I guess Mamita taught her to cook and iron and clean. Chucha was like a nun who had joined the convent of the de la Torre clan. She never married or went anywhere even on her days off. Instead, she'd close herself up in her room and pray for any de la Torre souls stuck up in purgatory.

Anyhow, that last day on the Island, we were in our side-by-side bedrooms, the four girls, setting out our clothes for going to the United States. The two creepy spies had left, and Mami and Tío Vic were in the bedroom. They were telling Papi, who was hidden in this secret closet, about how we would all be leaving in Tío Vic's limo for the airport for a flight he was going to get us. I know, I know, it sounds like something you saw on "Miami Vice," but all I'm doing is repeating what I've heard from the family.

But here's what I do remember of my last day on the island. Chucha came into our bedrooms with this bundle in her hands, and Nivea, who was helping us pack, said to her in a gruff voice, "What do you want, old woman?" None of the maids liked Chucha because they all thought she was kind of below them, being so black and Haitian and all. Chucha, though, just gave Nivea one of her spelling looks, and all of sudden, Nivea remembered that she had to iron our outfits for wearing on the airplane.

Chucha started to unravel her bundle, and we all guessed she was about to do a little farewell voodoo on us. Chucha always had a voodoo job going, some spell she was casting or spirit she was courting or enemy she was punishing. I mean, you'd open a closet door, and there, in the corner behind your shoes, would sit a jar of something wicked that you weren't supposed to touch. Or you'd find a candle burning in her room right in front of someone's picture and a little dish with a cigar on it and red and white crepe streamers on certain days crisscrossing her room. Mami finally had to give her a room to herself because none of the other maids wanted to steep with her. I can see why they were afraid. The maids said she got mounted by spirits. They said she cast spells on them. And besides, she slept in her coffin. No kidding. We were forbidden to go into her room to see it, but we were always sneaking back there to take a peek. She had her mosquito net rigged up over it, so it didn't look that strange like a real uncovered coffin with a dead person inside.

At first, Maim wouldn't let her do it, sleep in her coffin, I mean. She told Chucha civilized people had to sleep on beds, coffins were for corpses. But Chucha said she wanted to prepare herself for dying and couldn't one of the carpenters at Papito's factory measure her and build her a wooden box that would serve as her bed for now and her coffin later. Mami kept saying, Nonsense, Chucha, don't get tragic.

The thing was, you couldn't stand in Chucha's way even if you were Mami. Soon there were jars in Mami's closet, and her picture from when she was a baby being held by Chucha was out on Chucha's altar with mints on a little tin dish, and a constant votary candle going. Inside of a week, Mami relented. She said poor Chucha never asked for a blessed thing from the family, and had always been so loyal and good, and so, heavens to Betsy, if sleeping in her coffin would make the old woman happy, Mami would have a nice box built for her, and she did. It was plain pine, like Chucha wanted it, but inside, Mami had it lined in purple cushiony fabric, which was Chucha's favorite color, and bordered with white eyelet.

So here's the part I remember about that last day. Once Nivea left the room, Chucha stood us all up in front of her. "Chachas — " she always called us that, from *muchachas*, girls, which is how come we had ended up nicknaming her a play echo of her name for us, Chucha.

"You are going to a strange land." Something like that, I mean,

I don't remember the exact words. But I do remember the piercing look she gave me as if she were actually going inside my head. "When I was a girl, I left my country too and never went back. Never saw father or mother or sisters or brothers. I brought only this along." She held the bundle up and finished unwrapping it from its white sheet. It was a statue carved out of wood like the kind I saw years later in the anthro textbooks I used to pore over, as if staring at those little talismanic wooden carvings would somehow be my madeleine, bringing back my past to me like they say tasting that cookie did for Proust. But the textbook gods never triggered any four-volume memory in my head. Just this little moment I'm recalling here.

Chucha stood this brown figure up on Carla's vanity. He had a grimacing expression on his face, deep grooves by his eyes and his nose and lips, as if he were trying to go but was real constipated. On top of his head was a little platform, and on it, Chucha placed a small cup of water. Soon, on account of the heat I guess, that water started evaporating and drops ran down the grooves carved in that wooden face so that the statue looked as if it were crying. Chucha held each of our heads in her hands and wailed a prayer over us. We were used to some of this strange stuff from daily contact with her, but maybe it was because today we could feel an ending in the air, anyhow, we all started to cry as if Chucha had finally released her own tears in each of us.

They are gone, left in cars that came for them, driven by pale Americans in white uniforms with gold braids on their shoulders and on their caps. Too pale to be the living. The color of zombies, a nation of zombies. I worry about them, the girls, Doña Laura, moving among the

men the color of the living dead.

The girls all cried, especially the little one, clutching onto my skirts, Doña Laura weeping so hard into her handkerchief that I insisted on going back to her bureau and getting her a fresh one. I did not want her to enter her new country with a spent handkerchief because I know, I know what tears await her there. But let her be spared the knowledge that will come in time. That one's nerves have never been strong.

They have left — and only the silence remains, the deep and empty silence in which I can hear the voices of my *santos* settling into the rooms, of my *loa* telling me stories of what is to come.

After the girls and Doña Laura left with the American zombie whites, I heard a door click in the master bedroom, and I went out to the corridor to check for intruders. All in black, I saw the loa of Don Carlos putting his finger to his lips in mockery of the last gesture I had seen him make to me that morning. I answered with a sign and fell to my knees and watched him leave through the back door out through the guava orchard. Soon afterwards, I heard a car start up. And then the deep and empty silence of the deserted house.

I am to close up the house, and help over at Doña Carmen's until they go too, and then at Don Arturo's, who also is to go. Mostly, I am to tend to this house. Dust, give the rooms an airing. The others except for Chino have been dismissed, and I have been entrusted with the keys. From time to time, Don Victor, when he can get away from his young girls, will stop by to see to things and give me my monthly wages.

Now I hear the voices telling me how the grass will grow tall on the unkempt lawns; how Doña Laura's hanging orchids will burst their wire baskets, their frail blossoms eaten by bugs; how the birdcages will stand empty, the poor having poached the *tórtolas* and *guineas* that Don Carlos took so much trouble to raise; how the swimming pools will fill with trash and leaves and dead things. Chino and I will be left behind in these decaying houses until that day I can see now — when I shut my eyes — that day the place will be overrun by *guardias,* smashing windows and carting off the silver and plates, the pictures and the mirror with the winged babies shooting arrows, and the chairs with medallions painted on back, the box that makes music, and the magic one that gives pictures. They will strip the girls' shelves of the toys their grandmother brought them back from that place they were always telling me about with the talcum powder flowers falling out of the clouds and the buildings that touch Damballah's sky, a bewitched and unsafe place where they must now make their lives.

I have said prayers to all the *santos*, to the *loa*, and to the *Gran Poder de Dios*, visiting each room, swinging the can of cleaning smoke, driving away the bad spirits that filled the house this day, and fixing in my head the different objects and where they belong so that if any workman sneaks in and steals something I will know what is gone. In the girls' rooms I remember each one as a certain heaviness, now in my heart, now in my shoulders, now in my head or feet; I feel their losses pile up like dirt thrown on a box after it has been lowered into the earth. I see their future, the troublesome life ahead. They will be haunted by what they do and don't remember. But they have spirit in them. They will invent what they need to survive.

They have left, and the house is closed and the air is blessed. I lock the back door and pass the maid's room, where I see Imaculada and Nivea and Milagros packing to leave at dawn.

They do not need my goodbyes. I go in my own room, the one Doña Laura had special made for me so I could be with my *santos* at peace and not have to bear the insolence and annoyance of young girls with no faith in the spirits. I clean the air with incense and light the six candles — one for each of the girls, and one for Doña Laura, whose diapers I changed, and one for Don Carlos. And then, I do what I always do after a hard day, I wash my face and arms in *agua florida*. I throw out the water, saying the prayer to the *loa* of the night who watch with bright eyes from the darkened sky. I part the mosquito netting and climb into my box, arranging myself so that I am facing up, my hands folded on my waist.

Before sleep, for a few minutes, I try to accustom my flesh to the burial that is coming. I reach up for the lid and I pull it down, closing myself in. In that hot and tight darkness before I lift the lid back up for air, I shut my eyes and lie so still that the blood I hear pounding and the heart I hear knocking could be something that I have forgotten to turn off in the deserted house.

THINK ABOUT IT

1. What does Mami do to keep the guards from searching the house?
2. How does the presence of the guards affect the girls?

TALK ABOUT IT

3. Do you think that Mami and Papi love the girls? Cite examples from the story which prove your point.
4. What problems do you think the Garcia family will have adjusting to life in the United States? Do you think that they will find living here a positive or negative experience?

WRITE ABOUT IT

5. Interview an immigrant family. Describe the problems they have had adjusting to life in the United States.
6. Do you think that the United States should welcome immigrant families? Explain your reasons.

READ MORE ABOUT IT

Alvarez, Julia. *How the Garcia Girls Lost Their Accents.* Chapel Hill, NC: Algonquin Books of Chapel Hill, 1991.

Alvarez, Julia. *In the Time of Butterflies.* Chapel Hill, NC: Algonquin Books of Chapel Hill, 1994.

Chavez, Denise. *Face of an Angel.* New York: Farrar, Straus and Giroux, 1994.

Cisneros, Sandra. *Loose Woman.* New York: Alfred A. Knopf, 1994.

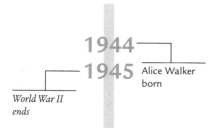

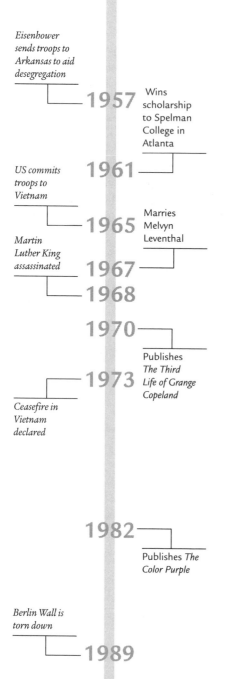

ALICE WALKER

Everyday Use

For Your Grandma

Alice Walker was born in Eatonton, Georgia, in 1944. She grew up in rural Georgia where most African Americans worked as tenant farmers. At eight, Walker was blinded in her right eye when her brother accidentally shot her with a BB gun. Because they did not have a car, her family was unable to seek medical attention for her for several days. The result was excessive scar tissue on her eye which was not removed until she was fourteen. This disfigurement led Walker to be withdrawn, but also gave her the opportunity to "begin to really see people and things, to really notice relationships and to be patient enough to care about how they turned out." This sensitivity is evident in her writing which includes novels, short stories, children's stories, and poetry. Her first novel, *The Third Life of Grange Copeland,* introduces a theme that recurs in her works: the domination of powerless women by equally powerless men. Her most famous work to date is *The Color Purple.* This novel won both the American Book Award and the Pulitzer Prize. Additionally, it was made into an Academy award-winning movie.

The following selection comes from her collection of short stories entitled *In Love and Trouble: Stories of Black Women,* published in 1973. It recounts one scene in the life of a family, but certainly emphasizes the power of intense emotions and their influence on family relationships.

I WILL WAIT FOR HER in the yard that Maggie and I floor and the fine sand around the edges lined with made so clean and wavy yesterday afternoon. A yard like this is more comfortable than most people know. It is not just a yard. It is like an extended living room. When the hard clay is swept clean as a tiny, irregular grooves, anyone can come and sit and look up into the elm tree and wait for the breezes that never come inside the house.

Maggie will be nervous until after her sister goes: she will stand hopelessly in corners, homely and ashamed of the burn scars down her arms and legs, eying her sister with a mixture of envy and awe. She thinks her sister has held life always in the palm of one hand, that "no" is a word the world never learned to say to her.

You've no doubt seen those TV shows where the child who has "made it" is confronted, as a surprise, by her own mother and father, tottering in weakly from backstage. (A pleasant surprise, of course: What would they do if parent and child came on the show only to curse out and insult each other?) On TV mother and child embrace and smile into each other's faces. Sometimes the mother and father weep, the child wraps them in her arms and leans across the table to tell how she would not have made it without their help. I have seen these programs.

Sometimes I dream a dream in which Dee and I are suddenly brought together on a TV program of this sort. Out of a dark and soft-seated limousine I am ushered into a bright room filled with many people. There I meet a smiling, gray, sporty man like Johnny Carson who shakes my hand and tells me what a fine girl I have. Then we are on the stage and Dee is embracing me with tears in her eyes. She pins on my dress a large orchid, even though she has told me once that she thinks orchids are tacky flowers.

In real life I am a large, big-boned woman with rough, man-working hands. In the winter I wear flannel nightgowns to bed and overalls during the day. I can kill and clean a hog as mercilessly as a man. My fat keeps me hot in zero weather. I can work outside all day, breaking ice to get water for washing; I can eat pork liver cooked over the open fire minutes after it comes steaming from the hog. One winter I knocked a bull calf straight in the brain between the eyes with a sledge hammer and had the meat hung up to chill before nightfall. But of course all this does not show on television. I am the way my daughter would want me to be: a hundred pounds lighter, my skin like an uncooked barley pancake. My hair glistens in the hot bright lights. Johnny Carson has much to do to keep up with my quick and witty tongue.

But that is a mistake. I know even before I wake up. Who ever knew a Johnson with a quick tongue? Who

can even imagine me looking a strange white man in the eye? It seems to me I have talked to them always with one foot raised in flight, with my head turned in whichever way is farthest from them. Dee, though. She would always look anyone in the eye. Hesitation was no part of her nature.

"How do I look, Mama?" Maggie says, showing just enough of her thin body enveloped in pink skirt and red blouse for me to know she's there, almost hidden by the door.

"Come out into the yard," I say.

Have you ever seen a lame animal, perhaps a dog run over by some careless person rich enough to own a car, sidle up to someone who is ignorant enough to be kind to him? That is the way my Maggie walks. She has been like this, chin on chest, eyes on ground, feet in shuffle, ever since the fire that burned the other house to the ground.

Dee is lighter than Maggie, with nicer hair and a fuller figure. She's a woman now, though sometimes I forget. How long ago was it that the other house burned? Ten, twelve years? Sometimes I can still hear the flames and feel Maggie's arms sticking to me, her hair smoking and her dress falling off her in little black papery flakes. Her eyes seemed stretched open, blazed open by the flames reflected in them. And Dee. I see her standing off under the sweet gum tree she used to dig gum out of; a look of concentration on her face as she watched the last dingy gray board of the house fall in toward the red-hot brick chimney. Why don't you do a dance around the ashes? I'd wanted to ask her. She had hated the house that much.

I used to think she hated Maggie, too. But that was before we raised the money, the church and me, to send her to Augusta to school. She used to read to us without pity; forcing words, lies, other folks' habits, whole lives

upon us two, sitting trapped and ignorant underneath her voice. She washed us in a river of make-believe, burned us with a lot of knowledge we didn't necessarily need to know. Pressed us to her with the serious way she read, to shove us away at just the moment, like dimwits, we seemed about to understand.

Dee wanted nice things. A yellow organdy dress to wear to her graduation from high school; black pumps to match a green suit she'd made from an old suit somebody gave me. She was determined to stare down any disaster in her efforts. Her eyelids would not flicker for minutes at a time. Often I fought off the temptation to shake her. At sixteen she had a style of her own: and knew what style was.

I never had an education myself. After second grade the school was closed down. Don't ask me why: in 1927 colored asked fewer questions than they do now. Sometimes Maggie reads to me. She stumbles along good-naturedly but can't see well. She knows she is not bright. Like good looks and money, quickness passed her by. She will marry John Thomas (who has mossy teeth in an earnest face) and then I'll be free to sit here and I guess just sing church songs to myself. Although I never was a good singer. Never could carry a tune. I was always better at a man's job. I used to love to milk till I was hooked[1] in the side in '49. Cows are soothing and slow and don't bother you, unless you try to milk them the wrong way.

I have deliberately turned my back on the house. It is three rooms, just like the one that burned, except the roof is tin; they don't make shingle roofs any more. There are no real windows, just some holes cut in the sides, like the portholes in a ship, but not round and not square, with

---

[1] i.e., by the horn of the cow being milked.

rawhide holding the shutters up on the outside. This house is in a pasture, too, like the other one. No doubt when Dee sees it she will want to tear it down. She wrote me once that no matter where we "choose" to live, she will manage to come see us. But she will never bring her friends. Maggie and I thought about this and Maggie asked me, "Mama, when did Dee ever *have* any friends?"

She had a few. Furtive boys in pink shirts hanging about on washday after school. Nervous girls who never laughed. Impressed with her they worshiped the well-turned phrase, the cute shape, the scalding humor that erupted like bubbles in lye. She read to them.

When she was courting Jimmy T she didn't have much time to pay to us, but turned all her faultfinding power on him. He *flew* to marry a cheap city girl from a family of ignorant flashy people. She hardly had time to recompose herself.

When she comes I will meet — but there they are!

Maggie attempts to make a dash for the house, in her shuffling way, but I stay her with my hand. "Come back here," I say. And she stops and tries to dig a well in the sand with her toe.

It is hard to see them clearly through the strong sun. But even the first glimpse of leg out of the car tells me it is Dee. Her feet were always neat-looking, as if God himself had shaped them with a certain style. From the other side of the car comes a short, stocky man. Hair is all over his head a foot long and hanging from his chin like a kinky mule tail. I hear Maggie suck in her breath. "Uhnnnh," is what it sounds like. Like when you see the wriggling end of a snake just in front of your foot on the road. "Uhnnnh."

Dee next. A dress down to the ground, in this hot weather. A dress so loud it hurts my eyes. There are yel-

lows and oranges enough to throw back the light of the sun. I feel my whole face warming from the heat waves it throws out. Earrings gold, too, and hanging down to her shoulders. Bracelets dangling and making noises when she moves her arm up to shake the folds of the dress out of her armpits. The dress is loose and flows, and as she walks closer, I like it. I hear Maggie go "Uhnnnh" again. It is her sister's hair. It stands straight up like the wool on a sheep. It is black as night and around the edges are two long pigtails that rope about like small lizards disappearing behind her ears.

"Wa-su-zo-Tean-o!" she says, coming on in that gliding way the dress makes her move. The short stocky fellow with the hair to his navel is all grinning and he follows up with "Asalamalakim,[2] my mother and sister!" He moves to hug Maggie but she falls back, right up against the back of my chair. I feel her trembling there and when I look up I see the perspiration falling off her chin.

"Don't get up," says Dee. Since I am stout it takes something of a push. You can see me trying to move a second or two before I make it. She turns, showing white heels through her sandals, and goes back to the car. Out she peeks next with a Polaroid. She stoops down quickly and lines up picture after picture of me sitting there in front of the house with Maggie cowering behind me. She never takes a shot without making sure the house is included. When a cow comes nibbling around the edge of the yard she snaps it and me and Maggie and the house. Then she puts the Polaroid in the back seat of the car, and comes up and kisses me on the forehead.

Meanwhile Asalamalakim is going through motions with Maggie's

---

2   Phonetic rendering of a Muslim greeting. "Wa-su-zo-Tean-o" is a similar rendering of an African dialect salutation.

hand. Maggie's hand is as limp as a fish, and probably as cold, despite the sweat, and she keeps trying to pull it back. It looks like Asalamalakim wants to shake hands but wants to do it fancy. Or maybe he don't know how people shake hands. Anyhow, he soon gives up on Maggie.

"Well," I say. "Dee."

"No, Mama," she says. "Not 'Dee,' Wangero Leewanika Kemanjo!"

"What happened to 'Dee'?" I wanted to know.

"She's dead," Wangero said. "I couldn't bear it any longer, being named after the people who oppress me."

"You know as well as me you was named after your aunt Dicie," I said. Dicie is my sister. She named Dee. We called her "Big Dee" after Dee was born.

"But who was she named after?" asked Wangero.

"I guess after Grandma Dee," I said.

"And who was she named after?" asked Wangero.

"Her mother," I said, and saw Wangero was getting tired. "That's about as far back as I can trace it," I said. Though, in fact, I probably could have carried it back beyond the Civil War through the branches.

"Well," said Asalamalakim, "there you are."

"Uhnnnh," I heard Maggie say.

"There I was not," I said, "before 'Dicie' cropped up in our family, so why should I try to trace it that far back?"

He just stood there grinning, looking down on me like somebody inspecting a Model A car. Every once in a while he and Wangero sent eye signals over my head.

"How do you pronounce this name?" I asked.

"You don't have to call me by it if you don't want to," said Wangero.

"Why shouldn't I?" I asked. "If that's what you want us to call you, we'll call you."

"I know it might sound awkward at first," said Wangero.

"I'll get used to it," I said. "Ream it out again."

Well, soon we got the name out of the way. Asalamalakim had a name twice as long and three times as hard. After I tripped over it two or three times he told me to just call him Hakim-a-barber. I wanted to ask him was he a barber, but I didn't really think he was, so I didn't ask.

"You must belong to those beef-cattle peoples down the road," I said. They said "Asalamalakim" when they met you, too, but they didn't shake hands. Always too busy: feeding the cattle, fixing the fences, putting up salt-lick shelters, throwing down hay. When the white folks poisoned some of the herd the men stayed up all night with rifles in their hands. I walked a mile and a half just to see the sight.

Hakim-a-barber said, "I accept some of their doctrines, but farming and raising cattle is not my style." (They didn't tell me, and I didn't ask, whether Wangero (Dee) had really gone and married him.)

We sat down to eat and right away he said he didn't eat collards and pork was unclean. Wangero, though, went on through the chitlins and corn bread, the greens and everything else. She talked a blue streak over the sweet potatoes. Everything delighted her. Even the fact that we still used the benches her daddy made for the table when we couldn't afford to buy chairs.

"Oh, Mama!" she cried. Then turned to Hakim-a-barber. "I never knew how lovely these benches are. You can feel the rump prints," she said, running her hands underneath her and along the bench. Then she gave a sigh and her hand closed over Grandma Dee's butter dish. "That's it!" she said. "I knew there was something I wanted to ask you if I could have." She jumped up from the table and went over in the corner where the churn stood, the milk in it clabber by now. She looked at the churn and looked at it.

"This churn top is what I need," she said. "Didn't Uncle Buddy whittle it out of a tree you all used to have?"

"Yes," I said.

"Uh huh," she said happily. "And I want the dasher, too."

"Uncle Buddy whittle that, too?" asked the barber.

Dee (Wangero) looked up at me.

"Aunt Dee's first husband whittled the dash," said Maggie so low you almost couldn't hear her. "His name was Henry, but they called him Stash."

"Maggie's brain is like an elephant's," Wangero said, laughing. "I can use the churn top as a centerpiece for the alcove table," she said, sliding a plate over the churn, "and I'll think of something artistic to do with the dasher."

When she finished wrapping the dasher the handle stuck out. I took it for a moment in my hands. You didn't even have to look close to see where hands pushing the dasher up and down to make butter had left a kind of sink in the wood. In fact, there were a lot of small sinks; you could see where thumbs and fingers had sunk into the wood. It was beautiful light yellow wood, from a tree that grew in the yard where Big Dee and Stash had lived.

After dinner Dee (Wangero) went to the trunk at the foot of my bed and started rifling through it. Maggie hung back in the kitchen over the dishpan. Out came Wangero with two quilts. They had been pieced by Grandma Dee and then Big Dee and me had hung them on the quilt frames on the front porch and quilted them. One was in the Lone Star pattern. The other was Walk Around the Mountain. In both of them were scraps of dresses Grandma Dee had worn fifty and more years ago. Bits and pieces of Grandpa Jarrell's Paisley shirts. And one teeny faded blue piece, about the size of a penny matchbox, that was from Great Grandpa Ezra's uniform that he wore in the Civil War.

"Mama," Wangero said sweet as a bird. "Can I have these old quilts?"

I heard something fall in the kitchen, and a minute later the kitchen door slammed.

"Why don't you take one or two of the others?" I asked. "These old things was just done by me and Big Dee from some tops your grandma pieced before she died."

"No," said Wangero. "I don't want those. They are stitched around the borders by machine."

"That'll make them last better," I said.

"That's not the point," said Wangero. "These are all pieces of dresses Grandma used to wear. She did all this stitching by hand. Imagine!" She held the quilts securely in her arms, stroking them.

"Some of the pieces, like those lavender ones, come from old clothes her mother handed down to her," I said, moving up to touch the quilts. Dee (Wangero) moved back just enough so that I couldn't reach the quilts. They already belonged to her.

"Imagine!" she breathed again, clutching them closely to her bosom.

"The truth is," I said, "I promised to give them quilts to Maggie, for when she marries John Thomas."

She gasped like a bee had stung her.

"Maggie can't appreciate these quilts!" she said. "She'd probably be backward enough to put them to everyday use."

"I reckon she would," I said. "God knows I been saving 'em for long enough with nobody using 'em. I hope she will!" I didn't want to bring up how I had offered Dee (Wangero) a quilt when she went away to college.

Then she had told me they were old-fashioned, out of style.

"But they're *priceless!*" she was saying now, furiously; for she has a temper. "Maggie would put them on the bed and in five years they'd be in rags. Less than that!" "She can always make some more," I said. "Maggie knows how to quilt."

Dee (Wangero) looked at me with hatred. "You just will not understand. The point is these quilts, *these* quilts!"

"Well," I said, stumped. "What would you do with them?"

"Hang them," she said. As if that was the only thing you could do with quilts.

Maggie by now was standing in the door. I could almost hear the sound her feet nude as they scraped over each other.

"She can have them, Mama," she said, like somebody used to never winning anything, or having anything reserved for her. "I can 'member Grandma Dee without the quilts."

I looked at her hard. She had filled her bottom lip with checkerberry snuff and it gave her face a kind of dopey, hangdog took. It was Grandma Dee and Big Dee who taught her how to quilt herself. She stood there with her scarred hands hidden in the folds of her skirt. She looked at her sister with something like fear but she wasn't mad at her. This was Maggie's portion. This was the way she knew God to work.

When I looked at her like that something hit me in the top of my head and ran down to the soles of my feet. just like when I'm in church and the spirit of God touches me and I get happy and shout. I did something I never had done before: hugged Maggie to me, then dragged her on into the room, snatched the quilts out of Miss Wangero's hands and dumped them into Maggie's lap. Maggie just sat there on my bed with her mouth open.

"Take one or two of the others," I said to Dee.

But she turned without a word and went out to Hakim-a-barber.

"You just don't understand," she said, as Maggie and I came out to the car.

"What don't I understand?" I wanted to know.

"Your heritage," she said. And then she turned to Maggie, kissed her, and said, "You ought to try to make something of yourself, too, Maggie. It's really a new day for us. But from the way you and Mama still live you'd never know it."

She put on some sunglasses that hid everything above the tip of her nose and her chin.

Maggie smiled; maybe at the sunglasses. But a real smile, not scared. After we watched the car dust settle I asked Maggie to bring me a dip of snuff. And then the two of us sat there just enjoying, until it was time to go in the house and go to bed.

THINK ABOUT IT

1. Describe the relationship between the women in the story. What factors have influenced the way they interact?

2. What causes the change in the mother's decision at the end of the story?

TALK ABOUT IT

3. Which relationship in the story is the most mature? Why?

4. Would the three African-American women react differently if they were from another ethnic or social background?

WRITE ABOUT IT

5. Write about the objects which mean the most to your sense of family identity. Do you put them to "everyday use?" Why or why not?

6. How do you think the quilt should be used — as an object of art or as an object of everyday use? Why?

READ MORE ABOUT IT

Walker, Alice. *In Love and Trouble: Stories of Black Women.* San Diego: Harcourt Brace Jovanovich, 1974.

Walker, Alice. *The Color Purple.* San Diego: Harcourt Brace Jovanovich, 1982.

Walker, Alice. *Goodnight Willie Lee, I'll See You in the Morning.* San Diego: Harcourt Brace Jovanovich, 1984.

ALICE ELLIOTT DARK

In the Gloaming

Alice Elliott Dark teaches writing at The Writer's Voice in New York City. In 1994, her short story, "In the Gloaming," was selected for *The Best American Short Stories of 1994.* In this anthology, Dark gives background on this story:

> After "In the Gloaming" was published, I got a lot of letters asking if it was really fiction; apparently it seemed autobiographical. I suppose it is, in the sense that I see it as a story about a woman trying to be a decent mother; a subject that was very much on my mind at the time I wrote it. I had recently become a mother, and was having bouts of vertigo whenever I thought of the scope of this new relationship. There were so many powerful, contradictory feelings to cope with: I wanted to encourage my son to have his own life, yet I hoped he would like me; I wanted to help him feel brave about going out into the world, yet when I imagined it, I instantly feared the harm that could come to him. Janet, the mother in the story, took on all this ambivalence and managed to behave with grace and honor toward her family under the worst of circumstances. I only wish I could do as well.
>
> I was also overwhelmed by the impending death of my grandfather. I'd never really been able to make sense of death, and my grandfather's would be particularly hard to fathom. One day the first line of the story came to me. Originally, it was: "He wanted to talk again, suddenly." I wrote it down and just kept writing. He became Laird .... The title came from my grandfather, the son of a Scotsman, who passed his love for the gloaming on to his family. There was some discussion about changing the title because the term was unfamiliar, but I asked to keep it and was glad at the pleasure my grandfather got from seeing one of his passions in the elegant *New Yorker* typeface before he died .... I never thought of it as an AIDS story; from what I've seen of AIDS, the end of the disease is not as gentle as this, nor do most victims have situations as idyllic as Laird's. I wish everyone could have as much love, comfort, and understanding. The story is a fantasy and a wish. During the writing, I felt the way I've heard actors describe their involvement with their parts; I took on the responsibility of speaking for these people and could not shake my awareness of them when I put my pen down for the day. Janet and Laird were completely real and absorbing to me, I missed them very much when I finished.

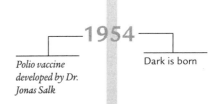

1954

Polio vaccine developed by Dr. Jonas Salk

Dark is born

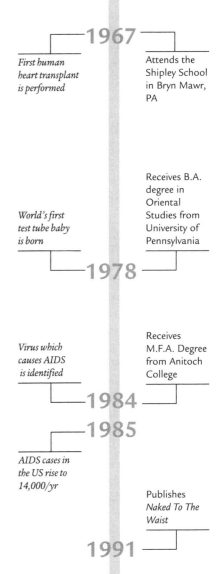

1967

First human heart transplant is performed

Attends the Shipley School in Bryn Mawr, PA

Receives B.A. degree in Oriental Studies from University of Pennsylvania

World's first test tube baby is born

1978

Virus which causes AIDS is identified

Receives M.F.A. Degree from Anitoch College

1984

1985

AIDS cases in the US rise to 14,000/yr

Publishes *Naked To The Waist*

1991

HER SON WANTED to talk again, suddenly. During the days, he still brooded, scowling at the swimming pool from the vantage point of his wheelchair, where he sat covered with blankets despite the summer heat. In the evenings, though, Laird became more like his old self — his *old* old self, really. He became sweeter, the way he'd been as a child, before he began to cloak himself with layers of irony and clever remarks. He spoke with an openness that astonished her. No one she knew talked that way — no man, at least. After he was asleep, Janet would run through the conversations in her mind, and realize what it was she wished she had said. She knew she was generally considered sincere, but that had more to do with her being a good listener than with how she expressed herself. She found it hard work to keep up with him, but it was the work she had pined for all her life.

A month earlier, after a particularly long and grueling visit with a friend who'd come up on the train from New York, Laird had declared a new policy: no visitors, no telephone calls. She didn't blame him. People who hadn't seen him for a while were often shocked to tears by his appearance, and, rather than having them cheer him up, he felt obliged to comfort them. She'd overheard bits of some of those conversations. The final one was no worse than the others, but he was fed up. He had said more than once that he wasn't cut out to be the brave one, the one who would inspire everybody to walk away from a visit with him feeling uplifted, shaking their heads in wonder. He had liked being the most handsome and missed it very much; he was not a good victim. When he had had enough he went into a self-imposed retreat, complete with a wall of silence and other ascetic practices that kept him busy for several weeks.

Then he softened. Not only did he want to talk again; he wanted to talk to *her*.

It began the night they ate outside on the terrace for the first time all summer. Afterward, Martin — Laird's father — got up to make a telephone call, but Janet stayed in her wicker chair, resting before clearing the table. It was one of those moments when she felt nostalgic for cigarettes. On nights like this, when the air was completely still, she used to blow her famous smoke rings for the children, dutifully obeying their commands to blow one through another or three in a row, or to make big, ropy circles that expanded as they floated up to the heavens. She did exactly what they wanted, for as long as they wanted, sometimes going through a quarter of a pack before they allowed her to stop. Incredibly, neither Anne nor Laird became smokers. Just the opposite; they nagged at her to quit, and were pleased when she finally did. She wished they had been just a little bit sorry; it was a part of their childhood coming to an end, after all.

Out of habit, she took note of the first lightning bug, the first star. The lawn darkened, and the flowers that had sulked in the heat all day suddenly released their perfumes. She laid her head back on the rim of the chair and closed her eyes. Soon she was following Laird's breathing, and found herself picking up the vital rhythms, breathing along. It was so peaceful, being near him like this. How many mothers spend so much time with their thirty-three year-old sons? she thought. She had as much of him now as she had had when he was an infant; more, in a way, because she had the memory of the intervening years as well, to round out her thoughts about him. When they sat quietly together she felt as close to him as she ever had. It was still him

in there, inside the failing shell. *She still enjoyed him.*

"The gloaming," he said, suddenly.

She nodded dreamily, automatically, then sat up. She turned to him. "What?" Although she had heard.

"I remember when I was little you took me over to the picture window and told me that in Scotland this time of day was called the 'gloaming.'"

Her skin tingled. She cleared her throat, quietly, taking care not to make too much of an event of his talking again. "You thought I said 'gloomy.'"

He gave a smile, then looked at her searchingly. "I always thought it hurt you somehow that the day was over, but you said it was a beautiful time because for a few moments the purple light made the whole world look like the Scottish Highlands on a summer night."

"Yes. As if all the earth were covered with heather."

"I'm sorry I never saw Scotland," he said.

"You're a Scottish lad nonetheless," she said. "At least on my side." She remembered offering to take him to Scotland once, but Laird hadn't been interested. By then, he was in college and already sure of his own destinations, which had diverged so thoroughly from hers. "I'm amazed you remember that conversation. You couldn't have been more than seven."

"I've been remembering a lot lately."

"Have you?"

"Mostly about when I was very small. I suppose it comes from having you take care of me again. Sometimes, when I wake up and see your face, I feel I can remember you looking in on me when I was in my crib. I remember your dresses."

"Oh, no!" She laughed lightly.

"You always had the loveliest expressions," he said.

She was astonished, caught off guard. Then, she had a memory, too — of her leaning over Laird's crib and suddenly having a picture of looking up at her own mother. "I know what you mean," she said.

"You do, don't you?"

He looked at her in a close, intimate way that made her self-conscious. She caught herself swinging her leg nervously, like a pendulum, and stopped.

"Mom," he said. "There are still a few things I need to do. I have to write a will, for one thing."

Her heart went flat. In his presence she had always maintained that he would get well. She wasn't sure she could discuss the other possibility.

"Thank you," he said.

"For what?"

"For not saying that there's plenty of time for that, or some similar sentiment."

"The only reason I didn't say it was to avoid the cliché, not because I don't believe it."

"You believe there is plenty of time?"

She hesitated; he noticed, and leaned forward slightly. "I believe there is time," she said.

"Even if I were healthy, it would be a idea."

"I suppose."

"I don't want to leave it until it's too late. You wouldn't want me to suddenly leave everything to the nurses, would you?"

She laughed, pleased to hear him joking again. "All right, all right, I'll call the lawyer."

"That would be great." There was a pause. "Is this still your favorite time of day, Mom?"

"Yes, I suppose it is," she said, "although I don't think in terms of favorites anymore."

"Never mind favorites, then. What else do you like?"

"What do you mean?" she asked.

"I mean exactly that."

"I don't know. I care about all the ordinary things. You know what I like."

"Name one thing."

"I feel silly."

"Please?"

"All right. I like my patch of lilies of the valley under the trees over there. Now can we change the subject?"

"Name one more thing."

"Why?"

"I want to get to know you."

"Oh, Laird, there's nothing to know."

"I don't believe that for a minute."

"But it's true. I'm average. The only extraordinary thing about me is my children."

"All right," he said. "Then let's talk about how you feel about me."

"Do you flirt with your nurses like this when I'm not around?"

"I don't dare. They've got me where they want me." He looked at her. "You're changing the subject."

She smoothed her skirt. "I know how you feel about church, but if you need to talk I'm sure the minister would be glad to come over. Or if you would rather have a doctor … "

He laughed.

"What?"

"That you still call psychiatrists 'doctors.'"

She shrugged.

"I don't need a professional, Ma." He laced his hands and pulled at them as he struggled for words.

"What can I do?" she asked.

He met her gaze. "You're where I come from. I need to know about you."

That night she lay awake, trying to think of how she could help, of what, aside from her time, she had to offer. She couldn't imagine.

She was anxious the next day when he was sullen again, but the next night, and on each succeeding night, the dusk worked its spell. She set dinner on the table outside, and afterward, when good Martin had vanished into the maw of his study, she and Laird began to speak. The air around them seemed to crackle with the energy they were creating in their effort to know and be known. Were other people so close, she wondered. She never had been, not to anybody. Certainly she and Martin had never really connected, not soul to soul, and with her friends, no matter how loyal and reliable, she always had a sense of what she could do that would alienate them. Of course, her friends had the option of cutting her off, and Martin could always ask for a divorce, whereas Laird was a captive audience. Parents and children were all captive audiences to each other; in view of this, it was amazing how little comprehension there was of one another's stories. Everyone stopped paying attention so early on, thinking they had figured it all out. She recognized that she was as guilty of this as anyone. She was still surprised whenever she went over to her daughter's house and saw how neat she was; in her mind, Anne was still a sloppy teenager who threw sweaters into the corner of her closet and candy wrappers under her bed. It still surprised her that Laird wasn't interested in girls. He had been, hadn't he? She remembered lying awake listening for him to come home, hoping that he was smart enough to apply what he knew about the facts of life, to take precautions.

Now she had the chance to let go of these old notions. It wasn't that she liked everything about Laird — there was much that remained foreign to her — but she wanted to know about all of it. As she came to her senses every morning in the moment or two after she awoke, she found herself aching with love and gratitude, as if he were a small, perfect creature again and she could look forward to a day of watching him grow. Quickly, she became greedy for their evenings. She replaced her half-facetious, half-hopeful reading of the horoscope in the daily newspaper with a new habit of tracking the time the sun would set, and drew satisfaction from seeing it come earlier as the summer waned; it meant she didn't have to wait as long. She took to sleeping late, shortening the day even more. It was ridiculous, she knew. She was behaving like a girl with a crush, behaving absurdly. It was a feeling she had thought she'd never have again, and now here it was. She immersed herself in it, living her life for the twilight moment when his eyes would begin to glow, the signal that he was stirring into consciousness. Then her real day would begin.

"Dad ran off quickly," he said one night. She had been wondering when he would mention it.

"He had a phone call to make," she said automatically.

Laird looked directly into her eyes, his expression one of gentle reproach. He was letting her know he had caught her in the central lie of her life, which was that she understood Martin's obsession with his work. She averted her gaze. The truth was that she had never understood. Why couldn't he sit with her for half an hour after dinner, or, if not with her, why not with his dying son?

She turned sharply to look at Laird. The word "dying" had sounded so loudly in her mind that she wondered if she had spoken it, but he showed no reaction. She wished she hadn't even thought it. She tried to stick to good thoughts in his presence. When she couldn't, and he had a bad night afterward, she blamed herself, as her efficient memory dredged up all the books and maga-

zine articles she had read emphasizing the effect of psychological factors on the course of the disease. She didn't entirely believe it, but she felt compelled to give the benefit of the doubt to every theory that might help. It couldn't do any harm to think positively. And if it gave him a few more months …

"I don't think Dad can stand to be around me."

"That's not true." It was true.

"Poor Dad. He's always been a hypochondriac — we have that in common. He must hate this."

"He just wants you to get well."

"If that's what he wants, I'm afraid I'm going to disappoint him again. At least this will be the last time I let him down."

He said this merrily, with the old, familiar light darting from his eyes. She allowed herself to be amused. He had always been fond of teasing, and held no subject sacred. As the de facto authority figure in the house — Martin hadn't been home enough to be the real disciplinarian — she had often been forced to reprimand Laird, but, in truth, she shared his sense of humor. She responded to it now by leaning over to cuff him on the arm. It was an automatic response, prompted by a burst of high spirits that took no notice of the circumstances. It was a mistake. Even through the thickness of his terrycloth robe, her knuckles knocked on bone. There was nothing left of him.

"It's his loss," she said, the shock of Laird's thinness making her serious again. It was the furthest she would go in criticizing Martin. She had always felt it her duty to maintain a benign image of him for the children. He had become a character of her invention, with a whole range of postulated emotions whereby he missed them when he was away on a business trip and thought of them

every few minutes when he had to work late. Some years earlier, when she was secretly seeing a doctor — a psychiatrist — she had finally admitted to herself that Martin was never going to be the lover she had dreamed of. He was an ambitious, competitive, self-absorbed man who probably should never have got married. It was such a relief to be able to face it that she wanted to share the news with her children, only to discover that they were dependent on the myth. They could hate his work, but they could not bring themselves to believe he had any choice in the matter. She had dropped the subject.

"Thank you, Ma. It's his loss in your case, too."

A throbbing began behind her eyes, angering her. The last thing she wanted to do was cry. There would be plenty of time for that. "It's not all his fault," she said when she had regained some measure of control. "I'm not very good at talking about myself. I was brought up not to."

"So was I," he said.

"Yes, I suppose you were."

"Luckily, I didn't pay any attention." He grinned.

"I hope not," she said, and meant it. "Can I get you anything?"

"A new immune system?"

She rolled her eyes, trying to disguise the way his joke had touched on her prayers. "Very funny. I was thinking more along the lines of an iced tea or an extra blanket."

"I'm fine. I'm getting tired, actually."

Her entire body went on the alert, and she searched his face anxiously for signs of deterioration. Her nerves darted and pricked whenever he wanted anything; her adrenaline rushed. The fight-or-flight response, she supposed. She had often wanted to flee, but had forced herself to stay, to fight with what few weapons she had. She responded to his needs, making sure there was a fresh, clean set of sheets ready when he was tired, food when he was hungry. It was what she could do.

"Shall I get a nurse?" She pushed her chair back from the table.

"O.K.," Laird said weakly. He stretched out his hand to her, and the incipient moonlight illuminated his skin so it shone like alabaster. His face had turned ashy. It was a sight that made her stomach drop. She ran for Maggie, and by the time they returned Laird's eyes were closed, his head lolling to one side. Automatically, Janet looked for a stirring in his chest. There it was: his shoulders expanded; he still breathed. Always, in the second before she saw movement, she became cold and clinical as she braced herself for the possibility of discovering that he was dead.

Maggie had her fingers on his wrist and was counting his pulse against the second hand on her watch, her lips moving. She laid his limp hand back on his lap. "Fast," she pronounced.

"I'm not surprised," Janet said, masking her fear with authority. "We had a long talk."

Maggie frowned. "Now I'll have to wake him up again for his meds."

"Yes, I suppose that's true. I forgot about that."

Janet wheeled him into his makeshift room downstairs and helped Maggie lift him into the rented hospital bed. Although he weighed almost nothing, it was really a job for two; his weight was dead weight. In front of Maggie, she was all brusque efficiency, except for the moment when her fingers strayed to touch Laird's pale cheek and she prayed she hadn't done any harm.

"Who's your favorite author?" he asked one night.

"Oh, there are so many," she said. "Your real favorite."

She thought. "The truth is there are certain subjects I find attractive more than certain authors. I seem to read in cycles, to fulfill an emotional yearning."

"Such as?"

"Books about people who go off to live in Africa or Australia or the South Seas."

He laughed. "That's fairly self-explanatory. What else?"

"When I really hate life I enjoy books about real murders. 'True crime,' I think they're called now. They're very punishing."

"Is that what's so compelling about them? I could never figure it out. I just know that at certain times I loved the gore, even though I felt absolutely disgusted with myself for being interested in it."

"You need to think about when those times were. That will tell you a lot." She paused. "I don't like reading about sex."

"Big surprise!"

"No, no," she said. "It's not for the reason you think, or not only for that reason. You see me as a prude, I know, but remember, it's part of a mother's job to come across that way. Although perhaps I went a bit far ..."

He shrugged amiably. "Water under the bridge. But go on about sex."

"I think it should be private. I always feel as though these writers are showing off when they describe a sex scene. They're not really trying to describe sex, but to demonstrate that they're not afraid to write about it. As if they're thumbing their noses at their mothers."

He made a moue.

Janet went on. "You don't think there's an element of that? I do question their motives, because I don't think sex can ever actually be portrayed — the sensations and the emotions are ... beyond language. If you only describe the mechanics, the effect is either clinical or pornographic, and if

you try to describe intimacy instead, you wind up with abstractions. The only sex you could describe fairly well is bad sex — and who wants to read about that, for God's sake, when everyone is having bad sex of their own?"

"Mother!" He was laughing helplessly, his arms hanging limply over the sides of his chair.

"I mean it. To me it's like reading about someone using the bathroom."

"Good grief!"

"Now who's the prude?"

"I never said I wasn't," he said. "Maybe we should change the subject."

She looked out across the land. The lights were on in other people's houses, giving the evening the look of early fall. The leaves were different, too, becoming droopy. The grass was dry, even with all the watering and tending from the gardener. The summer was nearly over.

"Maybe we shouldn't," she said. "I've been wondering. Was that side of life satisfying for you?"

"Ma, tell me you're not asking me about my sex life. "

She took her napkin and folded it carefully, lining up the edges and running her fingers along the hems. She felt very calm, very pulled together and all of a piece, as if she'd finally got the knack of being a dignified woman. She threaded her fingers and laid her hands in her lap. "I'm asking about your love life, " she said. "Did you love, and were you loved in return?"

"Yes."

"I'm glad."

"That was easy," he said.

"Oh, I've gotten very easy, in my old age."

"Does Dad know about this?" His eyes were twinkling wickedly.

" Don't be fresh," she said.

"You started it."

"Then I'm stopping it. Now."

He mad a funny face, and then another, until she could no longer keep from smiling. His routine carried her back to memories of his childhood efforts to charm her: watercolors of her favorite vistas (unrecognizable without the captions), bouquets of violets self-consciously flung into her lap, chores performed without prompting. He had always gone too far, then backtracked to regain even footing. She had always allowed herself to be wooed.

Suddenly she realized: Laird had been the love of her life.

One night it rained hard. Janet decided to serve the meal in the kitchen, since Martin was out. They ate in silence; she was freed from the compulsion to keep up the steady stream of chatter that she used to affect when Laird hadn't talked at all; now she could save her words for afterward. He ate nothing but comfort foods lately: mashed potatoes, vanilla ice cream, rice pudding. The days of his strict macrobiotic regime, and all the cooking classes she had taken in order to help him along with it, were past. His body was essentially a thing of the past, too; when he ate, he was feeding what was left of his mind. He seemed to want to recapture the cosseted feeling he'd had when he'd been sick as a child and she would serve him flat ginger ale, and toast soaked in cream, and play endless card games with him, using his blanket-covered legs as a table. In those days, too, there'd been a general sense of giving way to illness: then, he let himself go completely because he knew he would soon be better and active and have a million things expected of him again. Now he let himself go because he had fought long enough.

Finally, he pushed his bowl toward the middle of the table, signaling that he was finished. (His table manners had gone to pieces. Who

cared?) She felt a light, jittery excitement, the same jazzy feeling she got when she was in a plane that was picking up speed on the runway. She arranged her fork and knife on the rim of her plate and pulled her chair in closer. "I had an odd dream last night," she said.

His eyes remained dull.

She waited uncertainly, thinking that perhaps she had started to talk too soon. "Would you like something else to eat?"

He shook his head. There was no will in his expression; his refusal was purely physical, a gesture coming from the satiation in his stomach. An animal walking away from its bowl, she thought.

To pass the time, she carried the dishes to the sink, gave them a good rinse, and put them in the dishwasher. She carried the ice cream to the counter, pulled a spoon from the drawer and scraped off a mouthful of the thick, creamy residue that stuck to the inside of the lid. She ate it without thinking, so the sudden sweetness caught her by surprise. All the while she kept track of Laird, but every time she thought she noticed signs of his readiness to talk and hurried back to the table, she found his face still blank.

She went to the window. The lawn had become a floodplain and was filled with broad pools; the branches of the evergreens sagged, and the sky was the same uniform grayish yellow it had been since morning. She saw him focus his gaze on the line where the treetops touched the heavens, and she understood, there was no lovely interlude on this rainy night, no heathered dusk. The gray landscape had taken the light out of him.

"I'm sorry," she said aloud, as if it were her fault.

He gave a tiny, helpless shrug.

She hovered for a few moments, hoping, but his face was slack, and she gave up. She felt utterly forsaken, too disappointed and agitated to sit with him and watch the rain. "It's all right," she said. "It's a good night to watch television."

She wheeled him to the den and left him with Maggie, then did not know what to do with herself. She had no contingency plan for this time. It was usually the one period of the day when she did not need the anesthesia of tennis games, bridge lessons, volunteer work, errands. She had not considered the present possibility. For some time, she hadn't given any thought to what Martin would call "the big picture." Her conversation Laird had lulled her into inventing a parallel big picture of her own. She realized that a part of her had worked out a whole scenario: the summer evenings would blend into fall; then, gradually, the winter would arrive, heralding chats by the fire, Laird resting his feet on the pigskin ottoman in the den while she dutifully knitted her yearly Christmas sweaters for Anne's children.

She had allowed herself to imagine a future. That had been her mistake. This silent, endless evening was her punishment, a reminder of how things really were.

She did not know where to go in her own house, and ended up wandering through the rooms, propelled by a vague, hunted feeling. Several times, she turned around, expecting someone to be there, but, of course no one ever was. She was quite alone. Eventually, she realized that she was imagining a person in order to give material properties to the source of her wounds. She was inventing a villain. There should be a villain, shouldn't there? There should be an enemy, a devil, an evil force that could be driven out. Her imagination had provided it with aspects of a corporeal presence so she could pretend, for a moment, that there was a real enemy hovering around her, someone she could have the police come and take away. But the enemy was part of Laird, and neither he nor she nor any of the doctors or experts or ministers could separate the two.

She went upstairs and took a shower. She barely paid attention to her own body anymore, and only noticed abstractly that the water was too hot, her skin turning pink. Afterward, she sat on the chaise lounge in her bedroom and tried to read. She heard something; she leaned forward and cocked her head toward the sound. Was that Laird's voice? Suddenly she believed that he had begun to talk after all — She believed he was talking to Maggie. She dressed and went downstairs. He was alone in the den, alone with the television. He didn't hear or see her. She watched him take a drink from a cup, his hand shaking badly. It was a plastic cup with a straw poking through the lid, the kind used by small children while they are learning to drink. It was supposed to prevent accidents, but it couldn't stop his hands from trembling. He managed to spill the juice anyway.

Laird had always coveted the decadent pile of cashmere lap blankets she had collected over the years in the duty-free shops of the various British airports. Now he wore one around his shoulders, one over his knees. She remembered similar balmy nights when he would arrive home from soccer practice after dark, a towel slung around his neck.

"I suppose it has to be in the church," he said.

"I think it should," she said, "but it's up to you."

"I guess it's not the most timely moment to make a statement about my personal disbeliefs. But I'd like

you to keep it from being too lugubrious. No lilies, for instance."

"God forbid."

"And have some decent music."

"Such as?"

"I had an idea, but now I can't remember."

He pressed his hands to his eyes. His fingers were so transparent that they looked as if he were holding them over a flashlight.

"Please buy a smashing dress, something mournful yet elegant. And don't wait until the last minute."

She didn't reply.

Janet gave up on the idea of a rapprochement between Martin and Laird; she felt freer when she stopped hoping for it. Martin rarely came home for dinner anymore. Perhaps he was having an affair? It was a thought she'd never allowed herself to have before, but it didn't threaten her now. Good for him, she even decided, in her strongest, most magnanimous moments. Good for him if he's actually feeling bad and trying to do something to make himself feel better.

Anne was brave and chipper during her visits, yet when she walked back out to her car, she would wrap her arms around her ribs and shudder. " I don't know how you do it, Mom. Are you really all right?" she always asked, with genuine concern.

"Anne's become such a hopeless matron," Laird always said, with fond exasperation, when he and his mother were alone again later. Once, Janet began to tease him for finally coming to friendly terms with his sister, but she cut it short when she saw that he was blinking furiously.

They were exactly the children she had hoped to have: a companionable girl, a mischievous boy. It gave her great pleasure to see them together. She did not try to listen to their conversations but watched from

a distance, usually from the kitchen as she prepared them a snack reminiscent of their childhood, like watermelon boats or lemonade. Then she would walk Anne to the car, their similar good shoes clacking across the gravel. They hugged, pressing each other's arms, and their brief embraces buoyed them up — forbearance and grace passing back and forth between them like a piece of shared clothing, designated for use by whoever needed it most. It was the kind of parting toward which she had aimed her whole life, a graceful, secure parting at the close of a peaceful afternoon. After Anne left, Janet always had a tranquil moment or two as she walked back to the house through the humid September air. Everything was so still. Occasionally there were the hums and clicks of a lawnmower or the shrieks of a band of children heading home from school. There were the insects and the birds. It was a straightforward, simple life she had chosen. She had tried never to ask for too much, and to be of use. Simplicity had been her hedge against bad luck. It had worked for so long. For a brief moment, as she stepped lightly up the single slate stair and through the door, her legs still harboring all their former vitality, she could pretend her luck was still holding.

Then she would glance out the window and there would be the heart-catching sight of Laird, who would never again drop by for a casual visit. Her chest would ache and flutter, a cave full of bats.

Perhaps she had asked for too much, after all.

"What did you want to be when you grew up?" Laird asked.

"I was expected to be a wife and mother. I accepted that. I wasn't a rebel."

"There must have been something else."

"No," she said. "Oh, I guess I had all the usual fantasies of the day, of being the next Amelia Earhart or Margaret Mead, but that was all they were—fantasies. I wasn't even close to being brave enough. Can you imagine me flying across the ocean on my own?" She laughed and looked over for his laughter, but he had fallen asleep.

A friend of Laird's had somehow got the mistaken information that Laird had died, so she and Martin received a condolence letter. There was a story about a time a few years back when the friend was with Laird on a bus in New York. They had been sitting behind two older women, waitresses who began to discuss their income taxes, trying to decide how much of their tip income to declare to sound realistic so they wouldn't attract an audit. Each woman offered up bits of folk wisdom on the subject, describing in detail her particular situation. During a lull in the conversation, Laird stood up.

"Excuse me, I couldn't help overhearing," he said, leaning over them. "May I have your names and addresses, please? I work for the IRS."

The entire bus fell silent as everyone watched to see what would happen next. Laird took a small notebook and pen from the inside pocket of his jacket. He faced his captive audience. "I'm part of a new IRS outreach program," he told the group. "For the next ten minutes I'll be taking confessions. Does anyone have anything he or she wants to tell me?"

Smiles. Soon the whole bus was talking, comparing notes when they'd first realized he was kidding, and how scared they had been before they caught on. It was difficult to believe these were the same New Yorkers who were supposed to be so gruff and isolated.

"Laird was the most vital, funniest person I ever met," his friend wrote.

Now, in his wheelchair, he faced off against slow-moving flies, waving them away.

"The gloaming," Laird said.

Janet looked up from her knitting, startled. It was midafternoon, and the living room was filled with bright October sun. "Soon," she said.

He furrowed his brow. A little flash of confusion passed through his eyes, and she realized that for him it was already dark.

He tried to straighten his shawl, his hands shaking. She jumped up to help; then, when he pointed to the fireplace, she quickly laid the logs as she wondered what was wrong. Was he dehydrated? She thought she recalled that a dimming of vision was a sign of dehydration. She tried to remember what else she had read or heard, but even as she grasped for information, facts, her instincts kept interrupting with a deeper, more dreadful thought that vibrated through her, rattling her and making her gasp as she often did when remembering her mistakes, things she wished she hadn't said or done, wished she had the chance to do over. She knew what was wrong, and yet she kept turning away from the truth, her mind spinning in every other possible direction as she worked on the fire, only vaguely noticing how wildly she made the sparks fly as she pumped the old bellows.

Her work was mechanical — she had made hundreds of fires and soon there was nothing left to do. She put the screen up and pushed him close, then leaned over to pull his flannel pajamas down to meet his socks, protecting his bare shins. The sun streamed in around him, making him appear trapped between bars of light. She resumed her knitting, with mechanical hands.

"The gloaming," he said again. It did sound somewhat like "gloomy," because his speech was slurred.

"When all the world is purple," she said, hearing herself sound falsely bright. She wasn't sure whether he wanted her to talk. It was some time since he had talked — not long, really, in other people's lives, perhaps two weeks — but she had gone on with their conversations, gradually expanding into the silence until she was telling him stories and he was listening. Sometimes, when his eyes closed, she trailed off and began to drift. There would be a pause that she didn't always realize she was making, but if it went on too long he would call out "Mom?" with an edge of panic in his voice, as if he were waking from a nightmare. Then she would resume, trying to create a seamless bridge between what she had been thinking and where she had left off.

"It was really your grandfather who gave me my love for the gloaming," she said. "Do you remember him talking about it?" She looked up politely, expectantly, as if Laird might offer her a conversational reply. He seemed to like hearing the sound of her voice, so she went on, her needles clicking. Afterward, she could never remember for sure at what point she had stopped talking and had floated off into a jumble of her own thoughts, afraid to move, afraid to look up, afraid to know at which exact moment she became alone. All she knew was that at a certain point the fire was in danger of dying out entirely, and when she got up to stir the embers she glanced at him in spite of herself and saw that his fingers were making knitting motions over his chest, the way people did as they were dying. She knew that if she went to get the nurse, Laird would be gone by the time she returned, so she went and stood behind him, leaning over to press her face against his, sliding her hands down his busy arms, helping him along with his fretful stitches until he finished this last piece of work.

Later, after the most pressing calls had been made and Laird's body had been taken away, Janet went up to his old room and lay down on one of the twin beds. She had changed the room into a guest room when he went off to college, replacing his things with guest room decor, thoughtful touches such as luggage racks at the foot of each bed, a writing desk stocked with paper and pens, heavy wooden hangers and shoe trees. She made an effort to remember the room as it had been when he was a little boy; she had chosen a train motif, then had to redecorate when Laird decided trains were silly. He had wanted it to look like a jungle, so she had hired an art student to paint a jungle mural on the walls. When he decided that was silly, he hadn't bothered her to do anything about it, but had simply marked time until he could move on.

Anne came over, offered to stay, but was relieved to be sent home to her children.

Presently, Martin came in. Janet was watching the trees turn to mere silhouettes against the darkening sky, fighting the urge to pick up a true crime book, a debased urge. He lay down on the other bed.

"I'm sorry," he said.

"It's so wrong," she said angrily. She hadn't felt angry until that moment; she had saved it up for him. "A child shouldn't die before his parents. A young man shouldn't spend his early thirties wasting away talking to his mother. He should be out in the world. He shouldn't be thinking about me, or what I care about, or my opinions. He shouldn't have had to return my love to me — it was his to squander. Now I have it all back and I don't know what I'm supposed to do with it," she said.

She could hear Martin weeping in the darkness. He sobbed, and her anger veered away.

They were quiet for some time.

"Is there going to be a funeral?" Martin asked finally.

"Yes. We should start making the arrangements."

"I suppose he told you what he wanted."

"In general. He couldn't decide about the music. "

She heard Martin roll onto his side, so that he was facing her across the narrow chasm between the beds. He was still in his office clothes. "I remember being very moved by the bagpipes at your father's funeral."

It was an awkward offering, to be sure, awkward and late, and seemed to come from someone on the periphery of her life who knew her only slightly. It didn't matter; it was perfectly right. Her heart rushed toward it.

"I think Laird would have liked that idea very much," she said.

It was the last moment of the gloaming, the last moment of the day her son died. In a breath, it would be night; the moon hovered behind the trees, already rising to claim the sky, and she told herself she might as well get on with it. She sat up and was running her toes across the bare floor, searching for her shoes, when Martin spoke again, in a tone she used to hear on those long-ago nights when he rarely got home until after the children were in bed and he relied on her to fill him in on what they'd done that day. It was the same curious, shy, deferential tone that had always made her feel as though all the frustrations and boredom and mistakes and rushes of feeling in her days as a mother did indeed add up to something of importance, and she decided that the next round of telephone calls could wait while she answered the question he asked her: "Please tell me — what else did my boy like?"

THINK ABOUT IT

1. What is the gloaming? Why is it important in the story?
2. Why is the mother-son relationship in this story so different from the father-son relationship?

TALK ABOUT IT

3. Is the relationship between Janet and Laird a relationship based on dependency or on interdependency?
4. Should all families treat Laird as his family does? In other countries, would Laird receive more or less compassion than he does from his family?

WRITE ABOUT IT

5. Describe how you feel about AIDS victims.
6. Could you still love your child no matter what his/her lifestyle was? Explain your reasons.

READ MORE ABOUT IT

Dark, Alice Elliott. *Naked to the Waist.* Boston: Houghton Mifflin Company, 1991.

Reamer, Frederic G., ed. *AIDS and Ethics.* New York: Columbia University Press, 1991.

Wolff, Tobias, ed. *The Best American Short Stories of 1994.* Boston: Houghton Mifflin Company, - 1994.

Martin Niemöller

Kit Reed

Plato

Maya Angelou

Ernest J. Gaines

Francisco de Goya

Pablo Picasso

Salvador Dalí

Elie Wiesel

The UN Declaration of Human Rights

Christina Sommers

CHAPTER 5

Morality

T IS POSSIBLE to avoid many things during the course of a day. We can schedule our day so as not to meet certain people. We can control where we go or we can control our environment to avoid contact with germs and disease. We can spend an entire day without doing any work or, if we are feeling zealous, we can clean the garage. We can feast sumptuously or spend an entire day without food, fasting for inspiration or self-purification. No matter what we do or how hard we try to lose ourselves in everyday situations, however, we cannot avoid situations that place us squarely in the area known as morality. Morality

MARTIN NIEMÖLLER
Silence

First they came for the Jews.
I was silent. I was not a Jew.

Then they came for the Communists.
I was silent. I was not a Communist.

Then they came for the trade unionists.
I was silent. I was not a trade unionist.

Then they came for me.
There was no one left to speak for me.

deals with choices about what is right and what is wrong. Initially, Martin Niemöller, a Protestant pastor in Nazi Germany, did not think what he did was wrong by not acting, by not speaking out against the imprisonment of Jews, Communists, and trade unionists in Nazi Germany. Yet, he discovered that failure to speak out had serious consequences for him that he had not considered. Like Niemöller, we are confronted with moral choices every day. Morality is the science of human conduct, the way in which we decide what is right and what is wrong. As a science, morality has very specific rules of judging what are appropriate and inappropriate actions. As the basis for the choices we make, morality requires the examination of different possible courses of actions that will define what we think is right. Morality, thus, is an inescapable issue for all human beings. It requires that we assume responsibility for our behavior since our moral code is the product of the decisions and actions we take.

For as long as we can remember, people have tried to live together without conflict. Rules to protect small family groups or tribes became increasingly important as a means for group survival. Failure to abide by these rules meant the extinction of everyone, so the pressure to abide by the rules was paramount. From the day they were born, all the children in the group were taught the mores (customs) of that group so that they knew how they ought to act. Some mores remained polite customs, like deferring to elders when speaking, but others took on greater importance. For example, some customs required that members of the group refrain from stealing from one another and from harming each other. These rules formed the

moral identity of the group and came to reflect its concept of justice. Failure to follow these rules excluded the individual from the protection of and membership in the group. From these early origins, morality grew to be the customs and rules developed within particular cities and countries. Morality was seen as a matter of conforming to social conventions handed down through the years. Every member of the group would have to abide by these conventions, whether they related to sharing the same values or hating the same enemies. If another set of mores was encountered, it would be seen as foreign. It would not be binding; in fact, it would be seen as dangerous to the well-being of this community. But what of individuals within the group who do not accept the group's moral code? Can one person stand before the society that has given him or her the rules for behavior and say that they do not agree?

As a result of asking this question, many people have come to believe that morality does not come from society, but from the individual. They believe morality is and must be an individual concern. Jean-Paul Sartre, the noted twentieth-century philosopher, said that a moral theory does not make moral judgments, people do. When it comes time to act, it is not a theory, a principle, or a society that is acting, it is an individual doing what he or she has decided is right or wrong. Even in those situations where a person may feel compelled to act by an authority figure, the person must choose whether or not to conform. Thus, morality is the ability of the individual to make a decision as to what should be done and to take responsibility for that decision. In traditional terms, the individual forms his or her own conscience and allows that to guide behavior. From this perspective, society may offer advice and suggestions, but morality becomes the decision of individuals, working from their own consciences.

The issue of whether society or the individual defines morality can be debated. The truth probably lies somewhere in the middle of these two positions. No matter which position is chosen, many ethicists agree that to assess the morality of an action properly, at least three dimensions must be considered: the intention of the agent, the circumstances surrounding the act, and the act itself. The intention of the agent is the consideration of the individual's contribution to morality. In analyzing a person's intention, the question is raised: why did he or she do that? What was his or her motivation? Motivation involves ascertaining the reason for the action. In addition to the intention of the agent, the circumstances surrounding the action must also be considered. Circumstances take into consideration the external, societal input into the action. Performing a particular action is colored by the time, place, and what the moral agent knows about the situation. To ascertain the circumstances, one asks: what was going on prior to the action? What events are relevant to the action? Finally, the act itself and its impact on others must be considered. This raises the question, what is the most likely outcome of this action? Who will be affected? Thus a moral action results from careful consideration of one's intention, the circumstances surrounding the action, and the action itself. An action which cannot pass careful scrutiny on all these factors cannot be considered right.

For example, take the simple act of a young man giving his mother flowers. On the surface this would seem to be a good thing, since most people consider giving flowers an expression of love and affection. But what if the mother happens to be highly allergic to flowers and her son knows this? Then the act may be vicious and wrong because it is directed at harming her. Therefore, no action can be considered good unless the intentions of the agent and the circumstances surrounding the act, as well as its outcome, are considered. Take another version of this same situation. Maybe the flowers are his mother's favorite, but the young man robs a convenience store in order to get the money to buy them. Although the act of giving flowers to the mother is good and his intention is to please her, the circumstances show us that his action was wrong. A sound moral decision takes into account all three moral factors, intention, circumstances, and action. Recognizing the way in which these factors interact helps us understand the complexities involved in making moral judgments and equips us to consider our judgments more carefully.

In this chapter, different selections raise serious moral questions. For example, would a person ever act immorally if he or she could be invisible while acting? When is it right to kill? How are our standards of right and wrong affected by our prejudices? Can the atrocities of war ever be considered right? These questions affect us on the individual, as well as a social, level, and their answers are far from simple, War, racism, and even simple good deeds present challenges to investigate the basis for our own actions and to carefully examine the basis for our judgments about others' actions. However, like Niemöller, we have come to realize that it is immoral to maintain our silence when faced with these dilemmas. If we are silent in the face of difficult decisions, who will be left to speak for us?

THINK ABOUT IT

1. Describe the two basic ways in which morality is defined. What are the three elements in analyzing the morality of an action?

TALK ABOUT IT

3. Are there times when the individual should act against the conventions and customs of society?
4. Should we always abide by the dictum, "when in Rome, do as the Romans do"? Why or why not?

WRITE ABOUT IT

5. Take an item from the news and analyze the intentions, circumstances, and the actions of the people involved.
6. Have you ever had to take a stand against what everyone else said was right? What happened? Would you do this again? Why or why not?

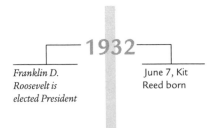

1932

Franklin D.
Roosevelt is
elected President

June 7, Kit
Reed born

Supreme Court
rules against
school
segregation

Receives B. A.
from Notre
Dame of
Maryland

1954

1958

Explorer I, first
American
satellite, is
launched

Named
New
England
Newspaper
Woman of
the Year

1964

Nelson Mandela
is sentenced to
life in prison

Awarded a
Guggenheim
Fellowship

1974

President Nixon
resigns in face of
Watergate
scandal

Works as
Visiting Writer
in India

Exxon Valdez
runs aground in
Alaska causing
worst ever
U.S. oil spill

Coordinates
Indo-U.S.
Writer's
Exchange

1989

1990

KIT REED

Winter

Lillian Craig Reed, Kit Reed, was born on June 7, 1932, in San Diego, California. In 1954, Reed earned a B.A. from the College of Notre Dame of Maryland. She married in 1955 and had three children. From 1954-55, Reed worked as a reporter and television editor in St. Petersburg, Florida. She was also a reporter for the *New Haven Register* from 1956-59. From 1974 to the present, she has been the visiting professor of English at Wesleyan University.

Reed has written many books including *Mother Isn't Dead, She's Only Sleeping* (1961), *Captain Grownup* (1976), *The Killer Mice* (1976), and *Magic Time* (1980). She has also written several short stories. "Winter" is an interesting story about two women, Maude and Lizzie, who fantasize about a young man, Arnold, who is a "guest" in their home during a harsh winter. Arnold spends time with each of the women, consuming their supply of winter food in record time. He wants to leave — but something keeps him there.

IT WAS LATE FALL when he come to us, there was a scum of ice on all the puddles and I could feel the winter cold and fearsome in my bones, the hunger inside me was already uncurling, it would pace through the first of the year but by spring it would be raging like a tiger, consuming me until the thaw when Maude could hunt again and we would get the truck down the road to town. I was done canning but I got the tomatoes we had hanging in the cellar and I canned some more; Maude went out and brought back every piece of meat she could shoot and all the grain and flour and powdered milk she could bring in one truckload, we had to lay in everything we could before the snow could come and seal us in. The week he come Maude found a jack-rabbit stone dead in the road, it was frozen with its feet sticking straight up, and all the meat hanging in the cold room had

froze. Friday there was rime on the grass and when I looked out I seen footprints in the rime, I said Maude, someone is in the playhouse and we went out and there he was. He was asleep in the mess of clothes we always dressed up in, he had his head on the velvet gown my mother wore to the Exposition and his feet on the satin gown she married Father in, he had pulled her feather boa around his neck and her fox fur was wrapped around his loins.

Before he come, Maude and me would pass the winter talking about how it used to be, we would call up the past between us and look at it and Maude would end by blaming me. I could of married either Lister Hoffman or Harry Mead and left this place for good if it hadn't been for you, Lizzie. I'd tell her, Hell, I never needed you. You didn't marry them because you didn't marry them, you was scared of it and you would use me for an excuse . She would get mad then. It's a lie. Have it your way, I would tell her, just to keep the peace.

We both knew I would of married the first man that asked me, but nobody would, not even with all my money, nobody would ask me because of the taint. If nobody had of known then some man might of married me, but I went down to the field with Miles Harrison once while Father was still alive, and Miles and me, we almost, except that the blackness took me, right there in front of him, and so I never did. Nobody needed to know, but then Miles saw me fall down in the field. I guess it was him that put something between my teeth, but when I come to myself he was gone. Next time I went to town they all looked at me funny, some of them would try and face up to me and be polite but they was all jumpy, thinking would I do it right there in front of them, would I froth much, would they be hurt, as soon as was decent they would say Excuse me, I got to, anything to get out of there fast. When I run into Miles that day he wouldn't look at me and there hasn't been a man near me since then, not in more than fifty years, but Miles and me, we almost, and I have never stopped thinking about that.

Now Father is gone and my mother is gone and even Lister Hoffman and Miles Harrison and half the town kids that used to laugh at me, they are all gone, but Maude still reproaches me, we sit after supper and she says if it hadn't been for you I would have grandchildren now and I tell her I would have had them before she ever did because she never liked men, she would only suffer them to get children and that would be too much trouble, it would hurt. That's a lie, Lizzie, she would say, Harry and me used to … and I would tell her you never, but Miles and me … Then we would both think about being young and having people's hands on us but memory turns Maude

bitter and she can never leave it at that, she says, It's all your fault, but I know in my heart that people make their lives what they want them, and all she ever wanted was to be locked in here with nobody to make demands on her, she wanted to stay in this house with me, her dried-up sister, cold and safe, and if the hunger is on her, it has come on her late.

After a while we would start to make up stuff: Once I went with a boy all the way to Portland … Once I danced all night and half the morning, he wanted to kiss me on the place where my elbow bends … We would try to spin out the winter but even that was not enough and so we would always be left with the hunger; no matter how much we laid in, the meat was always gone before the thaw and I suppose it was really our lives we was judging but we would decide nothing in the cans looked good to us and so we would sit and dream and hunger and wonder if we would die of it, but finally the thaw would come and Maude would look at me and sigh: If only we had another chance.

Well now perhaps we will.

We found him in the playhouse, maybe it was seeing him being in the playhouse, where we pretended so many times, asleep in the middle of my mother's clothes or maybe it was but there was this boy, or man, and something about him called up our best memories, there was promise wrote all over him. I am too old, I am all dried out, but I have never stopped thinking about that one time and seeing that boy there, I could pretend he was Miles and I was still young. I guess he sensed us, he woke up fast and went into a crouch, maybe he had a knife, and then I guess he saw it was just two big old ladies in Army boots, he said, I run away from the Marines, I needed a place to sleep.

Maude said, I don't care what you need, you got to get out of here, but when he stood up he wobbled. His hair fell across his head like the hair on a boy I used to know and I said, Maude,

why don't you say yes to something just this once.

He had on this denim shirt and pants like no uniform I ever seen and he was saying, Two things happened, I found out I might have to shoot somebody in the war and then I made a mistake and they beat me so I cut out of there. He smiled and he looked open. I stared hard at Maude and Maude finally looked at me and said, All right, come up to the house and get something to eat.

He said his name was Arnold but when we asked him Arnold what, he said Never mind. He was in the kitchen by then, he had his head bent over a bowl of oatmeal and some biscuits I had made, and when I looked at Maude she was watching the way the light slid across his hair. When we told him our names he said, You are both beautiful ladies. I could see Maude's hands go up to her face and she went into her room and when she come back I saw she had put colour on her cheeks. While we was alone he said how good the biscuits was and wasn't that beautiful silver, did I keep it polished all myself and I said well yes, Maude brings in supplies but I am in charge of the house and making all the food. She come back then and saw us with our heads together and said to Arnold, I guess you'll be leaving soon.

I don't know, he said, they'll be out looking for me with guns and dogs.

That's no never mind of ours.

I never done nothing bad in the Marines, we just had different ideas. We both figured it was something worse but he looked so sad and tired and besides, it was nice to have him to talk to, he said, I just need a place to hole up for a while.

Maude said, You could always go back to your family.

He said, They never wanted me. They was always mean-hearted, not like you.

I took her side and said, It wouldn't kill you to let him stay on, Maude, it's time we had a little life around here.

There won't be enough food for three.

He won't stay long. Besides, he can help you with the chores.

She was looking at his bright hair again, she said, like it was all my doing, If you want to let him stay I guess we can let him stay.

He was saying, I could work for my keep.

All right, I said, you can stay on until you get your strength.

My heart jumped. A man, I thought. A man. How can I explain it? It was like being young, having him around. I looked at Maude and saw some of the same things in her eyes, hunger and hope, and I thought, You are ours now, Arnold, you are all ours. We will feed you and take care of you and when you want to wander we will let you wander, but we will never let you go.

Just until things die down a little, he was saying.

Maude had a funny grin. Just until things die down.

Well it must of started snowing right after dark that afternoon, because when we all waked up the house was surrounded. I said, Good thing you got the meat in, Maude, and she looked out, it was still blowing snow and it showed no signs of stopping, she looked out and said, I guess it is.

He was still asleep, he slept the day through except he stumbled down at dusk and dreamed over a bowl of my rabbit stew, I turned to the sink and when I looked back the stew was gone and the biscuits was gone and all the extra in the pot was gone, I had a little flash of fright, it was all disappearing too fast. Then Maude come over to me and hissed, The food, he's eating all the food and I looked at his brown hands and his tender neck and I said, It don't matter, Maude, he's young and strong

and if we run short he can go out into the snow and hunt. When we looked around next time he was gone, he had dreamed his way through half a pie and gone right back to bed.

Next morning he was up before the light, we sat together around the kitchen table and thought how nice it was to have a man in the house, I could look at him and imagine anything I wanted. Then he got up and said, Look, I want to thank you for everything, I got to get along now and I said, You can't, and he said, I got things to do, I been here long enough, but I told him You can't, and took him over to the window. The sun was up by then and there it was, snow almost to the window ledges, like we have every winter, and all the trees was shrouded, we could watch the sun take the snow and make it sparkle and I said, Beautiful snow, beautiful, and he only shrugged and said, I guess I'll have to wait till it clears off some. I touched his shoulder. I guess it will. I knew not to tell him it would never clear off, not until late spring; maybe he guessed, anyway he looked so sad I gave him Father's silver snuffbox to cheer him up.

He would divide his time between Maude and me, he played Rook with her and made her laugh so hard she gave him her pearl earrings and the brooch Father brought her back from Quebec. I gave him Grandfather's diamond stickpin because he admired it, and for Christmas we gave him the cameos and Father's gold-headed cane. Maude got the flu over New Year and Arnold and me spent New Year's Eve together, I mulled some wine and he hung up some of Mama's jewelry from the centre light, and touched it and made it twirl. We lit candles and played the radio, New Year's Eve in Times Square and somebody's Make-believe Ballroom, I went to pour another cup of wine and his hand was on mine on the bottle, I knew my lips was red for once and next day I gave him Papa's fur-lined coat.

I guess Maude suspected there was something between us, she looked pinched and mean when I went in with her broth at lunch, she said, Where were you at breakfast and I said, Maude, it's New Year's Day, I thought I would like to sleep in for once. She was quick and spiteful. You were with him. I thought, If she wants to think that about me, let her, and I let my eyes go sleepy and I said, We had to see the New Year in, didn't we? She was out of bed in two days, I have never seen anybody get up so fast after the flu. I think she couldn't stand us being where she couldn't see what we was up to every living minute. Then I got sick and I knew what torture it must have been for her, just laying there, I would call Maude and I would call her, and sometimes she would come and sometimes she wouldn't come and when she finally did look in on me I would say, Maude, where have you been and she would only giggle and not answer. There was meat cooking all the time, roasts and chops and chicken fricassee, when I said Maude, you're going to use it up, she would only smile and say, I just had to show him who's who in the kitchen, he tells me I'm a better cook than you ever was. After a while I got up, I had to even if I was dizzy and like to throw up, I had to get downstairs where I could keep an eye on them. As soon as I was up to it I made a roast of venison that would put hair on an egg and after that we would vie with each other in the kitchen, Maude and me. Once I had my hand on the skillet handle and she come over and tried to take it away, she was saying, Let me serve it up for him. I said, you're a fool, Maude, I cooked this and she hissed at me, through the steam, it won't do you no good, Lizzie, it's me he loves, and I just pushed her away and said, you goddamn fool, he loves me, and I give him my amethysts just to prove it. A couple of days later I couldn't find neither of them nowhere, I thought I heard noises up in the back room and I went up there and if they was in there they wouldn't answer, the door was locked and they wouldn't say nothing, not even when I knocked and knocked and knocked. So the next day I took him up in my room and we locked the door and I told him a story about every piece in my jewel box, even the cheap ones, when Maude tapped and whined outside the door we would just shush, and when we did come out and she said, All right, Lizzie, what was you doing in there, I only giggled and wouldn't tell.

She shouldn't of done it, we was all sitting around the table after dinner and she looked at me hard and said, You know something, Arnold, I wouldn't get too close to Lizzie, she has fits. Arnold only tried to look like it didn't matter, but after Maude went to bed I went down to make sure it was all right. He was still in the kitchen, whittling, and when I tried to touch his hand he pulled away.

I said, Don't be scared, I only throw one in a blue moon.

He said, that don't matter.

Then what's the matter?

I don't know Miss Lizzie, I just don't think you trust me.

Course I trust you, Arnold, don't I give you everything?

He just looked sad. Everything but trust.

I owe you so much, Arnold, you make me feel so young.

He just smiled for me then. You look younger, Miss Lizzie, you been getting younger every day I been here.

You did it.

If you let me, I could make you really young.

Yes, Arnold, yes.

But I have to know you trust me.

Yes, Arnold.

So I showed him where the money was. By then it was past midnight and we was both tired, he said, Tomorrow, and I let him go off to get his rest.

I don't know what roused us both and brought us out into the hall but I bumped into Maude at dawn, we was

both standing in our nightgowns like two ghosts. We crept downstairs together and there was light in the kitchen, the place where we kept the money in was open, empty, and there was a crack of light in the door to the cold room. I remember looking through and thinking, The meat is almost gone. Then we opened the door a crack wider and there he was, he had made a sledge, he must of sneaked down there and worked on it every night. It was piled with stuff, our stuff, and now he had the door to the outside open, he had dug himself a ramp out of the snow and he was lashing some homemade snow-shoes on his feet, in another minute he would cut out of there.

When he heard us he turned.

I had the shotgun and Maude had the axe.

He said, You can have all your stuff.

We said, We don't care about the stuff, Arnold, how could we tell him it was our youth he was taking away?

He looked at us, wall-eyed. You can have it all, just let me out.

You said you loved us, Arnold.

He was scrabbling up the snow ramp. Never mind what I told you, let me out of here.

He was going to get away in another minute, so Maude let him have it with the axe.

Afterward we closed the way to the outside and stood there and looked at each other, I couldn't say what was in my heart so I only looked at Maude, we was both sad, sad, I said. The food is almost gone.

Maude said, Everything is gone. We'll never make it to spring.

Maude looked at him laying there. You know what he told me? He said, I can make you young.

Me too, I said, there was something in his eyes that made me believe it.

Maude's eyes was aglitter, she said, The food is almost gone.

I knew what she meant, he was going to make us young. I don't know how it will work in us, but he is going to make us young, it will be as if the fits had never took me, never in all them years. Maude was looking at me, waiting, and after a minute I looked square at her and I said, I know.

So we et him.

THINK ABOUT IT

1. Why do Maude and Lizzie welcome Arnold into their home? Why does he accept? What does each character gain from this?

2. Are Arnold's actions morally justifiable? What about Lizzie and Maude's actions?

TALK ABOUT IT

3. When is it justifiable to break moral codes?

4. Why is Reed's story shocking? Would it be as shocking to other cultures?

WRITE ABOUT IT

5. Describe a situation where someone was faced with the choice of either eating someone or of dying. Do you believe cannibalism can be morally justified?

6. Would you eat another human being if your life depended on it? Explain your reasons.

READ MORE ABOUT IT

Reed, Kit. *Captain Grownup*. New York: Dutton, 1976.

Reed, Kit. *Magic Time*. New York: Berkeley, 1980.

Reed, Kit."Winter." *The Norton Anthology of Contemporary Fiction*. R. V. Cassill ed. New York: W. W. Norton, 1988.

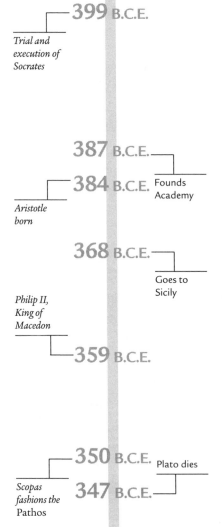

429 B.C.E.
Plato is
born

399 B.C.E.
Trial and
execution of
Socrates

387 B.C.E.
384 B.C.E. Founds
Academy
Aristotle
born

368 B.C.E.
Goes to
Sicily

Philip II,
King of
Macedon
359 B.C.E.

350 B.C.E. Plato dies
Scopas 347 B.C.E.
fashions the
Pathos

P L A T O

The Ring of Gyges

Plato, a Greek philosopher, was one of the most brilliant thinkers in the history of Western civilization. He was born into an old and important aristocratic Athenian family. Plato established a school for research which would include all fields of knowledge and explore their systematic interpretation. The result was the world's first university. Founded in 387 B.C.E., it was called the Academy.

The thesis of Plato's philosophy is his theory of Ideas, or Forms. He believed that human beings participate in two different worlds. One of these is the physical world that we experience through our bodily senses. The other world is one of immaterial and eternal essences that we can only experience through our minds. To Plato, the ideal world, sometimes called the world of Forms, is actually more real than the physical world, since he felt that the particular things that exist in the physical world are mere copies, or imitations, of this ideal world of Forms. For Plato, a Form is an eternal, unchangeable, and universal essence. Concepts such as justice, goodness, and truth exist as perfect forms in this ideal world. Justice became an idea Plato explored in detail after the trial and death of his mentor, Socrates.

In 399 B.C.E., the Athenian leaders believed Socrates was a danger to the people of Athens. They tried and then executed Socrates because he spoke out against established political leaders and their beliefs. Vigorously questioning the justice in executing an old man who loved only to teach and question, Plato wrote philosophical dialogues in vindication of Socrates' ideas. The following selection comes from Plato's famous work, the *Republic.* This selection asks whether there are any truly "just" people in the world.

NOW THE NATURE OF JUSTICE is this and of this sort, and it naturally grows out of these sorts of things. So the argument goes. That even those who practice it do so unwillingly, from an incapacity to do injustice, we would best perceive if we should in thought do something like this: give each, the just man and the unjust, license to do whatever he wants, while we follow and watch where his desire will lead each. We would catch the just man red-handed going the same way as the unjust man out of a desire to get the better; this is what any nature naturally pursues as good, while it is law which by force perverts it to honor equality. The license of which I speak would best be realized if they should come into possession of the sort of power that it is said the ancestor of Gyges, the Lydian, once got. They say he was a shepherd toiling in the service of the man who was then ruling Lydia. There came to pass a great thunderstorm and an earthquake; the earth cracked and a chasm opened at the place where he was pasturing. He saw it, wondered at it, and went down. He saw, along with other quite wonderful things about which they tell tales, a hollow bronze horse. It had windows; peeping in, he saw there was a corpse inside that looked larger than human size. It had nothing on except a gold ring on its hand; he slipped it off and went out. When there was the usual gathering of the shepherds to make the monthly report to the king about the flocks, he too came, wearing the ring. Now, while he was sitting with the others, he chanced to turn the collet of the ring to himself, toward the inside of his hand; when he did this, he became invisible to those sitting by him, and they discussed him as though he were away. He wondered at this, and, fingering the ring again, he twisted the collet toward the outside; when he had twisted it, he became visible. Thinking this over, he tested whether the ring had this power, and that was exactly his result: when he turned the collet inward, he became invisible, when outward, visible. Aware of this, he immediately contrived to be one of the messengers to the king. When he arrived, he committed adultery with the king's wife and, along with her, set upon the king and killed him. And so he took over the rule.

Now if there were two such rings, and the just man would put one on, and the unjust man the other, no one, as it would seem, would be so adamant as to stick by justice and bring himself to keep away from what belongs to others and not lay hold of it, although he had license to take what he wanted from the market without fear, and to go into houses and have intercourse with whomever he wanted, and to slay or release from bonds whomever he wanted, and to do other things as an equal to a god

among humans. And in so doing, one would act no differently from the other, but both would go the same way. And yet, someone could say that this is a great proof that no one is willingly just but only when compelled to be so. Men do not take it to be a good for them in private, since wherever each supposes he can do injustice, he does it. Indeed, all men suppose injustice is far more to their private profit than justice. And what they suppose is true, as the man who makes this kind of an argument will say, since if a man were to get hold of such license and were never willing to do any injustice and didn't lay his hands on what belongs to others, he would seem most wretched to those who were aware of it, and most foolish too, although they would praise him to each others' faces, deceiving each other for fear of suffering injustice. So much for that.

THINK ABOUT IT

1. How would Plato define "justice"?
2. Why would anyone want to be invisible?

TALK ABOUT IT

3. Are there any "just" people in the world today? If yes, would they change if they had the power of invisibility?
4. Why is sexual intercourse listed among the things that people would do if they were invisible? Does this tell us anything about Greek culture? Would this be the same in other cultures?

WRITE ABOUT IT

5. Make a list of the things you would do if you obtained the power of invisibility. Consider whether you would really do them.
6. What would you do if you had the ring of Gyges? Would you keep it, sell it, or give it to a museum?

READ MORE ABOUT IT

Annas, Julia. *An Introduction to Plato's Republic.* Oxford: Oxford University Press, 1981.

lias, Julius A. *Plato's Defense of Poetry.* New York: State University of N.Y. Press, 1984.

Teloh, Henry. *Socratic Education in Plato's Early Dialogue.* Notre Dame: University of Notre Dame Press, - 1986.

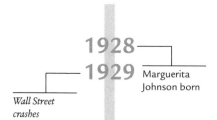

1928
1929 — Marguerita
Johnson born

Wall Street
crashes

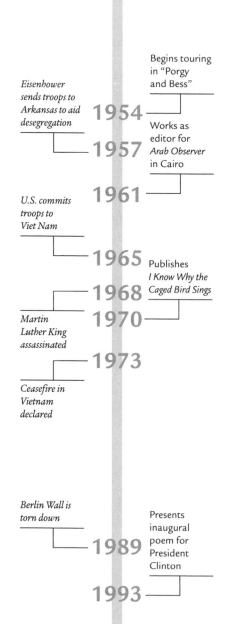

Eisenhower
sends troops to
Arkansas to aid
desegregation

Begins touring
in "Porgy
and Bess"

1954

Works as
editor for
Arab Observer
in Cairo

1957

1961

U.S. commits
troops to
Viet Nam

1965 — Publishes
*I Know Why the
Caged Bird Sings*

1968

1970

Martin
Luther King
assassinated

1973

Ceasefire in
Vietnam
declared

Berlin Wall is
torn down

Presents
inaugural
poem for
President
Clinton

1989

1993

MAYA ANGELOU

"Momma, the Dentist and Me"

Maya Angelou was born Marguerita Johnson on April 4, 1928, in St. Louis, Missouri. She attended public schools in Arkansas and California, but went on to lead a life that was far more complex than these simple beginnings would indicate. By the time she was in her twenties, Angelou had been a Creole cook, a streetcar conductor, a madam, a cocktail waitress, a dancer, and an unwed mother. In the early 1950s, she adopted the stage name Maya Angelou. Maya was a nickname her brother Bailey called her. Angelou was a variation on her married name from her first husband, Tosh Angelos. As Maya Angelou, she has become a woman of incredible diversity and ability. She appeared in several Off-Broadway productions as an actress and a singer, and later went on to write and produce her own plays. Angelou is best known, however, as a writer. She has had over twelve major works published, in addition to the many screenplays, articles, and poems she has written.

The following excerpt comes from Angelou's most successful work to date, *I Know Why the Caged Bird Sings,* which was nominated for the National Book Award in 1970. It tells of her experiences growing up, shuttling back and forth between her mother in St. Louis and her grandmother who ran a general store in Stamps, Arkansas. Stamps was a rural, highly segregated town, and this account of the trip to the dentist's office takes place there. Keep in mind, this story is set in the 1930s in Arkansas.

THE ANGEL OF the candy counter had found me out at last, and was exacting excruciating penance for all the stolen Milky Ways, Mounds, Mr. Goodbars and Hersheys with Almonds. I had two cavities that were rotten to the gums. The pain was beyond the bailiwick of crushed aspirins or oil of cloves. Only one thing could help me, so I prayed earnestly that I'd be allowed to sit under the house and have the building collapse on my left jaw. Since

there was no Negro dentist in Stamps, nor doctor either, for that matter, Momma had dealt with previous toothaches by pulling them out (a string tied to the tooth with the other end looped over her fist), pain killers and prayer. In this particular instance the medicine had proved ineffective; there wasn't enough enamel left to hook a string on, and the prayers were being ignored because the Balancing Angel was blocking their passage.

I lived a few days and nights in blinding pain, not so much toying with as seriously considering the idea of jumping in the well, and Momma decided I had to be taken to a dentist. The nearest Negro dentist was in Texarkana, twenty-five miles away, and I was certain that I'd be dead long before we reached half the distance. Momma said we'd go to Dr. Lincoln, right in Stamps, and he'd take care of me. She said he owed her a favor.

I knew that there were a number of whitefolks in town that owed her favors. Bailey and I had seen the books which showed how she had lent money to Blacks and whites alike during the Depression, and most still owed her. But I couldn't aptly remember seeing Dr. Lincoln's name, nor had I ever heard of a Negro's going to him as a patient. However, Momma said we were going, and put water on the stove for our baths. I had never been to a doctor, so she told me that after the bath (which would make my mouth feel better) I had to put on freshly starched and ironed underclothes from inside out. The ache failed to respond to the bath, and I knew then that the pain was more serious than that which anyone had ever suffered.

Before we left the Store, she ordered me to brush my teeth and then wash my mouth with Listerine. The idea of even opening my clamped jaws increased the pain, but upon her explanation that when you go to a doctor you have to clean yourself all over, but most especially the part that's to be examined, I screwed up my courage and unlocked my teeth. The cool air in my mouth and the jarring of my molars dislodged what little remained of my reason. I had frozen to the pain, my family nearly had to tie me down to take the toothbrush away. It was no small effort to get me started on the road to the dentist. Momma spoke to all the passers-by, but did-

n't stop to chat. She explained over her shoulder that we were going to the doctor and she'd "pass the time of day" on our way home.

Until we reached the pond the pain was my world, an aura that haloed me for three feet around. Crossing the bridge into whitefolks' country, pieces of sanity pushed themselves forward. I had to stop the moaning and start walking straight. The white towel, which was drawn under my chin and tied over my head, had to be arranged. If one was dying, it had to be done in style if the dying took place in whitefolks' part of town.

On the other side of the bridge the ache seemed to lessen as if a white-breeze blew off the whitefolks and cushioned everything in their neighborhood, including my law. The gravel road was smoother, the stones smaller and the tree branches hung down round the path and nearly covered us. If the pain didn't diminish then, the familiar yet strange sights hypnotized me into believing that it had.

But my head continued to throb with the measured insistence of a bass drum, and how could a toothache pass the calaboose, hear the songs of the prisoners, their blues and laughter, and not be changed? How could one or two or even a mouthful of angry tooth roots meet a wagonload of powhitetrash children, endure their idiotic snobbery and not feel less important?

Behind the building which housed the dentist's office ran a small path used by servants and those tradespeople who catered to the butcher and Stamps' one restaurant. Momma and I followed that lane to the backstairs of Dentist Lincoln's office. The sun was bright and gave the day a hard reality as we climbed up the steps to the second floor.

Momma knocked on the back door and a young white girl opened

it to show surprise at seeing us there. Momma said she wanted to see Dentist Lincoln and to tell him Annie was there. The girl closed the door firmly. Now the humiliation of hearing Momma describe herself as if she had no last name to the young white girl was equal to the physical pain. It seemed terribly unfair to have a toothache and a headache and have to bear at the same time the heavy burden of Blackness.

It was always possible that the teeth would quiet down and maybe drop out of their own accord. Momma said we would wait. We leaned in the harsh sunlight on the shaky railings of the dentist's back porch for over an hour.

He opened the door and looked at Momma. "Well, Annie, what can I do for you?"

He didn't see the towel around my jaw or notice my swollen face.

Momma said, "Dentist Lincoln. It's my grandbaby here. She got two rotten teeth that's giving her a fit."

She waited for him to acknowledge the truth of her statement. He made no comment, orally or facially.

"She had this toothache purt' near four days now, and today I said, 'Young lady, you going to the Dentist.'"

"Annie?"

"Yes, sit, Dentist Lincoln."

He was choosing words the way people hunt for shells. "Annie, you know I don't treat nigra, colored people."

"I know, Dentist Lincoln. But this here is just my little grandbaby, and she ain't gone be no trouble to you … "

"Annie, everybody has a policy. In this world you have to have a policy. Now, my policy is I don't treat colored people."

The sun had baked the oil out of Momma's skin and melted the Vaseline in her hair. She shone greasily as she leaned out of the dentist's shadow.

"Seem like to me, Dentist Lincoln, you might look after her, she ain't nothing but a little mite. And seems like maybe you owe me a favor or two."

He reddened slightly. "Favor or no favor. The money has all been repaid to you and that's the end of it. Sorry, Annie." He had his hand on the doorknob. "Sorry." His voice was a bit kinder on the second "Sorry," as if he really was.

Momma said, "I wouldn't press on you like this for myself but I can't take No. Not for my grandbaby. When you come to borrow my money you didn't have to beg. You asked me, and I lent it. Now, it wasn't my policy. I ain't no moneylender, but you stood to lose this building and I tried to help you out."

"It's been paid, and raising your voice won't make me change my mind. My policy …" He let go of the door and stepped nearer Momma. The three of us were crowded on the small landing. "Annie, my policy is I'd rather stick my hand in a dog's mouth than in a nigger's."

He had never once looked at me. He turned his back and went through the door into the cool beyond. Momma backed up inside herself for a few minutes. I forgot everything except her face which was almost a new one to me. She leaned over and took the doorknob, and in her everyday soft voice she said, "Sister, go on downstairs. Wait for me. I'll be there directly."

Under the most common of circumstances I knew it did no good to argue with Momma. So I walked down the steep stairs, afraid to look back and afraid not to do so. I turned as the door slammed and she was gone.

Momma walked in that room as if she owned it. She shoved that silly nurse aside with one hand and strode into the dentist's office. He was sitting in his chair, sharpening his mean instruments and putting extra sting into his medicines. Her eyes were blazing like live coals and her arms had doubled themselves in length. He looked up at her just before she caught him by the collar of his white jacket.

"Stand up when you see a lady, you contemptuous scoundrel." Her tongue had thinned and the words rolled off well enunciated. Enunciated and sharp like little claps of thunder.

The dentist had no choice but to stand at R.O.T.C.. attention. His head dropped after a minute and his voice was humble. "Yes, ma'am, Mrs. Henderson.

"You knave, do you think you acted like a gentleman, speaking to me like that in front of my granddaughter?" She didn't shake him, although she had the power. She simply held him upright.

"No, ma'am, Mrs. Henderson."

"No, ma'am, Mrs. Henderson, what?" Then she did give him the tiniest of shakes, but because of her strength the action set his head and arms to shaking loose on the ends of his body. He stuttered much worse than Uncle Willie. "No, ma'am, Mrs. Henderson, I'm sorry."

With just an edge of her disgust showing, Momma slung him back in his dentist's chair. "Sorry is as sorry does, and you're about the sorriest dentist I ever laid my eyes on." (She could afford to slip into the vernacular because she had such eloquent command of English.)

"I didn't ask you to apologize in front of Marguerite, because I don't want her to know my power, but I order you, now and herewith. Leave Stamps by sundown."

"Mrs. Henderson, I can't get my equipment …" He was shaking terribly now.

"Now, that brings me to my second order. You will never again practice dentistry. Never! When you get settled in your next place, you will be a vegetarian caring for dogs with mange, cats with cholera, and cows with epizootic. Is that clear?"

The saliva ran down his chin and his eyes filled with tears. "Yes, ma'am. Thank you for not killing me. Thank you, Mrs. Henderson."

Momma pulled herself back from being ten feet tall with eight-foot arms and said, "You're welcome for nothing, you varlet, I wouldn't waste a killing on the likes of you."

On her way out she waved her handkerchief at the nurse and turned her into a crocus sack of chicken feed.

Momma looked tired when she came down the stairs, but who wouldn't be tired if they had gone through what she had. She came close to me and adjusted the towel under my jaw (I had forgotten the toothache; I only knew that she made her hands gentle in order not to awaken the pain). She took my hand. Her voice never changed. "Come on, Sister."

I reckoned we were going home where she would concoct a brew to eliminate the pain and maybe give me new teeth too. New teeth that would grow overnight out of my gums. She led me toward the drugstore, which was in the opposite direction from the Store. "I'm taking you to Dentist Baker in Texarkana."

I was glad after all that I had bathed and put on Mum and Cashmere Bouquet talcum powder. It was a wonderful surprise. My toothache had quieted to solemn pain, Momma had obliterated the evil white man, and we were going on a trip to Texarkana, just the two of us.

On the Greyhound she took an inside seat in the back, and I sat beside her. I was so proud of being her granddaughter and sure that some of her magic must have come down to me. She asked if I was scared. I only shook my head and leaned over on her cool brown upper arm. There was no chance that a dentist, especially a Negro dentist, would dare hurt me there. Not with Momma there. The trip was uneventful, except that she put her arm around me, which was very unusual for Momma to do.

The dentist showed me the medicine and the needle before he deadened my gums, but if he hadn't I wouldn't have worried. Momma stood right behind him. Her arms were folded and she checked on everything he did. The teeth were extracted and she bought me an ice cream cone from the side window of a drug counter. The trip back to Stamps was quiet, except that I had to spit into a very small empty snuff can which she had gotten for me and it was difficult with the bus humping and jerking on our country roads.

At home, I was given a warm salt solution, and when I washed out my mouth I showed Bailey the empty holes, where the clotted blood sat like filling in a pie crust. He said I was quite brave, and that was my cue to reveal our confrontation with the peckerwood dentist and Momma's incredible powers.

I had to admit that I didn't hear the conversation, but what else could she have said than what I said she said? What else done? He agreed with my analysis in a lukewarm way, and I happily (after all, I'd been sick) flounced into the Store. Momma was preparing our evening meal and Uncle Willie leaned on the door sill. She gave her version.

"Dentist Lincoln got right uppity. Said he'd rather put his hand in a dog's mouth. And when I reminded him of the favor, he brushed it off like a piece of lint. Well, I sent Sister downstairs and went inside. I hadn't never been in his office before, but I found the door to where he takes out teeth, and him and the nurse was in there thick as thieves. I just stood there till he caught sight of me." Crash bang the pots on the stove. "He jumped just like he was sitting on a pin. He said, 'Annie, I done tole you, I ain't gonna mess around in no niggah's mouth.' I said, 'Somebody's got to do it then,' and he said, 'Take her to Texarkana to the colored dentist' and that's when I said, 'If you paid me my money I could afford to take her.' He said, 'It's all been paid.' I tole him everything but the interest had been paid. He said, ''Twasn't no interest.' I said, ''Tis now. I'll take ten dollars as payment in full.' You know, Willie, it wasn't no right thing to do, 'cause I lent that money without thinking about it.

"He tole that little snippity nurse of his'n to give me ten dollars and make me sign a 'paid in full' receipt. She gave it to me and I signed the papers. Even though by rights he was paid up before, I figger, he gonna be that kind of nasty, he gonna have to pay for it."

Momma and her son laughed and laughed over the white man's evilness and her retributive sin.

I preferred, much preferred, my version.

THINK ABOUT IT

1. As the story recounts it, what were the circumstances of Angelou's life as a young girl?
2. Why are there two explanations of the same event in the dentist's office? How are they different?

TALK ABOUT IT

3. Are there people today who find themselves in circumstances similar to Angelou's? Explain.
4. Why is racial intolerance so difficult to overcome? What countries do you think have the best and worst records at overcoming this intolerance?

WRITE ABOUT IT

5. Write about an instance of discrimination from the point of view of the victim. Describe the event in specific terms. Then write about the instance from the opposing viewpoint.
6. Have you ever found yourself in a humiliating situation because of bigotry, ignorance, or hatred? How did you respond? What would you have done differently?

READ MORE ABOUT IT

Angelou, Maya. *All God's Children Need Traveling Shoes*. New York: Random House, 1986.

Angelou, Maya. *I Know Why the Caged Bird Sings*. New York: Random House, 1970.

Angelou, Maya. *Poems: Maya Angelou*. New York: Bantam, 1986.

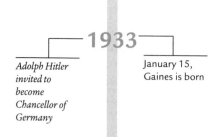

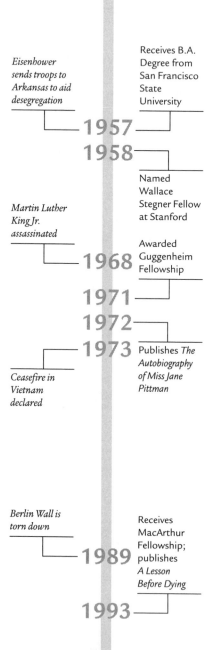

1933

January 15, Gaines is born

Adolph Hitler invited to become Chancellor of Germany

Eisenhower sends troops to Arkansas to aid desegregation

Receives B.A. Degree from San Francisco State University

1957
1958

Named Wallace Stegner Fellow at Stanford

Martin Luther King Jr. assassinated

Awarded Guggenheim Fellowship

1968
1971
1972
1973

Publishes *The Autobiography of Miss Jane Pittman*

Ceasefire in Vietnam declared

Berlin Wall is torn down

Receives MacArthur Fellowship; publishes *A Lesson Before Dying*

1989

1993

ERNEST J. GAINES

A Lesson before Dying

Ernest J. Gaines is a prize-winning African-American writer whose 1971 novel, *The Autobiography of Miss Jane Pittman,* became an Emmy-winning television movie. Born in Oscar, Louisiana, in 1933, he moved to San Francisco when he was fifteen. Even though he spent most of his teenage years in California, his years in rural Louisiana influence most of his fiction. Rural Louisiana has given Gaines the characters which populate his stories, as well as an intimate knowledge of life in a segregated society. Gaines' characters fight prejudice, discrimination, and a double standard of justice, yet develop strength and dignity. Gaines credits nineteenth-century Russian novelists with helping him develop his fiction. Gaines has said of Gogol, Turgenev, and Chekhov:

> I did not particularly find what I was looking for in the Southern writers. When they came to describing my own people, they did not do it the way that I knew my people to be. The Russians were not talking about my people, but about a peasantry for which they seemed to show such feeling. Reading them, I could find a way to write about my own people.

A Lesson Before Dying, winner of the National Book Critics Award for Fiction, is set in fictional Bayonne, Louisiana, which critics have compared to William Faulkner's Yoknapatawpha County. The Bayonne community is described by Gaines as a town of 6,000: 3,500 whites and 2,500 blacks. In 1948, the year of the story, Bayonne is the scene of a crime. A local storekeeper, Mr. Grope, is robbed by two black men, Brother and Bear. During the robbery, Mr. Grope, is fatally shot. Returning fire, he kills Brother and Bear. Jefferson, one of the two main characters in the novel, has innocently accepted a ride to the store with Brother and Bear. He then becomes an unwitting accomplice to the crime. Although he does not know of the plans for the robbery and does not participate in the murder, Jefferson does take money from the open cash register as he runs from the scene. He is caught and tried for murder.

Even though he is a grown man, Jefferson thinks and acts as a child throughout much of the novel. The story opens at Jefferson's trial where his attorney, appealing for mercy to an all-white jury, says, "I would just as soon put a hog in the electric chair as this," as he points to Jefferson. The plea falls on deaf ears, however, and Jefferson is sentenced to death by electrocution. As he awaits execution, Jefferson is visited by Grant Wiggins, the teacher in Bayonne's all-black school and the other main character in the novel. Wiggins has been sent by Jefferson's godmother, his "nannan," to "make him a man before he dies." Not knowing how to do this, Wiggins tries a number of things, but never feels comfortable with Jefferson or with his task. In the following chapter about their last meeting before his execution, Jefferson and Wiggins learn "a lesson before dying."

I WENT INTO THE CELL with a paper bag full of baked sweet potatoes. The deputy locked the heavy door behind me.

"How's it going, partner?" Jefferson nodded.

"How do you feel?" "I'm all right."

"I brought you a little something."

Jefferson was sitting on the bunk, with his hands clasped together. I put the bag beside him on the bunk and sat down. I could hear the radio, on the floor against the wall, playing a sad cowboy song. I saw the notebook and the pencil on the floor, next to the radio. This was my first visit since I'd given him the notebook and pencil, and I could see that the lead on the pencil was worn down to the wood. I could also see that he had used the eraser a lot. We were quiet awhile.

"Hungry?" I asked.

"Maybe later."

"I see you've been writing." He didn't answer.

"Personal, or can I look at it?"

"It ain't nothing."

"Do you mind?" I asked. "If you want."

I got the notebook and came back to the bunk. The fellow on the radio was saying what a beautiful day it was in Baton Rouge.

Jefferson had filled three-quarters of the first page. The letters were large and awkward, the way someone would write who could barely see. He had written across the lines instead of above them. He had used the eraser so much that in some places the paper was worn through. Nothing was capitalized, and there were no punctuation marks. The let-

ters were thin at the beginning, but became broader as the lead was worn down. *As closely as I could figure, he had written: I dreamt it again last night. They was taking me somewhere. I wasn't crying. I wasn't begging. I was just going, going with them. Then I woke up. I couldn't go back to sleep. I didn't want go back to sleep. I didn't want dream no more.* There was a lot of erasing, then he wrote: *If I ain't nothing but a hog, how come they just don't knock me in the head like a hog? Starb me like a hog? More erasing, then: Man walk on two foots; hogs on four hoofs.*

The last couple of words were barely visible, because the lead had been worn down all the way to the wood. I read it over a second time before closing the notebook. I didn't know what to say to him. He was staring at the wall, his hands clasped together.

"Do you want me to bring you a pencil sharpener?" I asked after a while. "The little ones you hold in your hand?"

"If you can find one."

"I'm sure I can," I said. "You know, Paul would have sharpened this pencil for you. He wouldn't mind."

Jefferson had unclasped his hands, and now he was scraping the ends of his left fingernails with the index finger of the right hand. His fingernails were hard and purplish.

"When's Easter?" he asked.

"Tomorrow is Good Friday."

"That's when He rose?"

"No. He rose on Easter."

"That's when He died," Jefferson said to himself. "Never said a mumbling word. That's right. Not a word."

"Did you talk to Reverend Ambrose when he came to visit you?" I asked Jefferson.

"Some. "

"You ought to talk to him. It's good for your nannan. She wants you to talk to him."

"He told me to pray."

"Do you?"

"No."

"It would be good for your nannan."

He looked at me. His eyes were large and sad and reddened.

"You think I'm going to heaven?" he asked.

"I don't know."

"You think Mr. Gropé went to heaven? You think Brother and Bear went to heaven?"

"I don't know."

"Then what I'm go'n pray for?"

"For your nannan. "

"Nannan don't need me to help her get to heaven. She'll make it if it's up there."

"She wants you there with her, where there's no pain and no sorrow."

He grinned at me, a brief cynical grin.

"You pray, Mr. Wiggins?"

"No, Jefferson, I don't."

He grunted.

"But then I'm lost, Jefferson," I said, looking at him closely. "At this moment I don't believe in anything. Like your nannan does, like Reverend Ambrose does, and like I want you to believe. I want you to believe so that one day maybe I will."

"In heaven, Mr. Wiggins?"

"If it helps others down here on earth, Jefferson."

"Reverend Ambrose say I have to give up what's down here. Say there ain't nothing down here on this earth for me no more."

"He meant possessions, Jefferson. Cars, money, clothes — things like that."

"You ever seen me with a car, Mr. Wiggins?"

"No."

"With more than a dollar in my pocket?"

"No."

"More than two pair shoes, Mr. Wiggins? One for Sunday, one for working in?"

"No, Jefferson."

"Then what on earth I got to give up, Mr. Wiggins?"

"You've never had any possessions to give up, Jefferson. But there is something greater than possessions — and that is love. I know you love her and would do anything for her. Didn't you eat the gumbo when you weren't hungry, just to please her? That's all we're asking for now, Jefferson — do something to please her."

"What about me, Mr. Wiggins? What people done to please me?"

"Hasn't she done many things to please you, Jefferson? Cooked for you, washed for you, taken care of you when you were sick? She is sick now, Jefferson, and she is asking for only one thing in this world. Walk like a man. Meet her up there."

"Y'all asking a lot, Mr. Wiggins, from a poor old nigger who never had nothing."

"She would do it for you."

"She go to that chair for me, Mr. Wiggins? You? Anybody?" He waited for me to answer him. I wouldn't.

"No, Mr. Wiggins, I got to go myself. Just me, Mr. Wiggins. Reverend Ambrose say God'd be there if I axe Him. You think He be there if I axe Him, Mr. Wiggins?"

"That's what they say, Jefferson."

"You believe in God, Mr. Wiggins?"

"Yes, Jefferson, I believe in God."

"How?"

"I think it's God that makes people care for people, Jefferson. I think it's God makes children play and people sing. I believe it's God that brings loved ones together. I believe it's God that makes trees bud and food grow out of the earth."

"Who make people kill people, Mr. Wiggins?"

"They killed His Son, Jefferson."

"And He never said a mumbling word."

"That's what they say."

"That's how I want to go, Mr. Wiggins. Not a mumbling word."

Another cowboy song was playing on the radio, but it was quiet and not disturbing. I could hear inmates down the cellblock calling to one another. Jefferson sat forward on the bunk, his big hands clasped together again. I still had the notebook. I started to open it, but changed my mind.

"You need anything, Jefferson?"

"No, I don't need nothing, Mr. Wiggins. Reverend Ambrose say I don't need nothing down here no more."

"I'll get you that sharpener," I said.

"I ain't got nothing more to say, Mr. Wiggins."

"I'm sure you have."

"I hope the time just hurry up and get here. Cut out all this waiting."

"I wish I knew what to do, Jefferson."

"I'm the one got to do everything, Mr. Wiggins. I'm the one."

He got up from the bunk and went to the window and looked up at the buds on the higher branches of the sycamore tree. Through the branches of the tree I could see the sky, blue and lovely and clear. "You Are My Sunshine" was playing on the radio. Jefferson turned his back to the window and looked at me. "Me, Mr. Wiggins. Me. Me to take the cross. Your cross, nannan's cross, my own cross. Me, Mr. Wiggins. This old stumbling nigger. Y'all axe a lot, Mr. Wiggins." He went to the cell door and grasped it with both hands. He started to jerk on the door, but changed his mind and turned back to look at me. "Who ever car'd my cross, Mr. Wiggins? My mama? My daddy? They dropped me when I wasn't nothing. Still don't know where they at this minute. I went in the field when I was six, driving that old water cart. I done pulled that cotton sack, I done cut cane, load cane, swung that ax, chop ditch banks, since I was six." He was standing over me now. "Yes, I'm youman, Mr. Wiggins. But nobody didn't know that 'fore now. Cuss for nothing. Beat for nothing. Work for nothing. Grinned to get by. Everybody thought that's how it was s'pose to be. You too, Mr. Wiggins. You never thought I was nothing else. I didn't neither. Thought I was doing what the Lord had put me on this earth to do." He went to the window and turned to look at me. "Now all y'all want me to be better than ever'body else. How, Mr. Wiggins? You tell me."

"I don't know, Jefferson."

"What I got left, Mr. Wiggins — two weeks?"

"I think it's something like that — if nothing happens."

"Nothing go'n happen, Mr. Wiggins. And it ain't 'something like that.' That's all I got on this here earth. I got to face that, Mr. Wiggins. It's all right for y'all to say 'something like that.' For me, it's 'that' — 'that,' that's all. And like Reverend Ambrose say, then I'll have to give up this old earth. But ain't that where I'm going, Mr. Wiggins, back in the earth?"

My head down, I didn't answer him.

"You can look at me, Mr. Wiggins; I don't mind."

I raised my head, and I saw him standing there under the window, big and tall, and not stooped as he had been in chains.

"I'm go'n do my best, Mr. Wiggins. That's all I can promise. My best."

"You're more a man than I am, Jefferson."

"'Cause I'm go'n die soon? That make me a man, Mr. Wiggins?"

"My eyes were closed before this moment, Jefferson. My eyes have been closed all my life. Yes, we all need you. Every last one of us."

He studied me awhile, then he turned his back and looked up at the window.

"So pretty out there," he said. "So pretty. I ain't never seen it so pretty." I looked at him standing there big and tall, his broad back toward me. "What it go'n be like, Mr. Wiggins?"

I thought I knew what he was talking about, but I didn't answer him. He turned around to face me.

"What it go'n feel like, Mr. Wiggins?"

I shook my head. I felt my eyes burning.

"I hope it ain't long."

"It's not long, Jefferson," I said.

"How you know, Mr. Wiggins?"

"I read it."

I was not looking at him. I was looking at the wall. It had been in the newspaper. The first jolt, if everything is right, immediately knocked a person unconscious.

He came back and sat down on the bunk.

"I'm all right, Mr. Wiggins."

I nodded without looking at him.

"Care for a 'tato, Mr. Wiggins?" he said, opening the paper bag. "Sure," I said.

THINK ABOUT IT

1. Describe specifically why Jefferson thinks he won't be able to face his execution.
2. Why does Jefferson keep referring to Jesus?

TALK ABOUT IT

3. What makes Wiggins conclude that Jefferson is a man?
4. Why does segregation breed injustice? What examples can you cite, from the United States as well as from other countries, that prove your point?

WRITE ABOUT IT

5. Write a dialogue between Wiggins and Jefferson's nannan. What would Wiggins tell her about his last meeting with Jefferson?
6. List and describe the qualities that make one a "man" or a "woman."

READ MORE ABOUT IT

Gaines, Ernest J. *The Autobiography of Miss Jane Pittman.* New York: Dial, 1971.

Gaines, Ernest J. *A Gathering of Old Men.* New York: Alfred A. Knopf, Inc. 1983.

Gaines, Ernest J. *In My Father's House.* New York: Alfred A. Knopf, Inc. 1983.

Gaines, Ernest J. *A Lesson Before Dying.* New York: Vintage Books, A Division of Random House, Inc.,1993.

1746 — Francisco de Goya is born in Spain

Napoleon's forces invade Spain

1802 — Goya paints *Tres de Mayo*

1814 —

1828 —

Andrew Jackson is elected President of the U.S.

Goya dies

War in South Africa won by Boers

Pablo Picasso is born in Spain

1881 —

Salvador Dali is born in Spain

1904 —

Franco assumes control of Spain

Dali paints *Soft Construction*

1936 —

1937 —

1939 —

Picasso paints *Guernica*

Ceasefire for Vietnam War signed

1973 —

Picasso dies

Berlin Wall comes down

1989 —

Dali dies

ROBERTA VANDERMAST

The Horrors of War:

Goya, Picasso, and Dali

Roberta Vandermast is coordinator and professor of Interdisciplinary Studies at Valencia Community College where she has been teaching interdisciplinary courses for twenty-six years. She has co-authored three humanities textbooks as well as a manual for the Interdisciplinary Studies Program at Valencia. After traveling to Spain, she became interested in Spanish painting and reflects that interest in the following article about the Spanish painters, Goya, Picasso, and Dali.

Goya, Picasso, and Dali have created visual images of the devastation and violence associated with war and the toll these take. Each of these artists depicts the brutality of war in a different way. Goya's style is naturalistic and resembles a photographic image; however, it conveys far more emotions than most photographs can. Picasso's style is Cubist and abstract. Cubist images depart from realism to portray people and objects as geometric shapes, often fragmented and superimposed. Cubism is a twentieth-century art style which was invented by Picasso and his friend, Georges Braque. Dali's style is Surrealist. Surrealism, another twentieth-century art style, uses the dream images of the painter as the source of its visual material, giving us paintings which are mysterious and provocative. These painters show us that violence, which is so much a part of modern life, is no stranger to art. In fact, they show us that art is uniquely equipped to display the immorality, as well as the horrors, of war.

WARFARE REMAINS the supreme act of inhumanity and immorality, for no matter how noble the cause, atrocities always follow in its wake. Today the horrors of modern warfare come directly into our living rooms on videotape shot live at the scene or in still shots as photographs of the latest carnage. In earlier times, battles and their aftermath were etched either in the minds of the survivors or captured on canvas by artists commissioned to paint the scenes. For most of the history of art, battles were recorded as noble endeavors, either because the artists sympathized with the victors or because the artists were commissioned by the winning side. However, in Spain in the early nineteenth and twentieth centuries, the art of the battlefield took a decidedly different turn.

Francisco de Goya (1746–1828) worked most of his adult life to gain a position at the court of the reigning Spanish monarch, Carlos IV, and had moved skillfully to rise to prominence as a portrait painter of the wealthy and powerful. His portraits are skillful and give insight into the characters of his subjects, but offer little new insight into either human nature or the art of painting. On May 2, 1808, however, Goya's art changed direction when Napoleon's forces seized control of Spain.

Assisted by the Prime Minister of Spain, Napoleon had convinced Carlos IV to abdicate in favor of his son, Fernando. He then convinced both the old and new king that it was in their best interests to station French troops in Spain to avoid a civil war. In addition, Napoleon convinced the Spanish royal family to come to France so that he could help them solve their family differences. Once in France, he appointed his brother-in-law, Joachim Murat, as commander of the French forces. Murat used French troops to enforce French authority over Spain. Rumors flew in Madrid, the capital of Spain, and on May 2, a fateful event took place.

The thirteen-year-old Spanish prince, Francisco de Paula, had been left in the Royal Palace with the family staff when the family left for France. With the rest of the royal family now in exile, Napoleon ordered that Prince Francisco be sent to join them. Rumors in Madrid portrayed the tearful prince refusing to leave Spain. A crowd formed at the palace in support of the young prince. At one point, French soldiers opened fire with muskets and a riot ensued.

Additional French troops were brought into the city to quell the riot and put down a possible revolt. Throughout the night and into the early morning hours, French firing squads summarily executed any *madrileños,* citizens of Madrid, found on the streets. The innocent as well as the guilty died during the night of May second and into the morning of May third. This incident, the massacre of innocent *madrileños,* became the rallying point for the Spanish people and the subject of one of Goya's masterpieces, *Tres de Mayo, 1808, en Madrid (The Third of May, 1808, in Madrid).*

Tres de Mayo is a large painting, measuring nine feet by twelve feet, which dramatizes the executions carried out by the French firing squads in a vivid and unforgettable way. At the top of the painting, the dark night sky contrasts with the ghostly outline of the skyline of Madrid. On the left side of the painting, silhouetted against a base of the mountain, is the line of *madrileños* awaiting their execution. At the center of the composition, illuminated by a lantern placed in front of them, the French firing squad has raised its rifles and taken aim. The innocent *madrileños,* react in fear, acceptance, and supplication. Priests, as well as peasants, face inevitable death. Below them, the ground is stained with blood and littered with corpses, marked by the bullet holes visible in their clothing and on their bodies. The central figure, whose white shirt is illuminated by the lantern, spreads his arms in a Christ-like pose, and looks straight into the faces of his executioners whose faces remain hidden. Visible on his face is a mixture of fear and courage. Thus, Goya personalizes the slaughter of the innocent, while having their executioners' faces known only to the victims. The soldiers, representing evil, are in the shadows, whereas the *madrileños,* representing

good, are fully illuminated. Goya uses these extreme contrasts of light and dark to convey the emotional importance of the event and to underline the immorality of the actions of the French soldiers.

Tres de Mayo is not only an emotional tour de force; it is also an artistic one. In this painting, Goya abandons the carefully detailed portrait painting and brighter palette which had been his artistic mainstays. Instead, he chooses a new compositional plan, a new painterly style, and a new, darker palette. The distribution of figures in *Tres de Mayo* represents an innovation for Goya. In his portraits, Goya had centered the subject in the middle of the canvas, keeping background detail to a minimum so that the subject would be the center of attention. Yet, in *Tres de Mayo,* he moves the two main groups of figures to either side of the center of the composition, allowing the line of rifles to be the central image on the canvas. In doing this, Goya suggests that the only thing that connects the two factions are the instruments of death. In addition, he arranges the groups of figures in two parallel lines: one of the Spaniards awaiting execution and the other of the French firing squad. This suggests the eternal separation of these two groups, divided by the gulf of injustice. To give the scene a spontaneous feeling, Goya applies the color in a painterly fashion; that is the brushwork is loose and the brush strokes are very visible. Surface details are formed by broad areas of color, rather than by exact drawing. In this way, Goya gives the impression that he was forced to make a quick sketch of the slaughter, even though this painting was composed in his studio and completed in 1814, six years after the incident. Although the center of the painting is illuminated by the lantern whose light is reflected in the peasant's white

ENTERRAR Y CALLAR, AFTER 1808
Francisco de Goya
Etching, approximately 9⅜ × 8¼ in.
Metropolitan Museum of Art, New York, NY

shirt, the general color scheme of the painting is somber. The darkness of the night, made even darker by its contrast with the ghostly skyline of Madrid, envelops the scene. The firing squad, cast in strong shadows, is engulfed by this darkness, as if overwhelmed by the evil which the darkness symbolizes. From 1814 until the end of his life, Goya continually used this darker palette as if convinced that darkness, and perhaps evil, was more powerful than light. *Tres de Mayo* represents not only a dramatic change in Goya's artistic style, it heralds in a new realism in painting and demonstrates the power of the artist to pro-

vide powerful visual images of the effects of human destructiveness.

While *Tres de Mayo* may indicate that the French were victorious, quite the reverse is true. The incidents of May second and third galvanized the Spanish people and, although lacking the fire power of the French, they fought on through sabotage and quick, unexpected strikes. Rail lines were dynamited, cafes bombed, and French officials assassinated. All of these activities were conducted by soldiers the Spanish called *guerrillas*, giving us a new form of warfare: guerilla warfare. To stop the spread of Napoleon's army and to curb his am-

bition, the British and Portuguese invaded Spain to fight the French and, aided by the guerrillas, they were successful. Led by the Duke of Wellington, these forces drove Napoleon from Spain and reestablished the Spanish monarchy. Eventually, Wellington defeated Napoleon's army at Waterloo, ending the reign of France's most ambitious dictator.

While Goya sympathized with the Spanish, he also knew that atrocities were committed by both sides. Traveling through the war zone, he probably witnessed some of these firsthand and it is certain that his

GRANDE HAZAÑA! CON MUERTOS!, AFTER 1808
Francisco de Goya
Etching, approximately 9⅜ × 8¼ in.
Metropolitan Museum of Art, New York, NY

friends from all over Spain brought him tales of rape, murder and mutilation. To record these brutalities, Goya produced a series of etchings, *Desastres de la guerra (The Horrors of War),* which depicted acts of butchery committed by both sides. In *Enterrar y callar (Bury them and be silent)* and in *Grande hazaña! Con muertos! (Wonderful heroism! Against dead men!)* Goya portrayed these atrocities. To underline their significance, Goya added inscriptions to the bottom of each etching. In the first etching,

Enterrar y callar, a man and woman weep over a field of corpses; each has been stripped of its clothing and possessions and left to rot. A lone shoe litters the foreground as a testament to brutality and greed. In *Grande hazaña!* a broken tree is hung with corpses and body parts. The inscription decries the belief that war is a noble, heroic act. These powerful images still echo the words of a traditional story told about them. While he was working on them, one of Goya's servants asked him, "Why do you paint

these barbarities that men commit?" Goya replied, "To tell men forever that they should not be barbarians."

One hundred years later, the horrors of war were repeated in Spain in a bloody civil war. This war was chronicled in two ways. Pablo Picasso (1881–1973) recorded an incident from this war in his Cubist painting, Guernica, and Salvador Dali (1904–1989) painted his premonition of the war in his Surrealist painting, Soft Construction With Boiled Beans. Both paintings were produced as battles were fought to determine what kind of Spanish government would prevail.

The Spanish Civil War (1936–1939) propelled Generalissimo Francisco Franco into power in Spain. He founded the Falange Party, a Spanish party which allied itself with the Italian Fascist and German Nazi parties. Backed by the Spanish military, Franco installed himself as dictator of Spain, but he was met with stiff opposition, especially in the Pyrenees Mountains in the Basque region of Northern Spain. For centuries, the Basques have sought recognition as an independent country and,

sandwiched between France and Spain, have fought both the French and the Spanish. Annoyed with their resistance and expertise at guerilla warfare, Franco called on the German air force for assistance.

Beginning at 4:40 P.M. on April 26, 1937 German pilots repeatedly bombed the Basque town of Guernica. It was market day and the town was crowded with people. Guernica was chosen for its symbolic significance. The Basques considered Guernica their unofficial capital and Franco felt that bombing this town would deal a serious blow to Basque morale. The German air force had

been practicing in Spain where it could go virtually unnoticed until the Nazis were ready for their conquest of Europe. Franco allowed them to use the town for target practice in order for the Germans to measure the effectiveness of their bombing techniques, as well as to eliminate the Basque stronghold. Thus thousands of innocent men, women and children were slaughtered in bombing raids on Guernica and, two days later, the town fell with no resistance.

Before the bombing, Picasso had issued a series of etchings in which he lampooned the Spanish dictator and, as a result, Picasso was commis-

sioned by the Spanish Republic, which opposed Franco, to paint a large mural for their pavilion at the 1937 Paris World's Fair. For two months, Picasso worked on ideas for the mural with no success, producing little more than portraits of his current mistress, Dora Maar. Reports of the bombing, however, gave him a new focus. For ten days after hearing and reading about the bombing in Paris newspapers, he sketched ideas for the mural, frantically recording images that would later emerge in the painting. On the eleventh day, he stretched a large canvas, eleven feet high by twenty-five feet long, and be-

gan to paint. The canvas was so large that it could not stand upright in his Paris studio and he was forced to leave it on a slant, leaning up against one wall. From ladders placed in front of the canvas, Picasso painted images that immortalized the senseless Basque slaughter which Picasso said has sunk Spain in an ocean of pain and death."

Picasso painted *Guernica* in black, white, and gray; he later said he used the color of the newsprint on which he had read accounts of the bombing. He chose to paint *Guernica* in the Cubist style which he had helped create in 1907. Cubism does not try to

represent objects or people as the camera sees them, rather it renders subjects geometrically, juxtaposing portions of different images so that the subject seems fragmented. In *Guernica,* Picasso makes skillful use of this technique. Portions of human figures, animals, and architectural elements are combined in a scene that conveys fragmentation, chaos and death. Beginning on the right side of the painting, a figure is trapped in a building and screams toward the ceiling. Light gray triangles protruding from around the window above the figure's head suggest the flames of the fires started by the exploding bombs. Slightly to the left and emerging from a window is the torso of a woman carrying a lamp. The light from her lamp, combined with the harsh light from the electric bulb, illuminates a jumbled mass of people, animals, and objects. The body of the screaming horse, ripped through by shrapnel, is covered in small lines, simulating the lines of print in the newspapers which reported the bombing. Below the horse, a young woman rushes in; however, it is too late for her to do anything but survey the destruction. A severed arm with

GUERNICA, 1937
Pablo Picasso
Oil on Canvas,
11 ft 5½ in. × 25 ft 5¾ in.
Prado, Madrid, Spain.

a broken sword litters the foreground, suggesting that it was once connected to the dead man whose face is seen simultaneously from the front and in profile. At the far left, a column of smoke rises from a hill while a bull stares directly out of the painting. Finally, a woman screams a silent scream as she holds the body of her dead child, forming a modern pieta- a universal symbol of human suffering. Death, destruction, and human misery reign in Guernica, a painting Picasso said represented the forces of "brutality and darkness" and which still stands as a memorial to the immorality of war.

Before Picasso painted Guernica in 1937, Salvador Dali recorded his premonition of the coming Spanish civil war in his painting, *Soft Construction With Boiled Beans: Premonition of the Spanish Civil War (Construcción suave con frijoles hervidos: Presentimiento de la guerra civil)*.[1] Unlike Guernica, whose impact comes from both its imagery and its size, Dali's *Soft Construction* is quite small, 39⅜ inches by 39 inches. This small, intimate size is typical of Dali's Surrealist works. Surrealism was a movement in painting, sculpture, poetry, and film which sought to tap into the subconscious and emotional world of the dream and to by-pass the conscious and rational parts of the mind. Influenced by the work of Sigmund Freud, Surrealists thought that the subconscious mind afforded a view into the unconscious workings of the human psyche that offered a heightened or "super" reality, a surreality, when compared with the traditional focus on conscious reality only. They felt that this dimension of human existence should be explored as fully as the rational dimension had been and sought to probe it in every conceivable way. Dali pursued Surrealism because it gave him the opportunity to explore his personal psyche, and so he created canvases which portray a fantastic landscape of fears, obsessions, and dreams, providing images which must be interpreted subjectively.

Dali's surrealist imagery features enigmatic figures in desolate, isolated landscapes drawn from his childhood in Spain. These landscapes are littered with mysterious symbols pulled from his dreams. In order to record his dreams, Dali often slept holding a spoon in one hand, with that hand stretched over the edge of his bed. When his hand relaxed and the spoon dropped, he would be awakened by the sound and would set to work recording the images from his most recent dream or nightmare. In an article he wrote, *Dali Proclaims Surrealism a Paranoiac Art*, he states:

I am the first to be surprised and often terrified by the extravagant images that I see appear with fatality on my canvas. In truth I am but the automaton which registers, without judgement and with all possible exactitude, the dictates of my subconscious, my dreams, the hypnagogical images and vision, my paranoiac hallucinations, and all those manifestations, concrete and irrational, of that sensational and obscure world discovered by Freud .... The fact that I myself at the moment of painting my pictures know nothing of their meaning is not to say that the images in question are without sense.

This is certainly true of *Soft Construction* which has been labeled "the memento of a cruel century .... comparable with the *Guernica* .... "

In this painting, a large, dismembered form dominates a desolate Spanish countryside. The form is composed of body parts arranged so that they give the impression that the figure is human. This figure is alternately full-fleshed and emaciated by decay. It gives the appearance of a diseased figure, literally tearing itself apart, an obvious symbol of the effects of any civil war. The painting's clouded sky, lit by a setting sun, is broken with patches of blue, and stretches over a barren, rocky landscape inhabited by the figure and one small man, half-hidden, behind the gnarled hand resting on the ground. An ossified foot and a closed crate support the figure, propping it up so to speak, while boiled beans dot the foreground. As the staple food of the Spanish lower class, their presence may indicate that it is the peasants who will suffer the most destruction. As a country tears itself apart in civil war, death and disease prevail, and the lower classes suffer the greatest losses. Thus, in its spirit, as well as in its imagery, *Soft Construction With Boiled Beans* is the direct descendant of Goya's *Desastres de la guerra* and the cousin of *Guernica*. Each of these works portrays the barbarity of war and its senseless immorality through unforgettable visual images. Goya portrays war as a struggle between the forces of good and the forces of evil, as well as showing the horrible mutilations that can occur in its wake. Picasso demonstrates how the lives of common people can be shattered by bombs raining down from above, and Dali dramatizes the fear of death and destruction inherent in the premonition of war.

Goya, Picasso, and Dali capture the brutality of war, its effects on people, and their hopelessness in its face. Since these images were painted, warfare has become even more horrible. Atomic and hydrogen bombs

---

1   The title of this painting is always given in English, however, a Spanish translation is provided. Dali titled some of his paintings in English, especially ones painted while he was in the United States, just as Picasso titled some of his paintings in French when he was living in France.

threaten death and destruction on a scale that Goya could not have dreamed of, although it is one that Dali wrote about. Dali said, "The atomic explosion of 6 August, 1945 shook me seismically ... Many of the landscapes painted in this period express the great fear inspired in me by the announcement of that explosion ..." Picasso hoped that the horrors of the World War II era would move mankind to adopt peace as a way of life, and he symbolized that hope with his popular image of the dove of peace. Our future is as uncertain as Spain's in either 1808 or in 1936. Will future generations enjoy a prosperous peace or will they be subjected to the murders, mutilations, and despair which are the real horrors of war?

THINK ABOUT IT

1. Which of the painters do you think best expresses the horrors of war? Why?
2. What is your reaction to the style of the modern painters, Picasso and Dali?

TALK ABOUT IT

3. Describe the images from the wars of our times, which are comparable to those created by Goya, Picasso, and Dali. What makes them similar?
4. What media do you think conveys the horrors of war more effectively: paintings, photographs, or films? Why?

WRITE ABOUT IT

5. Find a newspaper account of a war incident. Imagine what a person living through this account would experience. Write a narrative of the incident from his/her point of view.
6. Describe a painting that an artist might paint after a war fought with atomic weapons. What style would the artist choose? Why?

READ MORE ABOUT IT

Schickel, Richard, and the editors of Time-Life Books. *The World of Goya.* New York: Time-Life Books, 1968.

Wertenbarker, Lael, and the editors of Time-Life Books. *The World of Picasso.* New York: Time-Life Books, 1967.

Dail, Salvador. *Dali.* New York: Harry N. Abrams, Inc., 1968.

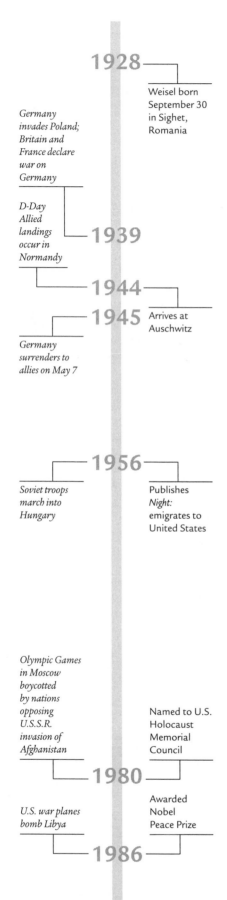

1928 — Weisel born September 30 in Sight, Romania

Germany invades Poland; Britain and France declare war on Germany

D-Day Allied landings occur in Normandy

1939

1944

1945 — Arrives at Auschwitz

Germany surrenders to allies on May 7

1956 — Publishes *Night;* emigrates to United States

Soviet troops march into Hungary

Olympic Games in Moscow boycotted by nations opposing U.S.S.R. invasion of Afghanistan

Named to U.S. Holocaust Memorial Council

1980

Awarded Nobel Peace Prize

U.S. war planes bomb Libya

1986

ELIE WIESEL

Night

For more than thirty-five years, Elie Wiesel's has been a tireless voice against the outrages of the Holocaust, the German genocide of Jews and other minorities during World War II. When he was fifteen, Wiesel, his parents, and three sisters were sent to the infamous German work camp at Auschwitz, Poland. Only Wiesel and two of his sisters survived. For ten years after his release, he was silent; then in 1956, with the publication of *Night,* Wiesel began speaking out in an attempt to bear witness for the dead. Subsequently, Wiesel has published more than thirty books and traveled throughout the world to give speeches and share his experiences. A number of awards and endowment funds have been established in Wiesel's name, and he has received many national and international honors, including the 1986 Nobel Peace Prize.

Night, from which this article is excerpted, is the story of a teen-age boy plagued with guilt for having survived the camps, a reaction that Wiesel still experiences. The boy is also devastated by the knowledge that the God he had so devoutly worshipped has abandoned him and his people. Indeed, Wiesel's previously deep faith in God was crushed by the atrocities he witnessed at Auschwitz. Thus, although *Night* and many of Wiesel's other writings are fictional accounts, they are essentially autobiographical. Through them, Wiesel has attempted to raise awareness of the need to maintain human dignity through peaceful means. He has consistently delivered a message of hope — the hope that the forces fighting evil in the world can be victorious if they are reminded of the horrors of which man is capable.

The powerful images of Käthe Kollwitz illustrate this article and convey the horrors of the type of "camp" life that Wiesel experienced. Kollwitz was a German artist and printmaker who used her work as a vehicle for social change. In the aftermath of World War I as Hitler rose to power, Kollwitz was one of the few brave Germans who dared to speak out against the Nazis. To punish her and set an example, the Nazis removed Kollwitz from her university position, forbade the exhibition of her work, and declared her a degenerate. She died in 1945, just days before the end of World War II.

THE CHERISHED OBJECTS we had brought with us thus far were left behind in the train, and with them, at last, our illusions.

Every two yards or so an SS man held his tommy gun trained on us. Hand in hand we followed the crowd.

An SS noncommissioned officer came to meet us, a truncheon in his hand. He gave the order:

"Men to the left! Women to the right!"

Eight words spoken quietly, indifferently, without emotion. Eight short, simple words. Yet that was the

THE PRISONERS, 1908.
Käthe Kollwitz
Etching and Soft Ground, 12⅞ × 16⅝ in.
Private Collection.

moment when I parted from my mother. I had not had time to think, but already I felt the pressure of my father's hand: we were alone. For a part of a second I glimpsed my mother and my sisters moving away to the right. Tzipora held Mother's hand. I saw them disappear into the distance; my mother was stroking my sister's fair hair, as though to protect her, while I walked on with my father and the other men. And I did not know that in that place, at that moment, I was parting from my mother and Tzipora forever. I went on walking. My father held onto my hand.

Behind me, an old man fell to the ground. Near him was an SS man, putting his revolver back in its holster.

My hand shifted on my father's arm. I had one thought not to lose him. Not to be left alone.

The SS officers gave the order: "Form fives!"

Commotion. At all costs we must keep together.

"Here, kid, how old are you?"

It was one of the prisoners who asked me this. I could not see his face, but his voice was tense and weary.

"I'm not quite fifteen yet."

"No. Eighteen."

"But I'm not," I said. "Fifteen."

"Fool. Listen to what I say."

Then he questioned my father, who replied:

"Fifty."

The other grew more furious than ever.

DEATH SEIZING A WOMAN, 1934.
Käthe Kollwitz
Lithograph, Printed in Black, 20 × 17¾ in.
The Museum of Modern Art, New York, N.Y.

"No, not fifty. Forty. Do you understand? Eighteen and forty."

He disappeared into the night shadows. A second man came up, spitting oaths at us.

"What have you come here for, you sons of bitches? What are you doing here, eh?"

Someone dared to answer him.

"What do you think? Do you suppose we've come here for our own pleasure? Do you think we asked to come?"

A little more, and the man would have killed him.

"You shut your trap, you filthy swine, or I'll squash you right now! You'd have done better to have hanged yourselves where you were than come here. Didn't you know what was in store for you at Auschwitz? Haven't you heard about it? In 1944?"

No, we had not heard. No one had told us. He could not believe his ears. His tone of voice became increasingly brutal.

"Do you see that chimney over there? See it? Do you see those flames? (Yes, we did see the flames.) Over there — that's where you're going to be taken. That's your grave, over there. Haven't you realized it yet? You dumb bastards, don't you understand anything? You're going to be burned. Frizzled away. Turned into ashes."

He was growing hysterical in his fury. We stayed motionless, petrified. Surely it was all a nightmare? An unimaginable nightmare?

I heard murmurs around me.

"We've got to do something. We can't let ourselves be killed. We can't go like beasts to the slaughter. We've got to revolt."

There were a few sturdy young fellows among us. They had knives on them, and they tried to incite the others to throw themselves on the armed guards.

One of the young men cried:

"Let the world learn of the existence of Auschwitz. Let everybody hear about it, while they can still escape ——"

But the older ones begged their children not to do anything foolish:

"You must never lose faith, even when the sword hangs over your head. That's the teaching of our sages .... "

The wind of revolt died down. We continued our march toward the square. In the middle stood the notorious Dr. Mengele (a typical SS officer: a cruel face, but not devoid of intelligence, and wearing a monocle); a conductor's baton in his hand, he was standing among the other officers. The baton moved unremittingly, sometimes to the right, sometimes to the left.

I was already in front of him:

"How old are you?" he asked, in an attempt at a paternal tone of voice.

"Eighteen." My voice was shaking.

"Are you in good health?"

"Yes."

"What's your occupation?"

Should I say that I was a student?

"Farmer," I heard myself say.

This conversation cannot have lasted more than a few seconds. It had seemed like an eternity to me.

The baton moved to the left. I took half a step forward. I wanted to see first where they were sending my father. If he went to the right, I would go after him.

The baton once again pointed to the left for him too. A weight was lifted from my heart.

We did not yet know which was the better side, right or left; which road led to prison and which to the crematory. But for the moment I was happy; I was near my father. Our procession continued to move slowly forward.

Another prisoner came up to us:

"Satisfied?"

"Yes," someone replied.

"Poor devils, you're going to the crematory."

He seemed to be telling the truth. Not far from us, flames were leaping up from a ditch, gigantic flames. They were burning something. A lorry drew up at the pit and delivered its load — little children. Babies! Yes, I saw it — saw it with my own eyes ... those children in the flames. (Is it surprising that I could not sleep after that? Sleep had fled from my eyes.)

So this was where we were going. A little farther on was another and larger ditch for adults.

I pinched my face. Was I still alive? Was I awake? I could not believe it. How could it be possible for them to burn people, children, and for the world to keep silent? No, none of this could be true. It was a nightmare .... Soon I should wake with a start, my heart pounding, and find myself back in the bedroom of my childhood, among my books ....

My father's voice drew me from my thoughts:

"It's a shame ... a shame that you couldn't have gone with your mother ... I saw several boys of your age going with their mothers .... "

His voice was terribly sad. I realized that he did not want to see what they were going to do to me. He did not want to see the burning of his only son.

My forehead was bathed in cold sweat. But I told him that I did not believe that they could burn people in our age, that humanity would never tolerate it ....

"Humanity? Humanity is not concerned with us. Today anything is allowed. Anything is possible, even these crematories .... "

His voice was choking.

"Father," I said, "if that is so, I don't want to wait here. I'm going to run to the electric wire. That would be better than slow agony in the flames."

He did not answer. He was weeping. His body was shaking convulsively. Around us, everyone was weeping.

Someone began to recite the Kaddish, the prayer for the dead. I do not know if it has ever happened before, in the long history of the Jews, that people have ever recited the prayer for the dead for themselves.

"*Yitgadal veyitkadach shmé raba* .... May His name be blessed and magnified .... " whispered my father.

For the first time, I felt revolt rise up in me. Why should I bless His name? The Eternal, Lord of the Universe, the All-Powerful and Terrible, was silent. What had I to thank Him for?

We continued our march. We were gradually drawing closer to the ditch, from which an infernal heat was rising. Still twenty steps to go. If I wanted to bring about my own death, this was the moment. Our line had now only fifteen paces to cover. I bit my lips so that my father would not hear my teeth chattering. Ten steps still. Eight. Seven. We marched slowly on, as though following a hearse at our own funeral. Four steps more. Three steps. There it was now, right in front of us, the pit and its flames. I gathered all that was left of my strength, so that I could break from the ranks and throw myself upon the barbed wire. In the depths of my heart, I bade farewell to my father, to the whole universe; and, in spite of myself, the words formed themselves and issued in a whisper from my lips: *Yitgadal veyitkadach shmé raba* .... May His name be blessed and magnified .... My heart was bursting. The moment had come. I was face to face with the Angel of Death ....

No. Two steps from the pit we were ordered to turn to the left and made to go into a barracks.

I pressed my father's hand. He said:

"Do you remember Madame Schachter, in the train? "

Never shall I forget that night, the first night in camp, which has turned my life into one long night, seven times cursed and seven times sealed.

Never shall I forget that smoke. Never shall I forget the little faces of the children, whose bodies I saw turned into wreaths of smoke beneath a silent blue sky.

Never shall I forget those flames which consumed my faith forever.

Never shall I forget that nocturnal silence which deprived me, for all eternity, of the desire to live. Never shall I forget those moments which murdered my God and my soul and turned my dreams to dust. Never shall I forget these things, even if I am condemned to live as long as God Himself. Never.

The barracks we had been made to go into was very long. In the roof were some blue-tinged skylights. The antechamber of Hell must look like this. So many crazed men, so many cries, so much bestial brutality!

There were dozens of prisoners to receive us, truncheons in their hands, striking out anywhere, at anyone, without reasons. Orders:

"Strip! Fast! *Los!* Keep only your belts and shoes in your hands .... "

We had to throw our clothes at one end of the barracks. There was already a great heap there. New suits and old, torn coats, rags. For us, this was the true equality, nakedness. Shivering with the cold.

Some SS officers moved about in the room, looking for strong men. If they were so keen on strength, perhaps one should try and pass oneself off as sturdy? My father thought the reverse. It was better not to draw attention to oneself. Our fate would then be the same as the others. (Later, we were to learn that he was right. Those who were selected that day were enlisted in the *Sonder-Kommando*, the unit which worked in the crematories. Bela Katz — son of a big tradesman from our town — arrived at Birkenau with the first transport, a week before us. When he heard of our arrival, he managed to get word to us that, having been chosen for his strength, he had himself put his father's body into the crematory oven.)

Blows continued to rain down.

"To the barber!"

Belt and shoes in hand, I let myself be dragged off to the barbers. They took our hair off with clippers, and shaved off all the hair on our bodies. The same thought buzzed all the time in my head — not to be separated from my father.

Freed from the hands of the barbers, we began to wander in the crowd, meeting friends and acquaintances. These meetings filled us with joy — yes, joy — "Thank God! You're still alive!"

But others were crying. They used all their remaining strength in weeping. Why had they let themselves be brought here? Why couldn't they have died in their beds? Sobs choked their voices.

Suddenly, someone threw his arms round my neck in an embrace: Yechiel, brother of the rabbi of Sighet. He was sobbing bitterly. I thought he was weeping with Joy at still being alive.

"Don't cry, Yechiel," I said. "Don't waste your tears ... "

"Not cry? We're on the threshold of death .... Soon we shall have crossed over ... Don't you understand? How could I not cry?"

Through the blue-tinged skylights I could see the darkness gradually fading. I had ceased to feel fear. And then I was overcome by an inhuman weariness.

Those absent no longer touched even the surface of our memories. We still spoke of them — "Who knows what may have become of them?" — but we had little concern for their fate. We were incapable of thinking of anything at all. Our senses were blunted; everything was blurred as in a fog. It was no longer possible to grasp anything. The instincts of self-preservation, of self-defense, of pride, had all deserted us. In one ultimate moment of lucidity it seemed to me that we were damned souls wandering in the half-world, souls condemned to wander through space till the generations of man came to an end, seeking their redemption, seeking oblivion — without hope of finding it.

Toward five o'clock in the morning, we were driven out of the barracks. The Kapos beat us once more, but I had ceased to feel any pain from their blows. An icy wind enveloped us. We were naked, our shoes and belts in our hands. The command: "Run!" And we ran. After a few minutes of racing, a new barracks.

A barrel of petrol at the entrance. Disinfection. Everyone was soaked in it. Then a hot shower. At high speed. As we came out from the water, we were driven outside. More running. Another barracks, the store. Very long tables. Mountains of prison clothes. On we ran. As we passed, trousers, tunic, shirt, and socks were thrown to us.

Within a few seconds, we had ceased to be men. If the situation had not been tragic, we should have roared with laughter. Such outfits! Meir Katz, a giant, had a child's trousers, and Stem, a thin little chap, a tunic which completely swamped him. We immediately began the necessary exchanges.

I glanced at my father. How he had changed! His eyes had grown dim. I would have liked to speak to him, but I did not know what to say.

The night was gone. The morning star was shining in the sky. I too had become a completely different person. The student of the Talmud, the child that I was, had been consumed in the flames. There remained only a shape that looked like me. A dark flame had entered into my soul and devoured it.

So much had happened within such a few hours that I had lost all sense of time. When had we left our houses? And the ghetto? And the train? Was it only a week? One night — one *single night*?

How long had we been standing like this in the icy wind? An hour? Simply an hour? Sixty minutes?

Surely it was a dream.

Not far from us there were some prisoners at work. Some were digging holes, others carrying sand. None of them so much as glanced at us. We were so many dried-up trees in the heart of a desert. Behind me, some people were talking. I had not the slightest desire to listen to what they were saying, to know who was talking or what they were talking about. No one dared to raise his voice, though there was no supervisor near us. People whispered. Perhaps it was because of the thick smoke which poisoned the air and took one by the throat ....

We were made to go into a new barracks, in the "gypsies' camp." In ranks of five.

"And now stay where you are!"

There was no floor. A roof and four walls. Our feet sank into the mud.

Another spell of waiting began. I went to sleep standing up. I dreamed of a bed, of my mother's caress. And I woke up: I was standing, my feet in the mud. Some people collapsed and lay where they were. Others cried:

"Are you mad? We've been told to stay standing. Do you want to bring trouble on us all?"

As if all the trouble in the world had not descended already upon our heads! Gradually, we all sat down in the mud. But we had to jump up constantly, every time a Kapo came in to see if anybody had a pair of new shoes. If so, they had to be given up to him. It was no use opposing this: blows rained down and in the final reckoning you had lost your shoes anyway.

I had new shoes myself. But as they were coated with a thick layer of mud, no one had noticed them. I thanked God, in an improvised prayer, for having created mud in His infinite and wonderful universe.

Suddenly the silence grew oppressive. An SS officer had come in and, with him, the odor of the Angel of Death. We stared fixedly at his fleshy lips. From the middle of the barracks, he harangued us:

"You're in a concentration camp. At Auschwitz ...." A pause. He observed the effect his words had produced. His face has stayed in my memory to this day. A tall man, about thirty, with crime inscribed upon his brow and in the pupils of his eyes. He looked us over as if we were a pack of leprous dogs hanging onto our lives.

"Remember this," he went on. "Remember it forever. Engrave it into your minds. You are at Auschwitz, and Auschwitz is not a convalescent home. It's a concentration camp. Here, you have got to work. If not, you will go straight to the furnace. To the crematory. Work or the crematory — the choice is in your hands."

We had already lived through so much that night, we thought nothing could frighten us any more. But his clipped words made us tremble. Here the word "furnace" was not a word empty of meaning: it floated on the air, mingling with the smoke. It was perhaps the only word which did have any real meaning here. He left the barracks. Kapos appeared, crying:

"All skilled workers — locksmiths, electricians, watchmakers — one step forward!"

The rest of us were made to go to another barracks, a stone one this time. With permission to sit down. A gypsy deportee was in charge of us.

My father was suddenly seized with colic. He got up and went toward the gypsy, asking politely, in German:

"Excuse me, can you tell me where the lavatories are?" The gypsy looked him up and down slowly, from head to foot. As if he wanted to convince himself that this man addressing him was really a creature of flesh and bone, a living being with a body and a belly. Then, as if he had suddenly woken up from a heavy doze, he dealt my father such a clout that he fell to the ground, crawling back to his place on all fours.

I did not move. What had happened to me? My father had just been struck, before my very eyes, and I had not flickered an eyelid. I had looked on and said nothing.

Yesterday, I should have sunk my nails into the criminal's flesh. Had I changed so much, then? So quickly? Now remorse began to gnaw at me. I thought only: I shall never forgive them for that. My father must have guessed my feelings. He whispered in my ear, "It doesn't hurt." His cheek still bore the red mark of the man's hand.

"Everyone outside!"

Ten gypsies had come and joined our supervisor. Whips and truncheons cracked round me. My feet were running without my being aware of it. I tried to hide from the blows behind the others. The spring sunshine.

"Form fives!"

The prisoners whom I had noticed in the morning were working at the side. There was no guard near them, only the shadow of the chimney ... Dazed by the sunshine and by my reverie, I felt someone tugging at my sleeve. It was my father. "Come on, my boy."

We marched on. Doors opened and closed again. On we went between the electric wires. At each step, a white placard with a death's head on it stared us in the face. A caption "Warning. Danger of death." Mockery: was there a single place here where you were not in danger of death?

The gypsies stopped near another barracks. They were replaced by SS, who surrounded us. Revolvers, machine guns, police dogs.

The march had lasted half an hour. Looking around me, I noticed that the barbed wires were behind us. We had left the camp.

It was a beautiful April day. The fragrance of spring was in the air. The sun was setting in the west.

But we had been marching for only a few moments when we saw the barbed wire of another camp. An iron door with this inscription over it:

'Work is liberty!'
Auschwitz.

THINK ABOUT IT

1. Summarize Wiesel's first night at Auschwitz. How did this experience change his attitude about life?
2. Why did the inscription over the camp entrance read "work is liberty"? Explain its meaning.

TALK ABOUT IT

3. Do similar "camp" situations exist in the world today? Where? Describe them.
4. Why were the Nazis and the other prisoners so cruel to the new arrivals?

WRITE ABOUT IT

5. Find two passages from the reading selection that could be used as captions for the Kollwitz drawings. Explain why they fit her images.
6. Have you ever failed to act to protect or come to the aid of a loved one? In what ways did your failure to act cause you to question your values?

READ MORE ABOUT IT

Against Silence: The Voice and Vision of Elie Wiesel. Ed. Irving Abrahamson. New York: Holocaust Library, 1985.

Wiesel, Elie. *Night, Dawn, Day.* New York: Farrar, Strauss, & Giroux, 1982.

Wiesel, Elie. *One Generation After.* New York: Random House, 1970.

Wiesel, Elie. *The Forgotten.* Trans. Stephen Becker. New York: Summit Books, 1992.

The United Nations Declaration of Human Rights

The United Nations Declaration of Human Rights was adopted by the United Nations General Assembly on December 10, 1948. It is an universal charter that sets out a common standard of ethical conduct to which all peoples and all nations are expected to adhere. The first twenty-one articles of the Declaration are similar to the first ten amendments, known as the Bill of Rights, of the Constitution of the United States. Articles twenty-two through twenty-seven, relating to economic and social rights, echo specific points in the constitution of the Soviet Union. Thus, the Declaration was intended to reflect key articles contained in the constitutions of the two most influential world powers at the time it was drafted.

The articles of the Declaration of Human Rights set out universal standards of social ethics for all societies. This document has been criticized for not respecting societies whose values are different from those inherent in this charter. Supporters of the Declaration have responded that the values contained in the charter's articles represent necessary standards for human conduct: all individuals in all societies should be expected to adhere to them.

Preamble

Whereas recognition of the inherent dignity and of the equal and inalienable rights of all members of the human family is the foundation of freedom, justice and peace in the world,

Whereas disregard and contempt for human rights have resulted in barbarous acts which have outraged the conscience of mankind, and the advent of a world in which human beings shall enjoy freedom of speech and belief and freedom from fear and want has been proclaimed as the highest aspiration of the common people,

Whereas it is essential, if man is not to be compelled to have recourse, as a last resort, to rebellion against tyranny and oppression, that human rights should be protected by the rule of law,

Whereas it is essential to promote the development of friendly relations between nations, Whereas the people of the United Nations have in the Charter reaffirmed their faith in fundamental human rights, in the dignity and worth of the human person and in the equal rights of men and women and have determined to promote social progress and better standards of life in larger freedom,

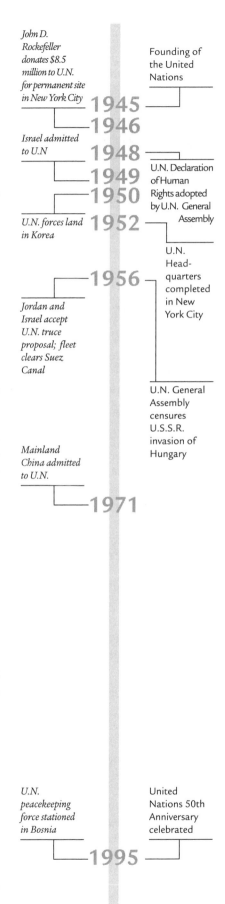

John D. Rockefeller donates $8.5 million to U.N. for permanent site in New York City

1945

Founding of the United Nations

1946

Israel admitted to U.N

1948

U.N. Declaration of Human Rights adopted by U.N. General Assembly

1949

1950

U.N. forces land in Korea

1952

U.N. Headquarters completed in New York City

1956

Jordan and Israel accept U.N. truce proposal; fleet clears Suez Canal

U.N. General Assembly censures U.S.S.R. invasion of Hungary

Mainland China admitted to U.N.

1971

U.N. peacekeeping force stationed in Bosnia

United Nations 50th Anniversary celebrated

1995

Whereas Member States have pledged themselves to achieve, in cooperation with the United Nations, the promotion of universal respect for and observance of human rights and fundamental freedoms,

Whereas a common understanding of these rights and freedoms is of the greatest importance for the full realization of this pledge,

Now, Therefore,

The General Assembly Proclaims

This Universal Declaration of Human Rights as a common standard of achievement for all peoples and all nations, to the end that every individual and every organ of society, keeping this Declaration constantly in mind, shall strive by teaching and education to promote respect for these rights and freedoms and by progressive measures, national and international, to secure their universal and effective recognition and observance, both among the peoples of Member States themselves and among the peoples of territories under their jurisdiction.

ARTICLE 1 All human beings are born free and equal in dignity and rights. They are endowed with reason and conscience and should act towards one another in a spirit of brotherhood.

ARTICLE 2 Everyone is entitled to all the rights and freedoms set forth in this Declaration, without distinction of any kind, such as race, colour, sex, language, religion, political or other opinion, national or social origin, property, birth or other status.

Furthermore, no distinction shall be made on the basis of the political, jurisdictional or international status of the country or territory to which a person belongs, whether it

be independent, trust, non-self-governing or under any other limitation of sovereignty.

ARTICLE 3 Everyone has the right to life, liberty and security of person.

ARTICLE 4 No one shall be held in slavery or servitude; slavery and the slave trade shall be prohibited in all their forms.

ARTICLE 5 No one shall be subjected to torture or to cruel, inhuman or degrading treatment or punishment.

ARTICLE 6 Everyone has the right to recognition everywhere as a person before the law.

ARTICLE 7 All are equal before the law and are entitled without any discrimination to equal protection of the law. All are entitled to equal protection against any discrimination in violation of this Declaration and against any incitement to such discrimination.

ARTICLE 8 Everyone has the right to an effective remedy by the competent national tribunals for acts violating the fundamental rights granted him by the constitution or by law.

ARTICLE 9 No one shall be subjected to arbitrary arrest, detention or exile.

ARTICLE 10 Everyone is entitled in full equality to a fair and public hearing by an independent and impartial tribunal, in the determination of his rights and obligations and of any criminal charge against him.

ARTICLE 11 (1) Everyone charged with a penal offence has the right to be presumed innocent until proved guilty according to law in a public trial at which he has had all the guarantees necessary for his defence.

(2) No one shall be held guilty of any penal offence on account of any act or omission which did not constitute a penal offence, under national or international law, at the time when it was committed. Nor shall a heavier penalty be imposed than the one that was applicable at the time the penal offence was committed.

ARTICLE 12 No one shall be subjected to arbitrary interference with his privacy, family, home or correspondence, nor to attacks upon his honour and reputation. Everyone has the right to the protection of the law against such interference or attacks.

ARTICLE 13 (1) Everyone has the right to freedom of movement and residence within the borders of each state.

(2) Everyone has the right to leave any country, including his own, and to return to his country.

ARTICLE 14 (1) Everyone has the right to seek and to enjoy in other countries asylum from persecution.

(2) This right may not be invoked in the case of prosecutions genuinely arising from non-political crimes or from acts contrary to the purposes and principles of the United Nations.

ARTICLE 15 (1) Everyone has the right to a nationality.

(2) No one shall be arbitrarily deprived of his nationality nor denied the right to change his nationality.

ARTICLE 16 (1) Men and women of full age, without any limitation due to race, nationality or religion, have the right to marry and to found a family. They are entitled to equal rights as to marriage, during marriage and at its dissolution.

(2) Marriage shall be entered into only with the free and full consent of the intending spouses.

(3) The family is the natural and fundamental group unity of society and is entitled to protection by society and the State.

ARTICLE 17 (1) Everyone has the right to own property alone as well as in association with others.

(2) No one shall be arbitrarily deprived of his property.

ARTICLE 18 Everyone has the right to freedom of thought, conscience and religion; this right includes freedom to change his religion or belief, and freedom, either alone or in community with others and in public or private, to manifest his religion or belief in teaching, practice, worship and observance.

ARTICLE 19 Everyone has the right to freedom of opinion and expression; this right includes freedom to hold opinions without interference and to seek, receive and impart information and ideas through any media and regardless of frontiers.

ARTICLE 20 (1) Everyone has the right to freedom of peaceful assembly and association.

(2) No one may be compelled to belong to an association.

ARTICLE 21 (1) Everyone has the right to take part in the government of his country, directly or through freely chosen representatives.

(2) Everyone has the right of equal access to public service in his country.

(3) The will of the people shall be the basis of the authority of government; this will shall be expressed in periodic and genuine elections which shall be by universal and equal suffrage and shall be held by secret vote or by equivalent free voting procedures.

ARTICLE 22 Everyone, as a member of society, has the right to social security and is entitled to realization, through national effort and international co-operation and in accordance with the organization and resources of each State, of the economic, social and cultural rights indispensable for his dignity and the free development of his personality.

ARTICLE 23 (1) Everyone has the right to work, to free choice of employment, to just and favourable conditions of work and to protection against unemployment.

(2) Everyone, without any discrimination, has the right to equal pay for equal work.

(3) Everyone who works has the right to just and favourable remu-

neration ensuring for himself and his family an existence worthy of human dignity, and supplemented, if necessary, by other means of social protection.

(4) Everyone has the right to form and to join trade unions for the protection of his interests.

ARTICLE 24 Everyone has the right to rest and leisure, including reasonable limitation of working hours and periodic holidays with pay.

ARTICLE 25 (1) Everyone has the right to a standard of living adequate for the health and wellbeing of himself and of his family, including food, clothing, housing and medical care and necessary social services, and the right to security in the event of unemployment, sickness, disability, widowhood, old age or other lack of livelihood in circumstances beyond his control.

(2) Motherhood and childhood are entitled to special care and assistance. All children, whether born in or out of wedlock, shall enjoy the same social protection.

ARTICLE 26 (1) Everyone has the right to education. Education shall be free, at least in the elementary and fundamental stages. Elementary education shall be compulsory. Technical and professional education shall be made generally available and higher education shall be equally accessible to all on the basis of merit.

(2) Education shall be directed to the full development of the human personality and to the strengthening of respect for human rights and fundamental freedoms. It shall promote understanding, tolerance and friendship among all nations, racial or religious groups, and shall further the activities of the United Nations for the maintenance of peace.

(3) Parents have a prior right to choose the kind of education that shall be given to their children.

ARTICLE 27 (1) Everyone has the right freely to participate in the cul-

tural life of the community, to enjoy the arts and to share in scientific advancement and its benefits.

(2) Everyone has the right to the protection of the moral and material interests resulting from any scientific, literary or artistic production of which he is the author.

ARTICLE 28 Everyone is entitled to a social and international order in which the rights and freedoms set forth in this Declaration can be fully realized.

ARTICLE 29 (1) Everyone has duties to the community in which alone the free and full development of his personality is possible.

(2) In the exercise of his rights and freedoms, everyone shall be subject only to such limitations as are determined by law solely for the purpose of securing due recognition and respect for the rights and freedoms of others and of meeting the just requirements of morality, public order and the general welfare in a democratic society.

(3) These rights and freedoms may in no case be exercised contrary to the purposes and principles of the United Nations.

ARTICLE 30 Nothing in this Declaration may be interpreted as implying for any State, group or person any right to engage in any activity or to perform any act aimed at the destruction of any of the rights and freedoms set forth herein.

THINK ABOUT IT

1. According to the Charter, what individual rights and freedoms are all humans entitled to? What social and economic rights must we be assured of?
2. Why should individuals and societies support and adhere to the rights set out in the Charter?

TALK ABOUT IT

3. Is there a society today where many of these rights are denied to individual members? What is being done to establish the rights?
4. Many critics of the Charter state that it has not been successfully enforced since its inception and, therefore, it is a meaningless document. Despite its lack of enforcement, do you think the Charter is valuable? Why or why not?

WRITE ABOUT IT

5. Which three articles do you think are the most important? Argue for their universal acceptance.
6. Write your own "Charter of Rights" that you think all members of your class should follow.

READ MORE ABOUT IT

Baier, Kurt. *The Moral Point of View*. Ithaca, NY: Cornell University Press, 1958.

Gert, Bernard. The Moral Rules: *A New Rational Foundation for Morality*. New York: Harper & Row, 1970.

Sommers, Christina, and Sommers, Fred. *Vice & Virtue in Everyday Life: Introductory Readings in Ethics*. Orlando, FL: Harcourt Brace Jovanovich, Inc., 1989.

CHRISTINA SOMMERS

Where Have All the Good Deeds Gone?

"Where Have All the Good Deeds Gone?" by Christina Sommers was selected for inclusion in the *Vice & Virtues in Everyday Life: Introductory Readings in Ethics* anthology published by Harcourt Brace Jovanovich in 1989. In the introduction that precedes this selection, it states:

> Christina Sommers (b. 1950) teaches philosophy at Clark University in Worcester, Massachusetts. She has written a number of articles on moral philosophy and is Director of the New England Society for Philosophy and Public Affairs.
>
> Sommers contends that social morality is replacing private moral initiative. The modern individual delegates too much moral responsibility to institutions . . . . Sommers maintains that social solutions [to matters of private ethics] are not sufficient. We badly need the individual "moral amateur."

In the following article, Christina Sommers addresses the conflict between group ethics, represented by institutions, and the moral responsibilities of the Individual, or "moral amateur." She uses the example of treatment of the elderly in an old-age home to explore which moral accountabilities rest with the institution and which with the individual.

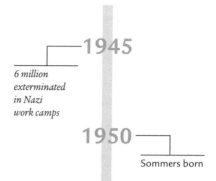

MILLER HOUSE is an old-age home in a well-to-do Boston suburb. As in many other homes for the elderly, conditions are grim. No matter how cold it is outside, old men sit downcast on the front porch. Sometimes one of them wanders over to a nearby fast-food restaurant where he will sit alone at a table for hours. One resident, Mr. Kelly, recently slipped out the front door and did not stop walking for three days. The police picked him up forty miles away, dazed from lack of sleep and still clutching his cardboard suitcase, and brought him back.

Mr. Richards, age eighty-four, sleeps more than twenty hours a day, waking only for meals and cigarette breaks. He hates Miller House. "I don't like fish cakes," he says. "We have them all the time and the director makes me eat them."

For the past seven years Miss Pickins, who is ninety-one, has lived in Miller House. Last year her doctor or-

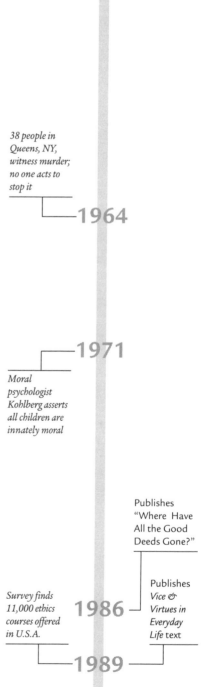

1945

6 million
exterminated
in Nazi
work camps

1950

Sommers born

38 people in
Queens, NY,
witness murder;
no one acts to
stop it

1964

1971

Moral
psychologist
Kohlberg asserts
all children are
innately moral

Publishes
"Where Have
All the Good
Deeds Gone?"

Publishes
Vice &
Virtues in
Everyday
Life text

Survey finds
11,000 ethics
courses offered
in U.S.A.

1986

1989

dered her to stop smoking. This upset a daily routine she had enjoyed — coffee and cigarettes in the lounge downstairs with the men. She became depressed, lost interest in leaving her room, and now spends most of her time there alone. The woman who runs the home makes Miss Pickins keep the sound of her radio so low that she cannot hear it. Once she did not finish her dessert, and as punishment she no longer gets any. These little injustices keep her in a constant rage.

Simone de Beauvoir has said, "By the fate it allots to its members who can no longer work, society gives itself away." Who is to blame for the fate that has been allotted to Miss Pickins, Mr. Kelly, and Mr. Richards? It is fashionable to condemn civic agencies and the government. But government agencies are responsible for enforcing standards of cleanliness and safety: should we also require that they meet standards of good-heartedness and neighborliness? What the Miller residents need is kindly attention: someone to talk to them, to take an interest in them, and to mitigate the little cruelties that seem always to tempt those in charge of helpless people. Should the state pay a social worker twenty dollars to make sure Miss Pickins gets her dessert? A few concerned neighbors could transform the residence into a much happier place. But that is not going to happen.

One reason, no doubt, is that a lot of people are uncaring and irresponsible, but far more important is the attitude of the responsible private individuals who no longer see themselves as the seat of moral initiative. Good deeds have been given over to experts: the acts that constitute the social morality of our time are being performed by paid professionals in large public agencies. Helping the needy, the sick, and the aged has be-

come an operation whose scale and character leave little room for the virtuous private person. Our ancestors in their idiosyncratic charitable endeavors look like moral amateurs.

Professionals who do use volunteers see them as incipient professionals. The assistant manager of the Greater Boston Red Cross observes: "Volunteers are there but you have to offer them something … career benefits and resumé experience." The Children's Museum of Boston offers the potential volunteer entries for a curriculum vitae — a volunteer fund raiser is called a "corporate membership marketing specialist," someone who helps paint walls, a "maintenance assistant." Since professionals look down on amateurs, executives of social institutions feel forced to counter the stigma of amateurism by conferring on the volunteer a quasi-professional status. The loss of confidence in private moral initiative is part of a general derogation of amateurism, a phenomenon that Christopher Lasch has called the "atrophy of competence."

Is it excessive to say that our society has become more morally passive? After all, the past few decades have seen the growth of liberal ideals and their realization in social programs that have benefited great numbers of people. Also, private moral initiative is not sufficient to guarantee a decent life to citizens in a complex society like our own. Without social security, Medicaid, and board of health regulations, the Miller residents would be much worse off.

The political diversion of moral energies, however, has given rise to a new kind of hypocrisy. It is now possible to consider ourselves morally exemplary simply because we adhere to an enlightened set of social principles. We may vote in accordance with these principles, but they require nothing of us personally: we need never lift a

finger to help anyone and we need take no active part in social reform movements. We can even permit ourselves to be ruthless in relations with other people. Because morality has been sublimated into ideology, great numbers of people, the young and educated especially, feel they have an adequate moral identity merely because they hold the "right" views on such matters as ecology, feminism, socialism, and nuclear energy. They may lead narrow, self-indulgent lives, obsessed with their physical health, material comforts, and personal growth, yet still feel a moral advantage over those who actively work to help the needy but who are, in their eyes, ideologically unsound.

The problems that arise from the imbalance of private morality and public policy transcend questions of liberal left versus conservative right. Where the left is directly responsible for the false and the unworkable doctrine that ethics is reducible to public policy, the right wishes to dismantle crucial institutions that protect people's rights to a sustainable existence. Conservatives too believe that one may discharge moral duties by holding and advocating "correct" views on public policy (against busing and gun control, for prayers in the school and the death penalty). If the extreme right proves effective, the indigent will have lost such protection as public policy now provides — and this in a society whose members have lost the will and the way to be their brothers' keeper. Moreover, in any number of situations direct action is simply inappropriate (housing for the elderly or disaster relief are prime examples) and the need for concerted social effort and sound public policy is clear. But being right and effective in social ethics is only half of the moral life; and the growing belief that it is more than half should be combated and dispelled.

Courses in ethics might be one place to begin.

A glance at a typical anthology of a college course in ethics reveals that most of what the student will read is directed toward analyzing and criticizing policies on such issues as punishment, recombinant DNA research, abortion, and euthanasia. Since the student is not likely to be personally involved in, say, inflicting the death penalty on anyone, the point is to learn how to form responsible opinions. Inevitably the student gets the idea that applying ethics to modern life is mainly a matter of being for or against some social policy. And since many of the articles read like briefs written for a judge or legislator, before long the student loses sight of him- or herself as a moral agent and begins to think like a proto-jurist or legislator.

The net effect of identifying normative ethics with public policy is to justify the moral passivity of the individual. But private benevolence continues to be badly needed in all areas of social concern. The paid functionaires who have virtually excluded the unpaid, well-meaning person are in no position to replace or repair the bonds that have been weakened by the atrophy of private moral initiative. Intellectuals, too, have lost their nerve. Consider the following, from Simone de Beauvoir's *The Coming of Age*:

> Once we have understood what the state of the aged really is, we cannot satisfy ourselves with calling for a more generous "old age policy," higher pensions, decent housing, and organized leisure. It is the whole system that is at issue and our claim cannot be otherwise than radical — change life itself.

Here is the mysterious and ultimately despairing demand of the contemporary social philosopher who has lost sight of the morally concerned citizen. The concrete need is not for revolutionizing society, perhaps not even for reforming it, but for finding a way to reach people like Miss Pickins and the other residents of Miller House.

THINK ABOUT IT

1. What standards exist at Miller House? Does the author think they are good or bad?
2. Why does Sommers say the "good deeds" have been given away? What must be done to reclaim them?

TALK ABOUT IT

3. According to Sommers, what does applying ethics to modern life mean?
4. Why has our society "lost the will and the way to be [our] brothers' keeper"? Name a culture where individuals reach out to the elderly.

WRITE ABOUT IT

5. Develop a plan of action for improving Mr. Richards' and Miss Pickens' daily routines.
6. What type of moral agent are you? Describe one of your commitments or activities as a moral agent.

READ MORE ABOUT IT

Kohlberg, Lawrence. *Essays on Moral Development,* vols. I and II. San Francisco: Harper and Row, 1981, 1984.

Sichel, Betty. *Moral Education: Character, Community and Ideals.* Philadelphia: Temple University Press, 1988.

Sommers, Christina, and Sommers, Fred. *Vice & Virtue in Everyday Life: Introductory Readings in Ethics.* Orlando, FL: Harcourt Brace Jovanovich, Inc., 1989.

Sommers, Christina. "Where Have All the Good Deeds Gone?" *Hastings Center Report* August 1982. Hastings-on-Hudson, NY.: Institute of Society, Ethics and the Life Sciences, 1982.

Emily Dickinson

Harold Kushner

Gautama Buddha

The Koran

The Sermon on the Mount

The Cathedral at Chartres

Gary Jennings

The Hopi

Annie Dillard

CHAPTER **6**

God

I T IS EASY to identify with Emily Dickinson's poem that expresses her desire to believe in god and at the same time to be skeptical of his existence. She adopts the voice of a child and asks, in all innocence, bold and basic questions relating to the adult world of religion. At some point in our lives, most of us have thought about whether god exists. Yet, every culture that has existed has believed in "someone" or "something" that transcends all human boundaries. God is a subject so vast that all our thoughts are lost in its immensity and so deep that our pride is quenched in its infinity. We wonder, "Is god one or many? Is god really good and perfect? Personal or impersonal? Do I need god?" When stated this way, these questions boggle the mind. Like these, Emily Dickinson's questions challenge one's belief in god.

EMILY DICKINSON

"Each Life Converges to Some Centre"

Each life converges to some centre
Expressed or still;
Exists in every human nature
A goal,

Admitted scarcely to itself, it may be,
Too fair
or credibility's temerity
To dare.

Adored with caution, as a brittle heaven,
To reach
Were hopeless as the rainbow's raiment
To touch,

Yet persevered toward, surer for the distance;
How high
Unto the saints' slow diligence
The sky!

Ungained, it may be, by a life's low venture,
But then,
Eternity enables the endeavoring
Again.

In her poem, she straddles heaven and earth, moving between a desire to believe in god and a skeptical disbelief of him which illustrates her courage in raising these questions. Her poetry challenges us to become as bold as innocent children and ask the questions that adults are sometimes unwilling to ask because they are afraid of the answers they might encounter. These questions force us to re-examine what we have heard about religion and grapple individually with its basic tenets. These questions force us to move beyond the surface of religion to its inner core — faith.

In our world there are many man-made gods and goddesses who often profess to be the ultimate authority and who seek to be the objects of our faith. Religious television programs, ads, books, and charismatic personalities preach to us that we are lost without their concepts of god.

As a result, millions of dollars are donated each year to self-styled prophets who attempt to indoctrinate us into their particular religion, church, or cult. These self-designated prophets stress the importance of following an external authority and hope we will follow them blindly. These prophets try to convince us that we should not ask the hard questions Emily Dickinson asks or have her discriminating and critical eye for truth. If these "prophets" can convince us to place our faith in them, they can profit from our obedience.

Yet beyond the hype of religious television and religious fads lies a deeper understanding of faith based on a more universal concept. Faith in god has threaded itself through human consciousness since the beginning of human history and has permeated all cultures. This faith has taken many forms. One of the most ancient of these is animism. Animists believe god is an all-pervading and living force, bringing life to everything that is. Sometimes this includes the belief that man is god, because god dwells in all men. Other times, animism produces a multiplicity of gods and goddesses, or it can give rise to the belief in one, infinite, impersonal, ultimate reality. Some other cultures believe in polytheism, the view that there is a presence of many "gods" as supernatural entities with different powers and functions. This belief is evident in Native American traditions, among others. Others, like Christianity, believe that there is one god, who is three persons: the Father, Jesus, and the Holy Spirit. The Christian's god is both personal and transcendent; involved with mankind and yet in absolute control. These characteristics are shared by the gods of Judaism and Islam. While Jews do not speak or write the sacred name of god, they conceive of god as the one absolute power in the universe. Islam, too, believes in the absolute unity of god who is named and called Allah. Yet another tradition, Buddhism, holds to the path of self-reliance or "enlightenment" which expects no help from a god. These expressions of faith, both polytheistic and monotheistic, are only a few of those which have arisen from the difficult questions humans have asked about a supreme presence in the universe.

Religions try to provide satisfying answers to the hard questions humans have asked by explaining how man should relate to god through faith. Faith is the inner facet that outwardly binds the believer to the particular religion. To some, faith is merely a verbal confession of some doctrinal statement. To others, faith is trusting in persons or things like religious figures and institutions. Or, faith can be a "leap into the dark," hoping god is there to catch us. Yet others see faith as a "leap into the light," resting upon the grounds of credible testimony. Faith involves an acknowledgment of someone or something which goes beyond the intellect and the emotions to change the nature of our lives, providing a sense of purpose and direction which we would otherwise lack. It explains how we came into being and why we are here, as well as connects us to a power and purpose greater than ourselves.

In this unit, authors and religious texts explore their concepts of god, and ultimately, their faith. Some of their concepts are monotheistic, others animistic. Still others hold to an eternal universe, or deify mankind. Included are representatives from some of the major world religions: Buddhism, Judaism, Christianity, and Islam. Some responses are personal, others are more universal. A Jewish Rabbi, for example, reexamines his faith in light of the death of his son; a Jewish Christian composes some of the most profound words about god ever written. A different perspective comes from the polytheistic Aztecs and Hopis who reveal a world far removed from traditional thought. Throughout these readings grapple with the difficult questions Emily Dickinson raises. Many of them come toward the answer she suggests. When faced with the question, "Does god exist?" Dickinson answers:

Each life converges to some centre
Expressed or still
Exists in every human nature
A goal, …

This center is reached by faith, whether it is in one god or in many.

THINK ABOUT IT

1. What are the different forms faith has taken?
2. Every society, past or present, has believed in a supreme being. Why do people feel they need a god in their lives?

TALK ABOUT IT

3. What other concepts of God exist in the world (other than those mentioned in the introduction)?
4. Why do some people choose not to believe in a supreme being?

WRITE ABOUT IT

5. Describe a famous person, past or present, whom you feel demonstrates a strong belief in god. How did that person show his or her faith?
6. What is the basis for your belief or disbelief in god?

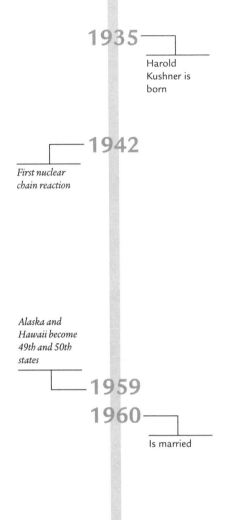

1935 — Harold Kushner is born

1942 — First nuclear chain reaction

Alaska and Hawaii become 49th and 50th states
1959
1960 — Is married

World Trade Center completed
1974

Writes *When Bad Things Happen to Good People*
1980

Beatle John Lennon murdered
1983

Writes *Who Needs God*
1989

HAROLD KUSHNER

When Bad Things Happen to Good People

Harold Samuel Kushner was born April 3, 1935, in Brooklyn, New York. He earned a B.A. and M.A. at Columbia University and an M.H.L. and D.H.L. from Jewish Theological Seminary. Kushner served as Assistant Rabbi from 1962–66 at the Temple Israel in New York and Rabbi at the Temple Israel in Natick, Massachusetts from 1966–90. He also served as a First Lieutenant in the Chaplin Corps from 1960-62. He was married in 1960 and had two children, Aaron (deceased) and Ariel Ann.

Rabbi Kushner poses some difficult questions about the nature of god and the importance of religion in everyday life in his best selling books, *When Children Ask About God* and *Who Needs God*. His best-selling book, *When Bad Things Happen to Good People,* introduces us to his own personal tragedy and suffering, and provides practical guidance for those in grief. Aaron, Kushner's oldest child, suffered from progeria, a disease that causes rapid aging and early death for its victims. Aaron died five days before his fourteenth birthday. Rabbi Kushner questioned how a fair and loving god could allow his son to suffer the injustice of inexplicable misfortune. If god is omnipotent (all powerful) and good, why doesn't he prevent human tragedy? Is it possible that God is powerless to prevent human suffering?

IN A SENSE, I have been writing this book for fifteen years. From the day I heard the word "progeria" and was told what it meant, I knew that I would one day have to face Aaron's declining and dying. And I knew that, after he died, I would feel the need to write a book, sharing with others the story of how we managed to go on believing in God and in the world after we had been hurt. I didn't know what I would call the book, and I wasn't to-

tally sure what I would say. But I knew that the page after the title page would carry a dedication to Aaron. I could visualize the dedication to him, and under it, in my mind's eye, I could see the quotation from the Bible, the words of King David after the death of his son: "Absalom, my son! Would that I had died instead of you!"

Then one day, a year and a half after Aaron's death, I realized that I was visualizing that page differently in my imagination. Now instead of the passage in which David wishes he were dead and his son alive, I saw in my mind's eye the words of David after the death of an earlier child, the passage that I have in fact used in part on the dedication page of this book:

> When David saw the servants whispering, he said to them, Is the child dead? And they said, He is ⌐ ead. And David rose and washed and changed his clothing and asked that food be set before him, and he ate. The servants said to him, What is this that you are doing? You fasted and wept for the child when he was alive, and now that he is dead, you get up and eat! And David said: While the child was yet alive, I fasted and wept, for I said, Who knows whether the Lord will be gracious to me and the child will live. But now that he is dead, why should I fast? Can I bring him back again? I shall go to him; but he will not return to me. (11 Samuel 12:19–23)

I knew then that the time had come for me to write my book. I had gone beyond self-pity to the point of facing and accepting my son's death. A book telling people how much I hurt would not do anyone any good. This had to be a book that would affirm life. It would have to say that no one ever promised us a life free from pain and disappointment. The most anyone promised us was that we would not be alone in our pain, and that we would be able to draw upon a source outside ourselves for the strength and courage we would need to survive life's tragedies and life's unfairness.

I am a more sensitive person, a more effective pastor, a more sympathetic counselor because of Aaron's life and death than I would ever have been without it. And I would give up all of those gains in a second if I could

have my son back. If I could choose, I would forego all the spiritual growth and depth which has come my way because of our experiences, and be what I was fifteen years ago, an average rabbi, an indifferent counselor, helping some people and unable to help others, and the father of a bright, happy boy. But I cannot choose.

I believe in God. But I do not believe the same things about Him that I did years ago, when I was growing up or when I was a theological student. I recognize His limitations. He is limited in what He can do by laws of nature and by the evolution of human nature and human moral freedom. I no longer hold God responsible for illnesses, accidents, and natural disasters, because I realize that I gain little and I lose so much when I blame God for those things. I can worship a God who hates suffering but cannot eliminate it, more easily than I can worship a God who chooses to make children suffer and die, for whatever exalted reason. Some years ago, when the "death of God" theology was a fad, I remember seeing a bumper sticker that read "My God is not dead; sorry about yours." I guess my bumper sticker reads "My God is not cruel; sorry about yours."

God does not cause our misfortunes. Some are caused by bad luck, some are caused by bad people, and some are simply an inevitable consequence of our being human and being mortal, living in a world of inflexible natural laws. The painful things that happen to us are not punishments for our misbehavior, nor are they in any way part of some grand design on God's part. Because the tragedy is not God's will, we need not feel hurt or betrayed by God when tragedy strikes. We can turn to Him for help in overcoming it, precisely because we can tell ourselves that God is as outraged by it as we are.

"Does that mean that my suffering has no meaning?" That is the most significant challenge that can be offered to the point of view I have been advocating in this book. We could bear nearly any pain or disappointment if we thought there was a reason behind it, a purpose to it. But even a lesser burden becomes too much for us if we feel it makes no sense: patients in a veterans' hospital who have been seriously wounded in combat have an easier time adjusting to their injuries than do patients with exactly the same injury sustained while fooling around on a basketball court or a swimming pool, because they can tell themselves that their suffering at least was in a good cause. Parents who can convince themselves that there is some purpose somewhere served by their child's handicap can accept it better for the same reason.

Do you remember the biblical story, in chapter 32 of Exodus, about Moses, how, when he came down from Mount Sinai and saw the Israelites worshipping the golden calf, he threw down the tablets of the Ten Commandments so that they shattered? There is a Jewish legend that tells us that while Moses was climbing down the mountain with the two stone tablets on which God had written the Ten Commandments, he had no trouble carrying them although they were large, heavy slabs of stone and the path was steep. After all, though they were heavy, they had been inscribed by God and were precious to him. But when Moses came upon the people dancing around the golden calf, the legend goes, the words disappeared from the stone. They were just blank stones again. And now they became too heavy for him to hold on to.

We could bear any burden if we thought there was a meaning to what we were doing. Have I made it harder for people to accept their illnesses, their misfortunes, their family tragedies by telling them that they are not sent by God as part of some master plan of His?

Let me suggest that the bad things that happen to us in our lives do not have a meaning when they happen to us. They do not happen for any good reason which would cause us to accept them willingly. But we can give them a meaning. We can redeem these tragedies from senselessness by imposing meaning on them. The question we should be asking is not, "Why did this happen to me? What did I do to deserve this?" That is really an unanswerable, pointless question. A better question would be "Now that this has happened to me, what am I going to do about it?"

Martin Gray, a survivor of the Warsaw Ghetto and the Holocaust, writes of his life in a book called *For Those I Loved.* He tells how, after the Holocaust, he rebuilt his life, became successful, married, and raised a family. Life seemed good after the horrors of the concentration camp. Then one day, his wife and children were killed when a forest fire ravaged their home in the south of France. Gray was distraught, pushed almost to the breaking point by this added tragedy. People urged him to demand an inquiry into what caused the fire, but instead he chose to put his resources into a movement to protect nature from future fires. He explained that an inquiry, an investigation, would focus only on the past, on issues of pain and sorrow and blame. He wanted to focus on the future. An inquiry would set him against other people — "was someone negligent? whose fault was it?" — and being against other people, setting out to find a villain, accusing other people of being responsible for your misery, only makes a lonely person lonelier. Life, he concluded, has to be lived for

something, not just against something.

We too need to get over the questions that focus on the past and on the pain — "why did this happen to me?" — and ask instead the question which opens doors to the future: "Now that this has happened, what shall I do about it?"

Let me once again cite Dorothee Soelle, the German theologian whom we quoted in Chapter 5, asking whose side we thought God was on in the concentration camps, the murderers' side or the victims' side. Soelle, in her book *Suffering*, suggests that "the most important question we can ask about suffering is whom it serves. Does our suffering serve God or the devil, the cause of becoming alive or being morally paralyzed?" Not "where does the tragedy come from?" but "where does it lead?" is the issue on which Soelle would have us focus. In this context she speaks of "the devil's martyrs." What does she mean by that phrase? We are familiar with the idea that various religions honor the memories of martyrs for God, people who died in such a way as to bear witness to their faith. By remembering their faith in the face of death, our own faith is strengthened. Such people are God's martyrs.

But the forces of despair and disbelief have their martyrs too, people whose death weakens other people's faith in God and in His world. If the death of an elderly woman in Auschwitz or of a child in a hospital ward leaves us doubting God and less able to affirm the world's goodness, then that woman and that child become "the devil's martyrs," witnesses against God, against the meaningfulness of a moral life, rather than witnesses in favor. But (and this is Soelle's most important point) it is not the circumstances of their death that makes them witnesses for or against God. It is our reaction to their death.

The facts of life and death are neutral. We, by our responses, give suffering either a positive or a negative meaning. Illnesses, accidents, human tragedies kill people. But they do not necessarily kill life or faith. If the death and suffering of someone we love makes us bitter, jealous, against all religion, and incapable of happiness, we turn the person who died into one of the "devil's martyrs." If suffering and death in someone close to us bring us to explore the limits of our capacity for strength and love and cheerfulness, if it leads us to discover sources of consolation we never knew before, then we make the person into a witness for the affirmation of life rather than its rejection.

This means, Soelle suggests, that there is one thing we can still do for those we loved and lost. We could not keep them alive. Perhaps we could not even significantly lessen their pain. But the one crucial thing we can do for them after their death is to let them be witnesses for God and for life, rather than, by our despair and loss of faith, making them "the devil's martyrs." The dead depend on us for their redemption and their immortality.

Soelle's words make it clear how we can act positively in the face of tragedy. But what about God's role? If God does not cause the bad things that happen to good people, and if He cannot prevent them, what good is He at all?

First of all, God has created a world in which many more good things than bad things happen. We find life's disasters upsetting not only because they are painful but because they are exceptional. Most people wake up on most days feeling good. Most illnesses are curable. Most airplanes take off and land safely. Most of the time, when we send our children out to play, they come home safely. The accident, the robbery, the inoperable tumor are life-shattering exceptions, but they are very rare exceptions. When you have been hurt by life, it may be hard to keep that in mind. When you are standing very close to a large object, all you can see is the object. Only by stepping back from it can you also see the rest of its setting around it. When we are stunned by some tragedy, we can only see and feel the tragedy. Only with time and distance can we see the tragedy in the context of a whole life and a whole world. In the Jewish tradition, the special prayer known as the Mourners' Kaddish is not about death, but about life, and it praises God for having created a basically good and livable world. By reciting that prayer, the mourner is reminded of all that is good and worth living for. There is a crucial difference between denying the tragedy, insisting that everything is for the best, and seeing the tragedy in the context of a whole life, keeping one's eye and mind on what has enriched you and not only on what you have lost.

How does God make a difference in our lives if He neither kills nor cures? God inspires people to help other people who have been hurt by life, and by helping them, they protect them from the danger of feeling alone, abandoned, or judged. God makes some people want to become doctors and nurses, to spend days and nights of self-sacrificing concern with an intensity for which no money can compensate, in the effort to sustain life and alleviate pain. God moves people to want to be medical researchers, to focus their intelligence and energy on the causes and possible cures for some of life's tragedies. When I was a boy, early summer was the most pleasant weather of the year in New York City, but it was a time of dread for young families because of the fear of a polio epidemic. But human beings used their God-given intelligence to eliminate that fear. Throughout human history, there have been plagues and epidemics that wiped out whole cities. People felt that they had to have six or eight children so that some at least would survive to adulthood. Human intelligence has come to understand more about the natural laws concerning sanitation, germs, immunization, antibiotics, and has succeeded in eliminating many of those scourges.

God, who neither causes nor prevents tragedies, helps by inspiring people to help. As a nineteenth-century Hasidic rabbi once put it, "human beings are God's language." God shows His opposition to cancer and birth defects, not by eliminating them or making them happen only to bad people (He can't do that), but by summoning forth friends and neighbors to ease the burden and to fill the emptiness. We were sustained in Aaron's illness by people who made a point of showing that they cared and understood: the man who made Aaron a scaled down tennis racquet suitable to his size, and the woman who gave him a small handmade violin that was a family heirloom; the friend who got him a baseball autographed by the Red Sox, and the children who overlooked his appearance and physical limitations to play stickball with him in the backyard, and who wouldn't let him get away with anything special. People like that were "God's language," His way of telling our family that we were not alone, not cast off.

In the same way, I firmly believe that Aaron served God's purposes, not by being sick or strange-looking (there was no reason why God should have wanted that), but by facing up so bravely to his illness and to the problems caused by his appearance. I know that his friends and schoolmates were affected by his courage and by the way he managed to live a full life despite his limitations. And I know that people who knew our family were moved to handle the difficult times of their own lives with more hope and courage when they saw our example. I take these as instances of God moving people here on earth to help other people in need.

And finally, to the person who asks "what good is God? Who needs religion, if these things happen to good people and bad people alike?" I would say that God may not prevent the calamity, but He gives us the strength and the perseverance to overcome it. Where else do we get these qualities which we did not have before? The heart attack which slows down a forty-six-year-old businessman does not come from God, but the determination to change his lifestyle, to stop smoking, to care less about expanding his business and care more about spending time with his family, because his eyes have been opened to what is truly important to him — those things come from God. God does not stand for heart attacks; those are nature's responses to the body's being overstressed. But God does stand for self-discipline and for being part of a family.

The flood that devastates a town is not an "act of God," even if the insurance companies find it useful to call it that. But the efforts people make to save lives, risking their own lives for a person who might be a total stranger to them, and the determination to rebuild their community after the flood waters have receded, do qualify as acts of God.

When a person is dying of cancer, I do not hold God responsible for the cancer or for the pain he feels. They have other causes. But I have seen God give such people the strength to take each day as it comes, to be grateful for a day full of sunshine or one in which they are relatively free of pain.

When people who were never particularly strong become strong in the face of adversity, when people who tended to think only of themselves become unselfish and heroic in an emergency, I have to ask myself where they got these qualities which they would freely admit they did not have before. My answer is that this is one of the ways in which God helps us when we suffer beyond the limits of our own strength.

Life is not fair. The wrong people get sick and the wrong people get robbed and the wrong people get killed in wars and in accidents. Some people see life's unfairness and decide, "There is no God; the world is nothing but chaos." Others see the same unfairness and ask themselves, "Where do I get my sense of what is fair and what is unfair? Where do I get my sense of outrage and indignation, my instinctive response of sympathy when I read in the paper about a total stranger who has been hurt by life? Don't I get these things from God? Doesn't He plant in me a little bit of His own divine outrage at injustice and oppression, just as He did for the prophets of the Bible? Isn't my feeling of compassion for the afflicted just a reflection of the compassion He feels when He sees the suffering of His creatures?" Our responding to life's unfairness with sympathy and with righteous indignation, God's compassion and God's anger working through us, may be the surest proof of all of God's reality.

Religion alone can affirm the afflicted person's sense of self-worth. Science can describe what has happened to a person; only religion can call it a tragedy. Only the voice of religion, when it frees itself from the need to defend and justify God for all that happens, can say to the afflicted person, "You are a good person, and you deserve better. Let me come and sit with you so that you will know that you are not alone."

None of us can avoid the problem of why bad things happen to good people. Sooner or later, each of us finds himself playing one of the roles in the story of Job, whether as victim of tragedy, as a member of the family, or as a friend-comforter. The questions never change; the search for a satisfying answer continues.

In our generation, the gifted poet Archibald MacLeish has given us his version of the job story in a modern setting. The first half of his poetic drama *J.B.* retells the familiar story. J.B., the Job-figure, is a successful businessman surrounded by an attractive, loving family. Then one by one, his children die. His business fails, his health fails. Finally, his whole city and much of the world are destroyed in a nuclear war.

Three friends come to "comfort" J.B., just as in the biblical story, and once again their words are more self-serving than comforting. In MacLeish's version, the first comforter is a Marxist who assures J.B. that none of his suffering is his fault. He just had the bad luck to be a member of the wrong economic class at the wrong time. He was a capitalist at the time of capitalism's decline. Had he lived the same life in another century, he would not have been punished. He is not suffering for any of his own sins. He just got in the way of the steamroller of historical necessity. J.B. is not comforted by this view. It takes his own personal tragedy too lightly, by seeing him only as a member of a certain class.

The second comforter is a psychiatrist. J.B. is not guilty, he tells him, because there is no such thing as guilt. Now that we understand what makes human beings tick, we know that we do not choose. We only think we choose. Really, we simply respond to instinct. We do not act; we are acted upon. Therefore we have no responsibility, and no guilt.

J.B. answers that such a solution, describing him as the passive victim of blind instincts, robs him of his humanity. "I'd rather suffer every unspeakable suffering God sends, knowing that it was … I that acted, I that chose, than wash my hands with yours in that defiling innocence."

The third and last comforter is a clergyman. When J.B. asks him for what sin he is being punished so harshly, he replies "Your sin is simple. You were born a man. What is your fault? Man's heart is evil. What you have done? Man's will is evil." J.B. is a sinner worthy of punishment not because of anything specific he has done, but because he is a human being, and human beings are inevitably imperfect and sinful. J.B. answers him, "Yours is the cruelest comfort of them all, making the Creator of the Universe the miscreator of mankind, a party to the crimes He punishes." J.B. cannot turn for help and comfort to a God who is described as making man imperfect and then punishing him for his imperfection.

Having rejected the explanations of the three comforters, J.B. turns to God Himself, and as in the Bible, God answers, overwhelming J.B. with His awesomeness, quoting lines directly from the biblical speech out of the whirlwind.

Up to this point, MacLeish has given us the biblical story of Job in a modern setting. His ending, however, is radically different. In the Bible, the story ends with God rewarding Job for having put up with so much suffering, and gives him new health, new wealth, and new children. In the play, there are no heavenly rewards in the closing scene. Instead, J.B. goes back to his wife, and they prepare to go on living together and building a new family. Their love, not God's generosity, will provide the new children to replace the ones who died.

J.B. forgives God and commits himself to going on living. His wife says to him, "You wanted justice, didn't you? There isn't any ... there is only love." The two narrators, representing the perspectives of God and Satan, are baffled. How could a person who has suffered so much in life want more life? "Who plays the hero, God or him? Is God to be forgiven?" "Isn't He? Job was innocent, you may remember." MacLeish's Job answers the problem of human suffering, not with theology or psychology, but by choosing to go on living and creating new life. He forgives God for not making a more just universe, and decides to take it as it is. He stops looking for justice, for fairness in the world, and looks for love instead.

In the play's moving last lines, Job's wife says:

The candles in churches are out,
The stars have gone out in the sky.
Blow on the coal of the heart
And we'll see by and by ....

The world is a cold, unfair place in which everything they held precious has been destroyed. But instead of giving up on this unfair world and life, instead of looking outward, to churches or to nature, for answers, they look inward to their own capacities for loving. "Blow on the coal of the heart" for what little light and warmth we will be able to muster to sustain us.

In *Dimensions of Job*, edited by Nahum N. Glatzer, MacLeish has written an essay explaining what he was trying to say in the ending of his Job-play. "Man depends on God for all things; God depends on man for one. Without Man's love, God does not exist as God, only as creator, and love is the one thing no one, not even God Himself, can command. It is a free gift, or it is nothing. And it is most itself, most free, when it is offered in spite of suffering, of injustice, and of death." We do not love God because He is perfect. We do not love Him be-

cause He protects us from all harm and keeps evil things from happening to us. We do not love Him because we are afraid of Him, or because He will hurt us if we turn our back on Him. We love Him because He is God, because He is the author of all the beauty and the order around us, the source of our strength and the hope and courage within us, and of other people's strength and hope and courage with which we are helped in our time of need. We love Him because He is the best part of ourselves and of our world. That is what it means to love. Love is not the admiration of perfection, but the acceptance of an imperfect person with all his imperfections, because loving and accepting him makes us better and stronger.

Is there an answer to the question of why bad things happen to good people? That depends on what we mean by "answer." If we mean "is there an explanation which will make sense of it all?" — why is there cancer in the world? Why did my father get cancer? Why did the plane crash? Why did my child die? — then there is probably no satisfying answer.

We can offer learned explanations, but in the end, when we have covered all the squares on the game board and are feeling very proud of our cleverness, the pain and the anguish and the sense of unfairness will still be there.

But the word "answer" can mean "response" as well as "explanation," and in that sense, there may well be a satisfying answer to the tragedies in our lives. The response would be Job's response in MacLeish's version of the biblical story — to forgive the world for not being perfect, to forgive God for not making a better world, to reach out to the people around us, and to go on living despite it all.

In the final analysis, the question of why bad things happen to good people translates itself into some very

different questions, no longer asking why something happened, but asking how we will respond, what we intend to do now that it has happened.

Are you capable of forgiving and accepting in love a world which has disappointed you by not being perfect, a world in which there is so much unfairness and cruelty, disease and crime, earthquake and accident? Can you forgive its imperfections and love it because it is capable of containing great beauty and goodness, and because it is the only world we have?

Are you capable of forgiving and loving the people around you, even if they have hurt you and let you down by not being perfect? Can you forgive them and love them, because there aren't any perfect people around, and because the penalty for not being able to love imperfect people is condemning oneself to loneliness?

Are you capable of forgiving and loving God even when you have found out that He is not perfect, even when He has let you down and disappointed you by permitting bad luck and sickness and cruelty in His world, and permitting some of those things to happen to you? Can you learn to love and forgive Him despite His limitations, as Job does, and as you once learned to forgive and love your parents even though they were not as wise, as strong, or as perfect as you needed them to be?

And if you can do these things, will you be able to recognize that the ability to forgive and the ability to love are the weapons God has given us to enable us to live fully, bravely, and meaningfully in this less-than-perfect world?

I think of Aaron and all that his life taught me, and I realize how much I have lost and how much I have gained. Yesterday seems less painful, and I am not afraid of tomorrow.

THINK ABOUT IT

1. According to Kushner, what purpose does religion serve?
2. Why did Kushner change his beliefs about God after his son died?

TALK ABOUT IT

3. How is one's view of God and suffering based on cultural or ethnic conditioning?
4. Should personal suffering alter one's view about God? Why or why not?

WRITE ABOUT IT

5. Name someone who has suffered a tragedy like Rabbi Kushner's. Describe how that person coped with the tragedy.
6. Describe a tragedy you have experienced. Did your suffering change any of your beliefs about God?

READ MORE ABOUT IT

Kushner, Harold. *When Bad Things Happen to Good People.* New York: Avon Books, 1983.

Kushner, Harold. *When Children Ask About God.* New York: Schocken Books, 1976.

kushner, Harold. *Who Needs God.* New York: Summit Books, 1989.

GAUTAMA BUDDHA

The Sermon on the Four Noble Truths

Siddhartha Gautama was born to royal parents in the year 563 B.C.E. in what is contemporary Nepal, near the Indian border. At his birth, his father inquired of fortunetellers who told him that his son was destined for greatness in one of two areas, either political or religious. Intent to have his son succeed as a great political leader, the king arranged for Siddhartha's training and care. All arrangements were made to protect the young prince from encountering any of the difficulties of life which would dissuade him from a political career, things like disease, old age, and death. The gods, however, had other plans for the prince, and on several trips outside the palace, Siddhartha experienced what are known as the Four Passing Sights. He encountered a sick man, an old man, a corpse, and finally a monk. Aware of these mysteries of life, he left the palace to seek answers for these questions.

Siddhartha spent the next six years in the woods, living a life of severe asceticism with five traveling monks who joined him. Near death from extreme hunger and privation, he made a serious decision. He had not found the answers in the luxury of the palace, nor had he found them in the life of severe asceticism. There must be a middle way. Thus, Siddhartha devoted his life to a less severe form of meditation. One day, he sat down under a bodhi tree and vowed never to rise again until he had discovered the truth. After many temptations to give up, Siddhartha became the Buddha, literally "one who woke up" or the "enlightened one." After three days of intense meditation on these insights, the Buddha arose and went to the Deer Park, just outside the city of Benares. There he delivered his first sermon to the five monks who had been with him before. This selection is an excerpt from that sermon.

REVERENCE TO THE Blessed One, the Holy One, the Fully Enlightened One!

Thus have I heard. The Blessed One was once staying at Benares, at the hermitage called Migadaya. The Blessed One addressed the company of the five monks, and said, "There are two extremes, O monks, which the man who has given up the world ought not to follow. The first is the habitual practice of those things whose attraction depends upon the passions. This is especially true of sensuality. It is a low and pagan way, unworthy, unprofitable, and fit only for the worldly minded. Second is the habitual practice of asceticism, which

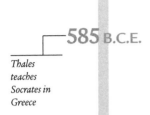

585 B.C.E.

Thales teaches Socrates in Greece

Siddhartha Guatama born

563 B.C.E.

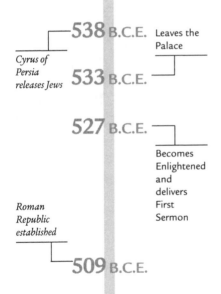

538 B.C.E. Leaves the Palace

Cyrus of Persia releases Jews 533 B.C.E.

527 B.C.E.

Becomes Enlightened and delivers First Sermon

Roman Republic established

509 B.C.E.

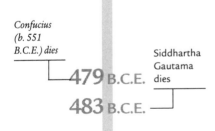

Confucius (b. 551 B.C.E.) dies

Siddhartha Gautama dies

479 B.C.E.

483 B.C.E.

is painful, unworthy, and unprofitable.

"There is a middle path, O monks, avoiding these two extremes, discovered by the Tathagata. This path opens the eyes, bestows understanding, leads to peace of mind, to the higher wisdom, to full enlightenment, and to Nirvana! What is that middle path, O monks, avoiding these two extremes, discovered by the Tathagata, the path that opens the eyes, and bestows understanding, which leads to peace of mind, to the higher wisdom, to full enlightenment, to Nirvana? Truly, it is this Noble Eightfold Path, that is to say: Right views; Right aspirations; Right speech; Right conduct; Right livelihood; Right effort; Right mindfulness; and Right contemplation ....

"Now this, O monks, is the noble truth concerning suffering. Birth brings pain, decay is painful, disease is painful, death is painful. Union with the unpleasant is painful, painful is separation from the pleasant. Any craving that is unsatisfied, that too is painful. In brief, the five aggregates that spring from attachment, the conditions of individuality and their cause, are painful. This, O monks, is the noble truth concerning suffering.

"Now this, O monks, is the noble truth concerning the origin of suffering. Truly, it is the thirst or craving, causing the renewal of existence, accompanied by sensual delight, seeking satisfaction now here, now there. That is to say, it is the craving for the gratification of the passions, or the craving for a future life, or the craving for success in this present life. This, O monks, is the noble truth concerning the origin of suffering.

"Now this, O monks, is the noble truth concerning the destruction of suffering. Truly, it is the destruction, in which no passion remains, of this very thirst. It is the laying aside of, the getting rid of, the being free from, the harboring no longer of this

SEATED BUDDHA
16th Century, Thailand

thirst. This, O monks, is the noble truth concerning the destruction of suffering.

"Now this, O monks, is the noble truth concerning the way which leads to the destruction of sorrow. Truly, it is this Noble Eightfold Path ....

"As long, O monks, as my knowledge and insight were not quite clear regarding each of these Four Noble Truths in this triple order, in this twelvefold manner, I was uncertain whether I had attained to the full insight of that wisdom that is unsurpassed in the heavens or on earth, among the whole race of Samanas and Brahmins, or of gods or men. But as soon as my knowledge and insight were quite clear regarding each of these four noble truths, in this triple order, in this twelvefold manner, then I became certain that I had attained to the full insight of that wisdom that is unsurpassed in the heavens or on earth, among the whole race of Samanas and Brahmins, or of gods or men. Now this knowledge and this insight has arisen within me. The emancipation of my heart is immovable. This is my last existence. Now there will be no rebirth for me!"

Thus spoke the Blessed One. The five monks praised the words of the Blessed One and were glad. When the discourse had been uttered, there arose within the venerable Kondanna the eye of truth, spotless, and without a stain. He saw that whatever has an origin also inherently must end.

And when the royal chariot wheel of the truth had been set rolling by the Blessed One, the gods of the earth ... the attendant gods of the four great kings ... and the gods in the highest heaven gave forth a shout. They said, "In Benares, at the hermitage of the Migadaya, the supreme wheel of the empire of Truth has been set rolling by the Blessed One. That wheel can never be turned back by any

Samana or Brahmin, nor by any god, nor by any Brahma or Mara, not by anyone in the universe!" In an instant, a second, a moment, this sound went up to the world of Brahma. This great ten-thousand-world-system quaked and trembled and was shaken violently. An immeasurably bright light appeared in the universe, beyond even the power of the gods!

THINK ABOUT IT

1. What does the Buddha believe is the critical insight for those seeking true peace and happiness?
2. Does the Buddha's description of the causes of suffering correspond to any experiences you have had?

TALK ABOUT IT

3. What examples from today's news would support or disprove the Buddha's theory of suffering?
4. Why is there suffering in the world? Are the causes of suffering the same everywhere in the world?

WRITE ABOUT IT

5. Write a sermon to a group of people looking to find happiness in the world today.
6. How have you dealt with suffering in your own life?

READ MORE ABOUT IT

Novak, Philip. *The World's Wisdom.* San Francisco: HarperCollins Publishers, 1994.

Sharma, Arvind. *Our Religions.* San Francisco: HarperCollins Publishers, 1993.

Smith, Huston. *The World's Religions.* San Francisco: HarperCollins Publishers, 1991.

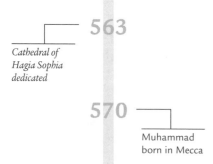

563

Cathedral of Hagia Sophia dedicated

570

Muhammad born in Mecca

The Koran

as revealed to Muhammad

One of the most common names in our world today is Muhammad, but the most famous person by that name was born in the city of Mecca in the year 570. His father died before he was born and his mother died when he was six. He was placed in the care of his grandfather and later his uncle until he married a wealthy widow and established his own household. While meditating privately in a cave in the year 610, Muhammad received a revelation through the angel Gabriel to call people to fidelity in the one God. He was to call people to *islam,* to surrender to the will of God. From rather humble beginnings, Islam has grown into a major religious tradition throughout the world.

The *Koran,* the sacred writings of Islam, are known as the standing miracle. While it is associated with Muhammad, it should not be seen as his work for he was illiterate. It is, instead, the recitation (the literal meaning of the word Koran) of the words of Allah (the name of God) to Muhammad. At first, the verses were memorized by those who heard them. Over the years, verses were written down on leaves and stones in a fragmentary way. The final collection and edition of the texts was not completed until twenty years after Muhammad's death. The style and language of the original Arabic text remains not only one of the great religious documents of the world, but also one of incomparable beauty and value as a literary text. Our selection is taken from Suras (chapters) 47, 55, and 56.

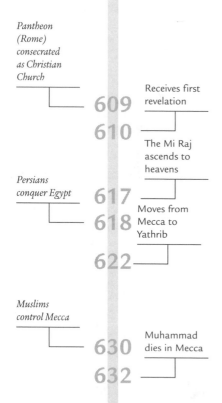

Pantheon (Rome) consecrated as Christian Church

Receives first revelation

609

610

The Mi Raj ascends to heavens

Persians conquer Egypt

617

618

Moves from Mecca to Yathrib

622

Muslims control Mecca

630

Muhammad dies in Mecca

632

GOD WILL BRING to nothing the deeds of those who disbelieve and debar others from His path. As for the faithful who do good works and believe in what is revealed to Muhammad — which is the Truth from their Lord — He will forgive them their sins and ennoble their state.

This, because the unbelievers follow falsehood, while the faithful follow the truth from their Lord. Thus God lays down for mankind their rules of conduct.

When you meet the unbelievers in the battlefield strike off their heads and, when you have laid them low, bind your captives firmly. Then grant them their freedom or take ransom from them, until War shall lay down her burdens.

Thus shall you do. Had God willed, He could Himself have punished them; but He has ordained it thus that He might test you, the one by the other.

As for those who are slain in the cause of God, He will not allow their works to perish. He will vouchsafe them guidance and ennoble their state; He will admit them to the Paradise He has made known to them.

Believers, if you help God, God will help you and make you strong.

But the unbelievers shall be consigned to perdition. He will bring their deeds to nothing. Because they have abhorred His revelations, He will frustrate their works.

Have they never journeyed through the land and seen what was the end of those who have gone before them? God destroyed them utterly. A similar fate awaits the unbelievers, because God is the protector of the faithful: because the unbelievers have no protector.

God will admit those who embrace the true Faith and do good works to gardens watered by running streams. The unbelievers take their fill of pleasure and eat as cattle eat: but the Fire shall be their home.

How many cities were mightier than your own city, which has cast you out![1] We destroyed them all, and there was none to help them.

Can he who follows the guidance of his Lord be compared to him who is led by his desires and whose foul deeds seem fair to him?

This is the Paradise which the righteous have been promised. Therein shall flow rivers of water undefiled, and rivers of milk for ever fresh; rivers of wine delectable to those that drink it, and rivers of clarified honey. They shall eat therein of every fruit and receive forgiveness from their Lord. Is this like the lot of those who shall abide in Hell for ever, and drink scalding water which will tear their bowels?

Some of them indeed listen to you, but no sooner do they leave your presence than they ask those endowed with knowledge: 'What did he say just now?' Such are the men whose hearts are sealed by God, and who follow their base desires.

As for those who follow the right path, He will increase their guidance and show them the way to righteousness.

Are they waiting for the Hour of Doom to overtake them unawares? Its portents have already come. How else will they be warned when it does overtake them?

Know that there is no deity but God. Implore Him to forgive your sins and to forgive the true believers, men and women. God knows your busy haunts and resting places.

The Merciful[2]

In the Name of God, the Compassionate, the Merciful

It is the Merciful who has taught the Koran.

He created man and taught him articulate speech. The sun and the moon pursue their ordered course. The plants and the trees bow down in adoration.

He raised the heaven on high and set the balance of all things, that you might not transgress that balance. Give just weight and full measure.

He laid the earth for His creatures, with all its fruits and blossom-bearing palm, chaff-covered grain and scented herbs. Which of your Lord's blessings would you[3] deny?

He created man from potter's clay, and the jinn from smokeless fire. Which of your Lord's blessings would you deny?

The Lord of the two easts[4] is He, and the Lord of the two wests. Which of your Lord's blessings would you deny?[5]

He has let loose the two oceans: they meet one another. Yet between them stands a barrier which they cannot overrun. Which of your Lord's blessings would you deny?

Pearls and corals come from both. Which of your Lord's blessings would you deny?

His are the ships that sail like mountains upon the ocean. Which of your Lord's blessings would you deny?

All that lives on earth is doomed to die. But the face of your Lord will abide for ever, in all its majesty and glory. Which of your Lord's blessings would you deny?

All who dwell in heaven and earth entreat Him. Each day some mighty task engages Him. Which of your Lord's blessings would you deny?

Mankind and jinn, We shall surely find the time to judge you! Which of your Lord's blessings would you deny?

Mankind and jinn, if you have power to penetrate the confines of heaven and earth, then penetrate them! But this you shall not do except with Our own authority. Which of your Lord's blessings would you deny?

Flames of fire shall be lashed at you, and molten brass. There shall be none to help you. Which of your Lord's blessings would you deny?

When the sky splits asunder, and reddens like a rose or stained leather (which of your Lord's blessings would you deny?), on that day neither man nor jinn will be asked about his sins. Which of your Lord's blessings would you deny?

The wrongdoers will be known by their looks; they shall be seized by their forelocks and their feet. Which of your Lord's blessings would you deny?

That is the Hell which the sinners deny. They shall wander between fire and water fiercely seething. Which of your Lord's blessings would you deny?

---

[1] Muhammad

[2] Compare this chapter with Psalm 126 of the Old Testament.

[3] The pronoun is in the dual number, the words being addressed to mankind and the jinn. This refrain is repeated no fewer than 31 times.

[4] The points at which the sun rises in summer and in winter.

[5] Salt water and fresh water.

But for those that fear the majesty of their Lord there are two gardens (which of your Lord's blessings would you deny?) planted with shady trees. Which of your Lord's blessings would you deny?

Each is watered by a flowing spring. Which of your Lord's blessings would you deny?

Each bears every kind of fruit in pairs. Which of your Lord's blessings would you deny?

They shall recline on couches lined with thick brocade, and within reach will hang the fruits of both gardens. Which of your Lord's blessings would you deny?

Therein are bashful virgins whom neither man nor jinn will have touched before. Which of your Lord's blessings would you deny?

Virgins as fair as corals and rubies. Which of your Lord's blessings would you deny?

Shall the reward of goodness be anything but good? Which of your Lord's blessings would you deny?

And beside these there shall be two other gardens (which of your Lord's blessings would you deny?) of darkest green. Which of your Lord's blessings would you deny?

A gushing fountain shall flow in each. Which of your Lord's blessings would you deny?

Each planted with fruit trees, the palm and the pomegranate. Which of your Lord's blessings would you deny?

In each there shall be virgins chaste and fair. Which of your Lord's blessings would you deny?

Dark-eyed virgins sheltered in their tents (which of your Lord's blessings would you deny?) whom neither man nor jinn will have touched before. Which of your Lord's blessings would you deny?

They shall recline on green cushions and fine carpets. Which of your Lord's blessings would you deny?

Blessed be the name of your Lord, the Lord of majesty and glory!

That Which Is Coming

In the Name of God, the Compassionate, the Merciful

When that which is coming comes – and no soul shall then deny its coming – some shall be abased and others exalted.

When the earth shakes and quivers, and the mountains crumble away and scatter abroad into fine dust, you shall be divided into three multitudes: those on the right (blessed shall be those on the right); those on the left (damned shall be those on the left); and those to the fore (foremost shall be those). Such are they that shall be brought near to their Lord in the gardens of delight: a whole multitude from the men of old, but only a few from the latter generations.

They shall recline on jewelled couches face to face, and there shall wait on them immortal youths with bowls and ewers and a cup of purest wine (that will neither pain their heads nor take away their reason); with fruits of their own choice and flesh of fowls that they relish. And theirs shall be the dark-eyed houris, chaste as hidden pearls: a guerdon for their deeds.

There they shall hear no idle talk, no sinful speech, but only the greeting, 'Peace! Peace!'

Those on the right hand – happy shall be those on the right hand! They shall recline on couches raised on high in the shade of thornless sidrs and clusters of talh[6] amidst gushing waters and abundant fruits, unforbidden, neverending.

We created the houris and made them virgins, loving companions for those on the right hand: a multitude from the men of old, and a multitude from the latter generations.

As for those on the left hand (wretched shall be those on the left hand!) they shall dwell amidst scorching winds and seething water: in the shade of pitch-black smoke, neither cool nor refreshing. For they have lived in comfort and persisted in the heinous sin,[7] saying: 'When we are once dead and turned to dust and bones, shall we be raised to life? And our forefathers, too?'

Say: 'Those of old, and those of the present age, shall be brought together on an appointed day. As for you sinners who deny the truth, you shall eat the fruit of the Zaqqum tree and fill your bellies with it. You shall drink scalding water: yet you shall drink it as the thirsty camel drinks.'

Such shall be their fare on the Day of Reckoning.

We created you: will you not believe then in Our power?

Behold the semen you discharge: did you create it, or We?

It was We that ordained death among you. Nothing can hinder Us from replacing you by others like yourselves or transforming you into beings you know nothing of.

You surely know of the First Creation. Why, then, do you not reflect? Consider the seeds you grow. Is it you that give them growth, or We? If We pleased, We could turn your harvest into chaff, so that, filled with wonderment, you would exclaim: 'We are laden with debts! Surely we have been robbed?'

Consider the water which you drink. Was it you that poured it from the cloud, or We? If We pleased, We could turn it bitter. Why, then, do you not give thanks?

---

6 Probably the banana fruit.

7 Idolatry

Observe the fire which you light,
Is it you that create its wood, or We?
We have made it a reminder for man,
and for the traveller a comfort.

Praise, then, the name of your Lord, the Supreme One. I swear by the shelter of the stars (a mighty oath, if you but knew it) that this is a glorious Koran, safeguarded in a book which none may touch except the purified; a revelation from the Lord of the Universe.

Would you scorn a scripture such as this, and earn your daily bread by denying it?

When under your very eyes a man's soul is about to leave him (We are nearer to him than you, although you cannot see Us), why do you not restore it, if you will not be judged hereafter? Answer this, if what you say be true!

Thus, if he is favoured, his lot will be repose and plenty, and a garden of delight. If he is one of those on the right hand, he will be greeted with, 'Peace be to you!' by those on the right hand.

But if he is an erring disbeliever, his welcome will be scalding water, and he will burn in Hell.

This is the indubitable truth. Praise, then, the name of your Lord, the Supreme One.

THINK ABOUT IT

1. What does the Koran tell us about the Islamic conception of God?
2. Are there similarities between the Islamic understanding of God and your own?

TALK ABOUT IT

3. What is the relationship between right action and judgment in the Koran? Does it still hold true today?
4. How does the description of paradise reflect Arabic culture? Does your description of heaven have a cultural basis?

WRITE ABOUT IT

5. Compare or contrast your concept of God's power to that written about in the Koran.
6. Describe the day of judgment in terms your friends can relate to.

READ MORE ABOUT IT

Abdalati, Hammudah. *Islam in Focus.* Indianapolis: American Trust Publications, 1993.

Mater, N. I. *Islam for Beginners.* New York: Writers & Readers, 1992.

Smith, Huston. *The World's Religions.* San Francisco: Harper Collins, 1991.

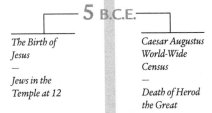

5 B.C.E.

The Birth of Jesus

—

Jews in the Temple at 12

Caesar Augustus World-Wide Census

—

Death of Herod the Great

Ministry of John the Baptist

Death, Burial. Resurrection

—

Ascension 40 days later

C.E. 26

C.E. 30

The Sermon on the Mount

The Sermon on the Mount was a message spoken by a Jewish carpenter from Nazareth, Israel, who claimed to be God. Jesus' sermon focuses on the issue of righteousness, or correct moral conduct. Jesus' thesis statement is, "For I say unto you, that except your righteousness shall exceed the righteousness of the scribes and Pharisees, you shall in no case enter into the kingdom of heaven." The Jewish religious leaders had an external righteousness based on observing the Laws of the Torah. But the righteousness Jesus described is a righteousness that begins internally, in the heart. Jesus felt that the Pharisees were concerned about minute details of the conduct, but neglected the major matter of character. He felt moral conduct flows out of character. The following outline will help the reader understand the Sermon on the Mount.

> Matt 5:1–16: What True Righteousness Is
> Matt. 5:17–20: How True Righteousness Comes
> Matt. 5:21–48: How Righteousness Works in Daily Life
> Matt. 6:1–18: Righteousness in Relation to Worship of God
> Matt. 6:19–34: Righteousness in Relation to Material Things
> Matt. 7:1–20: Righteousness in Relation to Other People

The Beatitudes

5 Now when he saw the crowds, he went up on a mountainside and sat down. His disciples came to him,[2] and he began to teach them, saying:

[3] "Blessed are the poor in spirit,
for theirs is the kingdom of heaven.

[4] Blessed are those who mourn,
for they will be comforted.

[5] Blessed are the meek,
for they will inherit the earth.

[6] Blessed are those who hunger and thirst for righteousness,
for they will be filled.

[7] Blessed are the merciful,
for they will be shown mercy.

[8] Blessed are the pure in heart,
for they will see God.

[9] Blessed are the peacemakers,
for they will be called sons of God.

[10] Blessed are those who are persecuted because of righteousness, for theirs is the kingdom of heaven.

[11] "Blessed are you when people insult you, persecute you and falsely say all kinds of evil against you because of me. [12] Rejoice and be glad, because great is your reward in heaven, for in the same way they persecuted the prophets who were before you.

Salt and Light

13 "You are the salt of the earth. But if the salt loses its saltiness, how can it be made salty again? It is no longer good for anything, except to be thrown out and trampled by men.

14 "You are the light of the world. A city on a hill cannot be hidden. 15 Neither do people light a lamp and put it under a bowl. Instead they put it on its stand, and it gives light to everyone in the house. 16 In the same way, let your light shine before men, that they may see your good deeds and praise your Father in heaven.

The Fulfillment of the Law

17 "Do not think that I have come to abolish the Law or the Prophets; I have not come to abolish them but to fulfill them. 18 I tell you the truth, until heaven and earth disappear, not the smallest letter, not the least stroke of a pen, will by any means disappear from the Law until everything is accomplished. 19 Anyone who breaks one of the least of these commandments and teaches others to do the same will be called least in the kingdom of heaven, but whoever practices and teaches these commands will be called great in the kingdom of heaven. 20 For I tell you that unless your righteousness surpasses that of the Pharisees and the teachers of the law, you will certainly not enter the kingdom of heaven.

Murder

21 "You have heard that it was said to the people long ago, 'Do not murder,ᵃ and anyone who murders will be subject to judgment 22 But I tell you that anyone who is angry with his brotherᵇ will be subject to judgment. Again, anyone who says to his brother, 'Raca,'ᶜ is answerable to the Sanhedrin. But anyone who says, 'You fool!' will be in danger of the fire of hell.

23 "Therefore if you are offering your gift at the altar and there remember that your brother has something against you, 24 leave your gift there in front of the altar. First go and be reconciled to your brother; then come and offer your gift.

25 "Settle matters quickly with your adversary who is taking you to court. Do it while you are still with him on the way, or he may hand you over to the judge, and the judge may hand you over to the officer, and you may be thrown into prison. 26 I tell you the truth, you will not get out until you have paid the last penny.

Adultery

27 "You have heard that it was said, 'Do not commit adultery.'ᵈ 28 But I tell you that anyone who looks at a woman lustfully has already committed adultery with her in his heart. 29 If your right eye causes you to sin, gouge it out and throw it away. It is better for you to lose one part of your body than for your whole body to be thrown into hell. 30 And if your right hand causes you to sin, cut it off and throw it away. It is better for you to lose one part of your body than for your whole body to go into hell.

31 "It has been said, 'Anyone who divorces his wife must give her a certificate of divorce.'ᵉ 32 But I tell you that anyone who divorces his wife, except for marital unfaithfulness, causes her to commit adultery, and anyone who marries a woman so divorced commits adultery.

Oaths

33 "Again, you have heard that it was said to the people long ago, 'Do not break your oath, but keep the oaths you have made to the Lord.' 34 But I tell you, Do not swear at all: either by heaven, for it is God's throne; 35 or by the earth, for it is his footstool; or by Jerusalem, for it is the city of the great King. 36 And do not swear by your head, for you cannot make even one hair white or black. 37 Simply let your 'Yes' be 'Yes,' and your 'No,' 'No'; anything beyond this comes from the evil one.

An Eye for an Eye

38 "You have heard that it was said, 'An eye for an eye, and a tooth for a tooth.'ᶠ 39 But I tell you, Do not resist an evil person. If someone strikes you on the right cheek, turn to him the other also. 40 And if someone wants to sue you and take your tunic, let him have your cloak as well. 41 If someone forces you to go one mile, go with him two miles. 42 Give to the one who asks you, and do not turn away from the one who wants to borrow from you.

Love for Enemies

43 "You have heard that it was said, 'Love your neighbor,ᵍ and hate your enemy.' 44 But I tell you, Love your enemiesʰ and pray for those who persecute you, 45 that you may be sons of your Father in heaven. He causes his sun to rise on the evil and the

---

a. Exodus 20:13.

b. Some MSS add *without cause*.

c. An Aramaic term of contempt.

d. Exodus 20:13.

e. Deut. 24:1.

f. Exodus 21:24; Lev. 24:20; Deut. 19:21.

g. Lev. 19:18.

h. Some late MSS add *bless those who curse you, do good to those who hate you*.

good, and sends rain on the righteous and the unrighteous. 46 If you love those who love you, what reward will you get? Are not even the tax collectors doing that? 47 And if you greet only your brothers, what are you doing more than others? Do not even pagans do that? 48 Be perfect, therefore, as your heavenly Father is perfect.

Giving to the Needy

6 "Be careful not to do your 'acts of righteousness' before men, to be seen by them. If you do, you will have no reward from your Father in heaven.

2 "So when you give to the needy, do not announce it with trumpets, as the hypocrites do in the synagogues and on the streets, to be honored by men. I tell you the truth, they have received their reward in full. 3 But when you give to the needy, do not let your left hand know what your right hand is doing, 4 so that your giving may be in secret. Then your Father, who sees what is done in secret, will reward you.

Prayer

5 "When you pray, do not be like the hypocrites, for they love to pray standing in the synagogues and on the street corners to be seen by men. I tell you the truth, they have received their reward in full. 6 When you pray, go into your room, close the door and pray to your Father, who is unseen. Then your Father, who sees what is done in secret, will reward you. 7 And when you pray, do not keep on babbling like pagans, for they think they will be heard because of their many words. 8 Do not be like them, for your Father knows what you need before you ask him.

9 "This is how you should pray:
'Our Father in heaven,
hallowed be your name,
10 your kingdom come,
your will be done
on earth as it is in heaven.
11 Give us today our daily bread.
12 Forgive us our debts,
as we also have forgiven our debtors.
13 And lead us not into temptation,
but deliver us from the evil one.i
14 For if you forgive men when they sin against you, your heavenly Father will also forgive you. 15 But if you do not forgive men their sins, your Father will not forgive your sins.

Fasting

16 "When you fast, do not look somber as the hypocrites do, for they disfigure their faces to show men they are fasting. I tell you the truth, they have received their reward in full. 17 But when you fast, put oil on your head and wash your face, 18 so that it will not be obvious to men that you are fasting, but only to your Father, who is unseen; and your Father, who sees what is done in secret, will reward you.

Treasures in Heaven

19 "Do not store up for yourselves treasures on earth, where moth and rust destroy, and where thieves break in and steal. 20 But store up for yourselves treasures in heaven, where moth and rust do not destroy, and where thieves do not break in and steal. 21 For where your treasure is, there your heart will be also.

22 "The eye is the lamp of the body. If your eyes are good, your whole body will be full of light. 23 But if your eyes are bad, your whole body will be full of darkness. If then the light within you is darkness, how great is that darkness!

24 "No one can serve two masters. Either he will hate the one and love the other, or he will be devoted to the one and despise the other. You cannot serve both God and Money.

Do Not Worry

25 "Therefore I tell you, do not worry about your life, what you will eat or drink; or about your body, what you will wear. Is not life more important than food, and the body more important than clothes? 26 Look at the birds of the air; they do not sow or reap or store away in barns, and yet your heavenly Father feeds them. Are you not much more valuable than they? 27 Who of you by worrying can add a single hour to his life?j

28 "And why do you worry about clothes? See how the lilies of the field grow. They do not labor or spin. 29 Yet I tell you that not even Solomon in all his splendor was dressed like one of these. 30 If that is how God clothes the grass of the field, which is here today and tomorrow is thrown into the fire, will he not much more clothe you, you of little faith? 31 So do not worry, saying, 'What shall we eat?' or 'What shall we drink?' or 'What shall we wear?', 32 For the pagans run after all these things, and your heavenly Father knows that you need them. 33 But seek first his kingdom and his righteousness, and all these things will be given to you as well. 34 Therefore do not worry about to-

---

i. Or from evil. Some late MSS add *for yours is the kingdom and the power and the glory forever. Amen.*

j. Or *Single cubit to his height*

morrow, for tomorrow will worry about itself. Each day has enough trouble of its own.

Judging Others

7 "Do not judge, or you too will be judged. ²For in the same way you judge others, you will be judged, and with the measure you use, it will be measured to you

3 "Why do you look at the speck of sawdust in your brother's eye and pay no attention to the plank in your own eye? ⁴ How can you say to your brother, 'Let me take the speck out of your eye,' when all the time there is a plank in your own eye? ⁵ You hypocrite, first take the plank out of your own eye, and then you will see clearly to remove the speck from your brother's eye.

6 "Do not give dogs what is sacred; do not throw your pearls to pigs. If you do, they may trample them under their feet, and then turn and tear you to pieces.

Ask, Seek, Knock

7 "Ask and it will be given to you; seek and you will find; knock and the door will be opened to you. ⁸ For everyone who asks receives; he who seeks finds; and to him who knocks, the door will be opened.

9 "Which of you, if his son asks for bread, will give him a stone? ¹⁰ Or if he asks for a fish, will give him a snake? ¹¹ If you, then, though you are evil, know how to give good gifts to your children, how much more will your Father in heaven give good gifts to those who ask him! ¹² In everything do to others what you would have them do to you, for this sums up the Law and the Prophets.

The Narrow and Wide Gates

13 "Enter through the narrow gate. For wide is the gate and broad is the road that leads to destruction, and many enter through it. ¹⁴ But small is the gate and narrow the road that leads to life, and only a few find it.

A Tree and its Fruit

15 "Watch out for false prophets. They come to you in sheep's clothing, but inwardly they are ferocious wolves. ¹⁶ By their fruit you will recognize them. Do people pick grapes from thornbushes, or figs from thistles? ¹⁷ Likewise every good tree bears good fruit, but a bad tree bears bad fruit. ¹⁸ A good tree cannot bear bad fruit, and a bad tree cannot bear good fruit. ¹⁹ Every tree that does not bear good fruit is cut down and thrown into the fire. ²⁰ Thus, by their fruit you will recognize them.

21 "Not everyone who says to me, 'Lord, Lord,' will enter the kingdom of heaven, but only he who does the will of my Father who is in heaven. ²² Many will say to me on that day, 'Lord, Lord, did we not prophesy in your name, and in your name drive out demons and perform many miracles?' ²³ Then I will tell them plainly, 'I never knew you. Away from me, you evildoers!'

The Wise and Foolish Builders

24 "Therefore, everyone who hears these words of mine and puts them into practice is like a wise man who built his house on the rock. ²⁵ The rain came down, the streams rose, and the winds blew and beat against that house; yet it did not fall, because it had its foundation on the rock. ²⁶ But everyone who hears these words of mine and does not put them into practice is like a foolish man who built his house on sand. ²⁷ The rain came down, the streams rose, and the winds blew and beat against that house, and it fell with a great crash."

28 When Jesus had finished saying these things, the crowds were amazed at his teaching, ²⁹ because he taught as one who had authority, and not as their teachers of the law.

THINK ABOUT IT

1. What kinds of actions does Jesus hold up as worthy of imitation? Are these kinds of actions universal, applicable to all people, or do they apply only to people with a certain religious outlook?
2. Are people today more concerned with the Pharisees' definition of morality or with Jesus' definition?

TALK ABOUT IT

3. Would living the principles Jesus outlines make one a better person?
4. Is it possible to be a successful business person and practice the principles Jesus outlines?

WRITE ABOUT IT

5. Can a religious person disregard the rules of her/his religion if s/he does not agree with them and still be considered a faithful member of that religion?
6. Is it realistic to expect people today to live by the principles Jesus outlines?

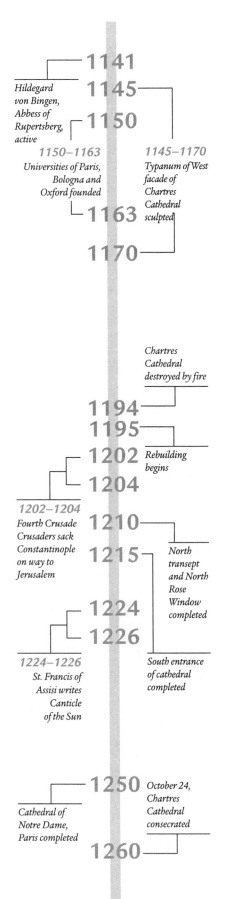

1141

1145

1150

Hildegard von Bingen, Abbess of Rupertsberg, active

1150–1163
Universities of Paris, Bologna and Oxford founded

1145–1170
Tympanum of West facade of Chartres Cathedral sculpted

1163

1170

Chartres Cathedral destroyed by fire

1194

1195

1202 *Rebuilding begins*

1204

1202–1204
Fourth Crusade Crusaders sack Constantinople on way to Jerusalem

1210

1215 *North transept and North Rose Window completed*

1224

1226

1224–1226
St. Francis of Assisi writes Canticle of the Sun

South entrance of cathedral completed

1250 *October 24, Chartres Cathedral consecrated*

Cathedral of Notre Dame, Paris completed

1260

ROBERTA VANDERMAST

The Cathedral at Chartres:

A Bible in Stone

Roberta Vandermast is coordinator and professor of Interdisciplinary Studies at Valencia Community College where she has been teaching interdisciplinary courses for twenty-six years. She has co-authored three humanities textbooks, as well as a manual for the Interdisciplinary Studies Program at Valencia. She studied art history and humanities in Florence, Italy, and has travelled to France several times to study its history, art, and architecture. Her interest in architecture as an expression of culture was stimulated by her visits to the Cathedral at Chartres.

Most modern pilgrims arrive at Chartres Cathedral faster than did their medieval counterparts. Most come today to marvel at its Gothic architecture, a relic of the cultural past, rather than to be inspired by the religiosity of the site. Yet few pilgrims can leave it without being touched by how beautifully this building speaks of the relationship between the human and the divine. Chartres is one of the many Gothic cathedrals which sprang up across Northern Europe in the twelfth and thirteenth centuries. In some ways, Chartres is special because it is one of the first of the great Gothic cathedrals; in other ways, it is typical of all churches of this type and stands as a living reminder of the relationship between man and God which existed in the latter part of the Middle Ages (1100-1300).

THE CATHEDRAL AT CHARTRES (1145-1260) began rising over the grain fields of northern France as its walls started to go up, and by the time it was completed, it literally towered over the countryside (Color Plate 11). Even today, it can be seen for miles before one actually arrives at the cathedral. Imagine how much more inspiring it must have been in the Middle Ages when people came by foot, cart, or horse. Then, the cathedral would have been seen for the better part of a day before the pilgrim arrived after an arduous journey. Yet then, as now, pilgrims came in large numbers to stand in awe at its architecture. Medieval pilgrims, however, also came to renew their faith and, perhaps, to witness a miracle.

In the Middle Ages, the pilgrimage and the pilgrimage church were the spiritual goals of every man, woman, or child. Life was focused on God and the people of this time believed that everything in their world had a direct and immediate relationship to him. God was not only the source of all creation, he was the divine power working in all created things. Every element of creation, from the most important person to the most common plant, had a place in God's ultimate design for the universe. Every stratum of life reaffirmed the presence of God. Thus, the role of God's church was to help man understand and participate in the spiritual dimension of life which lay in and beyond everyday existence. It followed that life on earth, even though temporal and finite, was a prelude to an eternal life in either Heaven or Hell. To the people of the Middle Ages, the church established their essential link with God by providing them with instruction in Christian beliefs and necessary rituals to be received into Heaven. Since most people in the Middle Ages could not read, a Gothic cathedral, such as Chartres, became a Bible in stone, with the building itself serving as a visual statement of their beliefs.

To make a pilgrimage to a church like Chartres during the Middle Ages meant considerable personal and financial hardship. Money was scarce and personal safety was jeopardized by the bands of armed robbers which preyed on defenseless travellers. Nevertheless, thousands came to Notre Dame de Chartres, "Our Lady of Chartres," to marvel at the magnificent church, to renew their faith, and to see first-hand its major relic, the tunic of the Virgin Mary. According to the legend recounted by Vincent Sablon in his *Historie* written in 1671: when the Virgin Mary, the Mother of Jesus, was

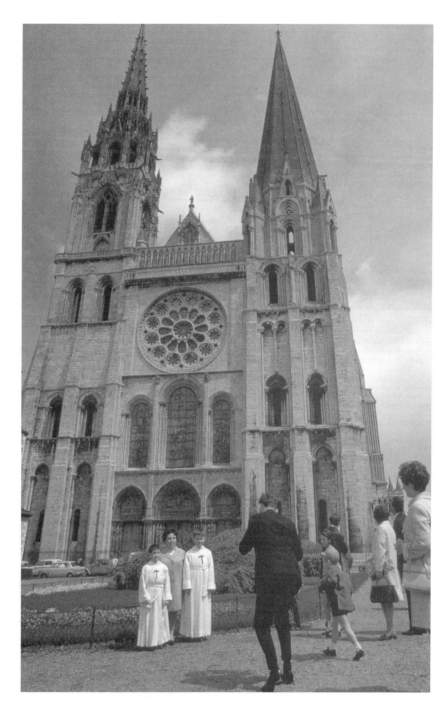

WEST FACADE
Exterior of the Cathedral Of Chartres, 1194-1240.

CROSS VAULTING
Interior of the Cathedral of Chartres, 1194–1240.

near death, she told the apostles gathered at her bed to give her clothes to a poor woman who had been attending her. From there, her tunic, a type of undergarment, passed through many hands, working miracles each time, until it fell into the hands of a Jewish woman. This woman had extended her hospitality to two brothers who were returning to Constantinople (modern Istanbul) after making a pilgrimage to Jerusalem to see its holy sites. The brothers repaid the kind woman's hospitality by stealing the tunic. They replaced the box in which the tunic was kept with a fake one and returned to Constantinople with the original. From there, the tunic in its reliquary, a jewel-encrusted box specially constructed to hold an important relic like this one, was given to the great Franco-German king, Charlemagne. His grandson, Charles the Bald, transferred the reliquary to Chartres where it continued to work miracles. The reliquary was reputed to have saved the city from invasion, healed the sick, and survived a disastrous fire which had levelled the previous cathedral. No wonder pilgrims made such sacrifices to see it! Undertaking such an arduous and dangerous journey in an era when roads were rutted trails and

robbers lurked at every bend would certainly be proof of one's faith and offered the chance of witnessing yet another miracle worked by the tunic of "Our Lady," the Virgin Mary.

The presence of a relic as important as the Virgin Mary's tunic brought thousands of travellers to the town. These travellers needed rooms to sleep in, meals to eat, and souvenirs to remind them of their journey. To live in a town where such an important relic was housed put one closer to the presence of God and, equally important to many, it led to economic gain. Economic benefits came from the medieval tourists who flocked to the site and also from the Catholic Church itself, which was the largest, most well-organized institution in this period. Attached to the great cathedrals were the schools whose job it was to produce the priests and clergymen needed to staff these great churches. The schools supplied the educated people of the era and attracted scholars from all over Europe. The Church also supported the local economy by sponsoring the most extensive building programs of the era which employed thousands of architects, sculptors, painters, stone masons, carpenters, and apprentices to construct these huge edifices. The

economic impact of a Gothic cathedral was enormous. It provided employment and job security for generations of local townspeople, as well as for skilled artists, craftsmen, and scholars throughout Europe. To a town like Chartres, the cathedral was the major factor in the local economy.

Aside from the economic conditions which accompanied the construction of these great churches, their primary function was religious — a fact no medieval pilgrim ever lost sight of. As one approached the church, the building itself testified to its religious purpose. Longer, wider, and taller than any other structure conceivable in the Middle Ages, the building itself seemed to ascend to heaven. A tall roof and elaborate external supports give the cathedral its vertical thrust. In addition, two tall towers rise on either side of the front of the church, each of which is topped with a large spire. At Chartres, the taller of these spires rises 377 feet (115 meters) into the air, the equivalent of a forty-story building!

The amazing height achieved by these cathedrals was made possible by the invention of cross vaulting and buttressing. In Northern Europe, stone was preferred for large buildings because of its fire-resistant capabilities. (The three major fires at Chartres which demolished earlier wooden churches give ample evidence of the need for fireproof stone buildings.) Since stone is dense and weighty, it requires heavy, thick walls for support. New building techniques invented during the Late Middle Ages allowed higher ceilings and larger windows. These building techniques originated with improvements to the system of cross vaulting, the basic system that was used to construct the ceilings of the cathedral. Cross vaulting occurs at the intersection of two barrel vaults, so named because they resemble a barrel cut in half and seen from the inside. The intersection of two barrel vaults creates a structure in which the downward thrust of the weight of the stone components is born by large piers or posts at the four "corners" of the intersection. This eliminates the need for thick stone walls, while creating a less weighty, highly stable structure. Originally, cross vaults were created with rounded barrel vaults, but in order to achieve the height wanted, medieval builders created vaults with "pointed" arches which allowed additional height. However, these pointed vaults created another structural problem which medieval architects had to solve.

While pointed vaults gave a greater distance from the floor to ceiling, they also made the structure less stable. Pointed vaults direct the thrust of the weight of their stones down, as well as out. If not counterbalanced, the weight of the pointed vaults can push the supporting walls out, causing the structure to collapse. To stabilize this outward thrust, buttressing was developed. A buttress is a heavy, thick, external "rib" which helps support the walls of the building. It is a tall, vertical member, constructed outside of main walls of the building, which pushes inward

ABRAHAM AND ISAAC
Detail from the Facade of the Cathedral of Chartres 1194-1240.

DEMON LEADING A MISER TO HELL
Column capital from the Interior of the Cathedral of Chartres, 1194-1240.

ures decorating the outside of the cathedral.

The outside of every Gothic cathedral is covered by the most elaborate sculptural display imaginable. Surrounding each of the major entrances, capping the buttresses, and protruding from along its roof are sculptures of people and animals, real and imagined. Famous among these are the gargoyles, imaginary monsters which often double as rain spouts. Since they represented the monsters waiting in Hell to torture the unfaithful, gargoyles must have struck terrible fear into the hearts of many medieval children and adults. These frightful monsters reminded medieval pilgrims to keep their eyes focused on Heaven. Along with the gargoyles, large sculptures of saints and holy persons offered the hope of paradise at each of the cathedral's main entrances. Medieval cathedrals were oriented so that the main entrances were on the north, south and west sides of the building. Over each set of doors were figures from the Old and New Testaments, accompanied by representations of the subjects studied in the cathedral's school. On these portals, a pilgrim could find Abraham, a man of faith, alongside Aristotle, a Greek philosopher. These figures served not only to remind pilgrims of the wisdom and learning which emanated from the Church, they also served as a stone "book" from which priests could dramatize the stories from the Bible, by pointing to the sculptures as they retold the stories from the Scriptures or informed listeners about the lives of the saints. Thus, the portals of the cathedral served to both usher in the faithful and to educate them in their religion.

While there were three entrances to Chartres Cathedral, most pilgrims would not have been deemed worthy enough to enter from either the north or the south. In the highly stratified

on these walls. Buttresses transfer to the ground the outward thrust of the pointed vaults, thus stabilizing the building. With buttressing, the main walls of the cathedral no longer have to bear the total weight and thrust of the ceiling; therefore, these walls can be made thinner and less weighty. This, in turn, permits greater height and the inclusion of more windows. In the Gothic cathedral, buttresses were topped with spires and were called "flying" buttresses because they appeared to be flying upward toward heaven. Chartres was one of the first

Gothic cathedrals to incorporate the use of these flying buttresses which have become hallmarks of Gothic architecture.

To the pilgrim approaching the Cathedral at Chartres, the height of the building, its twin towers and tall spires, as well as its flying buttresses, pointed to the direction that life should take. Life should focus not only on the everyday things of this world, it must prepare one for eternity which one hoped to spend above, in Heaven. This belief was reinforced by the representations of religious fig-

society of the Middle Ages, these entrances would have been reserved for the highest classes: clergy and royalty. "Commoners" would have entered the cathedral on its west side, through the cathedral's main entrance. Flanked by its twin towers and decorated with a rose window, the west facade is also the oldest portion of Chartres Cathedral. Its entrance is a remnant from an older church built on the same site and destroyed by fire. This is atypical of Gothic churches which were usually of one style. This Romanesque entrance depicts Jesus surrounded by symbols of the four apostles who recorded his life: Matthew, Mark, Luke, and John. Typically, a Gothic cathedral had at its entrance a depiction of the Last judgment when, according to Christian belief, Jesus would return to earth to separate the faithful from the unfaithful. (In a Romanesque church, the Last judgment is typically depicted inside the church, while in a Gothic church, the Last judgment appears on the outside.) Imagine what an impression a scene of the Last judgment made on these medieval pilgrims. As they entered the church, they could see graphic depictions of the damnation of the unbelievers and of the salvation of the faithful. From these sculptures, medieval pilgrims knew that both angels and devils hovered overhead, contending for their souls.

Inside the church, pilgrims could begin to glimpse the shape of the building and unravel its symbolism. Entering from the west placed them in the darkest portion of the church, although they would be facing the altar which was flooded with daylight. The journey to the altar represented the journey of the pilgrim from the darkness of sin to the presence of God or light. Symbolic, too, was the fact that the most significant religious services took place at the central al-

ARISTOTLE
Detail from the Facade of the Cathedral of Chartres, 1194–1240.

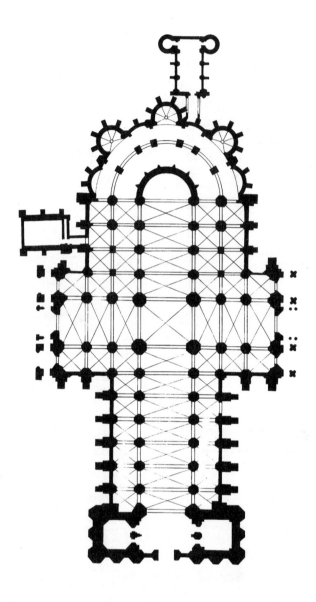

FLOOR PLAN
of the Cathedral of Chartres, 1194-1240.

windows of the clerestory. The clerestory forms the upper tier of the side walls and separates the inside and outside of the cathedral. The windows which light the nave of the church are located here. In addition to the main aisle of the church formed by the nave, there are two parallel aisles which are visible through the openings created by the cross vaults supporting these aisles. Above these aisles is the triforium gallery, supported by the roof of the aisles. The triforium gallery is an elevated platform which could be used to hold a choir or choirs. A special mass celebrated in the cathedral might include a pair of choirs singing either together or responsorially from either side of the nave. The inclusion of this music, echoing through the cavernous nave and drifting down from above, increased the pilgrims' feeling that they had come into the presence of God.

As the pilgrim approached the altar, the arms of the cross inscribed in the floor plan became visible. These arms are the transepts of the cathedral and at the end of each transept is a rose window. Rose windows, so called because they resemble the pattern of a fully-opened rose, are filled with beautifully colored and patterned stained glass. The light filtering through each window casts a kaleidoscope of colors across the grey stone of the interior. As the patterns of light cast by the rose windows continually changed, medieval pilgrims were reminded of the wondrous nature of God, the process of change in the universe, and the majesty and grandeur of the church which had been provided for their salvation (Color Plate 13).

At Chartres, the rose window in the north transept is referred to as the Rose of France. At its center, in a circular panel, is depicted the Virgin Mary, "Our Lady," holding the infant Jesus. This circular panel is resplen-

tar, attended by bishops and other important clergy. The altar, then, was the heart of the Gothic cathedral: the place symbolic of salvation. Salvation was signified not only by the presence of sunlight streaming in and the clergy at the altar, but also by the floor plan of the Gothic cathedral which traced the shape of a cross. Thus, the location of the altar approximated the position of Jesus' heart when he

died on the cross. Therefore, when the clergy offered the symbols of Jesus' Last Supper, the bread and the wine, to the congregation during the Mass, participants were literally standing at the heart of the church.

To arrive at the altar at Chartres, medieval pilgrims had to walk more than two hundred feet down the nave, the main aisle of the church, which was illuminated on either side by the

THE TRADEPT
of the Cathedral of Chartres, 1194–1240.

dent with red, blue, and gold — colors which were both popular and symbolic. Blue and gold represent the splendors and riches of heaven, while red represents the blood Jesus shed for the salvation of humanity. Surrounding this central circle containing Mary and Jesus are small semi-circles containing white fleur-de-lis, lilies of the valley, which were symbols of the French monarchy. These symbols identify the donor of the window, Blanche of Castile, mother of King Louis IX of France, who became St. Louis. The identification of the donor reveals another important aspect of the cathedral: that all facets of society played a part in its construction. This is evidenced, too, by the many stained glass windows signed by the various medieval guilds or trade unions. Signature windows show carpenters, barrel makers, and teamsters, as well as butchers, bakers, and candlestick makers. These donor signatures reminded pilgrims that it took all levels of society to build a church as great as this one — from the lowliest brick layer to the most exalted queen — and reflected the medieval belief that every social class played an essential role in God's great design.

Behind the altar is the apse, corresponding to the spot which held Jesus' head on the cross. This section of the church separated the clergy from the laity or non-clergy. This separation was very significant. In the Middle Ages, the clergy were not only the "heads" of the church, but also its "brains," in the sense that they were the most educated class in medieval society. Educated in religion and charged with the care of both parishioners and pilgrims, they were responsible for guiding souls to God and, thereby, to Heaven. This was a serious responsibility in an age when ascending to heaven was the focal point of every person's life. Thus, peo-

ple of the Middle Ages felt that the clergy deserved this honored spot in the cathedral.

Even though medieval pilgrims and parishioners could not sit in the apse during services, they could enter the many chapels behind it. A carved screen separated these chapels from the apse. Running behind this screen was an ambulatory, or passageway (Color Plate 12). On occasions when only a small congregation might be on hand for a marriage or baptism, these small chapels were used instead of the main nave of the church. The carved screen and the stained glass windows which decorated the chapels also provided lessons in religion for, like the outside of the church, they retold Biblical and other religious stories. For medieval pilgrims, a walk around the ambulatory and a return trip down the nave completed their viewing of the interior of the church. Walking around the church, both outside and inside, helped pilgrims learn about their religion and, in doing so, helped them trace a pathway to Heaven.

Every aspect of the medieval cathedral is designed to remind the viewer, medieval or modern, of the immanent presence of God. The size and shape of the church, and its sculpture and stained glass windows were all constructed to glorify the relationship between God and man. Without a doubt, the impact on medieval pilgrims was awe-inspiring. After journeying many difficult miles, the site of the Cathedral at Chartres, rising above the wheat fields of northern France, instilled the excitement and anticipation. Entering through the elaborately carved portal of the entrance reminded them of why they had come so far, and their reverent pilgrimage through the building drew them nearer to God. For the people of the Middle Ages, the Cathedral at Chartres was more than a Bible in

stone, it was the living embodiment of their relationship to God and an affirmation of His presence in all things.

THINK ABOUT IT

1. What are three of the most important ways in which a Gothic cathedral like Chartres emphasized the relationship between the pilgrim and God?
2. In your opinion, what is the most impressive feature of the Cathedral at Chartres?

TALK ABOUT IT

3. How do modern churches differ from the Cathedral at Chartres? What do these differences say about the modern relationship between people and God?
4. Why do religions feel the need to build structures as large as Chartres Cathedral? What other religions have buildings of comparable size and scope?

WRITE ABOUT IT

5. Compare the Cathedral at Chartres to a large structure from another religious tradition. What does each say about God?
6. Describe the ideal space in which to worship. What would it look like?

READ MORE ABOUT IT

Branner, Robert, editor. *Chartres Cathedral.* New York: W. W. Norton & Company, Inc., 1969.

Lee, Lawrence, et. al. *Stained Glass.* New York: Crown Publishers, Inc., 1976.

Miller, Malcolm. *Chartres Cathedral.* Andover, Great Britain: Pitkin Pictorials, 1985.

Salvadori, Mario. *Why Buildings Stand Up.* New York: W. W, Norton & Company, Inc., 1980.

GARY JENNINGS

The Dedication of the Great Pyramid of the Aztecs

Gary Jennings is best known for three monumental novels of historical fiction he wrote in the 1980s. These novels reflect his wide range of interests as well as his highly-developed research skills. *The Journeyer* recounts the "other half" of Marco Polo's adventures, the half withheld by the famous explorer so as not to offend the Europeans. In a totally different vein, *Spangle* is a novel that follows the adventures of a traveling circus immediately after the Civil War in the United States. Jennings is best known, however, for *Aztec*, a novel that relates the life of the Aztec people just before and during the Spanish conquest of Mexico in the sixteenth century. Jennings spent twelve years writing this novel; for ten of these years, he lived and conducted research in Mexico. Concerned about the anti-Indian bias he found in many of the contemporary accounts he read about the conquest, Jennings learned Nahuatl, the language of the Aztecs still spoken in modern Mexico, so he could present a balanced view of these fascinating people. He also travelled the country, seeking primary source materials and conducting interviews with Indians. Jennings's hard work paid off; *Aztec* was on the bestseller's list for many weeks and has been published in ten countries.

Aztec tells the life story of Mixtli, an elderly Indian. Mixtli, or Dark Cloud, has been commanded by the Spanish to relate all he knows about Indian life to an official of Emperor Charles I of Spain. His reminiscences begin with his life as a young boy and a student, then proceed as he becomes, in turn, a scribe, a soldier, a merchant, an advisor to noble rulers, and finally, the chronicler of his people's past for the victorious Spaniards. As his story is told, details of Aztec life and culture are revealed. Graphic descriptions of the capital at Tenochtítlan, the geography of the Aztec empire, the battles between warring nations, and the numerous religious festivals evoke vivid images of the Aztec world. Perhaps the most fascinating and unsettling aspect of this world is the Aztecs' religious ceremonies during which hundreds of prisoners of war, slaves, and others were sacrificed. The greatest event in Mixtli's world was the dedication of the Great Pyramid in Tenochtítlan where thousands were sacrificed to glorify the most splendid Aztec monument ever built.

1928
1929 — Birth of Gary Jennings

Diego Rivera paints "History of Mexico" murals 1

1938

Mexico achieves economic independence from foreign oil companies

American Civil Rights movement begins

1955

1958

Women given right to vote in Mexico

Publishes *Aztec*

1980

Publishes *The Journeyer*

Earthquake devastates Mexico City

1984

Publishes *Spangle*

1985
1987

YES, YOUR EXCELLENCY, I know that you are most particularly interested in our former religious observances, hence your attendance here today. Although I was never a priest, nor much of a friend to priests, I will explain the dedication of the Great Pyramid — the manner of it and the significance of it — as well as I can.

If that was not the most resplendent, populous, and awesome celebration ever held in the history of the Mexíca, it certainly outdid all others I beheld in my time. The Heart of the One World was a solid mass of people, of colorful fabrics, of perfumes, of feather plumes, of flesh, of gold, of body heat, of jewels, of sweat. One reason for the crowding was that lanes had to be kept open — by cordons of guards, their arms linked, struggling to contain the jostling mob — so the lines of prisoners could march to the pyramid and ascend to the sacrificial altar. But the spectator crush was also due to the fact that the standing room in the plaza had been reduced by the building of numerous new temples over the years, not to mention the gradually spreading bulk of the Great Pyramid itself.

Since Your Excellency never saw it, perhaps I had better describe that *icpac tlamanacáli*. Its base was square, one hundred and fifty paces from one corner to the next, the four sides sloping inward as they rose, until the pyramid's fiat summit measured seventy paces to a side. The staircase ascending its front or western incline was actually two stairways, one each for those persons climbing and descending, separated by an ornamental gutter for blood to flow down. Fifty and two stairs of steep risers and narrow treads led to a terrace that encircled the pyramid a third of the way up. Then another flight of one hundred and four steps culminated in the platform on top, with its temples and their appurtenances. At either side of every thir-

teenth step of the staircase stood the stone image of some god, major or minor, its stone fists holding aloft a tall pole from which floated a white feather banner.

To a man standing at the very bottom of the Great Pyramid, the structures on top were invisible. From the bottom he could see only the broad dual staircase ascending, appearing to narrow, and seeming to lead even higher than it did — into the blue sky or, on other occasions, into the sunrise. A *xochimíqui* trudging up the stairs toward his Flowery Death must have felt that he was truly climbing toward the very heavens of the high gods.

But when he reached the top, he would find first the small, pyramidal sacrificial stone and behind that the two temples. In a sense, those *teocáltin* represented war and peace, for the one on the right was the abode of Huitzilopóchtli, responsible for our military prowess, and in the one on the left dwelt *Tlaloc*, responsible for our harvests and peacetime prosperity. Perhaps there should rightly have been a third teocáli for the sun Tonatíu, but he already had a separate sanctuary on a more modest pyramid elsewhere in the plaza, as did several important gods. There was also in the plaza the temple in which were ranked the images of numerous gods of subordinate nations.

The new temples of Tlaloc and Huitzilopóchtli, atop the new Great Pyramid, were but square stone rooms, each containing a hollow stone statue of the god, his mouth wide open to receive nourishment. But each temple was made much taller and more impressive by a towering stone facade or roof comb: Huitzilopóchtli's indented with angular and red-painted designs, Tlaloc's indented with rounded and blue-painted designs. The body of the pyramid was predominantly a gleaming almost-silver gesso white, but the two serpentine banisters, one along

each flank of the dual staircase, were painted with reptilian scales of red, blue, and green, and their big snake heads, stretching out at the ground level, were entirely covered with beaten gold.

When the ceremony began, at the first full light of day, the chief priests of Tlaloc and Huitzilopóchtli, with all their assistants, were fussing around the temples at the top of the pyramid, doing whatever it is that priests do at the last moment. On the terrace encircling the pyramid stood the more distinguished guests: Tenochtítlan's Revered Speaker Ahuítzotl, naturally, with Texcóco's Revered Speaker Nezahualpíli and Tlácopan's Revered Speaker Chimalpopóca. There were also the rulers of other cities, provinces, and nations — from far-flung Mexíca domains, from the Tzapotéca lands, from the Mixtéca, from the Totonáca, from the Huaxtéca, from nations whose names I did not then even know. Not present, of course, was that implacably inimical ruler, old Xicoténca of Texcála, but Yquíngare of Michihuácan was there.

Think of it, Your Excellency. If your Captain-General Cortés had arrived in the plaza on that day, he could have accomplished our overthrow with one swift and easy slaughter of almost all our rightful rulers. He could have proclaimed himself, there and then, the lord of practically all of what is now New Spain, and our leaderless peoples would have been hard put to dispute him. They would have been like a beheaded animal which can twitch and flail only futilely. We would have been spared, I now realize, much of the misery and suffering we later endured. But *yyo ayyo!* On that day we celebrated the might of the Mexíca, and we did not even suspect the existence of such things as white men, and we supposed that our roads and our days led ahead into a limitless future. Indeed, we did have some years of vigor and glory still

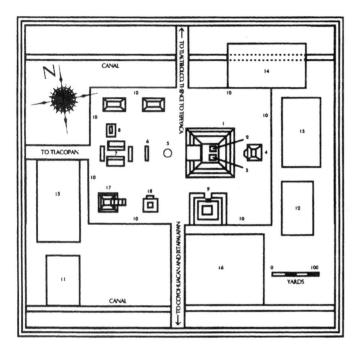

1. *The Great Pyramid*
2. *The Temple of Tlaloc*
3. *The Temple of Huitzilopochtli*
4. *Former Temple of Huitzilopochtli, Later (after completion of The Great Pyramid, 1487) the Coateocali, or catch-all temple of numerous minor gods, plus gods appropriated from other nations.*
5. *The Stone of Tixoc*
6. *The Tzompantli, Or Skull Rack*
7. *The Ceremonial Tlachtli Ball Court*
8. *The Platform of the Sun Stone*
9. *The Temple of Tezcatlipoca*
10. *The Snake Wall*
11. *The House of Song*
12. *The Menagerie*
13. *The Palace of Axayacatl, later of Cortes*
14. *The Palace of Ahuiltzol, ravaged by flood, 1499*
15. *The Palace of Motecuzoma I*
16. *The Palace of Motecuzoma II*
17. *The Temple of Xipe Totec*
18. *The Eagle Temple*

THE CENTRAL PLAZA OF TENOCHTÍTLAN, 1521

before us, so I am glad — even knowing what I know — I am glad that no alien intruder spoiled that splendid day.

The morning was devoted to entertainments. There was much singing and dancing by the troupes from this very House of Song in which we now sit, Your Excellency, and they were far more professionally skilled than any performers I had seen or heard in Texcáco or Xaltócan — though to me none equaled the grace of my lost Tzitzilíni. There were the familiar instruments: the single thunder drum, the several god drums, the water drums, the suspended gourds, the reed flutes and shinbone flutes and sweet-potato flutes. But the singers and dancers were also accompanied by other instruments of a complexity I had not seen elsewhere. One was called "the warbling waters," a flute which

sent its notes bubbling through a water jug, with an echo effect. There was another flute, made of clay, shaped rather like a thick dish, and its player did not move his lips or fingers; he moved his head about while he blew into the mouth-piece so that a small clay ball inside the flute rolled to stop one hole or another around its rim. And, of course, of every kind of instrument there were many. Their combined music must have been audible to any stay-at-homes in every community around all the five lakes.

The musicians, singers, and dancers performed on the lower steps of the pyramid and on a cleared space directly in front of it. Whenever they tired and required a rest, their place was taken by athletic performers. Strong men lifted prodigious weights of stone, or tossed nearly naked beautiful girls back and forth to each other

as if the girls had been feathers. Acrobats outdid grasshoppers and rabbits with their leaping, tumbling antics. Or they stood upon each other's shoulders — ten, then twenty, then forty men at a time — to form human representations of the Great Pyramid itself. Comic dwarfs performed grotesque and indecent pantomimes. Jugglers kept incredible numbers of *tlachtli* balls spinning aloft, from hand to hand, in intricate looping patterns ....

No, Your Excellency, I do not mean to imply that the morning's entertainments were a mere diversion (as you put it) to lighten the horror to come (as you put it), and I do not know what you mean when you mutter of "bread and circuses." Your Excellency must not infer that those merriments were in any wise irreverent. Every performer dedicated his particular trick or talent to the gods we honored that day. If the performances were not somber but frolicsome, it was to cajole the gods into a mood to receive with gratitude our later offerings.

Everything done that morning had some connection with our religious beliefs or customs or traditions, though the relation might not be immediately evident to a foreign observer like Your Excellency. For example, there were the *tocotíne*, come on invitation from the Totonáca oceanside lands where their distinctive sport had been invented—or perhaps god-inspired. Their performance required the erection of an exceptionally tall tree trunk in a socket specially drilled in the plaza marble. A live bird was placed in that hole, and mashed by the insertion of the tree trunk, so that its blood would lend the *tocotíne* the strength they would need for flying. Yes, flying.

The erected pole stood almost as tall as the Great Pyramid. At its top was a tiny wooden platform, no bigger than a man's circled arms. Twined all down the pole was a loose meshing of stout ropes. Five Totonáca men climbed the pole to its top, one carrying a flute and a small drum tied to his loincloth, the other four unencumbered except for a profusion of bright feathers. In fact, they were totally naked except for those feathers glued to their arms. Arriving at the platform, the four feathered men somehow sat around the edge of the wooden piece, while the fifth man slowly, precariously got to his feet and stood upon it.

There on that constricted space he stood, dizzyingly high, and then he stamped one foot and then the other, and then he began to dance, accompanying himself with flute and drum. The drum he pounded with one hand while his other manipulated the holes of the flute on which he blew. Though everyone watching from the plaza below was breathlessly quiet, the music

came down to us as only the thinnest tweedling and thumping. Meanwhile, the other four *tocotíne* were cautiously knotting the pole's rope ends around their ankles, but we could not see it, so high up they were. When they were ready, the dancing man made some signal to the musicians in the plaza.

Ba-ra-ROOM! There was a thunderous concussion of music and drumming that made every spectator jump, and, at the same instant, the four men atop the pole also jumped — into empty air. They flung themselves outward and spread their arms, the full length of which were feathered. Each of the men was feathered like a different bird: a red macaw, a blue fisher bird, a green parrot, a yellow toucan — and his arms were his outstretched wings. That first leap carried the *tocotíne* a distance outward from the platform, but then the ropes around their ankles jerked them up short. They would all have fallen back against the pole, except for the ingenious way the ropes were twined. The men's initial leap outward became a slow circling around the pole, each of the men equidistant from the others, and each still in the graceful posture of a spread-winged, hovering bird.

While the man on top went on dancing and the musicians below played a trifling, lilting, pulsing accompaniment, the four bird-men continued to circle and, as the ropes gradually unwound from the pole, they circled farther out and slowly came lower. But the men, like birds, could tilt their feathered arms so that they rose and dipped and soared up and down past each other as if they too danced — but in all the dimensions of the sky.

Each man's rope was wrapped thirteen times around and down the extent of the pole. On his final circuit, when his body was swinging in its widest and swiftest circle, almost touching the plaza pavement, he arched his body and backed his wings

against the air — exactly in the manner of a bird alighting — so that he skimmed to the ground feet first, and the rope came loose, and he ran to a stop. All four did that at the same moment. Then one of them held his rope taut for the fifth man to slide down to the plaza.

If Your Excellency has read some of my previous explanations of our beliefs, you will have realized that the sport of the *tocotíne* was not simply an acrobatic feat, but that each aspect of it had some significance. The four fliers were partly feathered, partly flesh, like Quetzalcóatl, the Feathered Serpent. The four circling men with the dancing man among them represented our five points of the compass: north, east, west, south, and center. The thirteen turns of each rope corresponded to the thirteen day and year numbers of our ritual calendar: And four times thirteen makes fifty and two, the number of years in a sheaf of years. There were more subtle relevances — the word *tocotíne* means "the sowers" — but I will not expatiate on those things, for I perceive that Your Excellency is more eager to hear of the sacrificial part of the dedication ceremony.

The night before, after they had all confessed to Filth Eater's priests, our Texcaltéca prisoners had been moved to the perimeter of the island and divided into three herds, so that they could move toward the Great Pyramid along the three broad avenues leading into the plaza. The first prisoner to approach, well forward of the rest, was my own: Armed Scorpion. He had haughtily declined to ride a litter chair to his Flowery Death, but came with his arms across the shoulders of two solicitous brother knights, though they were of course Mexíca. Armed Scorpion swung along between them, the remains of his legs dangling like gnawed roots. I was positioned at the base of the pyramid, where I fell in beside the three and accompanied them up the staircase to the terrace where all the nobles waited.

To my beloved son, the Revered Speaker Ahuítzotl said, "As our *xochimíqui* of highest rank and most distinction, Armed Scorpion, you have the honor of going first to the Flowery Death. However, as a Jaguar Knight of long and notable reputation, you may choose instead to fight for your life on the Battle Stone. What is your wish?"

The prisoner sighed. "I no longer have a life, my lord. But it would be good to fight one last time. If I may choose, then, I choose the Battle Stone."

"A decision worthy of a warrior," said Ahuítzotl. "And you will be honored with worthy opponents, our own highest-ranking knights. Guards, assist the esteemed Armed Scorpion to the stone and gird him for hand-to-hand combat."

I went along to watch. The Battle Stone, as I have earlier told, was the former Uey-Tlatoáni Tixoc's one contribution to the plaza: that broad, squat cylinder of volcanic rock situated between the Great Pyramid and the Sun Stone. It was reserved for any warrior who merited the distinction of dying as he had lived, still fighting. But a prisoner who chose to duel on the Battle Stone was required to fight not just one opponent. If, by guile and prowess, he bested one man, another Mexícatl knight would take up the fray, and another and another — four in all. One of those was bound to kill him ... or, at least that was the way the duels had always ended before.

Armed Scorpion was dressed in full battle armor of quilted cotton, plus his knightly regalia of jaguar skin and helmet. Then he was placed upon the stone where, having no feet, he could not even stand. His opponent, armed with an obsidian-bladed *maquáhuitl*, had the advantage of being able to leap on and off the pedestal, and to attack from any direction. Armed Scorpion was given two weapons with which to defend himself, but they were poor things. One was simply a wooden staff for warding off his attacker's blows. The other was a *maquáhuitl*, but the harmless play-kind used by novice soldiers in training: its obsidian flakes removed and replaced by tufts of feathery down.

Armed Scorpion sat near one edge of the stone, in a posture almost of relaxed anticipation, the bladeless sword in his right hand, the wooden staff gripped by his left and lying across his lap. His first opponent was one of the two jaguar Knights who had helped him into the plaza. The Mexícatl leapt onto the Battle Stone at the left side of Armed Scorpion; that is, on the side away from his offensive weapon, the *maquáhuitl*. But Armed Scorpion surprised the man. He did not even move the weapon, he used his defensive staff instead. He swung it, hard, in an up-curving arc. The Mexícatl, who could scarcely have expected to be attacked with a mere pole, caught it under his chin. His jaw was broken and he was knocked senseless. Some of the crowd murmured in admiration and others owl-hooted in applause. Armed Scorpion simply sat, the wooden staff held languidly resting on his left shoulder.

The second duelist was Armed Scorpion's other supporting Jaguar Knight. He, naturally supposing that the prisoner's first win had been only a caprice of fortune, also bounded onto the stone at Armed Scorpion's left, his obsidian blade poised to strike, his eyes fixed on the seated man's own *maquáhuitl*. That time, Armed Scorpion lashed overhand with his defensive staff, over the knight's uplifted weapon hand, and brought the pole crashing down between the ears of the Mexícatl's jaguar-head helmet. The man fell backward off the Battle Stone, his skull fractured, and he was dead

before he could be attended by any physician. The spectators' murmurs and hoots increased in volume.

The third opponent was an Arrow Knight, and he was justly wary of the Texcaltécatl's not at all harmless staff. He leapt onto the stone from the right, and swung his *maquáhuitl* in the same movement. Armed Scorpion again brought up his staff, but only to parry the swinging sword to one side. That time he also used his own maquáhuitl, though in an unusual way. He jabbed the hard blunt end of it upward, with all his strength, into the Arrow Knight's throat. It crushed that prominence of cartilage which you Spaniards call "the nut of the neck." The Mexícatl fell and writhed, and he strangled to death, right there on the Battle Stone.

As the guards removed that limp carcass, the crowd was going wild with shouts and hoots of encouragement — not for their Mexíca warriors, but for the Texcaltécatl. Even the nobles high on the pyramid were milling about and conversing excitedly. In the memory of no one present had a prisoner, even a prisoner with the use of all his limbs, ever bested as many as three opposing duelists.

But the fourth was the certain slayer, for the fourth was one of our rare left-handed fighters. Practically all warriors were naturally right-handed, had learned to fight right-handed, and had fought in that manner all their lives. So, as is well-known, a right-handed warrior is perplexed and confounded when he comes up against a left-handed combatant who is, in effect, a mirror image striking him.

The left-handed man, a knight of the Eagle Order, took his time climbing onto the Battle Stone. He came leisurely to the duel, smiling cruelly and confidently. Armed Scorpion still sat, his staff in his left hand, his *maquáhuitl* naturally in his right. The Eagle Knight, sword in his left hand,

TOLTEC, RECLINING FIGURE, C. 1000.
Castillo, Chichén Itzá, Mexico

made a distracting feint and then leapt forward. As he did so, Armed Scorpion moved as deftly as any of the morning's jugglers. He tossed his staff and *maquáhuitl* a little way into the air and caught them in the opposite hands. The Mexícatl knight, at that unexpected display of ambidexterity, checked his lunge as if to draw back and consider. He did not get the chance.

Armed Scorpion clapped his blade and staff together on the knight's left wrist, twisted them, and the man's *maquáhuitl* fell out of his hand. Holding the Mexícatl's wrist pinned between his wooden weapons, as in a parrot's strong beak, Armed Scorpion for the first time drew himself up from his sitting position, to kneel on his knees and stumps. With unbelievable strength, he twisted his two weapons still farther, and the Eagle Knight had to twist with them, and he fell on his back. The Texcaltécatl immediately laid the edge of his wooden blade across the supine man's throat. Placing one hand on either end of the wood, he knelt over and leaned heavily. The man thrashed under him, and Armed Scorpion lifted his head to look up at the pyramid, at the nobles.

Ahuítzotl, Nezahualpíli, Chimalpopópca, and the others on the terrace conferred, their gesticulations expressing admiration and wonderment. Then Ahuítzotl stepped to the edge of the platform and made a raising, beckoning movement with his hand. Armed Scorpion leaned back and lifted the *maquáhuitl* off the fallen man's neck. That one sat up, shakily, rubbing his throat, looking both unbelieving and embarrassed. He and Armed Scorpion were brought together to the terrace. I accompanied them, glowing with pride in my beloved son. Ahuítzotl said to him:

"Armed Scorpion, you have done something unheard of. You have fought for your life on the Battle Stone, under greater handicap than any previous duelist, and you have won. This swagger whom you last defeated will take your place as *xochimíqui* of the first sacrifice. You are free to go home to Texcála."

Armed Scorpion firmly shook his head. "Even if I could walk home, my Lord Speaker, I would not. A prisoner once taken is a man destined by his *tonáli* and the gods to die. I should shame my family, my fellow knights, all of Texcála, if I returned dishonorably alive. No, my lord, I have had what I requested — one last fight — and it was a good fight. Let your Eagle Knight live. A left-handed warrior is too rare and valuable to discard."

"If that is your wish," said the Uey-Tlatoáni, "then he lives. We are prepared to grant any other wish of yours. Only speak it."

"That I now be allowed to go to my Flowery Death, and to the warriors' afterworld."

"Granted," said Ahuítzotl and then, magnanimously, "The Revered Speaker Nezahualpíli and myself will be honored to bear you thither."

Armed Scorpion spoke just once more, to his captor, to me, as was customary, to ask the routine question, "Has my revered father any message he would like me to convey to the gods?"

I smiled and said, "Yes, my beloved son. Tell the gods that I wish only that you be rewarded in death as you have deserved in life. That you live the richest of afterlives, forever and forever."

He nodded, and then, with his arms across the shoulders of two Revered Speakers, he went up the remaining stairs to the stone block. The assembled priests, almost frenzied with delight at the auspicious events attendant on that first sacrifice of the day, made a great show of waving incense pots around, and throwing smoke colorings into the urn fires, and chanting invocations to the gods. The warrior Armed Scorpion was accorded two final honors. Ahuítzotl himself wielded the obsidian knife. The plucked-out heart was handed to Nezahualpíli, who took it in a ladle,

carried it into the temple of Huitzilopóchtli, and fed it into the god's open mouth.

That ended my participation in the ceremonies, at least until the coming night's feasting, so I descended the pyramid and stood off to one side. After the dispatch of Armed Scorpion, all the rest was rather anticlimactic, except for the sheer magnitude of the sacrifice: the thousands of *xochimíque*, more than ever had before been granted the Flowery Death in one day.

Ahuítzotl ladled the second prisoner's heart into the mouth of Tlaloc's statue, then he and Nezahualpíli descended again to the pyramid terrace. They and their fellow rulers also stood off to one side, out of the way, and, when they tired of watching the proceedings, idly talked among themselves of whatever Revered Speakers talk about. Meanwhile, the three long lines of captives shuffled in single file along the avenues Tlácopan, Ixtapalápan, and Tepeyáca, and into The Heart of the One World, and between the close-pressing ranks of spectators, and one behind another up the pyramid staircase.

The hearts of the first *xochimíque*, perhaps the first two hundred of them, were ceremoniously ladled into the mouths of Tlaloc and Huitzilopóchtli until the statues' hollow insides could hold no more, and the stone lips of the two gods drooled and dribbled blood. Of course, those hearts crammed into the statues' cavities would in time rot down to a sludge and make room for more. But that day, since the priests had an overabundance of hearts, the ones later plucked out were tossed into waiting bowls.

When the bowls were filled and heaped with hearts, still steaming, some still feebly pulsing, under-priests took them and hurried down the Great Pyramid, into the plaza and the streets of the rest of the island. They delivered the surplus bounty to every other pyra-

mid, temple, and god statue in both Tenochtítlan and Tlaltelóco — and, as the afternoon wore on, to temples in the mainland cities as well.

The prisoners endlessly ascended the right side of the pyramid's staircase, while the gashed bodies of their predecessors tumbled and rolled down the left side, kicked along by junior priests stationed at intervals, and while the gutter between the stairs carried a continuous stream of blood which puddled out among the feet of the crowd in the plaza. After the first two hundred or so of *xochimíque*, the priests abandoned all effort or pretense at ceremony. They laid aside their incense pots and banners and holy wands, they ceased their chanting, while they worked as quickly and indifferently as Swallowers on a battleground — meaning that they could not work very neatly.

The hurried ladling of hearts into the statues had spattered the interior of both temples until their walls and floors and even ceilings were coated with drying blood. The excess blood ran out their doors, while still more blood poured off the sacrificial stone, until the whole platform was awash with it. Also, many prisoners, however complacently they came to their fate, involuntarily emptied their bladders or bowels at the moment of lying down under the knife. The priests — who, that morning, had been clad in their usual vulturine black of robes, lank hair, and unwashed skin — had become moving clots of red and brown, of coagulated blood, dried mucus, and a plaster of excrement.

At the base of the pyramid, the meat cutters were working just as frantically and messily. From Armed Scorpion and a number of other Texcaltéca knights they had cut the heads, to be boiled down for their skulls, which would then be mounted on the plaza skull rack reserved to commemorate *xochimíque* of distinction. From those same bodies they had hacked off the thighs, to be broiled for that night's feast of the victorious warriors. As more and more cadavers tumbled down to them, the meat cutters sliced off just the choicest portions, to be fed immediately to the plaza menagerie's animals, or to be salted and smoked and stored for later feeding to the beasts, or to any distressed poor folk or masterless slaves who came begging for such a dispensation.

The mutilated bodies were then hastily carried by the butchers' boys to the nearest canal, the one that flowed under the Tepeyáca avenue. There they were dumped into big freight canoes which, as each was loaded, set off for various points on the mainland: the flower nurseries of Xochimílco, the orchards and produce farms elsewhere around the lakes, where the bodies would be buried for fertilizer. A separate, smaller *acáli* accompanied each fleet of scows. It carried fragments and chips of jadestone — bits too small to be of any other use — one of which would be put in the mouth or the fist of each dead man before he was interred. We never denied to our vanquished enemies that talisman of green stone which was necessary for admission to the afterworld.

And still the procession of prisoners went on. From the summit of the Great Pyramid, a mixture of blood and other substances ran in such torrents that, after a while, the stairway's disposal gutter could not contain it all. It cascaded like a slow, viscous waterfall down the steep steps themselves, it surged among the dead bodies flopping down. It bathed the feet of the live men plodding up, and made many slip and fall. It ran in sheets down smooth walls of the pyramid on all four sides. It spread out the entire extent of The Heart of the One World. That morning the Great Pyramid had gleamed like the snow-covered peak of Popocatépetl. In the afternoon, it

looked like a heap of fowl over which the cook had lavishly poured a thick red moli sauce. It looked like what it was providing: a great meal for the gods of great appetite.

An abomination, Your Excellency?

What horrifies and nauseates you, I think, is the number of men put to death at that one time. But how, my lord, can you set a measure to death, which is not an entity but a void? How can you multiply nothingness by any number known to arithmetic? When just one man dies, the whole living universe ends, as far as he is concerned. Every other man and woman in it likewise ceases to exist; loved ones and strangers, every creature, every flower, cloud, breeze, every sensation and emotion. Your Excellency, the world and every least thing in it dies every day, for somebody.

But what demonic gods, you ask, would countenance the obliteration of so many men in a single indiscriminate slaughter? Well, your own Lord God, for one …

No, Your Excellency, I do not think I blaspheme. I merely repeat what I was told by the missionary friars who instructed me in the rudiments of Christian history. If they spoke the truth, your Lord God was once displeased by the increasing corruption of the human beings He had created, so He drowned them in one great deluge. He left alive only a single boatman and his family to repopulate the earth. I have always thought the Lord God preserved a rather curious selection of humans, since the boatman was prone to drunkenness, and his sons to behavior I should judge peculiar, and all their progeny to quarrelsome rivalries.

Our world too, and every human in it, was once destroyed and also, be it noted, by a calamitous inundation of water — when the gods got dissatisfied with the men then inhabiting it.

However, our histories may go back further than yours, for our priests told us that this world had been previously scoured clean of humankind on three other occasions: the first time by all-devouring jaguars, the second time by all-destroying windstorms, the third time by a rain of fire from the skies. Those cataclysms happened, of course, sheaves of sheaves of years ago, and even the most recent one, the great flood, was so long ago that not the wisest *tlamatíni* could precisely calculate its date.

So the gods have four times created our One World and peopled it with human beings, and four times they have declared the creation a failure, wiped it out and started again. We here now, all of us living, constitute the fifth experiment of gods. But, according to the priests, we live just as precariously as any of those earlier unfortunates, for the gods will someday decide to end the world and all again — the next time by means of devastating earthquakes.

There is no knowing when they may commence. We of this land always thought it possible that the earthquakes might come during the five hollow days at the end of a year, which is why we made ourselves so inconspicuous during those days. It seemed even likelier that the world would end at the end of that most significant year, the fifty-second year of a sheaf of years. So it was at those times that we abased ourselves, and prayed for survival, and sacrificed even more abundantly, and celebrated the New Fire ceremony.

Just as we did not know when to expect the world-ending earthquakes, so we did not know how the earlier men on earth had brought down the wrath of the gods in the form of jaguars, winds, fire, and flood. But it seemed a safe assumption that those men had failed sufficiently to adore and honor and make offerings of nourishment to their creators. That is why we, in our time, tried our best not to be lax in those respects.

So, yes, we slew countless *xochimíque* to honor Tlaloc and Huitzilopóchtli on the day of the dedication of the Great Pyramid. But try to look at it as we did, Your Excellency. Not one man gave up more than his own one life. Each man of those thousands died only the once, which he would have done anyway, in time. And dying thus, he died in the noblest way and for the noblest reason we knew. If I may quote those missionary friars again, Your Excellency, though I do not recall their exact words, it seems there is a similar belief among Christians. That no man can manifest greater love than to surrender his life for his friends.

Thanks to your instructive missionaries, we Mexíca know now that, even when we did right things, we did them for the wrong reasons. But I regret to remind Your Excellency that there are still other nations in these lands, not yet subdued and absorbed into the Christian dominion of New Spain, where the unenlightened still believe that a sacrificial victim suffers only briefly the pain of the Flowery Death before entering a delightful and eternal afterlife. Those peoples know nothing of the Christian Lord God, Who does not confine misery to our brief lives on earth, but also inflicts it in the afterworld of Hell, where the agony is everlasting.

Oh, yes, Your Excellency, I know that Hell is only for the multitude of wicked men who deserve eternal torment, and that a select few righteous men go to a sublime glory called Heaven. But your missionaries preach that, even for Christians, the felicitous Heaven is a narrow place, hard to get to, while the terrible Hell is capacious and easily entered. I have attended many church and mission services since the one that converted me, and I have come to think that Christianity would be more attractive to the heathen if Your Excellency's priests were able to describe the delights of Heaven as vividly and gloatingly as they dwell upon the horrors of Hell.

Apparently His Excellency does not care to hear my unsolicited suggestions, not even to refute or debate them, and prefers instead to take his leave. Ah, well, I am but a novice Christian, and probably presumptuous in voicing opinions still unripened. I will drop the subject of religion, to speak of other things.

The warriors' feast, held in what was then the banquet hall of this very House of Song, on the night of the Great Pyramid's dedication, did have some religious connotations, but they were minor. It was believed that, when we victors dined on the broiled hams of the sacrificed prisoners, we thereby ingested some of the dead men's strength and fighting spirit. But it was forbidden that any "revered father" eat the flesh of his own "beloved son." That is, no one could eat of any prisoner he himself had captured, because, in religious terms, that would be as unthinkable as an act of incest. So, though all the other guests scrambled to seize a slice of the incomparable Armed Scorpion, I had to be content with the thigh meat of some less esteemed enemy knight.

The meat, my lords? Why, it was nicely spiced and well cooked and served with an abundance of side dishes: beans and tortillas and stewed tomatoes and chocolate to drink and—

The meat *nauseous,* my lords? Why, quite the contrary! It was most savory and tender and pleasing to the palate. Since the subject so excites your curiosity, I will tell you that cooked human flesh tastes almost exactly like the meat you call pork, the cooked flesh of those imported animals you call swine. Indeed, it is the similarity of texture and flavor which gave rise to the rumour that you Spaniards and your swine are closely related, that both Spaniards and pigs propagate their species by mutual intercourse, if not legal intermarriage.

Yya, do not make such faces, reverend friars! I never believed the rumor, for I could see that your swine are only domesticated animals akin to the wild boars of this land, and I do not think even a Spaniard would copulate with one of those. Of course, your pig meat is much more flavorsome and tender than the gamy, sinewy meat of our untamed boars. But the coincidental similarity of pork and human flesh is probably the reason why our lower classes early took to eating pig meat with such avidity, and probably also the reason why they welcomed your introduction of swine with rather greater enthusiasm than, for instance, they welcomed your introduction of Holy Church.

As was only fair, the guests at that night's banquet consisted mostly of Acólhua warriors who had come to Tenochtítlan in Nezahualpíli's retinue. There were a token few of Chimalpopóca's knights of the Tecpanéa, and of us Mexíca there were only three: myself and my immediate superiors in the field, the Cuachic Blood Glutton and the Arrow Knight Xococ. One of the Acólhua present was that soldier who had his nose cut off in the battle and replaced afterward, but it was gone again. He told us, sadly, that the physician's operation had not been a success; the nose had gradually turned black and finally fallen off. We all assured him that he looked not much worse without it than he had with it, but he was a mannerly man, and he sat well apart from the rest of us, not to spoil our appetites.

For each guest there was a seductively dressed *auyaními* woman to serve us tidbits from the platters of food, to fill the smoking tubes with *picíetl* and light them for us, to pour chocolate and *octli* for us, and, later, to retire with us to the curtained little bedrooms around the main chamber. Yes, I see the displeasure in your expressions, my lord scribes, but it is a fact. That feast of human meat and the subsequent enjoyment of casual copulation — they took place right here in this now sanctified diocesan headquarters.

I confess I do not remember everything that occurred, for I smoked my first *poquíetl* that night, and more than one of them, and I drank much *octli*. I had timidly tasted that fermented maguey juice before, but that night was the first time I indulged in enough of it to addle my senses. I remember that the gathered warriors did much boasting of their deeds in the recent war, and in wars past, and there were many toasts to my own first victory and my swift promotion upward through the ranks. At one point, our three Revered Speakers honored us with a brief appearance, and lifted a cup of *octli* with us. I have a vague recollection of thanking Nezahualpíli — drunkenly and fulsomely and possibly incoherently — for his gift of trade goods and trade currency, though I do not recall his reply, if he made any.

Eventually and not at all hesitantly, thanks perhaps to the *octli*, I retired to one of the bedrooms with one of the *auyaníme*. I remember that she

was a most comely young woman with hair artificially colored the red-yellow of the jacinth gem. She was exceptionally accomplished at what was, after all, her life's occupation—giving pleasure to victorious warriors. So, besides the usual acts, she taught me some things quite new to me, and I must say that only a soldier in his prime of vigor and agility could have kept up his part of them for long, or endured hers. In return, "I caressed her with flowers." I mean to say, I performed upon her some of the subtle things I had witnessed during the seduction of Something Delicate. The *auyaními* obviously enjoyed those attentions and marveled much at them. Having coupled always and only with men, and with rather crude men, she had never before known those particular titillations — and I believe she was pleased to learn of them and add them to her own repertory.

THINK ABOUT IT

1. Summarize the morning entertainments and the afternoon sacrifices of the dedication ceremonies. Based on these events, what adjectives would you use to describe Aztec religious practices?
2. Why does Mixtli say the Flowery Death is the most noble?

TALK ABOUT IT

3. The Aztec culture has been described as a brutal warrior culture. How does Armed Scorpion's final battle and death support this description? Describe other warrior cultures you have read or heard about. Are they as brutal as this one?
4. Why were the sacrificed prisoners' "hams" eaten at the banquet?

WRITE ABOUT IT

5. Find passages that allude to the Aztecs' view of their gods. How does this differ from your view of God?
6. What is the most noble way to die? Does this relate to your religious beliefs? Explain.

READ MORE ABOUT IT

Fuentes, Carlos. *The Buried Mirror: Reflections on Spain and the New World.* New York: Houghton Mifflin Company, 1992.

Jennings, Gary. *Aztec.* New York: Atheneum Publishers, 1980.

Leonard, Jonathan Norton, and the Editors of Time-Life Books. *Ancient America.* New York: Time, Inc., 1967.

MARGOT EDMONDS AND
ELLA E. CLARK

Creation Legends of the Hopi

Margot Edmonds and the late Ella E. Clark collaborated on several books and anthologies of Native American legends. Margot Edmonds, a freelance writer, still lives in California, where she first met Clark. Ella E. Clark had a long career at Washington State University as an English professor. She spent several years visiting Indian reservations and then wrote a number of books recounting American Indian legends. In 1979, Edmonds and Clark documented the story of the legendary Shoshoni Indian woman who served two explorers as a guide and interpreter in *Sacagawea of the Lewis and Clark Expedition.* Edmonds and Clark worked on their last joint undertaking, *Voices of the Winds: Native American Legends,* for ten years. Many of the tales recounted in this anthology were told to the authors by elderly storytellers and tribal historians.

   Voices of the Winds: Native American Legends is a comprehensive anthology of stories, myths, and religious practices of Native tribes in North America. The book is arranged by geographic area and includes more than one hundred selections from over sixty tribes. One of these, the Hopi (meaning "peaceful"), are a Pueblo Indian tribe of the southwestern United States. Their culture is regarded as one of the best preserved of all Native tribes. Today the Hopi live mainly in northeastern Arizona, a difficult desert environment of steep cliffs and desolate gorges. The Hopi's elaborate and all-pervasive religious system has helped them deal with the insecurities of living in such a harsh environment where they have often been forced to move to survive. The Hopi creation legends serve as an important part of their religious beliefs. Two of these legends are retold below.

How the Hopi Indians Reached Their World

   When the world was new, the ancient people and the ancient creatures did not live on the top of the earth. They lived under it. All was darkness, all was blackness, above the earth as well as below it.

   There were four worlds: this one on top of the earth, and below it three cave worlds, one below the other. None of the cave worlds was large enough for all the people and the creatures.

   They increased so fast in the lowest cave world that they crowded it.

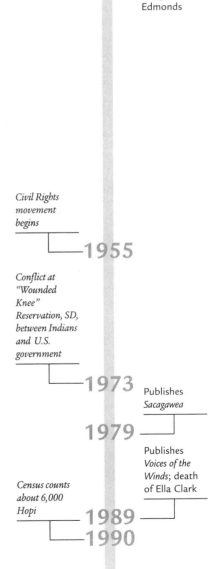

1882
Presidential order creates Hopi Reservation

1896
Birth of Ella Clark

c. 1910
Birth of Margot Edmonds

Civil Rights movement begins
1955

Conflict at "Wounded Knee" Reservation, SD, between Indians and U.S. government

1973
Publishes *Sacagawea*

1979
Publishes *Voices of the Winds*; death of Ella Clark

Census counts about 6,000 Hopi
1989
1990

HOPI INDIANS, *TABILITA*.

They were poor and did not know where to turn in the blackness. When they moved, they jostled one another. The cave was filled with the filth of the people who lived in it. No one could turn to spit without spitting on another. No one could cast slime from his nose without its falling on someone else. The people filled the place with their complaints and with their expressions of disgust.

Some people said, "It is not good for us to live in this way."

"How can it be made better?" one man asked.

"Let it be tried and seen!" answered another.

Two Brothers, one older and one younger, spoke to the priest-chiefs of the people in the cave world, "Yes, let it be tried and seen. Then it shall be well. By our wills it shall be well."

The Two Brothers pierced the roofs of the caves and descended to the lowest world, where people lived. The Two Brothers sowed one plant after another, hoping that one of them would grow up to the opening through which they themselves had descended and yet would have the strength to bear the weight of men and creatures. These, the Two Brothers hoped, might climb up the plant into the second cave world. One of these plants was a cane.

At last, after many trials, the cane became so tall that it grew through the opening in the roof, and it was so strong that men could climb to its top. It was jointed so that it was like a ladder, easily ascended. Ever since then, the cane has grown in joints as we see it today along the Colorado River.

Up this cane many people and beings climbed to the second cave world. When a part of them had climbed out, they feared that that cave also would be too small. It was so dark that they could not see how large it was. So they shook the ladder and caused those who were coming up it to fall back. Then they pulled the ladder out. It is said that those who were left came out of the lowest cave later. They are our brothers west of us.

After a long time the second cave became filled with men and beings, as the first had been. Complaining and wrangling were heard as in the beginning. Again the cane was placed under the roof vent, and once more men and beings entered the upper cave world. Again, those who were slow to climb out were shaken back or left behind. Though larger, the third cave was as dark as the first and second. The Two Brothers found fire. Torches were set ablaze, and by their light men built their huts and kivas, or traveled from place to place.

While people and the beings lived in this third cave world, times of evil came to them. Women became so crazed that they neglected all things for the dance. They even forgot their babies. Wives became mixed with wives, so that husbands did not know their own from others. At that time there was no day, only night, black night. Throughout this night, women danced in the kivas (men's "clubhouses"), ceasing only to sleep. So the fathers had to be the mothers of the little ones. When these little ones cried from hunger, the fathers carried them to the kivas, where the women were dancing. Hearing their cries, the mothers came and nursed them, and then went back to their dancing. Again the fathers took care of the children.

These troubles caused people to long for the light and to seek again an escape from darkness. They climbed to the fourth world, which was this world. But it too was in darkness, for the earth was closed in by the sky, just as the cave worlds had been closed in by their roofs. Men went from their lodges and worked by the light of torches and fires. They found the tracks of only one being, the single ruler of the unpeopled world, the tracks of Corpse Demon or Death. The people tried to follow these tracks, which led eastward. But the world was damp and dark, and people did not know what to do in the darkness. The waters seemed to surround them, and the tracks seemed to lead out into the waters.

With the people were five beings that had come forth with them from the cave worlds: Spider, Vulture, Swallow, Coyote, and Locust. The people and these beings consulted together, trying to think of some way of making light. Many, many attempts were made, but without success. Spider was asked to try first. She spun a mantle of pure white cotton. It gave some light but not enough. Spider therefore became our grandmother.

Then the people obtained and prepared a very white deerskin that had not been pierced in any spot. From this they made a shield case, which they painted with turquoise paint. It shed forth such brilliant light that it lighted the whole world. It made the light from the cotton mantle look faded. So the people sent the shield-light to the east, where it became the moon.

Down in the cave world Coyote had stolen a jar that was very heavy, so very heavy that he grew weary of carrying it. He decided to leave it behind, but he was curious to see what it contained. Now that light had taken the place of darkness, he opened the jar. From it many shining fragments and sparks flew out and upward, singeing his face as they passed him. That is why the coyote has a black face to this day. The shining fragments and sparks flew up to the sky and became stars.

By these lights the people found that the world was indeed very small and surrounded by waters, which made it damp. The people appealed to Vulture for help. He spread his wings and fanned the waters, which flowed away to the east and to the west until mountains began to appear.

Across the mountains the Two Brothers cut channels. Water rushed

TAOS PUEBLO, NEW MEXICO

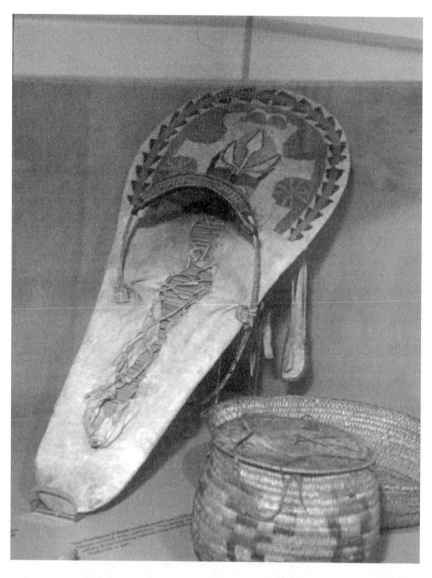

GREAT BASIN: CRADLE BOARD.

When people had followed in the tracks of Corpse Demon but a short distance, they overtook him. Among them were two little girls. One was the beautiful daughter of a great priest. The other was the child of somebody-or-other. She was not beautiful, and she was jealous of the little beauty. With the aid of Corpse Demon the jealous girl caused the death of the other child. This was the first death.

When people saw that the girl slept and could not be awakened, that she grew cold and that her heart had stopped beating, her father, the great priest, grew angry.

"Who has caused my daughter to die?" he cried loudly.

But the people only looked at each other.

"I will make a ball of sacred meal," said the priest. "I will throw it into the air, and when it falls it will strike someone on the head. The one it will strike I shall know as the one whose magic and evil art have brought my tragedy upon me."

The priest made a ball of sacred flour and pollen and threw it into the air. When it fell, it struck the head of the jealous little girl, the daughter of somebody-or-other. Then the priest exclaimed, "So you have caused this thing! You have caused the death of my daughter."

He called a council of the people, and they tried the girl. They would have killed her if she had not cried for mercy and a little time. Then she begged the priest and his people to return to the hole they had all come out of and look down it.

"If you still wish to destroy me, after you have looked into the hole," she said, "I will die willingly. "

So the people were persuaded to return to the hole leading from the cave world. When they looked down, they saw plains of beautiful flowers in a land of everlasting summer and

through the channels, and wore their courses deeper and deeper. Thus the great canyons and valleys of the world were formed. The waters have kept on flowing and flowing for ages. The world has grown drier, and continues to grow drier and drier.

Now that there was light, the people easily followed the tracks of Death eastward over the new land that was appearing. Hence Death is our greatest father and master. We followed his tracks when we left the cave worlds, and he was the only being

that awaited us on the great world of waters where this world is now.

Although all the water had flowed away, the people found the earth soft and damp. That is why we can see today the tracks of men and of many strange creatures between the place toward the west and the place where we came from the cave world.

Since the days of the first people, the earth has been changed to stone, and all the tracks have been preserved as they were when they were first made.

fruitfulness. And they saw the beautiful little girl, the priest's daughter, wandering among the flowers. She was so happy that she paid no attention to the people. She seemed to have no desire to return to this world.

"Look!" said the girl who had caused her death. "Thus it shall be with all the children of men."

"When we die," the people said to each other, "we will return to the world we have come from. There we shall be happy. Why should we fear to die? Why should we resent death?"

So they did not kill the little girl. Her children became the powerful wizards and witches of the world, who increased in numbers as people increased. Her children still live and still have wonderful and dreadful powers.

Then the people journeyed still farther eastward. As they went, they discovered Locust in their midst.

"Where did you come from?" they asked.

"I came out with you and the other beings," he replied. "Why did you come with us on our journey?" they asked.

"So that I might be useful," replied Locust.

But the people, thinking that he could not be useful, said to him, "You must return to the place you came from."

But Locust would not obey them. Then the people became so angry at him that they ran arrows through him, even through his heart. All the blood oozed out of his body and he died. After a long time he came to life again and ran about, looking as he had looked before, except that he was black.

The people said to one another, "Locust lives again, although we have pierced him through and through. Now he shall indeed be useful and shall journey with us. Who besides Locust has this wonderful power of renewing his life? He must possess

the medicine for the renewal of the lives of others. He shall become the medicine of mortal wounds and of war."

So today the locust is at first white, as was the first locust that came forth with the ancients. Like him, the locust dies, and after he has been dead a long time, he comes to life again — black. He is our father, too. Having his medicine, we are the greatest of men. The locust medicine still heals mortal wounds.

After the ancient people had journeyed a long distance, they became very hungry. In their hurry to get away from the lower cave world, they had forgotten to bring seed. After they had done much lamenting, the Spirit of Dew sent the Swallow back to bring the seed of corn and of other foods. When Swallow returned, the Spirit of Dew planted the seed in the ground and chanted prayers to it. Through the power of these prayers, the corn grew and ripened in a single day.

So for a long time, as the people continued their journey, they carried only enough seed for a day's planting. They depended upon the Spirit of Dew to raise for them in a single day an abundance of corn and other foods. To the Corn Clan, he gave this seed, and for a long time they were able to raise enough corn for their needs in a very short time.

But the powers of the witches and wizards made the time for raising foods grow longer and longer. Now, sometimes, our corn does not have time to grow old and ripen in the ear, and our other foods do not ripen. If it had not been for the children of the little girl whom the ancient people let live, even now we would not need to watch our cornfields whole summers through, and we would not have to carry heavy packs of food on our journeys.

As the ancient people traveled on, the children of the little girl tried

their powers and caused other troubles. These mischief-makers stirred up people who had come out of the cave worlds before our ancients had come. They made war upon our ancients. The wars made it necessary for the people to build houses whenever they stopped traveling. They built their houses on high mountains reached by only one trail, or in caves with but one path leading to them, or in the sides of deep canyons. Only in such places could they sleep in peace.

Only a small number of people were able to climb up from their secret hiding places and emerge into the Fourth World. Legends reveal the Grand Canyon is where these people emerged. From there they began their search for the homes the Two Brothers intended for them.

These few were the Hopi Indians that now live on the Three Mesas of northeastern Arizona.

How the Great Chiefs Made the Moon and the Sun

("Haliksai" was the usual beginning when a Hopi told a story in his own language. "Once upon a time" was his beginning when he told it in English.)

Once upon a time, when our people first came up from the villages of the underworld, there was no sun. There was no moon. They saw only dreary darkness and felt the coldness. They looked hard for firewood, but in the darkness they found little.

One day as they stumbled around, they saw a light in the distance. The Chief sent a messenger to see what caused the light. As the messenger approached it, he saw a small field containing corn, beans, squash, watermelons, and other foods. All around the field a great fire was burn-

HOPI INDIANS, *EAGLE KACHINA*.

Away from the fires it was still dark. The Great Chiefs, at a council with Skeleton, decided to make a moon like the one they had enjoyed in the underworld.

They took a piece of well-prepared buffalo hide and cut from it a great circle. They stretched the circle tightly over a wooden hoop and then painted it carefully with white paint. When it was entirely dry, they mixed some black paint and painted, all around its edge, completing the picture of the moon. When all of this was done, they attached a stick to the disk and placed it on a large square of white cloth. Thus they made a symbol of the moon.

Then the Great Chiefs selected one of the young men and bade him stand on top of the moon symbol. They took up the cloth by its corners and began to swing it back and forth, higher and higher. As they were swinging it, they sang a magic song. Finally, with a mighty heave, they threw the moon disk upward. It continued to fly swiftly, upward and eastward.

As the people watched, they suddenly saw light in the eastern sky. The light became brighter and brighter. Surely something was burning there, they thought. Then something bright with light rose in the east. That was the moon!

Although the moon made it possible for the people to move around with less stumbling, its light was so dim that frequently the workers in the fields would cut up their food plants instead of the weeds. It was so cold that fires had to be kept burning around the fields all the time.

Again the Great Chiefs held a council with Skeleton, and again they decided that something better must be done.

This time, instead of taking a piece of buffalo hide, they took a piece of warm cloth that they themselves

ing. Nearby stood a straight, handsome man wearing around his neck a turquoise necklace of four strands. Turquoise pendants hung from his ears.

"Who are you?" the owner of the field asked the messenger.

"My people and I have come from the cave world below," the messenger replied. "And we suffer from the lack of light and the lack of food."

"My name is Skeleton," said the owner of the field. He showed the stranger the terrible mask he often wore and then gave him some food. "Now return to your people and guide them to my field."

When all the people had arrived, Skeleton began to give them food from his field. They marveled that, although the crops seemed so small, there was enough food for everyone. He gave them ears of corn for roasting; he gave them beans, squashes, and watermelons. The people built fires for themselves and were happy.

Later, Skeleton helped them prepare fields of their own and to make fires around them. There they planted corn and soon harvested a good crop.

"Now we should move on," the people said. "We want to find the place where we will live always."

had woven while they were still in the underworld. They fashioned this as they had fashioned the disk of buffalo hide, except that this time they painted the face of the circle with a copper-colored paint.

They painted eyes and a mouth on the disk and decorated the forehead with colors that the Great Chiefs decided upon according to their desires. Around the circle, they then wove a ring of corn husks, arranged in a zig zag design. Around the circle of corn husks, they threaded a string of red hair from some animal. To the back of the disk, they fastened a small ring of corn husks. Through that ring they poked a circle of eagle feathers.

To the top of each eagle feather, the old Chief tied a few little red feathers taken from the top of the head of a small bird. On the forehead of the circle, he attached an abalone shell. Then the sun disk was completed.

Again the Great Chiefs chose a young man to stand on top of the disk, which they had placed on a large sheet. As they had done with the moon disk, they raised the cloth by holding its corners. Then they swung the sun disk back and forth, back and forth, again and again. With a mighty thrust, they threw the man and the disk far into the air. It traveled fast into the eastern sky and disappeared.

All the people watched it carefully. In a short time, they saw light in the east as if a great fire were burning. Soon the new sun rose and warmed the earth with its kindly rays.

Now with the moon to light the earth at night and the sun to light and warm it by day, all the people decided to pick up their provisions and go on. As they started, the White people took a trail that led them far to the south. The Hopis took one to the north, and the Pueblos took one midway between the two. Thus they wandered on to the places where they were to live.

The Hopis wandered a long time, building houses and planting crops until they reached the mesas where they now live. The ruins of the ancient villages are scattered to the very beginnings of the great river of the canyon — the Colorado.

THINK ABOUT IT

1. In what ways were insects, birds, and animals involved in helping create the Hopi world?
2. Why did the Hopi want to leave their home below the earth?

TALK ABOUT IT

3. The Hopi were often forced to move, owing to desert living conditions. How do forced migrations affect a group's outlook on life?
4. Why does the little girl who caused the first death have both "wonderful and dreadful" powers? How do other cultures describe death?

WRITE ABOUT IT

5. The Judeo-Christian creation story takes place over seven days, whereas creation of the Hopi world seems to evolve over a long period of time. Despite this difference, what are the similarities between the two creation stories?
6. Following the model of the Hopi legends, write a creation story that explains an important natural phenomenon.

READ MORE ABOUT IT

Edmonds, Margot, and Clark, Ella E. *Sacagawea of the Lewis and Clark Expedition.* Berkeley, CA: University of California Press, 1979.

Edmonds, Margot, and Clark, Ella E. *Voices of the Winds: Native American Legends.* New York: Facts on File, Inc., 1989.

Nequatewa, Edmund. *Truth of a Hopi: Stories Relating to the Myths and Clan Histories of the Hopi.* Flagstaff, AZ: Northland Press, 1967.

1945

World War II
ends

Birth of Annie
Dillard

A N N I E   D I L L A R D

Heaven and Earth in Jest

Annie Dillard is a writer and a teacher of poetry and creative writing. She has regularly contributed articles to such well-known journals and magazines as *Atlantic Monthly, American Scholar, Harper's, Antaeus,* and others. Dillard is best known for her poetic style of prose writing in which she explores the mysteries of life. She describes herself as "a poet and a walker with a background in theology and a penchant for quirky facts." Indeed, it is her unique perceptions of animals and nature that capture the imagination of her many avid readers. Her penetrating visions of the natural world first appeared in her reflections on life near a creek in rural Virginia.

Annie Dillard's first published prose work, *Pilgrim at Tinker Creek,* won instant acclaim and was awarded the prestigious Pulitzer Prize for general nonfiction in 1974. It is a detailed account of Dillard's meditations on life and nature. This beautifully written work achieves a pleasing harmony between her graphic descriptions of natural phenomena and the personal reflections they prompt. Dillard shares her sense impressions of the creek and its flora and fauna with the reader. She then interprets these impressions in the context of god's creation and regulation of the larger universe. Her underlying philosophical approach is that of animism, the belief that all life is produced by a spiritual force both separate from and evident in physical matter. The first chapter of *Pilgrim at Tinker Creek,* reproduced below, begins by considering why " . . . we're just set down here."

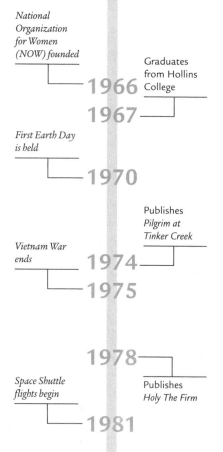

National
Organization
for Women
(NOW) founded

1966

Graduates
from Hollins
College

1967

First Earth Day
is held

1970

Publishes
*Pilgrim at
Tinker Creek*

Vietnam War
ends

1974

1975

1978

Space Shuttle
flights begin

Publishes
Holy The Firm

1981

I USED TO HAVE a cat, an old fighting tom, who would jump through the open window by my bed in the middle of the night and land on my chest. I'd half-awaken. He'd stick his skull under my nose and purr, stinking of urine and blood. Some nights he kneaded my bare chest with his front paws, powerfully, arching his back, as if sharpening his claws, or pummeling a mother for milk. And some mornings I'd wake in daylight to find my body covered with paw prints in blood; I looked as though I'd been painted with roses.

It was hot, so hot the mirror felt warm. I washed before the mirror in a daze, my twisted summer sleep still hung about me like sea kelp. What blood was this, and what roses? it could have been the rose of union, the blood of murder, or the rose of beauty bare and the blood of some unspeakable sacrifice or birth. The sign on my body could have been an emblem or a stain, the keys to the kingdom or the mark of Cain. I never knew. I never knew as I washed, and the blood streaked, faded, and finally disappeared, whether I'd purified myself or ruined the blood sign of the passover. We wake, if we ever wake at all, to mystery, rumors of death, beauty, violence ... " Seem like we're just set down here," a woman said to me recently, "and don't nobody know why."

These are morning matters, pictures you dream as the final wave heaves you up on the sand to the bright light and drying air. You remember pressure, and a curved sleep you rested against, soft, like a scallop in its shell. But the air hardens your skin; you stand; you leave the lighted shore to explore some dim headland, and soon you're lost in the leafy interior, intent, remembering nothing.

I still think of that old tomcat, mornings, when I wake. Things are tamer now; I sleep with the window shut. The cat and our rites are gone and my life is changed, but the memory remains of something powerful playing over me. I wake expectant, hoping to see a new thing. If I'm lucky I might be jogged awake by a strange birdcall. I dress in a hurry, imagining the yard flapping with auks, or flamingos. This morning it was a wood duck, down at the creek. It flew away.

I live by a creek, Tinker Creek, in a valley in Virginia's Blue Ridge. An anchorite's hermitage is called an anchor-hold; some anchor-holds were simple sheds clamped to the side of a church like a barnacle to a rock. I think of this house clamped to the side of Tinker Creek as an anchor-hold. It holds me at anchor to the rock bottom of the creek itself and it keeps me steadied in the current, as a sea anchor does, facing the stream of light pouring down. It's a good place to live; there's a lot to think

about. The creeks — Tinker and Carvin's — are an active mystery, fresh every minute. Theirs is the mystery of the continuous creation and all that providence implies: the uncertainty of vision, the horror of the fixed, the dissolution of the present, the intricacy of beauty, the pressure of fecundity, the elusiveness of the free, and the flawed nature of perfection. The mountains — Tinker and Brushy, McAfee's Knob and Dead Man — are a passive mystery, the oldest of all. Theirs is the one simple mystery of creation from nothing, of matter itself, anything at all, the given. Mountains are giant, restful, absorbent. You can heave your spirit into a mountain and the mountain will keep it, folded, and not throw it back as some creeks will. The creeks are the world with all its stimulus and beauty; I live there. But the mountains are home.

The wood duck flew away. I caught only a glimpse of something like a bright torpedo that blasted the leaves where it flew. Back at the house I ate a bowl of oatmeal; much later in the day came the long slant of light that means good walking.

If the day is fine, any walk will do; it all looks good. Water in particular looks its best, reflecting blue sky in the flat, and chopping it into graveled shallows and white chute and foam in the riffles. On a dark day, or a hazy one, everything's washed-out and lackluster but the water. It carries its own lights. I set out for the railroad tracks, for the hill the flocks fly over, for the woods where the white mare lives. But I go to the water.

Today is one of those excellent January partly cloudies in which light chooses an unexpected part of the landscape to trick out in gilt, and then shadow sweeps it away. You know you're alive. You take huge steps, trying to feel the planet's roundness are

between your feet. Kazantzakis says that when he was young he had a canary and a globe. When he freed the canary, it would perch on the globe and sing. All his life, wandering the earth, he felt as though he had a canary on top of his mind, singing.

... A couple of summers ago I was walking along the edge of the island to see what I could see in the water, and mainly to scare frogs. Frogs have an inelegant way of taking off from invisible positions on the bank just ahead of your feet, in dire panic, emitting a froggy "Yike!" and splashing into the water. Incredibly, this amused me, and, incredibly, it amuses me still. As I walked along the grassy edge of the island, I got better and better at seeing frogs both in and out of the water. I learned to recognize, slowing down, the difference in texture of the light reflected from mudbank, water, grass, or frog. Frogs were flying all around me. At the end of the island I noticed a small green frog. He was exactly half in and half out of the water, looking like a schematic diagram of an amphibian, and he didn't jump.

He didn't jump; I crept closer. At last I knelt on the island's winterkilled grass, lost, dumbstruck, staring at the frog in the creek just four feet away. He was a very small frog with wide, dull eyes. And just as I looked at him, he slowly crumpled and began to sag. The spirit vanished from his eyes as if snuffed. His skin emptied and drooped; his very skull seemed to collapse and settle like a kicked tent. He was shrinking before my eyes like a deflating football. I watched the taut, glistening skin on his shoulders ruck, and rumple, and fall. Soon, part of his skin, formless as a pricked balloon, lay in floating folds like bright scum on top of the water: it was a monstrous and terrifying thing. I gaped bewildered, appalled. An oval shadow hung in the water behind the drained frog; then the shadow glided away. The frog skin bag started to sink.

I had read about the giant water bug, but never seen one. "Giant water bug" is really the name of the creature, which is an enormous, heavy-bodied brown beetle. It eats insects, tadpoles, fish, and frogs. Its grasping forelegs are mighty and hooked inward. It seizes a victim with these legs, hugs it tight, and paralyzes it with enzymes injected during a vicious bite. That one bite is the only bite it ever takes. Through the puncture shoot the poisons that dissolve the victim's muscles and bones and organs — all but the skin — and through it the giant water bug sucks out the victim's body, reduced to a juice. This event is quite common in warm fresh water. The frog I saw was being sucked by a giant water bug. I had been kneeling on the island grass; when the unrecognizable flap of frog skin settled on the creek bottom, swaying, I stood up and brushed the knees of my pants. I couldn't catch my breath.

Of course, many carnivorous animals devour their prey alive. The usual method seems to be to subdue the victim by downing or grasping it so it can't flee, then eating it whole or in a series of bloody bites. Frogs eat everything whole, stuffing prey into their mouths with their thumbs. People have seen frogs with their wide jaws so full of live dragonflies they couldn't close them. Ants don't even have to catch their prey: in the spring they swarm over newly hatched, featherless birds in the nest and eat them tiny bite by tiny bite.

That it's rough out there and chancy is no surprise. Every live thing is a survivor on a kind of extended emergency bivouac. But at the same time we are also created. In the Koran, Allah asks, "The heaven and the earth and all in between, thinkest thou I made them *in jest?*" It's a good question. What do we think of the created

universe, spanning an unthinkable void with an unthinkable profusion of forms? Or what do we think of nothingness, those sickening reaches of time in either direction? If the giant water bug was not made in jest, was it then made in earnest? Pascal uses a nice term to describe the notion of the creator's, once having called forth the universe, turning his back to it: *Deus Absconditus.* Is this what we think happened? Was the sense of it there, and God absconded with it, ate it, like a wolf who disappears round the edge of the house with the Thanksgiving turkey? "God is subtle," Einstein said, "but not malicious." Again, Einstein said that "nature conceals her mystery by means of her essential grandeur, not by her cunning." It could be that God has not absconded but spread, as our vision and understanding of the universe have spread, to a fabric of spirit and sense so grand and subtle, so powerful in a new way, that we can only feel blindly of its hem. In making the thick darkness, a swaddling band for the sea, God "set bars and doors" and said, "Hitherto shalt thou come, but no further." But have we come even that far? Have we rowed out to the thick darkness, or are we all playing pinochle in the bottom of the boat?

Cruelty is a mystery, and the waste of pain. But if we describe a world to compass these things, a world that is a long, brute game, then we bump against another mystery: the inrush of power and light, the canary that sings on the skull. Unless all ages and races of men have been deluded by the same mass hypnotist (who?), there seems to be such a thing as beauty, a grace wholly gratuitous. About five years ago I saw a mockingbird make a straight vertical descent from the roof gutter of a four-story building. It was an act as careless and spontaneous as the curl of a stem or the kindling of a star.

The mockingbird took a single step into the air and dropped. His wings were still folded against his sides as though he were singing from a limb and not falling, accelerating thirty-two feet per second through empty air. Just a breath before he would have been dashed to the ground, he unfurled his wings with exact, deliberate care, revealing the broad bars of white, spread his elegant, white-banded tail, and so floated onto the grass. I had just rounded a corner when his insouciant step caught my eye; there was no one else in sight. The fact of his free fall was like the old philosophical conundrum about the tree that falls in the forest. The answer must be, I think, that beauty and grace are performed whether or not we will or sense them. The least we can do is try to be there.

Another time I saw another wonder: sharks off the Atlantic coast of Florida. There is a way a wave rises above the ocean horizon, a triangular wedge against the sky. If you stand where the ocean breaks on a shallow beach, you see the raised water in a wave is translucent, shot with lights. One late afternoon at low tide a hundred big sharks passed the beach near the mouth of a tidal river in a feeding frenzy. As each green wave rose from the churning water, it illuminated within itself the six- or eight-foot-long bodies of twisting sharks. The sharks disappeared as each wave rolled toward me; then a new wave would swell above the horizon, containing in it, like scorpions in amber, sharks that roiled and heaved. The sight held awesome wonders: power and beauty, grace tangled in a rapture with violence.

We don't know what's going on here. If these tremendous events are random combinations of matter run amok, the yield of millions of monkeys at millions of typewriters, then what is it in us, hammered out of those same typewriters, that they ignite? We don't know. Our life is a faint tracing on the surface of mystery, like the idle, curved tunnels of leaf miners on the face of a leaf. We must somehow take a wider view, look at the whole landscape, really see it, and describe what's going on here. Then we can at least wall the right question into the swaddling band of darkness, or, if it comes to that, choir the proper praise.

At the time of Lewis and Clark, setting the prairies on fire was a well-known signal that meant, "Come down to the water." It was an extravagant gesture, but we can't do less. If the landscape reveals one certainty, it is that the extravagant gesture is the very stuff of creation. After the one extravagant gesture of creation in the first place, the universe has continued to deal exclusively in extravagances, flinging intricacies and colossi down aeons of emptiness, heaping profusions on profligacies with ever-fresh vigor. The whole show has been on fire from the word go. I come down to the water to cool my eyes. But everywhere I look I see fire; that which isn't flint is tinder, and the whole world sparks and flames.

... I walk out; I see something, some event that would otherwise have been utterly missed and lost; or something sees me, some enormous power brushes me with its clean wing, and I resound like a beaten bell.

... Something pummels us, something barely sheathed. Power broods and lights. We're played on like a pipe; our breath is not our own. James Houston describes two young Eskimo girls sitting cross-legged on the ground, mouth on mouth, blowing by turns each other's throat cords, making a low, unearthly music. When I cross again the bridge that is really the steers' fence, the wind has thinned to the delicate air of twilight; it crumples the water's skin. I watch the running sheets of light raised on the creek's surface. The sight has the appeal of the purely passive, like the racing of light under clouds on a field, the beautiful dream at the moment of being dreamed. The breeze is the merest puff, but you yourself sail headlong and breathless under the gale force of the spirit.

THINK ABOUT IT

1. Describe specifically what the author finds beautiful in nature. What does she find violent?
2. How does Annie Dillard describe the spiritual force she finds present in animals and nature?

TALK ABOUT IT

3. What quote does the author use from the Koran? How does she connect this thought to her ideas about the spiritual force in nature?
4. Do you think Dillard believes in god? Why or why not?

WRITE ABOUT IT

5. If Dillard lived in New York City, what types of phenomena might she describe? Would she be likely to find a similar "beauty and violence"? Why or why not?
6. Take a long, meditative walk in a natural area near your home. Describe in detail the natural forces you perceive.

READ MORE ABOUT IT

Dillard, Annie. *Pilgrim at Tinker Creek.* New York: Harper's Magazine Press, 1974.

Dillard, Annie. *Holy the Firm.* New York: Harper & Row, 1978.

Acknowledgments

CHAPTER 1 "Theme for English B": from *The Collected Poems of Langston Hughes* by Langston Hughes, copyright 1994 by The Estate of Langston Hughes. Used by permission of Alfred A. Knopf, a division of Random House, Inc. "Mirrorings" first appeared in *Harper's Magazine.* Copyright 1994 by *Harper's Magazine.* "Beethoven's Silent Testment": The Heiligenstadt Testament by Ludwig van Beethoven is reprinted from Classical Music: The Era of Haydn, Mozart and Beethoven by Philip G. Downs. Copyright 1992 W. W. Norton & Co. Used by permission of W.W. Norton & Company, Inc. "I Was a Slave": from *Narrative of the Life of Frederick Douglass,"* courtesy of the Library of America. "How Don Quixote Became a Knight": from *Don Quixote,* by Miguel de Cervantes, reprinted from *Don Quixote: A Norton Critical Edition— The Ormsby Translation* by Joseph Jones and Kenneth Douglas. Copyright 1981 W. W. Norton & Co. "Martha Graham: Dancer": reprinted from *Deep Song: The Dance Story of Martha Graham* by Ernestine Stodelle. Schirmer Books, a division of Macmillan. Copyright 1984 Ernestine Stodelle. Used by permission. "The Bicentennial Man" reprinted from *Bicentennial Man and Other Stories,* by Isaac Asimov. Copyright 1976 Doubleday, a division of Random House. Reprinted by permission.

CHAPTER 2 "The Giant Pyramids": from *The Complete Pyramids,* by Mark Lehner. Copyright 1997 Thames & Hudson Ltd., London. Published with permission of the publisher. "Dorothea Lange, Photographer": The introductory essay by Christopher Cox from *Dorothea Lange: Aperture Masters of Photography number 5,* Aperture, New York, 1987. "The Samurai Warrior," by D. T. Suzuki: Reprinted from *Zen & Japanese Culture.* Copyright 1959 by Bollingen Foundation, Inc., NY, NY, PUP. Reprinted by permission of Princeton University Press. "The Myth of Sisyphus": From *The Myth of Sisyphus* by Albert Camus,

translated by Justin O'Brien, copyright 1995 by Alfred A. Knopf, a division of Random House, Inc. Used by permission of Alfred A. Knopf, a division of Random House, Inc. "Liberation Management": From *Liberation Management* by Tom Peters, copyright 1992 by Excel, a California Limited Partnership. Used by permission of Alfred A. Knopf, a division of Random House, Inc.

CHAPTER 3 "The Falconer and the Lady": Translated by Mark Musa and Peter Bondanella, from *The Decameron* by Giovanni Boccaccio, translated by Peter Bondanella & Marc Musa, copyright 1982 by Mark Musa and Peter Bondanella. Used by permission of Dutton Signet, a division of Penguin Putnum Inc. "A Summer Tragedy" by *Arna Bontemps* first appeared in *Harper's Magazine.* Copyright 1965 *Harper's Magazine.* "Frida's Love Letter": Reprinted from *Famous Love Letters* by Ronald Tamplin. Copyright 1995 Reader's Digest Press. "The Tragedy of Love": Reprinted from *The Aeneid* by Virgil, translated by W. F. Jackson-Knight (Penguin Classics, 1956) Copyright 1983 by Penguin Books, Ltd. "Hills Like White Elephants": Reprinted with permission of Scribner, a division of Simon and Schuster, Inc., from *Men Without Women* by Ernest Hemingway. Copyright 1927 Charles Scribner's Sons. Copyright renewed 1955 by Ernest Hemingway. "Othello" is reprinted from *The Tragedy of Othello, Moor of Venice,* by William Shakespeare, edited by Barbara A. Mowat and Paul Werstice. Reprinted by permission of Pocket Books, a division of Simon & Schuster Adult Publishing Group. Copyright 1993 by The Folger Shakespeare Library. All rights reserved.

CHAPTER 4 "The Making of a Scientist": From *"What Do You Care What Other People Think?" Further Adventures of a Curious Character* by Richard Feynman as told to Ralph Leighton. Copyright 1988 by Gweneth Feynman and Ralph Leighton. Used by

permission of W.W. Norton & Company. "Waiting for the Mahatma": Copyright 1955 University of Chicago Press. Reprinted by permission. "Hector and Andromache": Reprinted from *The Illiad of Homer,* Richard Lattimore, trans. Copyright 1951 University of Chicago Press. "The Blood of the Conquistadores": Reprinted from *How the Garcia Girls Lost their Accents* by Julia Alvarez. Copyright 1991 by Julia Alvarez. Published by Plume,an imprint of the The Penguin Group (USA), and originally in hardcover by Algonquin Books of Chapel Hill. Reprinted by permission of Susan Bergholz Literary Services, New York. All rights reserved. "Everyday Use": From *In Love & Trouble: Stories of Black Women* by Alice Walker. Copyright 1973. Reprinted by permission of Harcourt. "In the Gloaming" reprinted with the permission of Simon & Schuster Adult Publishing Group, from *In the Gloaming* by Alice Elliot Dark. Copyright 2000 by Alice Elliot Dark. All rights reserved.

CHAPTER 5 "Winter": Reprinted from *The Norton Anthology of Contemporary Fiction.* Copyright Kit Reed. Reprinted by permission. "The Ring of Gyges": Reprinted from *The Republic* by Plato. Copyright Basic Books. "Momma, the Dentist and Me": Reprinted from *I Know Why the Caged Bird Sings.* Copyright 1960 Maya Angelou and renewed 1997. Used by permission of Random House, Inc. "A Lesson before Dying": Copyright 1993 Ernest Gaines. Reprinted by permission of Alfred A. Knopf, a division of Random House, Inc. "Night": Excerpts from *Night* by Elie Wiesel and translated by Stella Rodway. Translation copyright 1960 by MacGibbon & Kee, renewed 1988 by the Collins Publishing Group. Reprinted by permission of Hill and Wang, a division of Farrar, Strauss & Giroux, Inc. "Where Have All the Good Deeds Gone?": Reprinted from *Vice and Virtue in Everyday Life* by Christina Sommers. Copyright 1989 Harcourt Brace Jovanovich.

CHAPTER 6   "Each Life Converges to Some Centre": Reprinted by permission of the publishers and the Trustees of Amherst College from *The Poems of Emily Dickinson*, Thomas H. Johnson, ed., Cambridge, Mass.: The Belknap Press of Harvard University Press, Copyright 1951, 1955, 1979 by the President and Fellows of Harvard College. "When Bad Things Happen to Good People": From *When Bad Things Happen to Good People* by Harold S. Kushner, copyright 1981 by Harold S. Kushner. Preface copyright 2001 by Harold S. Kushner. Used by permission of Schocken Books, a division of Random House, Inc. "The Sermon on the Four Noble Truths": Reprinted from *Anthology of World Scriptures* by Robert E. Van Voost. Copyright 1994 Wadsworth Publishing. Reprinted by permission. Wadsworth is an imprint of Thomson Global Rights Group. Excerpts from The Koran: From The Koran. London: J. M . Dent & Sons, 1909. "The Dedication of the Great Pyramid of the Aztecs": From *Aztecs* by Gary Jennings. Copyright 1980 MacINtosh & Otis. "Creation Legends of the Hopi": From *Voices of the Winds* by Margot Edmonds and Ella E. Clark. Copyright 1989 by Margot Edmonds and the Association on American Indian Affairs, Inc. Reprinted by permission of Facts On File, Inc. "Heaven and Earth in Jest": Reprinted from *Pilgrim at Tinker Creek* by Annie Dillard. Copyright 1974 by Annie Dillard. Reprinted by permission of Harper Collins Publishers, Inc.

Photographs and Illustrations

Page i: (top left) Corbis, *(top center)* Library of Congress; *(top right)* ©Nimtallah/Art Resource NY, *(bottom left)* ©Topham/The Image Works, *(bottom center)* Burstein Collection/ Corbis, *(bottom right)* Hulton Archive.

CHAPTER 1   *Page 13:* ©Underwood & Underwood/Corbis. *Page 23:* British Museum. *Pages 31, 32:* Corbis.

CHAPTER 2   *Page 68:* Library of Congress. *Page 71:* Copyright the Dorothea Lange Collection, Oakland Museum of California, City of Oakland. *Page 72,74:* Library of Congress. *Page 82:* Courtesy the Dorothea Lange Collection, Oakland Museum of California, City of Oakland. Gift of Paul S. Taylor. *Page 75:* Copyright the Dorothea Lange Collection, Oakland Museum of California, City of Oakland.

CHAPTER 3   *Page 91:* © AFP/CORBIS. *Page 92: (left)* Nimatallah/Art Resource, NY; *(right)* © Bettmann/CORBIS. *Page 99:* © Bettmann/CORBIS. *Page 101:* © Pramod Mistry/Dinodia Picture Agency. *Page 102:* ©Superstock Inc. *Page 109:* © Bettmann/CORBIS. *Page 110:* Instituto Nacional de Bellas Artes y Litura/Gelman Collection/Centro Arte Contemporaneo A.C., Mexico. Banco de Mexico, Fiduciario en el Fideicomiso relativo a los Museos Diego Rivera y Frida Kahlo. *Page 111:* Banco de Mexico, Fiduciario en el Fideicomiso relativo a los Museos Diego Rivera y Frida Kahlo.

CHAPTER 4   *Page 136:* ©Dinodia Photo Library/The Image Works. *Page 145: (top)* © Dave Bartruff/CORBIS; *(bottom)* SEF/Art Resource, NY. *Page 146: (top)* © Vanni Archive/CORBIS; *(bottom)* © Roger-Viollet. *Page 148: (top)* ©Scala/Art Resource; *(bottom)* © Araldo de Luca/CORBIS. *Page 149: (top)* ©SEF/Art Resource; *(bottom)* © Christel Gerstenberg/CORBIS. *Page 152:* National Portrait Gallery, Smithsonian Institution. *Page 154:* Metropolitan Museum of Art. Gift of Paul J. Sachs, 1916 (16.2.9). All rights reserved, The Metropolitan Museum of Art.

CHAPTER 5   *Page 206:* The Metropolitan Museum of Art, Harris Brisbane Dick Fund, 1932 (32.62.12). All rights reserved, The Metropolitan Museum of Art. *Page 207:* The Metropolitan Museum of Art, Purchase, Rogers Fund and Jacob H. Schiff Bequest, 1922 (22.60.25(39)). All rights reserved, The Metropolitan Museum of Art. *Pages 208–209:* Centro de Arte Reina Sofia, Madrid, Spain/Giraudon, Paris/Superstock. *Page 213:* Reproduced by permission of the Artist Rights Society. *Page 214:* The Museum of Modern Art, New York. Abby Aldrich Rockefeller Fund. Photograph © 2001 The Museum of Modern Art, Ne w York.

CHAPTER 6   *Page 238.* Photodisc. *Page 249:* © Dean Conger/CORBIS. *Page 251:* © Paul Almasy/CORBIS. *Page 252:* ©Foto Marburg/Art Resource. *Page 253:* ©Scala/Art Resource. *Pages 254, 255.* © Collection Viollet/Roger Viollet. *Page 262.* © Yann Arthus-Bertrand/CORBIS. *Pages 268, 269, 270.* © Marilyn "Angel" Wynn, nativestock.com. *Page 272.* ©Larry Mangino / The Image Works.

COLOR PLATES   *Color Plate 1A:* Jonathan Blair/Corbis. *Color Plate 1B:* Carmen Redondo/Corbis. *Color Plate 2:* National Gallery, London, England/Corbis. *Color Plate 3:* © Francis G. Mayer/CORBIS. *Color Plate 4:* National Gallery, London, England/Corbis. *Color Plate 5:* © Joe Carini/The Image Works. *Color Plate 6:* © Vatican Museums and Galleries, Vatican City, Italy/Bridgeman Art Library, London. *Color Plate 7:* © Vatican Museums and Galleries, Vatican City, Italy/Bridgeman Art Library, London. *Color Plate 8:* Travel Ink/Corbis. *Color Plates 9, 10:* Mimmo Jodice/Corbis. *Color Plate 11:* Jean Claude N'Diaye/Imapress/The Image Works. *Color Plate 12:* ©John Elke III. *Color Plate 13:* Angelo Hornak/Corbis. *Color Plate 14:* The Philadelphia Museum of Art, Philadelphia, PA/Corbis. *Color Plate 15:* Archivo Iconografico, S.A./Corbis. *Color Plate 16:* Banco de Mexico, Fiduciario en el Fideicomiso relativo a los Museos Diego Rivera y Frida Kahlo. *Color Plate 17:* Metropolitan Museum of Art, H.O. Havemeyer Collection, Bequest of Mrs. H.O. Havemeyer, 1929 (29.100.48). Photograph ©1997 The Metropolitan Museum of Art. *Color Plate 18:* The Philadelphia Museum of Art, Philadelphia, PA/W.P. Wilstach Collection.